EXPERIENCING
GOD

KNOWING *and* DOING THE WILL OF GOD

REVISED AND EXPANDED

HENRY & RICHARD BLACKABY
CLAUDE KING

LifeWay Press®
Nashville, Tennessee

Published by LifeWay Press®
© 2007 Henry Blackaby, Richard Blackaby, and Claude King
Eighth printing 2013

ISBN 978-1-4158-5838-7
Item 005084536

Dewey decimal classification: 231
Subject heading: GOD—WILL

Cover art: Mike Wimmer is one of the nation's leading illustrators. He has done numerous book covers, movie posters, and images used in major national advertising campaigns. When he was asked to paint the portrait of Moses for *Experiencing God,* Mike's extensive research, talent, and commitment led to a classic rendition of the prophet's experience with God at the burning bush.

To order additional copies of this resource, write to LifeWay Church Resources Customer Service; One LifeWay Plaza; Nashville, TN 37234-0113; email *orderentry@lifeway.com;* fax 615.251.5933; phone toll free 800.458.2772; order online at *www.lifeway.com;* or visit the LifeWay Christian Store serving you.

Printed in the United States of America

Adult Ministry Publishing
LifeWay Church Resources
One LifeWay Plaza
Nashville, TN 37234-0152

CONTENTS

THE AUTHORS

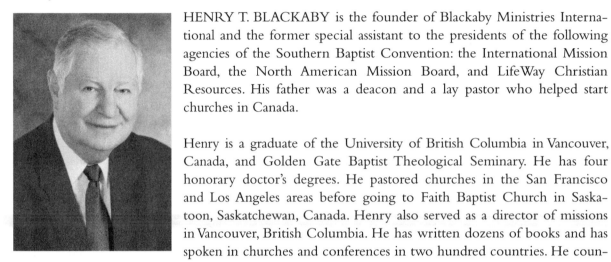

HENRY T. BLACKABY is the founder of Blackaby Ministries International and the former special assistant to the presidents of the following agencies of the Southern Baptist Convention: the International Mission Board, the North American Mission Board, and LifeWay Christian Resources. His father was a deacon and a lay pastor who helped start churches in Canada.

Henry is a graduate of the University of British Columbia in Vancouver, Canada, and Golden Gate Baptist Theological Seminary. He has four honorary doctor's degrees. He pastored churches in the San Francisco and Los Angeles areas before going to Faith Baptist Church in Saskatoon, Saskatchewan, Canada. Henry also served as a director of missions in Vancouver, British Columbia. He has written dozens of books and has spoken in churches and conferences in two hundred countries. He counsels Christian CEOs of major companies and has spoken in the White House and the United Nations.

Henry's wife is the former Marilynn Sue Wells. They have five children: Richard, Thomas, Melvin, Norman, and Carrie. All five children serve in full-time Christian ministry.

For further information about Henry Blackaby and his ministry, contact Blackaby Ministries International; P.O. Box 1035; Jonesboro, GA 30237; 770.471.2332; *www.blackaby.org.*

CLAUDE V. KING is a discipleship specialist at LifeWay Christian Resources. In addition to this course, Claude worked with T. W. Hunt to develop *The Mind of Christ.* He is the author or coauthor of more than 20 books and courses, including *Growing Disciples: Pray in Faith, Fresh Encounter, The Call to Follow Christ, Come to the Lord's Table, Meet Jesus Christ,* and *Concentric Circles of Concern.* Claude serves as the president on the board of directors for Final Command Ministries. He is a graduate of Belmont College and New Orleans Baptist Theological Seminary.

RICHARD BLACKABY, Henry's oldest son, holds a PhD in history as well as an honorary doctorate. He has served as a pastor and a seminary president and is currently the president of Blackaby Ministries International. He and his wife, Lisa, have three children: Mike, Daniel, and Carrie. Richard is the author of *CrossSeekers, Putting a Face on Grace,* and *Unlimiting God* and has coauthored a dozen books with his father.

Editor's note: Henry Blackaby is the primary author of the content of this course. Claude King wrote the learning activities to assist you in your study. Richard contributed material to the revised edition.

The illustrations of the authors are written solely from their personal viewpoints. Others who were involved, if given the opportunity, could write different and more complete accounts.

PREFACE

When we first wrote *Experiencing God* in 1990, we didn't realize the enormity of the spiritual hunger in the hearts and lives of God's people to experience God. God's people had head knowledge but little heart and life experience with God. They knew there had to be much more to the Christian life than more and more activity, but they didn't know what was missing, nor did they know what to do about it. They longed to experience God.

God had granted me an understanding of Himself and His ways. He had also brought Avery Willis and Claude King into my life. God was ready to hear the cry of His people:

Show me Your ways, O LORD;
Teach me Your paths.
Lead me in Your truth and teach me,
For You are the God of my salvation;
On You I wait all the day (Ps. 25:4-5, NKJV).

Experiencing God was my life message. This is how I had always understood and walked with God. This is how I had pastored and guided God's people. I had shared these truths in many places where I was asked to speak. Over and over again people asked, "Have you ever written anything on what you are teaching? God's people need to hear these truths." Avery Willis, the person responsible for adult discipleship training at the time, gave me the encouragement and opportunity to put my message in writing in the workbook *Experiencing God: Knowing and Doing the Will of God*.

Since 1990 God has used this study to touch and change millions of lives and thousands of churches around the world. At the 10th anniversary more than three million copies of the workbook had been distributed, and God was using other *Experiencing God* resources. This workbook is now published in 47 languages and has been used in almost every denomination. We are amazed that God, in His mercy and grace, would use such a modest work by ordinary people! He has chosen to grant His favor on His truth expressed in this study. The original workbook has given birth to many *Experiencing God* resources, listed at the right.

We have been overwhelmed by the response to the truths shared in *Experiencing God*. So many lives have been radically changed—in prisons; in the military; and in all walks of life, including lawyers, judges, CEOs, professional athletes, and politicians. Thousands of churches, high schools, colleges, and seminaries have been greatly helped and radically changed. God has used these truths to affect people around the world, including leaders of countries, government officials, and diplomats. Hundreds of missionaries are on the fields of the world because of this study, and hundreds of others are now serving as pastors, evangelists, and faithful servants. Only heaven really knows how God has chosen to use *Experiencing God*.

This resource has also had a profound effect on our lives and the lives of our family. We have all received God's grace as a continuing affirmation of His hand on us for His purposes, and we continue to obey God as He directs us. As we seek to be good stewards of His grace, we cry out, "Let a man so consider us, as servants of Christ and stewards of the mysteries of God. Moreover it is required in stewards that one be found faithful" (1 Cor. 4:1-2, NKJV).

As God has granted us—especially as a family—many open doors to share with God's people, we beg our friends and the many friends of *Experiencing God* to pray for each of us: Marilynn and me; Richard and Lisa, Michael, Daniel, and Carrie; Tom and Kim, Erin, Matthew, and Connor; Mel and Gina, Christa, Stephen, and Sarah; Norm and Dana, Emily, Douglas, and Anne; Carrie and Wendell, Elizabeth, and Joshua.

Thanks must also go to Claude King, who helped develop the first workbook and who continues to remain faithful to the Lord in serving Him, and to those at LifeWay Christian Resources who continually improve and provide *Experiencing God*.

The Blackabys

Other Experiencing God Resources

Experiencing God trade books and audio book
Experiencing God Day-by-Day devotional book
Experiencing God at Home
Experiencing God Audio Devotional CD Set
Experiencing God: A Documentary
Experiencing God: The Musical
Seven Truths from Experiencing God booklet
When God Speaks: How to Recognize God's Voice and Respond in Obedience
Experiencing God: God's Invitation to Young Adults
Experiencing God: Youth Edition
Seven Steps to Knowing, Doing, and Experiencing the Will of God: For Teens
Audio and video downloads, *www.lifeway.com/eg*

UNIT I

VERSE TO MEMORIZE

"I AM THE VINE; YOU ARE THE
BRANCHES. IF A MAN REMAINS IN
ME AND I IN HIM, HE WILL BEAR
MUCH FRUIT; APART FROM ME
YOU CAN DO NOTHING."

JOHN 15:5

God's Will and Your Life

Vancouver World's Fair

When the World's Fair was coming to Vancouver, our association of churches was convinced God wanted us to try to reach the 22 million people who would come to our city. We had about 2,000 members in our churches. How in the world could our little group make much impact on such a mass of tourists from all over the world?

Two years before the fair, we began to set our plans in motion. The total income for our association was $9,000. The following year it grew to $16,000. The year of the World's Fair, we set a budget for $202,000.[1] We had commitments that would provide 35 percent of that budget. Sixty-five percent of it depended on prayer. Can you operate a budget on prayer? Yes. But when you do that, you are attempting something only God can do. What do most of us do? We set the practical budget, which represents what we can do. Then we might set a second hope or faith budget. The budget we really trust and use, however, is the one we can reach by ourselves. We do not really trust God to make a practical difference in what we do.

As an association of churches, we decided God had definitely led us to the work that would cost $202,000. That became our operating budget. All of our people began praying for God to provide for everything we believed He had led us to do during the World's Fair. At the end of the year, I asked our treasurer how much money we had received. From Canada, the United States, and other parts of the world we had received $264,000. People from all over North America assisted us. During the fair we became a catalyst to see almost 20,000 people accept Jesus Christ. You cannot explain that except in terms of God's intervention. Only God could have done that. He accomplished it with a people who had determined to be servants and were moldable and available for their Master's use.

---

1. Throughout this book I will give illustrations that sometimes mention amounts of money. Don't get caught up in the amounts, since they are relative to the year when the event took place. Some amounts may seem small by current standards, while other amounts may seem inconceivably large in other cultures or economies. Focus instead on the faith required or the miraculous timing and provision of the Lord in regard to the need. In the case above, the amounts merely indicate the size of the faith required when the people compared the proposed budget to their previous experience.

DAY I

Jesus Is Your Way

AS YOU FOLLOW JESUS ONE DAY AT A TIME, HE WILL KEEP YOU IN THE CENTER OF GOD'S WILL.

Real Christianity is not merely a religion; it is a relationship with a Person.

1 Corinthians 2:14

"The man without the Spirit does not accept the things that come from the Spirit of God, for they are foolishness to him, and he cannot understand them, because they are spiritually discerned."

Jesus said, "This is eternal life: that they may know you, the only true God, and Jesus Christ, whom you have sent" (John 17:3). The essence of eternal life and of this study is for you to know God and to know Jesus Christ, whom He has sent. Knowing God does not come through a program or a method. Real Christianity is not merely a religion; it is a relationship with a Person. It is an intimate love relationship with God. Through this relationship God reveals His will and invites you to join Him where He is at work. When you obey, God accomplishes through you something only He can do. Then you come to know God in a more intimate way by experiencing Him at work through your life.

I want to help you move into the kind of relationship with God through which you will experience eternal life to the fullest degree possible. Jesus said, "I have come that they may have life, and have it to the full" (John 10:10). Would you like to experience life in its fullest measure? You can if you are willing to respond to God's invitation to an intimate love relationship with Him.

A Prerequisite—A Relationship with Jesus

In this course I assume you have already trusted Jesus Christ as your Savior and have acknowledged Him as the Lord of your life. If you have not made this important decision, the rest of the course will have little meaning for you because spiritual matters can be understood only by those who have the Spirit of Christ dwelling in them (see **1 Cor. 2:14**).

1 **If you sense a need to accept Jesus as your Savior and Lord, now is the time to settle this matter with God. Ask God to speak to you as you read the following Scriptures.**
   ❑ Romans 3:23: All have sinned.
   ❑ Romans 6:23: Eternal life is a free gift of God.
   ❑ Romans 5:8: Because of His love for you, Jesus paid the death penalty for your sins.
   ❑ Romans 10:9-10: Confess Jesus as Lord and believe that God raised Him from the dead.
   ❑ Romans 10:13: Ask God to save you, and He will.

To place your faith in Jesus and receive His gift of eternal life, you must—
   • recognize you are a sinner who needs a saving relationship with Jesus Christ;
   • confess (agree with God about) your sins;
   • repent of your sins (turn from sin to God);
   • ask Jesus to save you by His grace;
   • turn over the rule of your life to Jesus, letting Him be your Lord.

2 **If you need help, call on your minister or a Christian friend for help. If you have just made this important decision, tell someone the good news of what God has done in your life. Then notify your church about**

your decision so they can celebrate with you and help you grow in your relationship with Christ.

Looking for More in Your Experience of God?

You may have been frustrated in your Christian experience because you know God has a more abundant life for you than you have experienced so far. Perhaps you have been a believer for many years, but your Christian life has become dry and monotonous. Maybe you have heard others excitedly talking about what God is doing in their lives, and you long to have a dynamic walk with God too. Or you may earnestly desire God's directions for your life and ministry. You may have experienced tragedy in your life. Standing bewildered in the middle of a broken life, you don't know what to do. Whatever your present circumstances may be, my earnest prayer is that during this study you will be able to—

- hear when God is speaking to you;
- clearly identify His activity in your life;
- believe Him to be and do everything He has promised;
- adjust your beliefs, character, and behavior to Him and His ways;
- recognize a direction He is taking in your life and identify what He wants to do through your life;
- clearly know what you need to do in response to His activity in your life;
- experience God doing through you what only He can do!

It is impossible for this course to achieve these goals in your life. These are things only God can do. I will serve as your guide, encourager, and catalyst (someone who assists in bringing about an action or a reaction) for a deeper walk with God. I will share with you the biblical truths by which God guides my life and ministry. I will tell you about some wonderful works the Lord has done as God's people have applied biblical truths to following Him. In the learning activities I will invite you to interact with God so He can reveal to you the ways He wants you to apply these truths in your life, ministry, and church.

The Holy Spirit will be your personal Teacher (see **John 14:26**) during this study. He will guide you to apply these truths according to God's will. He will work to reveal God, His purposes, and His ways to you. Jesus said, "If anyone chooses to do God's will, he will find out whether my teaching comes from God or whether I speak on my own" (John 7:17). This will be true of this course as well. The Holy Spirit working in you will confirm in your heart the truth of Scripture. When I present what I see as a biblical truth, you can depend on the Holy Spirit to confirm whether that teaching comes from God. Therefore, your intimate relationship with God, cultivated through prayer, meditation, and Bible study, will be an indispensable part of this course.

The Bible is God's Word to you. The Holy Spirit honors and uses God's Word in speaking to you. The Scriptures are your source of authority for your faith and practice. You cannot depend on traditions, your experience, or others' experiences to be accurate authorities on God's will and ways. As you study this resource, use the suggested Scriptures to examine your experience and tradition against God's Word of truth.

Anything significant that happens in your life during this study will be the result of God's activity in your life. Let the Spirit of God lead you into an intimate relationship with the God of the universe, "who is able to do immeasurably more than all we ask or imagine, according to his power that is at work within us" (Eph. 3:20).

The Holy Spirit will be your personal Teacher.

___

John 14:26

"The Counselor, the Holy Spirit, whom the Father will send in my name, will teach you all things."

The Scriptures are your Source of Authority.

___

> The goal is not to finish this course but to have a life-transforming encounter with God.

This book is different from most material with which you may be familiar. It is not designed for you to sit down and read from cover to cover. I want you to study, understand, and apply biblical truths to your life. This challenging exercise takes time. To get the most from this course, you must take your time by studying only one day's lesson at a time. Do not try to study several lessons in a single day. You need time to let these truths sink into your understanding and practice. The goal is not to finish this course but to have a life-transforming encounter with God as you study these materials. You want to experience a Person—Jesus Christ. Time, meditation, and personal application are necessary to allow the Holy Spirit to make Christ real in your life.

Do not skip any learning activities. They are designed to help you learn and apply the truths to your life. They will help you establish a personal, daily walk with God. Many activities will lead you to interact with God through prayer, meditation, and Bible study. If you leave out these activities, you may miss an encounter with God that could radically change your life. You will learn that your relationship with God is the most important part of knowing and doing God's will. Without an intimate relationship with Him, you will miss what He wants to do in and through your life.

 The learning activities are indicated by the symbol that appears beside this paragraph. Follow the instructions given. After you have completed the activity, continue reading.

Normally, you will be given answers following the activity so you can check your work. Write your own answer before reading mine. Sometimes your response to the activity will be your own opinion, and no right or wrong answer can be given. If you have difficulty with an activity or if you question the answers given, write a note in the margin. Discuss your concern with your leader or small group.

Once each week you should attend a small-group session designed to help you discuss the content you studied the previous week, share insights and testimonies, encourage one another, and pray together. Small groups should not have more than 10 members for maximal effectiveness. Larger groups will experience less closeness, less intimate sharing, more absenteeism, and more dropouts. If more than 10 persons want to study the course, enlist additional leaders for each group of 6 to 10.

If you have started studying *Experiencing God* but are not involved in a small group, enlist some friends or family to study the course with you. Other members of the body of Christ can help you more fully know and understand God's will. Apart from a small-group experience, you will miss much of the intended learning from this course.

Jesus Is Your "Map"

For 12 years I pastored a church in a city surrounded by farming communities. One day a farmer invited me to visit him at his farm. His directions went something like this: "Go a quarter mile past the edge of the city, and you will see a big, red barn on your left. Go to the next road and turn to your left. Take that road for ¾ of a mile. You'll see a large poplar tree. Go right for about 4 miles, and then you will see a big rock …" I wrote all of this down, and only by God's grace did I eventually manage to find the farm!

The next time I went to the man's house, he was with me in the vehicle. Because there was more than one way to get to his house, he could have taken me any way he wanted to. You see, he was my map. What did I have to do? I simply had to listen to him and do what he said. Every time he said, "Turn," I did what he said. He took me a way I had never been and could not have discovered on my own. I could never retrace that route by myself. The farmer was my map; he knew the way.

4 **When you come to the Lord Jesus to seek His will for your life, which of the following requests more closely resembles the way you generally ask? Check your response.**

❏ a. Lord, what do You want me to do? When do You want me to do it? How shall I do it? Where shall I do it? Whom do You want me to involve along the way? And please tell me what the outcome will be.

❏ b. Lord, as You go with me, tell me what to do one step at a time. I will do it.

Isn't the first response typical? We always ask God for a detailed road map. We say, "Lord, if You could just tell me where I am heading, then I will be able to set my course and go."

He says, "You don't need to. You need to follow Me one day at a time." This response comes only from those who have learned to walk closely with God and to trust Him to care for the details of their lives. We need to come to the place where the second response is ours. Who really knows the way for you to go to fulfill God's purpose for your life? Who knows how you can experience abundant life? God. Jesus said, "I am the way" (**John 14:6**).

- He did not say, "I will show you the way."
- He did not say, "I will give you a road map."
- He did not say, "I will tell you which direction to go."
- He said, "I am the way." Jesus knows the way; He is your way. ✓

John 14:6
"I am the way and the truth and the life."

5 **If you do everything Jesus tells you one day at a time, will you always be in the center of where God wants you to be? Check your response.**

❏ No, Jesus does not guide people specifically.

❏ No, by seeking to follow Jesus, I could end up going the wrong way.

❏ It is much wiser to wait until God tells me all the details before I begin moving my life in a particular direction.

☑ Yes, if I follow Jesus one day at a time, I will be right in the center of God's will for my life.

When you get to the place in your life where you trust Jesus to guide you one step at a time, you experience tremendous freedom. If you don't trust Him to guide you this way, what happens if you don't know the way you should go with your life? You worry every time you make a decision. You may become immobilized with worry. This is not the way God intends for you to live.

I have found that when I release my way to God, then I immediately respond to everything He tells me each day. He gives me plenty to do to fill every day with meaning and purpose. If I do what He says, I am in the center of His will when He wants to use me for a special assignment. My primary concern should not be, What should I do with my life tomorrow? but, What does God want me to do today? As you follow Jesus one day at a time, He will keep you in the center of God's will.

Following One Day at a Time

Abram (later God changed his name to Abraham) is a good example of this approach to following God. He walked by faith and not by sight.

6 Read about Abram's call to do God's will. Notice how much detail he was given before God asked him to follow Him. Underline where he was to go and what he was to do.

"The LORD had said to Abram, 'Leave your country, your people and your father's household and go to the land I will show you.

'I will make you into a great nation
  and I will bless you;
I will make your name great,
  And you will be a blessing.
I will bless those who bless you,
  and whoever curses you I will curse;
and all peoples on earth
  will be blessed through you.'

"So Abram left, as the LORD had told him; and Lot went with him. Abram was seventy-five years old when he set out from Haran. He took his wife Sarai, his nephew Lot, all the possessions they had accumulated and the people they had acquired in Haran, and they set out for the land of Canaan, and they arrived there" (Gen. 12:1-5).

What did God say? How specific was He? "Leave" and "go." Go where? "To a land I will show you."

7 Are you ready to follow God's will that way? Check your response.
❏ No, I don't think God will ask me to go anywhere without showing me ahead of time where I am going.
❏ I'm not sure.
❏ Yes, I am willing to follow Him by faith and not by sight.
☑ Other: *I am, but I am not the leader of my family. It's hard to be married to a non-Christian wife*

doesn't care about the will or calling of god.

Many times, as with Abram, God called people to simply follow Him. (Tomorrow you will read about several.) He is much more likely to ask you to follow Him one day at a time than He is to spell out all the details before you begin to obey Him. As we continue our study together, you will see this truth illustrated in the lives of many people in the Bible.

Matthew 6:33-34

"Seek first his kingdom and his righteousness, and all these things will be given to you as well. Therefore do not worry about tomorrow, for tomorrow will worry about itself. Each day has enough trouble of its own."

8 Read Matthew 6:33-34 in the margin; then pause and pray.
• Agree that God is absolutely trustworthy. ✓
• Agree with God that you will follow Him one day at a time. ✓
• Agree to follow Him even when He does not spell out all the details. ✓
• Agree that you will let Him be your Way.

If you cannot agree to these now, openly confess your struggles to Him. Ask Him to help you want to do His will in His way. Claim the promise "It is God who works in you to will and to act according to his good purpose" (Phil. 2:13).

Daily Review

At the end of each day's lesson, I will ask you to review the lesson and pray. Ask God to identify for you one or more statements or Scriptures from the material that He wants you to understand, learn, or practice. This is a personal-application question that has no wrong answer. If God makes a statement or Scripture meaningful to you, that is the correct response. I will also ask you to reword that statement or Scripture into a prayer of response for your life. Pray about what God wants you to do in response to that truth. This should become a time of prayer and meditation each day as you ask God what He wants you to do in response to the truths you encountered in the lesson. You may want to take notes in the margin each day as you study. God may reveal several responses He wants you to make to a particular lesson. Don't let those thoughts get away from you. Write them down so you can review them. When God speaks, it is important to write down what He says. You may want to keep a notebook for recording your spiritual journey. I will talk to you more about journaling in a later unit.

After today's lesson a person might have responded like this:
- What was the most meaningful statement or Scripture you read today? "Jesus is my Way. I don't need a complete road map to stay in the center of God's will."
- Reword the statement or Scripture into a prayer of response to God. "Lord, I will follow You even if I don't know where You are leading."
- What does God want you to do in response to today's study? "I need to quit worrying about tomorrow and trust Jesus to guide me one day at a time."

9 **Each week I have given you a verse of Scripture to memorize. You will find memory cards for these Scriptures in the back of the book. Cut out the card for unit 1 (John 15:5). If you prefer, you may use a different translation for the memory verses in this study. The verses on the cards are from the New International Version. Read through John 15:5 several times. Then begin memorizing it one phrase at a time. Write your memory verse for this unit. Practice your memory verses daily.** _I am the vine and you are the branches. If you remain in me, and I in you, you will bear much fruit. Apart from me, you can do nothing!_

Review today's lesson. Pray and ask God to identify one or more statements or Scriptures He wants you to understand, learn, or practice. Underline them. Then respond to the following.

What was the most meaningful statement or Scripture you read today?	Reword the statement or Scripture into a prayer of response to God.	What does God want you to do in response to today's study?
God is absolutely trustworthy.	_Lord, I praise & thank you for being the God who does me. You know what I need & have never forsaken me. Peace._	_I don't need to simply cling to God — I abide in God — I need to cling to him._

**DAY
2**

JESUS WATCHED TO
SEE WHERE THE FA-
THER WAS AT WORK
AND JOINED HIM.

Look to see
what God
says and how
He works in
the Scriptures.
Make your
decisions and
evaluate your
experiences
based on bibli-
cal truths.

Malachi 3:6

"I the LORD do not change."

Jesus Is Your Model

During this course and throughout your life, you will have times when you want to respond to situations based on your own experiences or your own wisdom. Such an approach will get you in trouble. This should be your guideline: always go to the Bible and ask the Holy Spirit to reveal the truth of your situation to you. Look to see what God says and how He works in the Scriptures. Make your decisions and evaluate your experiences based on biblical truths.

When you study the Scriptures, do not base your decision on one isolated verse or story. Look to see how God generally works throughout the Scriptures. When you learn how God has consistently related to people throughout history, you can expect Him to work in a similar way with you. Your experience is valid only as it is confirmed in the Scriptures. I never deny anyone's personal experience. I always reserve the right, however, to interpret it according to what I understand from Scripture. At times individuals get upset with me and say, "I don't care what you say. I've experienced this." I kindly respond, "I do not deny your experience, but I question your interpretation of what happened because it is contrary to what I see in God's Word." Our experiences cannot be our guide. Every event in your life must be understood and interpreted by the Scriptures, for the God revealed in Scripture does not change (see **Mal. 3:6**).

1 **Mark the following statements *T* (true) or *F* (false).**

_F_ a. I can trust my experiences as an effective way to know and follow God.

_T_ b. I should always evaluate my experiences based on the truths I find in God's Word.

_T_ c. I may get a distorted understanding of God if I do not check my experiences against the truths of Scripture.

_T_ d. I can trust God to work in my life similarly to ways I see Him working throughout the Scriptures.

Statements b, c, and d are true. The first statement is false because your experiences must be interpreted in light of the Scriptures. Experience alone is not a trustworthy guide. You must be cautious about isolating a single event from the context of Scripture. Instead, observe the way God works throughout the Bible. You will never go wrong if, under the Holy Spirit's instruction, you let the Bible be your guide.

The Bible Is Your Guide

Christians are becoming more and more unfamiliar with the Bible as a guide for their daily living. Consequently, they turn to worldly solutions, programs, and methods that appear to be answers to spiritual problems. I use God's Word as a guide to what I should do. Some people say, "Henry, that is not practical." They want me to disregard the Bible and to rely on the world's ways or on personal experience. But as a Christian disciple, I cannot abandon the guidance I find in the Bible. The Bible is my guide for how to relate to God and how to live my life.

How do you let God's Word become your guide? When I seek God's direction, I insist on following the directives I see in His Word. Yesterday's lesson is an example. Does God call people to follow Him without giving them all the details in advance? We know He called Abram to follow that way. Is that pattern consistent in the Scriptures?

 Read the following Scriptures about Jesus' call for people to follow Him. Write what Jesus told these people to do.

Matthew 4:18-20: _follow me_
Matthew 4:21-22: _called them → follow me_
Matthew 9:9: _follow me_
Acts 9:1-20: _Arise & Go_

In some cases God gave more details than in others. We will look at Moses' call and discover God gave him a bigger picture of the assignment than He usually revealed. In every case, however, the individual had to stay close to God for His daily guidance. For Moses and the children of Israel, God led through a cloud by day and fire by night. For Peter, Andrew, James, John, Matthew, and Saul, God disclosed little detail about their assignments. He basically said, "Follow Me, and I will show you."

What Is God's Will?

When people seek to know and do God's will, many ask the question, What is God's will for my life? One of my seminary professors, Gaines S. Dobbins, used to say, "If you ask the wrong question, you will get the wrong answer." Sometimes we assume every question is legitimate. However, when we ask the wrong question, we may find an answer but remain disoriented to God and His activity. Always check to see whether you have asked the right question before you pursue the answer.

<u>What is God's will for my life? is *not* the right question. I think the proper question is, What is God's will? Once I know God's will, then I can adjust my life to Him</u>. In other words, what is it God is purposing to accomplish where I am? Once I know what God is doing, then I know what I need to do. The focus needs to be on *God*, not on *my life!*

When I want to learn how to know and do God's will, I can find no better model than Jesus' life. During His approximately 33 years on earth, He perfectly completed every assignment the Father gave Him. He never failed to do the will of the Father. He never sinned. Would you like to understand how Jesus came to know and do His Father's will?

 Read John 5:17,19-20 in the margin and answer the questions.
a. Who is always at work? _the Father_
b. How much can the Son do by Himself? _nothing_
c. What does the Son do? _whatever the Father does_
d. Why does the Father show the Son what He is doing? _b/c He loves him_

Some people read these verses and have difficulty understanding that Jesus Christ was fully God and fully human. Our minds can't fully grasp the truth that Jesus and the Father are one (John 15:9). We will look at their oneness more later. But make no mistake. Jesus is God and He lived on earth in human flesh. In these verses Jesus clearly states how He knew what to do. Jesus watched to see where His Father was at work and joined Him. Jesus' approach to knowing and doing His Father's will can be outlined like this:

The proper question is, What is God's will?

John 5:17,19-20

[17] "My Father is always at his work to this very day, and I, too, am working. [19] I tell you the truth, the Son can do nothing by himself; he can do only what he sees his Father doing, because whatever the Father does the Son also does. [20] For the Father loves the Son and shows him all he does. Yes, to your amazement he will show him even greater things than these."

Watch to see where God is working and join Him!

REALITY 1

GOD'S WORK

SUMMARY STATEMENTS

The Bible is my guide for faith and practice.

The right question is, What is God's will?

Watch to see where God is working and join Him.

God is always at work around me.

Jesus' Example

1. The Father has been working right up until now.
2. Now the Father has Me working.
3. I do nothing on My own initiative.
4. I watch to see what the Father is doing.
5. I do what I see the Father doing.
6. The Father loves Me.
7. He shows Me everything He is doing.

This model applies to your life personally and also to your church. It is not a step-by-step approach for knowing and doing God's will. It describes a love relationship through which God accomplishes His purposes. I sum it up this way: watch to see where God is working and join Him!

God Is Always at Work Around You

Right now God is working all around you, as well as in your life. One of the greatest tragedies among God's people is that, although they deeply long to experience God, they are encountering Him day after day but do not recognize Him. By the end of this course, you will have learned many ways to clearly identify God's activity in and around your life. The Holy Spirit and God's Word will instruct you and will help you know when and where God is working. Once you know where He is active, you will adjust your life to join Him in His activity.

You will experience God accomplishing His purposes through your life. When you enter this kind of intimate love relationship with God, you will know and do His will and experience Him in ways you have never known before. You cannot achieve this by following a spiritual formula. Only God can bring you into this kind of relationship.

4 Turn to the diagram inside the back cover of this book. Read all seven of the realities of experiencing God. Personalize the *first* statement and write it below, using *me* instead of *you*.

God is always at work around me.

Later this week we will take a closer look at these seven truths.

Review today's lesson. Pray and ask God to identify one or more statements or Scriptures He wants you to understand, learn, or practice. Underline them. Then respond to the following.

What was the most meaningful statement or Scripture you read today?

My life doesn't mattee. Gods will for my life is the wrong question.

Reword the statement or Scripture into a prayer of response to God.

God help me to see your will in youe work around me.

What does God want you to do in response to today's study?

Open my eyes to see the week as god sees it.

Learning to Be a Servant of God

TO BE A SERVANT OF GOD, YOU MUST BE MOLDABLE AND REMAIN IN THE HAND OF THE MASTER.

Many Scripture passages describe Jesus as God's Servant. He came as a Servant to accomplish God's will to redeem humanity. Here is what Paul said about Jesus: "Your attitude should be the same as that of Christ Jesus: Who, being in very nature God, did not consider equality with God something to be grasped, but made himself nothing, taking the very nature of a *servant,* being made in human likeness. And being found in appearance as a man, he humbled himself and became obedient to death—even death on a cross!" (Phil. 2:5-8, emphasis added).

In His instructions to His disciples about servanthood, Jesus (the Son of man) described His own role of service this way: "Whoever wants to become great among you must be your servant, and whoever wants to be first must be your slave—just as the Son of Man did not come to be served, but *to serve,* and to give his life as a ransom for many" (Matt. 20:26-28, emphasis added). Jesus also identified what our relationship with Him should be like: "As the Father has sent me, I am sending you" (John 20:21).

1 **Based on these Scriptures and others you may be familiar with, do you believe you should be God's servant?** ☑ Yes ❑ No

2 **Have you ever given your best effort to serve God and felt frustrated when nothing lasting resulted from your work?** ❑ Yes ❑ No

→ I have never thought about it before.

3 **What is a servant? Define *servant* in your own words.** *Someone who helps others - not always as their first choice.*

Did your definition sound something like this: "A servant is one who finds out what his master wants him to do and then does it"? The world's concept of a servant is that a servant goes to the master and says, "Master, what do you want me to do?" The master tells him, and the servant goes off *by himself* and does it. That is not the biblical concept of being a servant of God. Being a servant of God is different from being a servant of a human master. A servant of a human master works *for* his master. God, however, works *through* His servants.

Potter and Clay

My understanding of a servant is depicted by the potter and the clay (see **Jer. 18:1-6**). The clay must do two things:
1. The clay has to be molded. It has to be responsive to the potter so he can make it into an instrument of his choosing.
2. The clay has to remain in the potter's hand. When the potter has finished making the instrument of his choosing, that instrument has no ability to do what it wants. It has to remain in the potter's hand to be effective. Suppose the potter molds the clay into a cup. The cup has to remain in the potter's hands so he can use that cup the way he chooses.

Jeremiah 18:1-6
"This is the word that came to Jeremiah from the Lord: 'Go down to the potter's house, and there I will give you my message.' So I went down to the potter's house, and I saw him working at the wheel. But the pot he was shaping from the clay was marred in his hands; so the potter formed it into another pot, shaping it as seemed best to him. Then the word of the Lord came to me: 'O house of Israel, can I not do with you as this potter does?' declares the Lord. 'Like clay in the hand of the potter, so are you in my hand, O house of Israel.' "

Forgive me, Lord, when I don't want to be shaped by you.

17

To be God's servant, you must be moldable and remain in the hand of the Master.

These characteristics are quite different from the world's view of a servant. When you come to God as His servant, He first wants you to allow Him to mold and shape you into the instrument of His choosing. Then He takes your life where He wills and works through it to accomplish His purposes. Just as a cup cannot do anything on its own, you do not have the ability to carry out the Lord's command except to be where He wants you to be.

4 **Answer the following questions about being a servant of God.**
   a. How much can a servant do by himself or herself? _nothing_

   b. When God works through a servant, how much can that servant do? _whatever God has intended_

   c. What are two things a servant must do to be used by God? _1) be moldable, 2) remain in the hand of the Master_

To be God's servant, you must be moldable and remain in the hand of the Master. Then the Master will use you, the instrument, as He chooses. The servant can do nothing of Kingdom value alone, just as Jesus said, "The Son can do nothing by himself" (John 5:19) and "Apart from me you can do nothing" (John 15:5). With God working through a servant, however, he or she can do anything God can do. Wow! Unlimited potential! Servanthood requires obedience. Servants must do what they are instructed but must remember it's God who is accomplishing all the work.

If you have been working from the human approach to being a servant, this concept should change your approach to serving God. You do not get your orders and then go out to accomplish them on your own. You relate to God, respond to Him, and adjust your life to Him so that from your relationship with Him, He does what He wants to do through your life. Let's look at how God worked through His servant Elijah.

When **Elijah** challenged the prophets of Baal (a Canaanite fertility idol) to prove once and for all whose God was the true God, he took a big risk as God's servant.

5 **Read 1 Kings 18:15–39 and answer the following questions.**
   a. Elijah was God's servant. How many false prophets did he face at Mount Carmel? _850_

   b. What test did Elijah propose to prove whose God was the one true God? _to see which God would send fire from Heaven to consume a sacrifice_

   c. What did Elijah do to the altar of the Lord? _repaired it_

   d. At whose initiative did Elijah offer this challenge? _?_

   e. What did he intend to prove through this experience? _to prove the LORD is God_

   f. How did the people respond? _It's a reasonable contest._

   g. What was God's work in this event? _He sent the fire._

   h. What was Elijah's work in this event? _He listened to God_

Elijah was outnumbered 850 to 1. If God had not displayed His power by coming in fire and consuming the sacrifice (and altar) as Elijah had proposed, Elijah would have utterly failed. That would have cost him his life. Elijah repaired the altar of the Lord. He had to stay with God and do everything God commanded him to do. He was acting in obedience to God's command, not on his own initiative. He went where God guided him when God told him and did what God instructed him. Then God accomplished His purposes through him. God wanted the people to identify the Lord as the true God. As God worked through His prophet Elijah, that is exactly how the people responded.

Did Elijah or God bring down the fire from heaven? God did. What was Elijah doing? Being obedient. Elijah had no ability to preform the miraculous. When God did something only He could do, all the people knew He was the true God. God convinced people of His powerful presence through His obedient servant.

6 **As your study time permits, read the following questions. Try to answer each one before moving to the next one. You may want to jot down some notes on the response lines.**

a. What will be the difference between the quality of service and the quantity of lasting results when God is working and when you are working?

What God intends will happen & will have a deep and lasting impact.

b. What are you doing in your life personally and in your church *– I'm not "churched"* that you know <u>cannot be accomplished</u> unless God intervenes?

my marriage + family, my sanity

c. What are we doing in our lives and in our churches that could be done without reference to God at all? *→ making purchases, financial decisions, taking jobs – although I did pray for that!*

d. Why do you think we often experience meager lasting fruit from our efforts?

For me, I get set on bringing glory to myself.

Don't Just Do Something

We are a doing people. We always want to be doing something. Every now and then someone will exclaim, "Don't just stand there; do something!"

In contrast, I think God is crying out to us, "<u>Don't just do something. Stand there! Enter a love relationship with Me. Get to know Me.</u> Adjust your life to Me. Let Me love you and reveal Myself through you to a watching world." A time will come when doing will be called for, but we cannot skip the relationship. The relationship with God must come first.

Jesus said, "I am the vine; you are the branches. If a man remains in me and I in him, he will bear much fruit; apart from me you can do nothing" (John 15:5). Do you believe Him? <u>Without Him you can do nothing.</u> He means that.

7 **Turn to the diagram inside the back cover. Read again all seven realities listed there. Personalize the *last* (seventh) reality and write it below, using *I* and *me* instead of *you*.** *I come to know God by experience as I obey Him, and He accomplishes His work through me.*

> "Don't just do something. Stand there!"

God can do anything through me.

When I find out where the Master is working, then I know that is where I need to be.

I come to know God by experience as I obey Him, and He accomplishes His work through me.

God wants you to come to a greater knowledge of Him by experience. He wants to develop a growing, deepening love relationship with you. He wants to involve you in His Kingdom purposes. He wants to accomplish His will through you.

Do you want to be a servant of God? Find out what is on the Master's heart. Discover where the Master is working; that is where you need to be. Find out what the Master is doing; that is what you need to do. Jesus said, "Whoever serves me must follow me; and where I am, my servant also will be. My Father will honor the one who serves me" (John 12:26).

8 **Practice quoting your Scripture-memory verse aloud and/or write it on a separate sheet of paper.**

I am the vine & you are the branches. If you remain in me & I in you, you will bear much fruit. Apart from me, you can do nothing.

Review today's lesson. Pray and ask God to identify one or more statements or Scriptures He wants you to understand, learn, or practice. Underline them. Then respond to the following.

What was the most meaningful statement or Scripture you read today?

But the pot he was shaping me from the clay was marred in his hands so the potter formed it into another pot, shaping it as it seemed best to him.

Reword the statement or Scripture into a prayer of response to God.

Father, I was marred in your hands but you didn't throw me out—you formed me into something new as seemed best to you—thank you, Lord.

What does God want you to do in response to today's study?

Love Him more, seek him – be molded by Him & remain in his hand.

Disbanding Church Revitalized

A church in an inner city had suffered years of decline as its neighborhood transitioned and church members moved to the suburbs. When only a remnant was left, they concluded they should disband their church. As a final activity the members decided to study *Experiencing God.* At the conclusion of the study, they would close the church doors for the last time. At the beginning of the course, the people learned that God is always at work around them. They chuckled at the thought, since nothing unusual had happened in their church for years. Nevertheless, they decided to watch during the week to see where God might be working.

That week an apartment manager approached a church member and asked if her church could do anything about all the kids in the apartment block with nothing to do. He offered the free use of the apartment's common room if the church would provide activities. The church decided to offer a children's program during the final few months of its existence. This soon brought several unwed mothers to their attention. Then some drug addicts were attracted to the church, as well as some gang members. Before this little group of people realized what was happening, they had launched several new ministries and were seeing people come to faith in Christ almost every week. At the close of the 13-week study, instead of disbanding, the church, now revitalized, began to minister powerfully to its community. Rather than remaining discouraged, the people realized they were in the center of God's activity. He had been working in their community all along.

God Works Through His Servants, Part I

We often act as though God tells us what He wants us to do and then sends us off by ourselves to try and do it. Then anytime we need Him, we can call on Him, and He comes to help us. That is not the biblical picture. When God is about to do something, He reveals it to His people. He wants to accomplish His work through His people or His servant.

When God is about to do something through you, He has to get you from where you are to where He is, so He tells you what He is doing. (Later, I will help you understand how you can clearly know when God is speaking to you.) When you know what God is doing, then you know what you need to do: you need to join Him. The moment you know God is doing something where you are, your life and its activity will be thrown in contrast to God and His activity. You cannot stay the way you are and go with God.

Seven Realities of Experiencing God

The illustration below (and inside the back cover) summarizes the way you should respond to God's initiative in your life. The text of the realities is in the margin.

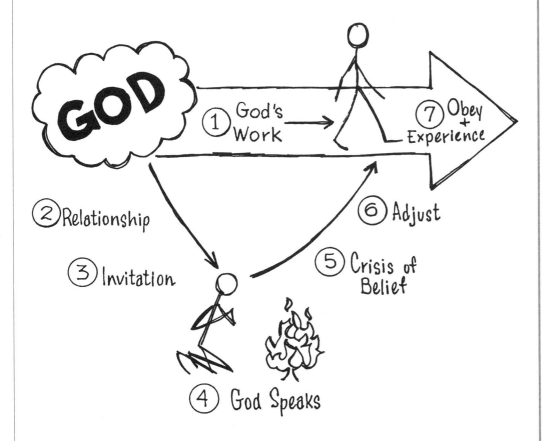

YOU CANNOT STAY THE WAY YOU ARE AND GO WITH GOD.

1. God is always at work around you.
2. God pursues a continuing love relationship with you that is real and personal.
3. God invites you to become involved with Him in His work.
4. God speaks by the Holy Spirit through the Bible, prayer, circumstances, and the church to reveal Himself, His purposes, and His ways.
5. God's invitation for you to work with Him always leads you to a crisis of belief that requires faith and action.
6. You must make major adjustments in your life to join God in what He is doing.
7. You come to know God by experience as you obey Him, and He accomplishes His work through you.

Complete the following to begin learning the seven realities. Use the text of the realities in the margin on page 21.

a. Underline key words or phrases that help you recall the seven realities.

b. Write the key words or phrases on the following lines. ¹God works. ²God pursues. ³God invites. ⁴God speaks ⁵) Crisis of belief. ⁶) Major adjustments. ⁷) Know God.

[handwritten in margin: —I don't think every decision has to be a crisis of belief.]

c. Slowly read each reality. Write in the margin questions about any of the realities you do not fully understand.

d. Using only the words or phrases you recorded, see if you can mentally summarize all seven realities. Review before moving to the next question.

e. On a separate sheet of paper, try writing each of the seven realities from memory. They do not have to be word for word, but they should cover the important information. Start with your key words or phrases if that helps.

Most of this course will focus on one or more of these realities to help you understand them more completely. You may notice that I frequently repeat different aspects of this cycle. I use the repetition in different situations to help you learn how you can respond to God's activity in your life.

In the assignment above, you could have selected various words or phrases. Yours may be different, but I chose *God/work, love relationship, involved with Him, God speaks, crisis of belief, adjustments, obey.* You may have asked questions like these:
- What is involved in a love relationship with God?
- How can I know when God is speaking?
- How do I know where God is at work?
- What kinds of adjustments does God require me to make?
- What is the difference between adjustment and obedience?

As I've worked with people in many settings, I've been asked questions like these. I will answer as many questions as possible during the remaining units of this course. Richard and I will address other issues in the DVD messages that accompany this course.

We can identify three similarities in the lives of Bible characters through whom God worked:
1. When God spoke, they knew it was God.
2. They knew what God was saying.
3. They knew what they were to do in response.

[handwritten: there is no crisis here.]

Wouldn't you like for your walk with God to be such that He worked through you that way? He wants to move you into that kind of relationship. I trust this course will help you grow in your understanding of God.

Moses' call and ministry are good examples of the way God worked with people in the Bible. Exodus 2–4 describes his early life and call to ministry. Other passages of Scripture also help us see how Moses came to know and follow God's will. Using the seven realities, let's look at Moses' call and response. (You may want to read Ex. 2–4 first.)

Reality 1. God was already at work around Moses.

> "The Israelites groaned in their slavery and cried out, and their cry for help because of their slavery went up to God. God heard their groaning and he remembered his covenant with Abraham, with Isaac and with Jacob. So God looked on the Israelites and was concerned about them" (Ex. 2:23-25).

Reality 2. God pursued a continuing love relationship with Moses that was real and personal. God took the initiative to come to Moses and initiate a love relationship with him at the burning bush. God told Moses He would go with him into Egypt. Many texts throughout Exodus, Leviticus, Numbers, and Deuteronomy illustrate the way God pursued a continuing love relationship with Moses. Here is one example:

> "The LORD said to Moses, 'Come up to me on the mountain and stay here, and I will give you the tablets of stone, with the law and commands I have written for their instruction.' When Moses went up on the mountain, the cloud covered it, and the glory of the LORD settled on Mount Sinai. Moses entered the cloud as he went on up the mountain. And he stayed on the mountain forty days and forty nights" (Ex. 24:12,15-16,18).

Reality 3. God invited Moses to become involved with Him in His work.

> "I have come down to rescue them [the Israelites] from the hand of the Egyptians and to bring them up out of that land into a good and spacious land. So now, go. I am sending you to Pharaoh to bring my people the Israelites out of Egypt" (Ex. 3:8,10).

2 **Answer the following questions about the three preceding statements.**
a. Reality 1: What was God already doing for Israel? _Fulfilling His part of the covenant_

b. Reality 2: What evidence demonstrates God wanted a real and personal relationship with Moses? _Ex 3:10 - God says, "I will send you" He also gets mad at Moses._

c. Reality 3: How did God want to involve Moses in the work He was already doing? _He sent Moses to talk to Pharoah._

(1) God had a purpose He was accomplishing in Moses' world. Even though Moses was an exile in the desert, he was on God's schedule, in the fullness of God's timing, in the middle of God's will. When God was about to deliver the children of Israel, the important factor was not God's will for Moses. The critical truth was God's will for Israel. (2) God's purpose was to deliver the children of Israel. Moses was the one through whom God wanted to work to accomplish His purposes. (3) Time and again God invited Moses to talk with Him and to be with Him. God initiated and maintained a growing relationship with Moses. This relationship was based on love, and God daily fulfilled His purposes through His friend Moses. (For other examples of the love relationship, see Ex. 33:7–34:10; Num. 12:6-8.)

Whenever God prepares to do something, He reveals to a person or His people what He is going to do (see **Amos 3:7**). God accomplishes His work through His

Amos 3:7

"Surely the Sovereign LORD does nothing without revealing his plan to his servants the prophets."

people. This is the way God will work with you. The Bible is designed to help you understand God's ways. Then when God starts to act in that manner in your life, you will recognize that it is He who is working.

This is a two-part lesson, so we will continue with statement 4 tomorrow. This two-part lesson will be summarized at the end of day 5.

Review today's lesson. Pray and ask God to identify one or more statements or Scriptures He wants you to understand, learn, or practice. Underline them. Then respond to the following.

What was the most meaningful statement or Scripture you read today?

Whenever God perposis to do something, he reveals to them what it is about to do.

Reword the statement or Scripture into a prayer of response to God.

Father, reveal your work to me if & when there is something for me to do. Let me do it. Lead me to it.

What does God want you to do in response to today's study?

Think about it & read tomorrow's lesson with an open heart.

DAY 5

God Works Through His Servants, Part 2

GOD REVEALS WHAT HE IS ABOUT TO DO. THAT REVELATION BECOMES AN INVITATION TO JOIN HIM.

Yesterday you studied the first three realities of God's working with Moses. Now look at the last four.

Reality 4. God spoke to reveal Himself, His purposes, and His ways.

"There the angel of the LORD appeared to him in flames of fire from within a bush. … God called to him from within the bush, 'Moses! Moses!' And Moses said, 'Here I am.'

'Do not come any closer,' God said. 'Take off your sandals, for the place where you are standing is holy ground.' Then he said, 'I am the God of your father, the God of Abraham, the God of Isaac and the God of Jacob.'

"The LORD said, 'I have indeed seen the misery of my people in Egypt. I have heard them crying out because of their slave drivers, and I am concerned about their suffering. So I have come down to rescue them from the hand of the Egyptians and to bring them up out of that land into a good and spacious land' " (Ex. 3:2-8).

"When a prophet of the LORD is among you,
    I reveal myself to him in visions,
    I speak to him in dreams.
But this is not true of my servant Moses;
    he is faithful in all my house.
With him I speak face to face" (Num. 12:6-8).

Reality 5. God's invitation for Moses to work with Him led to a crisis of belief that required faith and action. Moses expressed a crisis of belief when he made the following statements to God.

> "Who am I, that I should go to Pharaoh and bring the Israelites out of Egypt?"
>
> "Suppose I go to the Israelites and say to them, 'The God of your fathers has sent me to you,' and they ask me, 'What is his name?' Then what shall I tell them?"
>
> "What if they do not believe me or listen to me and say, 'The LORD did not appear to you' "?
>
> "O Lord, I have never been eloquent, neither in the past nor since you have spoken to your servant. I am slow of speech and tongue."
>
> "O Lord, please send someone else to do it" (Ex. 3:11,13; 4:1,10,13).

Reality 6. Moses had to make major adjustments in his life to join God in what He was doing. Moses' crisis called for faith and action.

> "By faith Moses, when he had grown up, refused to be known as the son of Pharaoh's daughter. He chose to be mistreated along with the people of God rather than to enjoy the pleasures of sin for a short time. ... By faith he left Egypt, not fearing the king's anger; he persevered because he saw him who is invisible. By faith he kept the Passover and the sprinkling of blood, so that the destroyer of the firstborn would not touch the firstborn of Israel. By faith the people passed through the Red Sea as on dry land; but when the Egyptians tried to do so, they were drowned" (Heb. 11:24-29).

> "The LORD had said to Moses in Midian, 'Go back to Egypt, for all the men who wanted to kill you are dead.' So Moses took his wife and sons, put them on a donkey and started back to Egypt" (Ex. 4:19-20).

Reality 7. Moses came to know God by experience as he obeyed God, and God accomplished His work through Moses. Many texts throughout Exodus, Leviticus, Numbers, and Deuteronomy illustrate how God revealed His nature and His purposes to Moses. As Moses obeyed God, God accomplished through Moses what Moses could not do in his own strength. Here is one example in which Moses and the people came to know God as their Deliverer.

> "Then the LORD said to Moses, 'Why are you crying out to me? Tell the Israelites to move on. Raise your staff and stretch out your hand over the sea to divide the water so that the Israelites can go through the sea on dry ground. I will harden the hearts of the Egyptians so that they will go in after them. And I will gain glory through Pharaoh and all his army. ...'
>
> "Then Moses stretched out his hand over the sea, and all that night the LORD drove the sea back with a strong east wind and turned it into dry land. The waters were divided, and the Israelites went through the sea on dry ground, with a wall of water on their right and on their left. The Egyptians pursued them.
>
> "Then the LORD said to Moses, 'Stretch out your hand over the sea so that the waters may flow back over the Egyptians and their chari-

ots and horsemen.' Moses stretched out his hand over the sea, and at daybreak the sea went back to its place.

"But the Israelites went through the sea on dry ground, with a wall of water on their right and on their left. That day the LORD saved Israel from the hands of the Egyptians, and Israel saw the Egyptians lying dead on the shore. And when the Israelites saw the great power the LORD displayed against the Egyptians, the people feared the LORD and put their trust in him and in Moses his servant" (Ex. 14:15-17,21-23,26-27,29-31).

1 **Answer the following questions about the last four realities.**

a. Reality 4: What did God reveal about Himself, His purposes, and His ways?
He is holy. He is concerned for us. He hears our cries. He acts on our behalf.

b. Reality 5: What did Moses have trouble believing about God? _____
That God could use a person like him.

c. Reality 5: How would you summarize Moses' faith as it is described in Hebrews 11? *An active faith*

d. Reality 6: What adjustments did Moses have to make? *give up comforts - be willing to suffer*

e. Reality 7: How do you think Moses felt when God delivered the Israelites through him? *Exhausted & amazed! Whew! grateful, humbled.*

God reveals what He is about to do. That revelation becomes an invitation to join Him. (4) God talked to Moses about His will. God wanted Moses to go to Egypt to be His instrument to deliver the Israelites from their bondage. God revealed to Moses His holiness, His mercy, His power, His name, and His purpose to keep His promise to Abraham and to give Israel the promised land. (5) Moses offered many objections. He questioned whether God could do such a great work through someone like him (see Ex. 3:11), whether the Israelites would believe God had appeared to him (see Ex. 4:1), and whether he was capable of speaking eloquently enough to accomplish the task (see Ex. 4:10). In each case Moses was really doubting God more than himself. Moses faced a crisis of belief: is God really able to do what He says? (5) Moses' faith is described in Hebrews, however, as a model of self-sacrifice and trust in almighty God. Once God let Moses know what He was about to do, that revelation became Moses' invitation to join Him. (6) Moses made the necessary adjustments to orient his life to God. Moses had to come to the place where he believed God could do everything He said He would do. Then he had to leave his job and in-laws and move to Egypt. After making these adjustments, he was in a position to obey God. That did not mean he was going to do something all by himself for God. It meant he was going to be where God was working so God would do what He had purposed to do in the first place. Moses was a servant who was *moldable,* and he *remained* at God's disposal to be used as God chose. God accomplished His purposes through him. When God does a God-sized work through your life, you will be humbled before Him. (7) Moses must have felt unworthy to be used in such a significant way. Moses obeyed and did everything God told him. Then God accomplished through Moses all He intended. Every step of obedience brought Moses (and Israel) to a greater knowledge of God (see Ex. 6:1-8).

What Can One Ordinary Person Do?

A wonderful Scripture that has helped me at this point is "Elijah was a man just like us. He prayed earnestly that it would not rain, and it did not rain on the land for three and a half years. Again he prayed, and the heavens gave rain, and the earth produced its crops" (Jas. 5:17-18). Elijah was an ordinary man just like us. He prayed, and God responded powerfully.

When God healed the crippled beggar through Peter, **Peter and John** were called before the Sanhedrin (the highest Jewish court in the land) to give an account of their actions. Filled with the Holy Spirit, Peter boldly spoke to the religious leaders. Notice the leaders' response: "When they saw the courage of Peter and John and realized that they were unschooled, *ordinary men,* they were astonished and they took note that these men had been with Jesus" (Acts 4:13, emphasis added).

The people you generally see in the Scriptures were ordinary. Their relationships with God and the activity of God made them extraordinary. Did you notice this statement: the leaders recognized Peter and John "had been with Jesus"? Anyone who takes the time to enter an intimate relationship with God can see Him do extraordinary things through his or her life.

Dwight L. Moody was a poorly educated, unordained shoe salesman who felt God's call to preach the gospel. Early one morning he and some friends gathered for prayer, confession, and consecration. They heard Henry Varley say, "The world has yet to see what God can do with and for and through and in a man who is fully and wholly consecrated to Him."

Moody was deeply moved by those words. Later he listened to the great preacher Charles H. Spurgeon. Moody thought:

> "The world had yet to see! with and for and through and in! A man!" Varley meant *any* man! Varley didn't say he had to be educated, or brilliant, or anything else! Just a *man*! Well, by the Holy Spirit in him, he'd [Moody] be *one* of those men. And then suddenly, in that high gallery, he saw something he'd never realized before,—it was not Mr. Spurgeon, after all, who was doing that work: it was God. And if God could use Mr. Spurgeon, why should He not use the rest of us, and why should we not all just lay ourselves at the Master's feet, and say to Him, "Send me! use me!"

Dwight L. Moody was an ordinary person who sought to be fully and wholly consecrated to Christ. One ordinary Christian in the hand of almighty God can do *anything* God commands. Through this one common life God began to do the extraordinary. Moody became one of the greatest evangelists of modern times. He preached in revival services across Britain and America, where thousands and thousands came to Christ.

2 **Could God work in extraordinary ways through your life to accomplish significant things for His kingdom?** ☑ Yes ❑ No

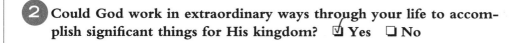

You might say, "I'm not a D. L. Moody." You don't have to be. God doesn't want you to be a D. L. Moody. God wants you to be you and to let Him do through you whatever He chooses. When you believe nothing significant can happen through you, you have said more about your belief in God than you have declared about yourself. You have said that God is incapable of doing anything significant through you. The truth is, He

"The world has yet to see what God can do with and for and through and in a man who is fully and wholly consecrated to Him."

When you believe nothing significant can happen through you, you have said more about your belief in God than you have declared about yourself.

is able to do anything He pleases with one ordinary person who is fully consecrated to Him. Would you be willing to make yourself available to Him? Do it!

God's Standards Are Different from Ours

Don't be surprised that God's standards of excellence are different than the world's. How long was the public ministry of John the Baptist? Perhaps six months. What was Jesus' estimate of John's life? Jesus said, "I tell you, among those born of women there is no one greater than John" (Luke 7:28). None greater! John had six months wholly yielded to God, and the Son of God declared that his contribution to the kingdom of God was unsurpassed.

Don't measure your life by the world's standards. Many denominations are doing it. Many pastors and churches are doing it. Think about it. By the world's standards, a person or a church may look pretty good yet, in God's sight, be utterly detestable. Similarly, a person or a church may be wholly yielded to God and pleasing to Him yet be insignificant in the world's eyes. Could a pastor who faithfully serves where God placed him in a small, rural community be pleasing to the Lord? Certainly, if that is where God placed him. God will look for and reward faithfulness, whether the person has been given responsibility for little or much.

God delights in using ordinary people to accomplish His purposes. Paul said God deliberately seeks the weak things and the despised things because from them He receives the greatest glory (see 1 Cor. 1:26-31). Then everyone knows only God could have done something through them. If you feel weak, limited, or ordinary, you are the best material through which God works.

3 **Review your Scripture-memory verse and be prepared to recite it to a partner in your small-group session this week.**

4 **Spend a few minutes in prayer for your small group. Pray that the Lord will have complete freedom to mold and shape and guide each one to be perfectly in the middle of His will.**

SUMMARY STATEMENTS

God reveals what He is about to do.

The revelation becomes an invitation to join Him.

I can't stay where I am and go with God.

God is able to do anything He pleases with one ordinary person who is fully consecrated to Him.

God's standards of excellence are different from ours.

Review today's lesson. Pray and ask God to identify one or more statements or Scriptures He wants you to understand, learn, or practice. Underline them. Then respond to the following.

What was the most meaningful statement or Scripture you read today?

God deliberately seeks weak and despised things because from these He receives the greatest glory.

Reword the statement or Scripture into a prayer of response to God.

Dear Lord, use my weakness to glorify you. Not myself. Keep me molded & humble in the centre of your will.

What does God want you to do in response to today's study?

Lord, help me to understand what you will reveal to me through this study. Draw me closer to you.

This is the end of this unit's lessons. The following page will be used in your small-group session this week. It includes notes from the DVD messages and a review of the content you have studied this week.

GOD'S WILL AND YOUR LIFE

DVD Message Notes

1. The Bible is God-centered.
2. God has assigned the Holy Spirit to be our Teacher.
3. To know God, you have to experience Him.
4. There is a DNA in every believer to know and do the will of God.
5. When you get your life God-oriented, you begin to see how God had an agenda you knew nothing about.
6. God's goal is to conform you to the image of His Son.
7. God is always at work around you.
8. You need to see where He is at work and join Him.
9. The servant doesn't have the agenda. The Master does.
10. The question is not "What do You want me to do for You?" The question is "What are You doing?"

Scriptures Referenced

Romans 8:28
Amos 7:14
Hebrews 4:15
John 5:17,19-20

Testimony

Lock Sourinthone

Your Notes

The pattern for following the will of God is the Lord Jesus—depend on the Holy Spirit, depend on the Scriptures.

John 5:19-20 → the Son only does what the Father does & the Father shows us what He is doing

What's on your plan sheet?
When God writes on it, we're going to do it.

God doesn't need us to do anything for Him. He wants to do something through us.

Unit Review

Write a key word or words for each of the seven realities of experiencing God. If you need help, you may peek at the inside back cover.

1. God's work
2. Relationship
3. Invitation
4. God Speaks
5. Crisis of Belief
6. Adjust
7. Obey & Experience

Check your answers, using the inside back cover of your book.

Get Acquainted

1. My name is …
2. My immediate family includes …
3. The thing I liked best about my home-town was …
4. Something interesting you might not know about me is …
5. I chose to study this course on knowing and doing the will of God because …

For Makeup or Review

Audio and video downloads are available at *www.lifeway.com*.

UNIT 2

VERSE TO MEMORIZE

"SOME TRUST IN CHARIOTS
AND SOME IN HORSES,
BUT WE TRUST IN THE NAME
OF THE LORD OUR GOD."

PSALM 20:7

Looking to God

COLLEGE CAMPUS BIBLE STUDIES

A church I pastored began to sense God leading us to an outreach ministry to the university campus. Neither I nor our church had done student work before. Our denominational student-ministries department recommended we begin with a Bible study in the dormitories. For over a year we tried to start one, but it did not work.

One Sunday I pulled our students together and said, "This week I want you to go to the campus, watch to see where God is working, and join Him." They asked me to explain. God had impressed on my heart these two Scriptures:

- "There is no one righteous, not even one; there is no one who understands, no one who seeks God" (Rom. 3:10-11).
- "No one can come to me [Jesus] unless the Father who sent me draws him" (John 6:44).

I explained, "According to these passages, people don't seek God on their own initiative. They won't ask about spiritual matters unless God is working in their lives. When you encounter someone who is seeking God or asking about spiritual matters, you are seeing God at work."

I also told our students, "If someone asks you spiritual questions, whatever else you have scheduled, cancel your plans. Go with that individual and look to see what God is doing in that person's life." That week our students went out to see where God was at work on their campus and to join Him.

On Wednesday one of the young women reported, "Pastor, a girl who has been in classes with me for almost two years came to me after class today. She said, 'I think you might be a Christian. I need to talk to you.' I remembered what you said. I had a class at that time, but I skipped it. We went to the cafeteria to talk. She said, 'Eleven of us girls have been studying the Bible, and none of us are Christians. Do you know somebody who can lead us in a Bible study?' "

As a result of that contact, we started three Bible-study groups in the women's dorms and two in the men's dorm. For two years we had tried to do something for God and failed. For three days we looked to see where God was working and joined Him. What a difference that made!

Day 1

To know and do God's will, you must deny self and return to a God-centered life.

God-Centered Living

Part of the Book of Genesis is the record of God's accomplishing His purposes through Abraham. It is not the record of Abraham's walk with God. Can you see the difference in focus? The focus of the Bible is God. The essence of sin is a shift from God-centeredness to self-centeredness. The essence of salvation is denying self instead of affirming self. We must deny ourselves and return to God-centeredness in our lives. Then God has us in a place where He will accomplish His eternal purposes through us.

A Self-Centered Life

- Is focused on self
- Is proud of self and self's accomplishments
- Is self-confident
- Depends on self and abilities
- Affirms self
- Seeks to be acceptable to the world and its ways
- Looks at circumstances from a human perspective
- Chooses selfish and ordinary living

A God-Centered Life

- Places confidence in God
- Depends on God and His ability and provision
- Focuses on God and His activity
- Is humble before God
- Denies self
- Seeks first the kingdom of God and His righteousness
- Seeks God's perspective in every circumstance
- Chooses holy and godly living
  To know and do God's will, you must deny self and return to a God-centered life.

1 **In your own words write definitions of the following terms.**
Self-centered: <u>needing to be important</u>

God-centered: <u>serving God without a need for honor or recognition</u>

2 **In each pair of biblical examples, write *G* before the one that illustrates God-centeredness. Write *S* before the one that illustrates self-centeredness.**

S 1a. God placed Adam and Eve in a beautiful, bountiful garden. He told them not to eat from the tree of the knowledge of good and evil. Eve saw that the fruit was pleasing to the eye and desirable for gaining wisdom, so she ate it (see Gen. 2:16-17; 3:1-7).

G 1b. Potiphar's wife daily begged Joseph to go to bed with her. He told her he could not do such a wicked thing and sin against God. When she tried to force him, he fled the room and went to prison rather than yield to temptation (see Gen. 39).

God promised to give the land of Canaan to Israel. Moses sent 12 men into the promised land to explore it and to bring back a report. The land was bountiful, but the people living there appeared to be giants (see Num. 13–14).

S 2a. Ten of the spies said, "We can't attack those people; they are stronger than we are" (13:31).

G 2b. Joshua and Caleb said, "If the Lord is pleased with us, he will lead us into that land. … Do not be afraid of the people of the land" (14:8-9).

G 3a. King Asa was facing Zerah the Cushite's army in battle. He prayed, "LORD, there is no one like you to help the powerless against the mighty. Help us, O LORD our God, for we rely on you, and in your name we have come against this vast army. O LORD, you are our God; do not let man prevail against you" (2 Chron. 14:11).

S 3b. King Asa and Judah were being threatened by Baasha, the king of Israel. Asa sent gold and silver from the temple and his own palace to Ben-Hadad, the king of Aram, asking for his help in this conflict (see 2 Chron. 16:1-3).

Self-centeredness is a subtle trap because it makes sense from a human perspective. Like King Asa, you can avoid it at one time and fall into its trap at another. God-centeredness requires the daily death of self and submission to God (see **John 12:23-25**). Illustrations of God-centeredness are 1b, 2b, and 3a. The others illustrate self-centeredness.

God's Purposes, Not Our Plans

To live a God-centered life, you must focus your life on God's purposes, not on your own plans. You must seek to view situations from God's perspective rather than from your own distorted human outlook. When God starts to do something in the world, He takes the initiative to reveal His will to people. For some divine reason He has chosen to involve His people in accomplishing His purposes.

3 **Answer the following questions. Find and read the Scriptures listed if you do not already know the answers.**

a. What was God about to do when He asked Noah to build an ark (see Gen. 6:5-14)? ___destroy mankind___

b. What was God about to do to Sodom and Gomorrah when He came to Abraham (see Gen. 18:16-21; 19:13)? ___destroy it___

c. What was God about to do when He came to Gideon (see Judg. 6:11-16)? ___to deliver Israel from the Midianites___

d. What was God about to do when He came to Saul (later called Paul) on the road to Damascus (see Acts 9:1-16)? ___About to make Saul his chosen vessel___

John 12:23-25
"Unless a kernel of wheat falls to the ground and dies, it remains only a single seed. But if it dies, it produces many seeds. The man who loves his life will lose it, while the man who hates his life in this world will keep it for eternal life."

SUMMARY STATEMENTS

To know and do God's will, I must deny self and return to a God-centered life.

I must focus my life on God's purposes, not on my own plans.

I must seek to see from God's perspective rather than from my own distorted human outlook.

I must wait until God shows me what He is about to do through me.

I will watch to see what God is doing around me and join Him.

e. At each of these moments, what was the most important factor? Check one.
- ☐ a. What the individual wanted to do for God
- ☑ b. What God was about to do

God was about to destroy the world with a great flood when He approached Noah. When God prepared to destroy Sodom and Gomorrah, He told Abraham. God came to Gideon when He was about to deliver the Israelites from the oppression of Midian. God encountered Saul when He wanted to carry the gospel message to the Gentiles around the known world. Without a doubt the most important factor in each situation was what God was about to do (b).

Let's use Noah as an example. What about his plans to serve God? They would not make much sense in light of the coming destruction, would they? Noah was not calling God in to help him accomplish what he was dreaming of doing for God. God never asks people to dream up something to do for Him. We do not sit down and dream what we want to do for God and then call God in to help us accomplish it. The pattern in Scripture is that we submit ourselves to God. Then we wait until God shows us what He is about to do, or we watch to see what God is already doing around us and join Him.

4 Write your Scripture-memory verse for this week. Then review your verse from last week.

Don't trust in chariots and others in horses, but we trust in the name of the Lord of our God.

Review today's lesson. Pray and ask God to identify one or more statements or Scriptures He wants you to understand, learn, or practice. Underline them. Then respond to the following.

What was the most meaningful statement or Scripture you read today?	Reword the statement or Scripture into a prayer of response to God.	What does God want you to do in response to today's study?
God's purposes — not my plans.	Father in Heaven, I do have to die daily to myself for this to happen. Why do we have a self at all?	Acknowledge total depravity.

From Death Row to Life Row

God-centered living always affects other lives. Being certain God is always at work around you will affect your relationships with others.

When Karla Faye Tucker was on death row in the Gatesville Women's prison in Texas, she became a Christian. Some faithful Christians led her through *Experiencing God*. Her life was so changed, she began to teach other inmates on death row. So many came to know Jesus as Savior, the women themselves renamed it Life Row because they came to know true life in Christ. Eventually, Karla was executed for her crime, but her testimony affected a nation and touched a world.

God's Plans Versus Our Plans

Who delivered the children of Israel from Egypt—Moses or God? God did. God chose to bring Moses into a relationship with Himself so that He [God] could deliver Israel. Did Moses ever try to take matters into his own hands? Yes.

In **Exodus 2:11-15** Moses began to assert himself on behalf of his people. What might have happened if Moses had tried to deliver the children of Israel through a human approach? Thousands of his countrymen would have been slain in battle. Moses tried to personally deliver one Israelite, and that cost him 40 years of exile in Midian working as a shepherd and reorienting his life to God-centered living.

When God delivered the children of Israel, how many Israelite lives were lost? None. In the process God even led the Egyptians to give the Israelites their gold, silver, and clothes. Egypt was plundered, the Egyptian army was destroyed, and the Israelites did not lose a single person.

Why do we not realize that it is always best to do things God's way? We cause some of the wreck and ruin in our churches because we have a plan. We implement the plan and accomplish only what we can do. We ask God to bless our plans, and then we promise to give Him the glory when He does. Yet God is not glorified by making our plans succeed. He receives glory when *His* will is done in His way. Christ is the Head of the body—the church. What a difference it would make if we obeyed Christ as the Head of that body! He could accomplish more in six months through a people yielded to Him than we could do in 60 years without Him.

Following God's Ways

1 **Read the following Scripture and look for God's response to those who will not follow His ways. Then answer the questions that follow.**

"I am the LORD your God,
  who brought you up out of Egypt.
  Open wide your mouth and I will fill it.
But my people would not listen to me;
  Israel would not submit to me.
So I gave them over to their stubborn hearts
  to follow their own devices" (Ps. 81:10-12).

a. What had God already done for Israel? *brought them out of Egypt*
b. What did God promise His people? *fill their mouths*
c. How did the people respond? *didn't listen or submit*
d. What did God do? *left them to their own devices*

2 **Now read the next two verses to see what could have been true for Israel.**

UNDERSTANDING WHAT GOD IS ABOUT TO DO WHERE I AM IS MORE IMPORTANT THAN TELLING GOD WHAT I WANT TO DO FOR HIM.

Exodus 2:11-15
"One day, after Moses had grown up, he went out to where his own people were and watched them at their hard labor. He saw an Egyptian beating a Hebrew, one of his own people. Glancing this way and that and seeing no one, he killed the Egyptian and hid him in the sand. The next day he went out and saw two Hebrews fighting. He asked the one in the wrong, 'Why are you hitting your fellow Hebrew?'

"The man said, 'Who made you ruler and judge over us? Are you thinking of killing me as you killed the Egyptian?' Then Moses was afraid and thought, 'What I did must have become known.'

"When Pharaoh heard of this, he tried to kill Moses, but Moses fled from Pharaoh and went to live in Midian.'"

"If my people would but listen to me,
    if Israel would follow my ways,
  how quickly would I subdue their enemies
    and turn my hand against their foes!" (Ps. 81:13-14).

What could have been true if Israel had listened to and followed God?
He would have defeated all their enemies.

3 Locate in your Bible and read Hebrews 3:7-19. Why were the children of Israel denied entrance into the promised land?
they did not believe, they hardened their hearts & rebelled

We adjust our lives to God so *He* will do through us what *He* wants to accomplish. God is not our servant to adjust His activity to our plans. We are His servants, and we adjust our lives to what He is about to do. If we do not submit, God will allow us to follow our own devices. In following them, however, we will never experience what God wanted to do on our behalf or through us for others.

God brought Israel out of Egypt with many miraculous signs and wonders. Wouldn't you think the Hebrews would trust God to do anything after that? When they arrived in the promised land, however, they could not trust Him to deliver it to them. For that reason they spent the next 40 years wandering in the wilderness. In Psalm 81 God reminded Israel that He would have conquered their enemies quickly if they had only followed His plans rather than trusting in their own devices and wisdom.

4 Answer the following questions.
  a. Has God changed the way He works with people as He carries out His plans and purposes? ☑ Yes ☐ No

  b. Why are we ever satisfied to pursue our plans when God has so much more for us to experience? _We don't know how to listen to the Holy Spirit as he leads us._

You Need to Know What God Is About to Do

One year denominational leaders came to our city to discuss long-range plans for an emphasis we had scheduled in the metropolitan area. Top denominational executives were going to work with us to achieve the goals we had set. Yet I was asking myself, *What if God calls our nation to judgment before that time?* I realized how much I needed to know what God had in mind for my city. Planning what I wanted to do in the future would have been irrelevant if God intended to do something else.

When God called the prophets, He often had a twofold message. God's first desire was "Call the people to return to Me." If the people failed to respond, they needed to hear God's second message: "Let them know that they are closer to judgment than they have ever been." God's word to the prophet was "Tell the people: this is what I have done. This is what I am doing right now. This is what I am about to do. Then call them to respond."

Do you suppose it was crucial for the prophets to understand what God was preparing to do? When God was about to bring a terrible judgment on Jerusalem and destroy the entire city, was it important to know what God was about to do? Certainly!

We are His servants, and we adjust our lives to what He is about to do.

5 **How close do you think your country is to God's judgment? Check one.**

❏ I do not believe God will bring judgment on my country.

❏ I believe God's judgment is a long time off.

☑ I cannot understand why God has waited this long. I believe we are on the verge of a major judgment from God.

❏ I believe we are already experiencing a disciplinary judgment like that described in Isaiah 5:1-7.

❏ I believe we have already experienced part of God's judgment.

What evidence can you give to support your answer? *wars & rumors) of wars – his children, his chosen people are tearing themselves apart*

What effect does your belief have on the way you live? *pray more, love more*

Understanding what God is about to do where you are is more important than telling God what you want to do for Him. What good would it have done for Abraham to tell God about his plans to take a survey of Sodom and Gomorrah and go door-to-door witnessing the day after God was going to destroy the cities? What good would you do by making long-range plans in your church if God brings judgment on your nation or church before you implement them?

You need to know what God has on His agenda for your church, community, and nation at this time in history. Then you and your church can adjust your lives to God so He can move you into the mainstream of His activity before it is too late. Though God will probably not give you a detailed schedule, He will let you know one step at a time how you and your church need to respond to what He is doing.

6 **Pray now, asking God to guide your response to Him ...**

• in your personal life; ✓
• in your work; ✓
• in your family; ✓
• in your community; ✓
• in your church; ✓
• in our nation. ✓

I don't have to do this ... god is doing it.

You may want to make notes in the margin or on a separate sheet of paper.

In 1209 Francis of Assisi heard a sermon on Matthew 10:7-10. He immediately recognized it was God's word to him to sell all he had and devote his life to preaching the gospel and ministering to the poor. As Francis obeyed, others were soon attracted to his ministry. Ultimately, many thousands of men and women devoted their lives to this cause and blessed countless thousands of people in need. God's word to one young man impacted thousands of people across Europe and around the world.

When God began to speak to John and Charles Wesley, He was preparing to bring a sweeping revival across England that would save the nation from a bloody revolution like the one France suffered. Through these men, along with George Whitefield and others, God was able to do a mighty work and completely turn England around spiritually.

In your community some things are about to happen in the lives of others. God wants to intercept those people to bring about His purposes. Suppose He wants to do

Understanding what God is about to do where you are is more important than telling God what you want to do for Him.

SUMMARY STATEMENTS

Do things God's way.

God will accomplish more in six months through a people yielded to Him than we could do in 60 years without Him.

I am God's servant. I adjust my life to what He is about to do.

it through you! He comes to you and talks to you. But if you are self-centered, you may respond, "I don't think I have time. I don't think I am able to do it. And I …"

Do you see what happens? The focus is on self. The moment you sense God is moving in your life, you give Him an extensive list of reasons He has enlisted the wrong person or the time is not convenient (see Ex. 3:11; 4:1). You always need to seek God's perspective. God knows you can't do it! He wants to do it Himself *through* you.

> Understanding what God is about to do where I am is more important than telling God what I want to do for Him.

Review today's lesson. Pray and ask God to identify one or more statements or Scriptures He wants you to understand, learn, or practice. Underline them. Then respond to the following.

What was the most meaningful statement or Scripture you read today?

God knows I
can't do it.

Reword the statement or Scripture into a prayer of response to God.

God, I can't raise
my kids. They
are yours. Raise
them through me

What does God want you to do in response to today's study?

DAY 3

God Takes the Initiative

✓

GOD'S REVELATION OF HIS ACTIVITY IS AN INVITATION FOR YOU TO JOIN HIM.

Philippians 2:13
"It is God who works in you to will and to act according to his good purpose."

Throughout Scripture God takes the initiative. When He comes to a person, He reveals Himself and His activity. That revelation is always an invitation for individuals to adjust their lives to God. None of the people God encountered could remain the same afterward. They had to make major adjustments in their lives to walk obediently with Him.

God is the Sovereign Lord. Strive to keep your life God-centered because He is the One who sets the agenda. He is always the One who takes the initiative to accomplish what He wants to do. When you are God-centered, even the desires to do the things that please Him come from God's activity in your life (see Phil. 2:13).

What often happens when we see God at work? We immediately become self-centered rather than God-centered. We must reorient our lives to God. We should learn to see things from His perspective. We need to allow Him to develop His character in us. We must let Him reveal His thoughts to us. Only then can we gain a proper perspective on life.

God's revelation of His activity is an invitation for you to join Him. If you keep your life God-centered, you will immediately join His activity. When you see God at work around you, your heart will leap within you and say, "Thank You, Father, for letting me be involved where You are." When you are in the middle of God's activity and He lets you see where He is working, you know God wants you to join Him.

1 **Answer the following questions by checking your responses.**
  a. Who takes the initiative in your knowing and doing God's will?
  ❏ (1) I do. God waits for me to decide what I want to do and then helps
     me accomplish it.
  ☑ (2) God does. He invites me to join Him in what He is about to do.

  b. Which of the following are ways God may reveal His plan or purpose
     to you? Check all that apply.
  ❏ (1) He lets me see where He is already working around me.
  ❏ (2) He speaks to me through Scripture and impresses on me a practical
     application of the truth to my life.
  ❏ (3) He gives me an earnest desire that grows stronger as I pray.
  ❏ (4) He creates circumstances around me that open a door of opportunity.

God always takes the initiative (a–2). He does not wait to see what we want to do for Him. After He has taken the initiative to come to us, He waits until we respond to Him by adjusting ourselves to Him and making ourselves available to Him. In question b, all four are ways God may reveal His plan or purpose to you. There are others as well. The last two (3 and 4), however, must be carefully watched. A self-centered life tends to confuse its selfish desire with God's will. In addition, circumstances do not always indicate a clear direction for God's leadership. Open and closed doors do not always indicate God's guidance. Check to see that prayer, the Scriptures, and circumstances agree on the direction you sense God leading you.

Learning to Walk with God

You may be thinking, *That all sounds good, but I need practical help in learning how to apply these concepts.* In every situation God demands that you depend on Him rather than a method. The key is not a method but a relationship with God. Let me illustrate by telling you about someone who learned to walk with God by prayer and faith.

George Müller, a minister in England during the 19th century, was concerned that God's people had become discouraged. They no longer looked for God to do anything unusual in their midst. They were not trusting God to answer their prayers. They had little faith.

God led Müller to pray. Müller's prayers were for God to lead him to a work people could explain only as an act of God. Müller wanted people to learn that God was a faithful, prayer-answering God. He discovered Psalm 81:10, which you read in yesterday's lesson: "Open wide your mouth and I will fill it." God led him in a walk of faith that became an outstanding testimony of faith to all who hear his story.

When Müller felt led by God to minister, he prayed for the needed resources and told no one else. He wanted everyone to know that God had provided for the need in answer to prayer and faith. During his ministry in Bristol, Müller started the Scriptural Knowledge Institute for the distribution of Scripture and for religious education. He also began an orphanage. By the time of Müller's death, God had used him to build four orphan houses that cared for 2,000 children at a time. The orphanages had provided for more than 10,000 children. He had distributed more than eight million dollars that had been given to him in answer to prayer. Yet when he died at 93, his own worldly possessions were valued at eight hundred dollars.[1]

How did Müller know and do God's will?

Read the following statement by George Müller and list things he did that helped him know what to do. Then list things that led him to make mistakes in knowing God's will.

> I never remember ... a period ... that I ever SINCERELY AND PATIENTLY sought to know the will of God by *the teaching of the Holy Ghost,* through *the instrumentality of the Word of God,* but I have been ALWAYS directed rightly. But if *honesty of heart* and *uprightness before God* were lacking, or if I did not *patiently* wait upon God for instruction, or if I preferred *the counsel of my fellow men* to the declarations of *the Word of the living God,* I made great mistakes.[2]

a. What helped George Müller know God's will? honest & sincere before God – HS, word of God.

b. What led to mistakes in knowing God's will?
- listening to others
- impatience

Müller mentioned these things that helped him:
- He sincerely sought God's direction.
- He patiently waited on God until he had a word from Him.
- He looked to the Holy Spirit to teach him through the Word.

The following things led to mistakes.
- Lacking honesty of heart
- Lacking uprightness before God
- Impatience to wait for God
- Preferring the counsel of men over the declarations of Scripture

Here is how Müller summed up the way he entered a heart relationship with God and learned to discern His voice:

1. I seek at the beginning to get my heart into such a state that it has no will of its own in regard to a given matter. Nine-tenths of the trouble with people generally is just here. Nine-tenths of the difficulties are overcome when our hearts are ready to do the Lord's will, whatever it may be. When one is truly in this state, it is usually but a little way to the knowledge of what His will is.
2. Having done this, I do not leave the result to feeling or simple impression. If so, I make myself liable to great delusions.
3. I seek the Will of the Spirit of God through, or in connection with, the Word of God. The Spirit and the Word must be combined. If I look to the Spirit alone without the Word, I lay myself open to great delusions also. If the Holy Ghost guides us at all, He will do it according to the Scriptures and never contrary to them.
4. Next I take into account providential circumstances. These often plainly indicate God's Will in connection with His Word and Spirit.
5. I ask God in prayer to reveal His Will to me aright.

6. Thus, through prayer to God, the study of the Word, and reflection, I come to a deliberate judgment according to the best of my ability and knowledge, and if my mind is thus at peace, and continues so after two or three more petitions, I proceed accordingly.[3]

3 Check the correct answer for each of the following questions.

a. How did Müller begin his search for God's will?
 ❑ (1) He tried to determine what he wanted to do for God.
 ❑ (2) He made sure he had no will of his own.
 ❑ (3) He tried to get to the place he wanted only God's will.
 ☑ (4) Both 2 and 3

b. What did Müller say leads to possible delusions or false directions?
 ❑ (1) Basing a decision on feelings alone
 ❑ (2) Following the slightest impressions
 ❑ (3) Looking to the Spirit alone for direction
 ☑ (4) All of the above

c. In which of the following pairs of things did Müller look for agreement?
 ❑ (1) His desires and circumstances
 ☑ (2) The Spirit and the Word
 ❑ (3) The counsel of others and his desires
 ❑ (4) Circumstances and a sense of peace

d. What was the final test by which Müller came to understand God's will?
 ❑ (1) He identified whether the door was open or closed.
 ❑ (2) He submitted his decision to his local minister.
 ❑ (3) He went with his best guess and hoped it worked.
 ☑ (4) He used prayer, Bible study, and reflection to find lasting peace about a proposed direction.

#3 answers: a–4, b–4, c–2, d–4

I hope Müller's example has helped. Don't get discouraged if the way to know God's will still seems vague. We have much more time to study together.

4 Practice quoting aloud your Scripture-memory verses or write them on separate paper. *Some trust in chariots. Others in horses. But we trust in the Name of the Lord our God.*

Review today's lesson. Pray and ask God to identify one or more statements or Scriptures He wants you to understand, learn, or practice. Underline them. Then respond to the following.

What was the most meaningful statement or Scripture you read today?

Reword the statement or Scripture into a prayer of response to God.

What does God want you to do in response to today's study?

DAY 4

God Speaks to His People

GOD HAS NOT CHANGED. HE STILL SPEAKS TO HIS PEOPLE.

Years ago I spoke to a group of young pastors. When I finished the first session, a pastor took me aside and said, "I vowed to God I would never again listen to a man like you. You talk as though God is personal and talks to you. I just despise that."

I asked him, "Are you having difficulty letting God speak to you?" He and I talked, and before long we were on our knees. He wept and thanked God that He had spoken to him. Don't let anyone intimidate you about hearing from God.

1 **Read the following Scriptures and answer the questions that follow.**

Hebrews 1:1—"In the past God spoke to our forefathers through the prophets at many times and in various ways, but in these last days he has spoken to us by his Son."

John 14:26—"The Counselor, the Holy Spirit, whom the Father will send in my name, will teach you all things and will remind you of everything I have said to you."

John 16:13-14—"When he, the Spirit of truth, comes, he will guide you into all truth. He will not speak on his own; he will speak only what he hears, and he will tell you what is yet to come. He will bring glory to me by taking from what is mine and making it known to you."

John 8:47—"He who belongs to God hears what God says. The reason you do not hear is that you do not belong to God."

a In the Old Testament ("times past") how and through whom did God speak?
prophets

b. In New Testament times ("these last days") how did God speak?
Son

c. In John 14:26 whom did Jesus promise the Father would send in His name?
_HS_

d. What is the work of the Holy Spirit as described in John 14:26; 16:13-14?
teach us, Remind us of Jesus' word, guide us to know Christ's will

e. Who is the one who hears what God says? _He who belongs to God._

f. What does John 8:47 say about a person who does not hear what God says?
he doesn't belong to God

2 **Write a summary in the margin of what these Scriptures say about God's speaking.**

The HS speaks to us, teaches us, tells us what Jesus wants to reveal to us — if we are in Christ — the HS will teach us & we will know his will.

In the Old Testament God spoke at many times and in a variety of ways. Through Jesus, God spoke to His people. Now God speaks through the Holy Spirit. The Holy Spirit will teach you all things, call to your memory the things Jesus said, guide you into all truth, speak what He hears from the Father, tell you what is yet to come, and glorify Christ as He reveals Christ to you.

the work of the Holy Spirit

Does God really speak to people today? Will He reveal to you where He is working when He wants to use your life? Yes! God has not changed. He still speaks to people. If you have trouble hearing God speak, you are in trouble at the heart of your Christian experience.

Hearing God's Voice

Sin has so affected us (see Rom. 3:10-11) that you and I cannot understand God's truth unless the Holy Spirit reveals it. He is the Teacher. When He teaches you the Word of God, carefully listen to Him and respond to Him. As you pray, watch to see how He uses Scripture to confirm in your heart a word from God. Watch what He is doing around you and in your circumstances. The God who is speaking to you as you pray and the God who is speaking to you in the Scriptures is the God who is also working around you.

③ Look on the inside back cover at the fourth reality. Then answer the following questions.

a. When Jesus returned to heaven, which Person of the Trinity was sent to speak to God's people? Check one.
❏ God the Father ❏ Jesus ☑ The Holy Spirit

b. What are four ways He speaks? _calls to memory what Jesus said, guides us into all truth, tells us what will come, glorifies Christ_

c. When He speaks, what does He reveal? _He reveals Christ to us._

God speaks by the Holy Spirit through the Bible, prayer, circumstances, and the church to reveal Himself, His purposes, and His ways. Later we will study the ways God speaks. I cannot give you a formula, however, and say this is how you can know for certain when God is speaking to you. I will share with you what the Bible says. The Scriptures can encourage you at this point. When God chose to speak to people in the Bible, they knew it was God, and they knew what God was saying.

In John 10:2-4,14 Jesus said:
• "The man who enters by the gate is the shepherd of his sheep.
• The sheep listen to his voice.
• His sheep follow him because they know his voice.
• I am the good shepherd; I know my sheep and my sheep know me."

The key to knowing God's voice is not a formula, nor is it a method you can follow. Knowing God's voice comes from an intimate love relationship with God. That is why those who do not have the relationship ("do not belong to God," John 8:47) do not hear what God is saying. You must watch to see how God uniquely communicates with you. You will not be able to rely on other people's walks with God. You will have to depend on God alone. Your relationship with Him is of upmost importance.

If you have trouble hearing God speak, you are in trouble at the heart of your Christian experience.

Knowing God's voice comes from an intimate love relationship with God.

4 **Which of the following best describes the way you will know God's voice when He speaks? Check your response.**
❑ a God will give me a miraculous sign. Then I will know God has spoken to me.
☑ b. In an intimate relationship with God, I will come to recognize His voice.
❑ c. When I learn and follow the correct formula, I will hear God speaking.
❑ d. If a verse in the Bible jumps out at me, it must be God's word for my life.

5 **What is the key to knowing God's voice?** *Knowing God*

The *relationship* is the key to knowing God's voice, to hearing when God speaks. The correct answer is b. What about a, c, and d? Sometimes in Scripture God gave a miraculous sign to assure the person that the word was from Him. Gideon is one example (see Judg. 6). Asking God for a sign often indicates unbelief. When the scribes and Pharisees asked Jesus for a miraculous sign, Jesus condemned them as a "wicked and adulterous generation" (Matt. 12:38-39). They were so self-centered and sinful they could not recognize when God was in their midst (see Luke 19:41-44).

A formula is not the way to recognize God's voice either. How many other burning bushes did God use besides the one with Moses? None. God does not want you to become an expert at using a formula. If there was a formula to hearing from God, you would not have to seek God with all your heart. You could mindlessly use the formula and neglect your relationship with God. He wants an intimate love relationship with you. He insists you depend on Him alone. Hearing God does not depend on a method or a formula but on a relationship.

Some may wonder why answer d is not acceptable. They may ask, Can't I get a word from the Bible? Yes, you can! But only the Holy Spirit can reveal to you which truth of Scripture is a word from God for a particular circumstance. The Holy Spirit must help you understand how a particular verse specifically applies to you. Even if the biblical circumstance is similar to yours, only God can reveal His word for your circumstance.

You also need to be careful about claiming you have a word from God. Claiming to have a word from God is a serious matter. If God has spoken to you, you must continue responding to that word until it comes to pass (even 25 years, like Abram). If you have not been given a word from God but say you have, you stand in judgment as a false prophet: "You may say to yourselves, 'How can we know when a message has not been spoken by the Lord?' If what a prophet proclaims in the name of the Lord does not take place or come true, that is a message the Lord has not spoken. That prophet has spoken presumptuously" (Deut. 18:21-22). In the Old Testament, the penalty for being a false prophet was death (see Deut. 18:20). That certainly is a serious charge. Do not take a word from God lightly.

God loves you. He wants to have an intimate relationship with you. He wants you to depend on Him when you seek a word from Him. He wants you to learn to hear His voice and know His will. Your relationship with Him is the key to hearing when God speaks to you.

6 **Consider praying this prayer: "God, I pray that I will grow in my relationship with You so much that when you speak, I will immediately hear and respond."**

SUMMARY STATEMENTS

God has not changed. He still speaks to His people.

If I have trouble hearing God speak, I am in trouble at the very heart of my Christian experience.

God speaks by the Holy Spirit through the Bible, prayer, circumstances, and the church to reveal Himself, His purposes, and His ways.

Knowing God's voice comes from an intimate love relationship with God.

Review today's lesson. Pray and ask God to identify one or more statements or Scriptures He wants you to understand, learn, or practice. Underline them. Then respond to the following.

What was the most meaningful statement or Scripture you read today?	Reword the statement or Scripture into a prayer of response to God.	What does God want you to do in response to today's study?
The HS reveals himself thru the Bible, prayer, circumstances & the church to reveal Himself, His purposes & His ways.	Lord, Keep me in prayer, in the word, in obedience & in the church so that the HS can perform his revealing work in me.	Remain in the vine. Apart from God, we can do nothing.

God Speaks with a Purpose

GOD DEVELOPS CHARACTER TO MATCH THE ASSIGNMENT.

We usually want God to speak to us so He can give us a devotional thought to make us feel good for the rest of the day. If you want the God of the universe to speak to you, you need to be ready for Him to reveal what He is doing where you are. In Scripture God is not often seen coming and speaking to people just for conversation's sake. He was always working to accomplish His purposes. When God speaks to you through the Bible, prayer, circumstances, the church, or another way, He has a purpose in mind for your life.

When God spoke to Abram (see Gen. 12), what was God about to do? He was about to begin building a nation. Notice God's timing. Why did God speak to Abram when He did? Because it was then God wanted to start building the nation. The moment Abram knew what God was about to do, he had to adjust his life to God. He had to immediately follow what God said.

The moment God speaks to you is the time He wants you to respond to Him. Don't think you have the next three or four months to decide whether this is really God's timing. The moment God speaks to you *is* God's timing. That is why He chooses to speak when He does. He speaks to His servant when He is ready to move. Otherwise, He wouldn't speak to you. As God enters the mainstream of your life, the timing of your response is crucial. When God speaks to you, you need to believe and obey Him.

Do not assume, however, that the moment God calls you, you are prepared for the assignment. How long was it from the time God spoke to Abram (later named Abraham) until Isaac, the child of promise, was born? Twenty-five years (see Gen. 12:4; 21:5)! Why did God wait 25 years? Because it took God 25 years to make Abraham a father suitable for Isaac. God was concerned not so much about Abram but about founding a nation. The quality of the father will affect the quality of following generations. As goes the father, so go the next several generations. God took time to build Abram into a man of character. Abram immediately began adjusting his life to God's

> The moment God speaks to you is the time He wants you to respond to Him.

ways. He could not wait until Isaac was born and then try to become the kind of father required to raise a patriarch of God's people.

How long was it after God (through Samuel) anointed David king before David mounted the throne? Maybe 10 or 12 years. What was God doing in the meantime? He was building David's relationship with Himself. As goes the king, so goes the nation. You cannot bypass character.

How long was it after the living Lord called the Apostle Paul until Paul went on his first missionary journey? Maybe 10 or 11 years. The focus was not on Paul; the focus was on God. God wanted to redeem a lost world, and He wanted to redeem the Gentiles through Paul. God took that much time to prepare Paul for the assignment.

1 Mark the following statements _T_ (true) or _F_ (false).
  _F_ a. God speaks to me primarily so I can have a devotional thought to encourage me throughout the day.
  _T_ b. God speaks to me when He has a purpose in mind for my life.
  _F_ c. When God speaks to me, I should take plenty of time to decide when and how I should respond.
  _T_ d. When God speaks to me, I must immediately respond by adjusting my life to Him, His purposes, and His ways.
  _T_ e. The moment God speaks is God's timing.

We are so oriented to a quick response we abandon the word from God long before He has developed our character. When God speaks, He has a purpose in mind for our lives. The moment He speaks is the time we need to begin responding to Him. False: a and c. True: b, d, and e.

Character That Matches the Assignment

When God called Abram, He said, "I will make your name great" (Gen. 12:2). That means "I will develop your character to match your assignment." Nothing is more pathetic than having a small character when you have a big assignment. Many of us don't want to give attention to the development of our characters; we just want God to give us a big assignment.

Suppose a pastor is waiting for a big church to call him to be their pastor. Then a small church calls and asks, "Will you come and serve bivocationally to help us here on the west side of Wyoming?"

"Well, no," the prospective pastor responds because he thinks, _I am waiting for God to give me a significant assignment. I have done so much training, I can't waste my life by working a secular job when I want to serve in a church full-time. I think I deserve something much more substantial than that._

2 How would you classify that response? Check one.
❏ God-centered   ☑ Self-centered

Do you see how self-centered that viewpoint is? Human reasoning will not give you God's perspective. If you can't be faithful in a little, God will not give you a larger assignment. He may want to adjust your life and character in smaller assignments first to prepare you for the larger ones. That is where God starts to work. When you make the adjustments and start to obey Him, you come to know Him by experience. This is the goal of God's activity in your life—that you come to know Him. Do you want to experience God mightily working in and through your life? Then adjust your life to God and pursue the kind of relationship in which you follow Him wherever He leads you—even if the assignment seems to be small or insignificant. One day you will hear it said of you, "Well done, good and faithful servant!" (Matt. 25:21).

Should you automatically assume every small assignment is from God? No. Whether the assignment is large or small in your eyes, you must still find out whether it is from God. However, always let God tell you. Do not rule out an assignment, large or small, on the basis of your preconceived ideas. Remember, you will know what you should do through your relationship with God. Never bypass the relationship.

3 **Suppose you had planned to go fishing or watch football or go to the mall. Then God confronts you with an opportunity to join Him in something He wants to do. What would you do? Check your response.**
- ❏ I would finish my plans and then fit God's plans into the next available time in my schedule.
- ❏ I would assume that, because God already knew my plans, this new assignment must not be from Him.
- ❏ I would try to find a way to do both what I want and God's will.
- ☑ I would adjust my plans to join God in what He was about to do.

I have known some people who wouldn't interrupt a fishing trip or a football game for anything. In their minds they say they want to serve God, but they eliminate from their lives anything that would interfere with their plans. They are so self-centered they do not recognize the times when God comes to them with a divine invitation. On the other hand, if you are God-centered, you will adjust your life to what God wants to do.

God has a right to interrupt your life anytime He wants to! He is Lord. When you accepted Him as Lord, you gave Him the right to help Himself to your life. In Jesus' parable of the talents in Matthew 25:14-30, suppose that 5 times out of 10 when the master had something for the servant to do, the servant said, "I'm sorry. That's not on my schedule." What do you suppose the master would do? He would discipline the servant. If the servant did not respond to discipline, sooner or later the master would no longer assign any tasks.

You may wish you could experience God working through you the way He works through someone else. But every time God goes to that person, he adjusts his life to God and obeys. When he has been faithful in little assignments, God has given him more important assignments.

If you are not willing to be faithful in a little, God will not give you larger assignments. God uses the smaller assignments to develop character. God always builds character to match His assignment. If God has a great task for you, He will expand your character to match that assignment.

4 **Answer the following.**
a. What kind of assignments have you wanted the Lord to give you?

I don't know that I want any.

b. Have you been frustrated or disappointed in this area of your life? Why?

I can't even take good care of my own kids.

Matthew 25:21

"Well done, good and faithful servant! You have been faithful with a few things; I will put you in charge of many things. Come and share your master's happiness!"

If God has a great task for you, He will expand your character to match that assignment.

---

c. Can you think of a time when God probably wanted to use you in an assignment and you chose not to follow His leading? If so, briefly describe the situation. *I'm too far out of Xn circles for this discussion.*

d. Is the Holy Spirit saying anything to you now about your character? If so, what is He saying? *I still need to work on remaining in the Vine. I'm not ready for any kind of ministry.*

e. Do your actions acknowledge Christ as Lord of your life? If not, what response should you make to His claims on your life right now? *Yes. Lord, draw me close to you. Keep me close. I surrender. That's what I need to do.*

SUMMARY STATEMENTS

The moment God speaks to me is the moment God wants me to respond to Him.

The moment God speaks to me is God's timing.

God develops my character to match the assignment He has for me.

God has a right to interrupt my life. He is Lord. When I accepted Him as Lord, I gave Him the right to help Himself to my life anytime He wants.

When God tells you a direction, you accept it, and you understand it clearly, <u>then give God all the time He wants to make you the kind of person He can trust with that assignment.</u> Is it for your sake God takes time to prepare you for His assignments? No, not for you alone but also for the sake of those He wants to influence through you. For their sake, give yourself to an obedient love relationship with God. Then when He gives you an assignment, He will achieve everything He wants in the lives of those around you.

5 **Write your Scripture-memory verse (Ps. 20:7) on the following lines.** *Some trust in horses, and others in chariots but we trust in the name of the Lord Our God.*

6 **Review your other Scripture-memory verses and be prepared to recite them to a partner in your small-group session this week.**

Review today's lesson. Pray and ask God to identify one or more statements or Scriptures He wants you to understand, learn, or practice. Underline them. Then respond to the following.

What was the most meaningful statement or Scripture you read today? *Give God all the time He wants to make you the kind of person He can trust with that assignment.*

Reword the statement or Scripture into a prayer of response to God. *Lord, take all the time you need because I'm messed up.*

What does God want you to do in response to today's study? *It's okay. God's timing is not our timing. I believe in a sovereign Lord.*

---
1. For further reading on George Müller, see A. E. C. Brooks, comp., *Answers to Prayer from George Müller's Narratives* (Chicago: Moody Press) and Faith Coxe Bailey, George Müller (Moody Press).
2. Basil Miller, *George Müller, The Man of Faith* (Grand Rapids: Zondervan, 1941), 51.
3. George Müller, *Answers to Prayer*, 6.

LOOKING TO GOD

DVD Message Notes

1. If the Christian life is radically God-centered, then it is important that we constantly look to God, listen to God, and watch to see what His directives are going to be.
2. Is it possible to become so involved in doing things we think are God-centered that we completely go against the activity of God?
3. Right on schedule when God has everything in place, He then initiates something in the life of an individual.
4. The timing of God is always with eternal dimensions.
5. I wonder if there's anything God wants to do through me to address this issue.
6. Watch to see what God does next.
7. What God initiates, He also completes. He never purposes anything He doesn't bring to pass.
8. If what you're thinking makes sense to you, it's probably not from God.
9. When God reveals what He's about to do, it probably won't make any sense at all.
10. "With God nothing is impossible."
11. "Do unto me according to Your word."
12. God's ways are not man's ways.
13. One of the ways of God is interdependence.
14. Often God will deliberately ask you to do what you failed to do in your own strength. Now you will do it in His strength.

Your Notes

_____

_____

_____

_____

_____

Unit Review

Mark the following statements *T* (true) or *F* (false).

___ 1. God asks people to dream up what they want to do for Him (p. 34).
___ 2. God always takes the initiative in my relationship with Him (p. 39).
___ 3. I know God's will by following the correct formula (p. 44).
___ 4. The moment God speaks is God's timing (p. 45).

Choose from the following words to fill in the blanks in the statements.

ability   *belief*   *character*   *unbelief*

a. Asking God for a sign often indicates _____ (p. 44).
b. God develops _____ to match the assignment (p. 46).

Check your answers, using the pages cited in parentheses.

Scripture Referenced

Isaiah 55:8-9

Testimony

John Robson
Angola Prison

Sharing Time

- The questions about God's judgment, activity 5, page 37
- The questions on lordship and character building, activity 4, pages 47–48
- One of the most meaningful statements or Scriptures from this unit's lessons and your prayer response to God. Choose one from pages 34, 38, 41, 45, and 48.

For Makeup or Review

Audio and video downloads are available at *www.lifeway.com*.

UNIT 3

VERSE TO MEMORIZE

"Jesus replied: '"Love the Lord your God with all your heart and with all your soul and with all your mind." This is the first and greatest commandment.'"

Matthew 22:37-38

God Pursues a Love Relationship

CARRIE'S CANCER

When one of my children could not get his own way, he used to say, "You don't love me." Was that true? No, my love had not changed. At that moment, however, my love was expressing itself differently than he wanted it to.

When our only daughter, Carrie, was 16, the doctors told us she had an advanced case of cancer. We had to take her through chemotherapy and radiation. We suffered along with Carrie as we watched her experience the severe sickness that accompanies the treatments. Some people face such an experience by blaming God and questioning why He doesn't love them anymore. Carrie's cancer treatments could have been a devastating experience for us. Did God still love us? Yes. Had His love changed? No, He still cared for us with an infinite love.

When you face circumstances like this, you can ask God to explain what is happening. We did that. We asked Him what we should do. I raised all of those questions, but I never said, "Lord, I guess You don't love me."

Long before this experience with Carrie, I had made a determination: no matter what my circumstances, I would never look at my situation except against the backdrop of the cross. In the death and resurrection of Jesus Christ, God forever convinced me that He loved me. For this reason during Carrie's illness I could go before the Heavenly Father and see behind my daughter the cross of Jesus Christ. I said, "Father, don't ever let me look at my life and question Your love for me. Your love for me was settled on the cross. That has never changed and will never change." Our love relationship with the Heavenly Father sustained us through an extremely difficult time.

No matter what your circumstances are, God's love never changes. The cross, the death of Jesus Christ, and His resurrection are God's final, total, and complete expression that He loves you. Never allow your heart to question God's love. Settle it on the front end of your desire to know Him and experience Him. He loves you. He created you for a love relationship. He has been pursuing you in that love relationship. Every encounter He has with you is an expression of His love for you. God would cease to be God if He expressed Himself in any way other than *perfect love!*[1]

Created for a Love Relationship

A LOVE RELATION-
SHIP WITH GOD IS
MORE IMPORTANT
THAN ANY OTHER
SINGLE FACTOR IN
YOUR LIFE.

*God pursues
a continuing
love relationship
with me that
is real and
personal.*

In the first two units I introduced you to some basic truths for knowing and doing the will of God. The seven realities you have examined summarize the kind of relationship through which God works to accomplish His purposes. As I said earlier, this course was not written to teach you a program, a method, or a formula for knowing and doing God's will. It was written to point you to a *relationship* with God. God will then work through that relationship to accomplish through you whatever He pleases.

1 **By way of review, see if you can fill in the blanks in the seven reali- ties below with the correct words. If you need help, look on the inside back cover.**
Reality 1: _____God_____ is always at work around you.

Reality 2: God pursues a continuing love ___Relationship___ with you that is real and ___personal___.

Reality 3: God invites you to become ___involved___ with Him in His ___work___.

Reality 4: God speaks by the ___Holy___ ___Spirit___ through the Bible, ___prayer___, circumstances, and the ___church___ to reveal Himself, His ___plan___, and His ways.

Reality 5: God's invitation for you to work with Him always leads you to a crisis of ~~faith~~ belief that requires ___faith___ and action.

Reality 6: You must make major ___adjustments___ in your life to join God in what He is doing.

Reality 7: You come to know God by ___experiencing___ as you ___obey___ Him, and He accomplishes His work through you.

2 **This unit will focus on the second reality. Write the second reality in the margin, but replace the word *you* with *me*.**

REALITY 2

RELATIONSHIP

With All Your Heart

In this unit I want to help you see that God Himself pursues a love relationship with you. He takes the initiative to bring you into this relationship. He created you for fellowship with Himself. That is the purpose of your life. This love relationship can and should be real and personal to you.

3 **If you were standing before God, could you describe your relation- ship with Him by saying, "I love You with all my heart and all my soul and all my mind and all my strength"?** ⬇ **Yes** ❑ **No**

One of our church members was always having difficulty in his personal life, with his family, at work, and in the church. In a church meeting he became extremely angry and stormed out of the room. It was obvious his life was filled with anger. Soon after, I met with him and asked, "Can you describe your relationship with God by sincerely saying, 'I love You with all my heart'?"

The strangest look came over his face. He said, "Nobody has ever asked me that. No, I could not describe my relationship with God that way. I could say I obey Him, I serve Him, I worship Him, and I fear Him. But I cannot say I love Him." This man had a father who never told him he loved him. The son feared his father, but he didn't love him. The man had wrongly assumed God was the same kind of Father. I helped this man realize God loved him and wanted to have loving fellowship with him. That truth set the man free to experience the love of His Heavenly Father.

Everything in this man's life was out of order because God's basic purpose for his life was missing. God created us for a love relationship with Him. If you cannot describe your relationship with God by saying that you love Him with all your being, you need to ask the Holy Spirit to bring you into that kind of a relationship.

4 **If you need to and are willing, pause now and ask the Holy Spirit to bring you into a wholehearted love relationship with God.**

Spend time in prayer expressing your love to God. Thank Him for the ways He has shown His love to you. Be specific in naming what God has done. You may want to list some ways in the margin. Praise Him for His lovingkindness.

If I tried to summarize the entire Old Testament, it would be expressed in this verse: "Hear, O Israel: The Lord our God, the Lord is one. Love the Lord your God with all your heart and with all your soul and with all your strength" (Deut. 6:4-5).

This heart-cry of God is expressed throughout the Old Testament. The essence of the New Testament is the same. Quoting from Deuteronomy, Jesus said the greatest commandment in the law is "Love the Lord your God with all your heart and with all your soul and with all your mind and with all your strength" (Mark 12:30). Everything in your Christian life, everything about knowing Him and experiencing Him, everything about knowing His will depends on the quality of your love relationship with God. If that is not settled, nothing in your life will be right.

5 **Read the following Scriptures, which describe a love relationship with God. As you read, circle the word *love* (or any form of it, such as *loves*) each time it appears.**

"This day I call heaven and earth as witnesses against you that I have set before you life and death, blessings and curses. Now choose life, so that you and your children may live and that you may love the Lord your God, listen to his voice, and hold fast to him. For the Lord is your life" (Deut. 30:19-20).

"God so loved the world that he gave his one and only Son, that whoever believes in him shall not perish but have eternal life" (John 3:16).

Can you describe your relationship with God by sincerely saying, "I love You with all my heart"?

I have always known god loves me - always!

Everything in your Christian life, everything about knowing Him and experiencing Him, everything about knowing His will depends on the quality of your love relationship with God.

"Whoever has my commands and obeys them, he is the one who loves me. He who loves me will be loved by my Father, and I too will love him and show myself to him" (John 14:21).

"Who shall separate us from the love of Christ? Shall trouble or hardship or persecution or famine or nakedness or danger or sword? No, in all these things we are more than conquerors through him who loved us. [Nothing] will be able to separate us from the love of God that is in Christ Jesus our Lord" (Rom. 8:35,37,39).

"This is how we know what love is: Jesus Christ laid down his life for us. And we ought to lay down our lives for our brothers" (1 John 3:16).

"This is how God showed his love among us: He sent his one and only Son into the world that we might live through him. This is love: not that we loved God, but that he loved us and sent his Son as an atoning sacrifice for our sins. We love because he first loved us" (1 John 4:9-10,19).

6 **Using the preceding Scriptures, answer the following questions.**
a. Who is your life? _Jesus Christ_
b. In what ways has God demonstrated His love for us? _He sent His Son to lay down His life for our sins._
c. How can we show our love for Him? _obeying him – doing likewise for our brothers_
d. What does God promise to do in response to our loving Him? _love will Reveal himself to us_
e. Who loved first—we or God? _God_

Answers: (a) The Lord is your life. (b) He has drawn us to Himself. He sent His only Son to provide eternal life for us. Jesus laid down His life for us. (c) Choose life, listen to His voice, hold fast to Him, believe in His only Son, obey His commands and teachings, be willing to lay down our lives for our brothers. (d) We and our children will live under His blessings. By believing in Jesus, we have eternal life. The Father will love us. God will come to make His home with us. He will make us more than conquerors over all our difficulties. We will never be separated from His love. (e) God loved us first. "God is love" (1 John 4:16). His very nature is love.

What is the one thing God wants from you? He wants you to love Him with all your being. Your experiencing God depends on your having this relationship of love. A love relationship with God is more important than any other single factor in your life.

7 **Write your Scripture-memory verses for this unit on the following lines and review your verses from other units. Remember, you may select a different verse to memorize or a different translation.**
Thou shalt love the Lord your God with all your heart, and with all your heart and with all your soul. This is the first command meet with promise.

8 **Day 3's assignment may require advance planning. Turn to page 60 and read activity 2 so you can prepare.**

A love relationship with God is more important than any other single factor in your life.

SUMMARY STATEMENTS

My Christian life depends on the quality of my love relationship with God.

God created me for a love relationship with Him.

Everything God says and does is an expression of love.

A love relationship with God is more important than any other single factor in my life.

Review today's lesson. Pray and ask God to identify one or more statements or Scriptures He wants you to understand, learn, or practice. Underline them. Then respond to the following.

What was the most meaningful statement or Scripture you read today?

_____
_____
_____
_____
_____
_____

Reword the statement or Scripture into a prayer of response to God.

_____
_____
_____
_____
_____
_____

What does God want you to do in response to today's study?

_____
_____
_____
_____
_____
_____

A Love Relationship with God

DAY 2

Picture in your mind a tall ladder leaning against a wall. Now think about your life as a process of climbing that ladder. Wouldn't it be a tragedy to ascend to the top and find you had placed the ladder against the wrong wall? One life to live, and you missed it! Earlier in the course we talked about your life being God-centered. That means your life must be properly related to God. This is the love relationship for which you were created—a God-centered love relationship. Your walk with God (Father, Son, and Spirit) is the single most important aspect of your life. If it is not as it should be, nothing else will function properly.

If you knew all you had was a relationship with God, would you be totally and completely satisfied? Many people would say, "I would like to have that relationship, but I would also like to do something" or "I would like for Him to give me a ministry or something to do." We are a doing people. We feel worthless or useless if we are not busy doing something. Scripture leads us to understand that God is saying, "I want you to love Me above everything else. When you are in a relationship of love with Me, you have everything there is." To be loved by God is the highest relationship, the greatest achievement, and the noblest position in life.

That does not mean you will never accomplish anything as an expression of your love for God. He will call you to obey Him and do whatever He asks of you. However, you do not need to do something to feel fulfilled. You are completely fulfilled in a relationship with God. When you are filled with Him, what else do you need?

1 Read the following hymn by Rhea Miller and circle everything that may compete with Jesus for a person's love and attention.

I'd rather have Jesus than silver or gold,
I'd rather be His than have riches untold;
I'd rather have Jesus than houses or lands,
I'd rather be led by His nail-pierced hand.

TO BE LOVED BY GOD IS THE HIGH-EST RELATIONSHIP, THE HIGHEST ACHIEVEMENT, AND THE HIGHEST POSITION IN LIFE.

I'd rather have Jesus than men's applause,
I'd rather be faithful to His dear cause;
I'd rather have Jesus than worldwide fame,
I'd rather be true to His holy name.
He's fairer than lilies of rarest bloom,
He's sweeter than honey from out the comb;
He's all that my hungering spirit needs,
I'd rather have Jesus and let Him lead.

Refrain
Than to be the king of a vast domain
Or be held in sin's dread sway;
I'd rather have Jesus than anything
This world affords today.[2]

2 **Reflect on the meanings of the words. If you could have only one or the other in each of the following pairs, which would you honestly choose? Check your response.**
I would rather have: ❏ Jesus. ❏ silver, gold, riches untold, houses and lands.
I would rather have: ❏ Jesus. ❏ men's applause and worldwide fame.
I would rather: ❏ have Jesus. ❏ be the king of a vast domain.

3 **If you chose *Jesus* for each answer, is this the way you have been living your life?**
❏ Yes ❏ No

Do you really want to love the Lord your God with all your heart? He will allow no competitors, not money and things, not fame and popularity, and not power or authority. God says:
- "No one can serve two masters. Either he will hate the one and love the other, or he will be devoted to the one and despise the other. You cannot serve both God and Money" (Matt. 6:24).
- "When the Lord your God brings you into the land he swore to your fathers, to Abraham, Isaac and Jacob, to give you—a land with large, flourishing cities you did not build, houses filled with all kinds of good things you did not provide, wells you did not dig, and vineyards and olive groves you did not plant—then when you eat and are satisfied, be careful that you do not forget the Lord, who brought you out of Egypt, out of the land of slavery. Fear the Lord your God, serve him only and take your oaths in his name. Do not follow other gods, the gods of the peoples around you; for the Lord your God, who is among you, is a jealous God" (Deut. 6:10-15).
- From His love for you, God will provide everything else you need—when you love Him and Him alone (see **Matt. 6:31-33**).

Created for Eternity

God did not create you for time; He created you for eternity. Time—your lifetime on earth—provides the opportunity for you to become acquainted with Him. It provides occasions for Him to develop your character into His likeness. Then eternity will hold its fullest dimensions for you.

Matthew 6:31-33

"Do not worry, saying, 'What shall we eat?' or 'What shall we drink?' or 'What shall we wear?' For the pagans run after all these things, and your heavenly Father knows that you need them. But seek first his kingdom and his righteousness, and all these things will be given to you as well."

If you live only for time—the here and now—you will miss the ultimate purpose of creation. If you live for time, you will allow your past to shape your life today. Your life as a child of God ought to be shaped by the future—what you will be one day. God uses your present experiences to mold you for future usefulness here on earth and in eternity.

4 **What are some things in your past that have a strong limiting influence on your life today? These may include handicaps; a troubled family background; failures; shame over a personal or family secret; past abuse; or things like pride, success, fame, recognition, or excessive wealth.**

poverty, bipolar disorder, divorce

5 **Do you think you are primarily being shaped by your past or by your future? Why?** _my past — I'm trying not to repeat it._

I was speaking at a conference when a woman approached me and recounted the heartbreaking story of how her father had abandoned her and her family. She described her feelings of worthlessness, abandonment, and rejection. For years she was consumed with finding her father and convincing him she was not worthless and he should take her back. "Then one day I found my Father," she said. "He was at the back of the *Experiencing God* book." She had been studying *Experiencing God* and had come to the list of the names of God. She realized her Heavenly Father had always loved her and had been seeking a love relationship with her. Her Heavenly Father set her free from the bondage to which her earthly father had consigned her.

Paul had to overcome his difficult personal history too. Here was his approach to dealing with his past and present:

> [4]If anyone else thinks he has reasons to put confidence in the flesh, I have more: [5]circumcised on the eighth day, of the people of Israel, of the tribe of Benjamin, a Hebrew of Hebrews; in regard to the law, a Pharisee; [6]as for zeal, persecuting the church; as for legalistic righteousness, faultless.
>
> [7]But whatever was to my profit I now consider loss for the sake of Christ. [8]What is more, I consider everything a loss compared to the surpassing greatness of knowing Christ Jesus my Lord, for whose sake I have lost all things. I consider them rubbish, that I may gain Christ [9]and be found in him, not having a righteousness of my own that comes from the law, but that which is through faith in Christ—the righteousness that comes from God and is by faith. [10]I want to know Christ and the power of his resurrection and the fellowship of sharing in his sufferings, becoming like him in his death, [11]and so, somehow, to attain to the resurrection from the dead.
>
> [12]Not that I have already obtained all this, or have already been made perfect, but I press on to take hold of that for which Christ Jesus took hold of me. [13]Brothers, I do not consider myself yet to have taken hold of it. But one thing I do: Forgetting what is behind and straining toward what is ahead, [14]I press on toward the goal to win the prize for which God has called me heavenward in Christ Jesus (Phil. 3:4-14).

Matthew
6:19-21,33

"Do not store up for yourselves treasures on earth,
where moth and rust destroy,
and where thieves break
in and steal. But store up
for yourselves treasures in
heaven, where moth and
rust do not destroy, and
where thieves do not break
in and steal. For where
your treasure is, there your
heart will be also. But seek
first his kingdom and his
righteousness, and all these
things will be given to you
as well."

SUMMARY STATEMENTS

To be loved by God is the
highest relationship, the
highest achievement, and
the highest position in life.

God did not create me
for time; He created me
for eternity.

I will let my present be
molded and shaped by what
I am to become in Christ.

"Seek first his kingdom
and his righteousness."

I will make sure I am investing in things that are lasting.

6 **Answer the following questions, based on Paul's statement in Philippians 3:4-14.**

a. What are some things in Paul's past that could have influenced his present? *His Jewish heritage, persecution of Christians, his role/pride as a Pharisee*

b. How did Paul value these things (v. 8)? *He counted them all as loss*

c. Why did Paul discredit his past this way (vv. 8-11)? *He wanted to be faithful to share in the suffering of Christ.*

d. What did Paul do to prepare for a future prize (vv. 13-14)?
Forget *what lies behind*
Strain toward *what is ahead*
Press on toward *the goal to win the prize to which god has called me heavenward*

Answers: (a) Paul was true and faithful to his heritage as a Jew from the tribe of Benja-min. He was faultless in keeping the laws of the Pharisees. He was zealous for God. (b) He considered them rubbish and loss. (c) Paul wanted to know Christ, to be found in Him, and to become like Him to attain a future blessing (resurrection from the dead). (d) He forgot the past. He strained toward the future. He pressed toward the future goal of a heavenly prize.

Paul's desire was to know Christ and to become like Him. You too can so order your life under God's direction that you come to know Him, love Him, and become like Christ. Let your present be molded and shaped by what you are to become in Christ. You were created for eternity!

Investing in the Future

Begin orienting your life to God's will. His purposes go far beyond time and into eternity. Make sure you are investing your life, time, and resources in things that will last, not in things that will pass away. If you don't recognize that God created you for eternity, you will invest in the wrong priorities. You need to store up treasures in heaven (see **Matt. 6:19-21,33**).

This is why a love relationship with God is so important. He loves you. He knows what is best for you. Only He can guide you to invest your life in worthwhile ways. This guidance will come as you walk with Him and listen to Him.

7 **In what are you investing your life, your time, and your resources? Make two lists below. On the left list things that will pass away. On the right list things that have eternal value.**

Passing Away	Eternal
This job, this apartment, titles, wealth, Riches, clothes.	*My soul & my childrens souls & my husbands soul*

8 Think and pray about any adjustments you may need to make in the way you invest your life. Ask God for His perspective on your life. Write any adjustments you sense God wants you to make.

Only God can guide me to invest my life in worthwhile ways.

Be patient & love my children — don't be so selfish

Review today's lesson. Pray and ask God to identify one or more statements or Scriptures He wants you to understand, learn, or practice. Underline them. Then respond to the following.

What was the most meaningful statement or Scripture you read today?	Reword the statement or Scripture into a prayer of response to God.	What does God want you to do in response to today's study?
Passion — Seek first the kingdom of God — all these things will be given unto us —	*Lord, first I seek your kingdom above all else — break my heart & help me love the unloveable.*	*Help me love my kids the way they need to be loved, not the way I think I need to love them.*

Walking with God

God created the first man and woman, **Adam and Eve**, for a love relationship with Himself. After Adam and Eve sinned, they heard God walking in the garden in the cool of the day. They hid from Him because of their fear and shame. Try to sense the heart of a loving Father when He asked that wonderful love question "Where are you?" (Gen. 3:9). God knew something had happened to the love relationship.

When your relationship is as it ought to be, you will always be in fellowship with the Father. You will be in His presence expecting and anticipating the relationship of love. When Adam and Eve were not there, something had gone wrong.

WHEN YOUR RELATIONSHIP IS AS IT OUGHT TO BE, YOU WILL ALWAYS BE IN FELLOWSHIP WITH THE FATHER.

Quiet Time with God

Early each day I have an appointment with God. I often wonder what happens when the God who loves me comes to meet with me. How does He feel when He asks, "Henry, where are you?" and I am not there (see Jer. 7:13). I have found this to be true in my walk with the Lord: I keep that time alone with God, not in order to have a relationship but because I have a relationship. Because I have that love relationship with my Lord, I want to meet with Him and spend time with Him. Time with Him enriches and deepens the relationship I already have with Him.

I hear many people say, "I really struggle trying to have time alone with God." If that is a problem you face, let me suggest something: make the priority in your life to love Him with all your heart. That will solve most of your problem with your quiet time. People who struggle to spend time with God don't have a scheduling problem; they have a love problem. You have a quiet time because you know Him and therefore love Him, not just because you want to learn more about Him. The Apostle Paul said Christ's love compelled or constrained him (see 2 Cor. 5:14).

1 **Suppose you were dating someone you loved and intended to marry. What is the primary reason you would date (spend time with) that person? Check only one response.**
❑ Because I would want to find out about his likes and dislikes
❑ Because I would want to find out about her family background
❑ Because I would want to find out about his knowledge and education
❑ Because I would love her and would enjoy being with her

When two persons love each other and plan to marry, they want to find out information about each other. However, that is not the primary reason they date. They spend time together because they love each other and enjoy being together.

Similarly, you will learn much about God, His Word, His purposes, and His ways as you spend time with Him. You will come to know Him during the day as you experience Him working in and through your life. But learning about Him is not why you should want to have a quiet time with Him. The more you know Him and experience His unfathomable love, the more you will love Him. You will want time alone with God because you love Him and enjoy His fellowship.

Today's lesson is shorter than normal to allow time for the following assignment. You may be able to do it today, but you might choose to set aside time later in the week. Plan to complete the assignment prior to your next small-group session. This assignment may require some planning or adapting. Feel free to adjust the assignment to your personal needs and circumstances. Many people have told me the following exercise was one of the most meaningful aspects of this study.

2 **Just as Adam and Eve walked with God in the cool of the day, set aside at least 30 minutes for a time to walk with God. If your location, physical condition, and weather permit, find a place outside to walk. Use this time to get out of your routine. You may even want to plan a special trip for part of a day to be alone with God. The place could be: in your neighborhood, a wooded area in the country, a city park, a beach, a garden, a mountain road, a lakeshore, or anywhere.**

Spend time walking and talking with God. If the location permits, you may even want to talk out loud. Focus your thoughts on your Heavenly Father's love for you and your love for Him. Praise Him for His love and mercy. Thank Him for expressions of His love to you. Be specific. Express your love for Him. Take time to worship Him and adore Him.

3 **After your walk, use the space below, in the margin, or in your journal to write about your feelings. Answer some of the following:**
• How did you feel as you walked and talked with God?
• What aspect of your love relationship with God did you become aware of?
• If this was a difficult or an emotionally uneasy time, why do you think it was?
• What happened that was especially meaningful or joyful?

Thou shalt love the Lord thy God with all thy heart, soul, mind & strength.

God Pursues a Love Relationship

God always takes the initiative in our love relationship. The witness of the entire Bible testifies that God pursues us and orchestrates ways for us to experience Him. He came to Adam and Eve in the garden. In love He had fellowship with them and they with Him. He came to Noah, Abraham, Moses, and the prophets. God took the initiative for each person in the Old Testament to experience Him in a personal fellowship of love. In the New Testament Jesus approached His disciples and chose them to be with Him and to experience His love. He came to Paul on the Damascus road.

In our natural human state we do not seek God on our own initiative.

GOD TAKES THE INITIATIVE. HE CHOOSES US, LOVES US, AND REVEALS HIS ETERNAL PURPOSES FOR OUR LIVES.

1 Read Romans 3:10-12 in the margin and answer these questions.
a. How many people are naturally righteous? ___*none*___
b. How many people understand spiritual truths on their own? ___*none*___
c. How many people naturally seek God? ___*none*___
d. How many people instinctively do good? ___*none*___

No one! Not even one! Sin has marred us so deeply no one seeks God on his own initiative. Therefore, if we are to have a relationship with Him and His Son, God must take the initiative. This is exactly what He does.

2 Read John 6:44-45,65 in the margin and answer these questions.
a. Who can come to Jesus without being drawn by the Father? ___*no one*___

b. What does a person do who listens to the Father and learns from Him?
___*comes to Christ Jesus*___

c. What is the only way a person can come to Jesus? ___*if enabled by the Father*___

> "The LORD appeared to us in the past saying:
> 'I have loved you with an everlasting love;
>   I have drawn you with loving-kindness' " (Jer. 31:3).
>
> I led them with cords of human kindness,
>   with ties of love;
> I lifted the yoke from their neck
>   and bent down to feed them (Hos. 11:4).

Romans 3:10-12
"There is no one righteous, not even one; there is no one who understands, no one who seeks God. All have turned away, they have together become worthless; there is no one who does good, not even one."

John 6:44-45,65
"No one can come to me [Jesus] unless the Father who sent me draws him. Everyone who listens to the Father and learns from him comes to me. This is why I told you that no one can come to me unless the Father has enabled him."

The love God focuses on your life is an everlasting love. From that love He has pursued you. He has drawn you with cords of love when you were not His friend but His enemy. He gave His own Son to die for you. To firmly anchor your experiencing God and knowing His will, you must be absolutely convinced of God's love for you.

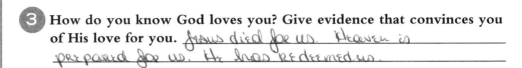

3 **How do you know God loves you? Give evidence that convinces you of His love for you.** *Jesus died for us. Heaven is prepared for us. He has redeemed us.*

God came to Saul, later known as **Paul** (see Acts 9:1-19). Saul was opposing God and His people and was fighting against God's Son, Jesus. Jesus came to Saul and revealed the Father's purposes of love for him. This is also true in our lives. We do not choose Him. He chooses us, loves us, and reveals His eternal purposes for our lives (see Rom. 8:29-30).

Jesus said to His **disciples**, "You did not choose me, but I chose you and appointed you. As it is, you do not belong to the world, but I have chosen you out of the world" (John 15:16,19). Didn't Peter choose to follow Jesus? No. Jesus chose Peter. Peter responded to God's invitation. God took the initiative.

Jesus said **Peter** was responding to God's initiative in his life (see **Matt. 16:13-17**). Jesus asked the disciples who people said He was. Then He asked them who they thought He was. Peter correctly answered, "You are the Christ." Then Jesus made a profound statement to Peter: "This was not revealed to you by man, but by my Father in heaven."

4 **Who had revealed to Peter that Jesus was the Christ, the promised Messiah?** *God in Heaven.*

In essence Jesus said, "Peter, you could never have known and confessed that I am the Christ unless My Father had been at work in your life. He caused you to know who I am. You are responding to the Father's activity in your life."

Do you realize God determined to love you? Apart from that, you never would have become a Christian. He had something in mind when He called you. He began to work in your life. You experienced a love relationship with God when He took the initiative. He opened your understanding. He drew you to Himself.

5 **What did you do when God took the initiative? Check your response.**
❏ I responded to His invitation to a love relationship.
❏ I rejected His offer of a love relationship.

When you responded to His invitation, He brought you into a love relationship with Himself. You would never know that love, be in the presence of that love, or experience that love if God had not first reached out to you. You cannot know God's activity unless He takes the initiative to reveal it to you.

6 **Number the following items from 1 to 4 in the order they occur in the development of a love relationship with God.**
_4_ a. God comes into my life and fellowships with me.
_3_ b. I respond to God's activity in my life and invite Him
      to do in my life what He pleases.
_2_ c. God shows me His love and reveals Himself to me.
_1_ d. God chooses me because of His love.

Some of these actions almost seem to happen at the same time. Yet we can be sure of this: God takes the initiative; then we respond. I numbered the items a–4, b–3, c–2, d–1. God *always* takes the initiative in loving us.

Matthew 16:13-17

"When Jesus came to the region of Caesarea Philippi, he asked his disciples, 'Who do people say the Son of Man is?'

"They replied, 'Some say John the Baptist; others say Elijah; and still others, Jeremiah or one of the prophets.'

" 'But what about you?' he asked. 'Who do you say I am?'

"Simon Peter answered, 'You are the Christ, the Son of the living God.'

"Jesus replied, 'Blessed are you, Simon son of Jonah, for this was not revealed to you by man, but by my Father in heaven.' "

7 The following Scriptures speak of God's initiative in the love relationship. Read each verse. Then briefly summarize how God acts (acted) or what He does (did) to take the initiative.

"The LORD your God will circumcise your hearts and the hearts of your descendants, so that you may love him with all your heart and with all your soul, and live" (Deut. 30:6).

He set aside my hearts.

"All things have been committed to me by my Father. No one knows who the Son is except the Father, and no one knows who the Father is except the Son and those to whom the Son chooses to reveal him" (Luke 10:22).

He revealed Himself to me through Jesus.

"You did not choose me, but I chose you and appointed you to go and bear fruit—fruit that will last" (John 15:16).

He chose me to bear fruit.

"It is God who works in you to will and to act according to his good purpose" (Phil. 2:13).

He works in me to do his good purpose.

"This is how we know what love is: Jesus Christ laid down his life for us" (1 John 3:16).

He died for me.

"Here I am! I stand at the door and knock. If anyone hears my voice and opens the door, I will come in and eat with him, and he with me" (Rev. 3:20).

He came into my life to fellowship with me.

8 Write one of these words in the blank to make the following statement true: *never   sometimes   frequently   always*

God ___always___ takes the initiative to establish a love relationship with me.

Review today's lesson. Pray and ask God to identify one or more statements or Scriptures He wants you to understand, learn, or practice. Underline them. Then respond to the following.

What was the most meaningful statement or Scripture you read today?

Reword the statement or Scripture into a prayer of response to God.

What does God want you to do in response to today's study?

Day 5

A Real, Personal, Practical Relationship

GOD'S PLAN FOR THE ADVANCEMENT OF HIS KINGDOM DEPENDS ON HIS RELATIONSHIP WITH HIS PEOPLE.

The relationship God wants to have with you will be real and personal. Some people ask, Can a person actually have a real, personal, and practical relationship with God? They seem to think God is far off and unconcerned about their day-to-day living. That is not the God we see in the Scriptures.

1 **Read each Scripture passage and describe at least one fact indicating the relationship the person(s) had with God was real, personal, and/or practical. If you are already familiar with the account, you may answer from your present knowledge of the passage. I have completed the first as an example.**

a. Adam and Eve after they sinned (see Gen. 3:20-21): _They were naked. God made garments of skin for them._

b. Hagar when she fled from Sarai (see Gen. 16:1-13): _God directly addressed her & he blessed her. He wanted to engage in conversation with her._

c. Solomon and his request for discernment (see 1 Kings 3:5-13; 4:29-30): _God asked Solomon what he wanted & God gave it to him beyond measure._

d. Twelve Jesus sent out to preach (see Mark 6:7-13): _Jesus equipped them for their jobs & gave them instruction._

e. Peter in prison awaiting trial (see Acts 12:1-17): _An angel spoke to Peter & walked him out of jail in safety_

f. John on the island of Patmos (see Rev. 1:9-20): _Jesus appeared in all his glory to John & told him not to be afraid. He wanted to see his glory._

From Genesis to Revelation we see God relating to people in real, personal, intimate, and practical ways. God had wonderful fellowship with **Adam and Eve**, walking in the garden with them in the cool of the day. When they sinned, God pursued them to restore the love relationship. He met a practical need by providing clothing to cover their nakedness.

Hagar fled for her life after Sarai used, mistreated, and abused her. At a time when she had reached the end of her resources, when she had nowhere else to turn, when all hope was gone, when everyone else had forsaken her, God came to Hagar. In her relationship with God, she learned that God saw her, knew her needs, and would lovingly provide for her. God is extremely personal.

Solomon's father, David, had been a man who sought the Lord with his whole heart. **Solomon** had a heritage of faith and obedience to follow. He had the opportunity to ask and receive anything he wanted from God. Solomon demonstrated his love for God's people by asking for a discerning heart. God granted his request and gave him wealth and fame as well. Solomon found his relationship with God to be very practical.

The disciples also had a real, personal, and practical relationship with Jesus, the Son of God. Jesus had chosen them to be with Him. What a joy it must have been to have such an intimate relationship with Jesus! When Jesus gave them a difficult assignment, He did not send them out helpless. He gave them authority they had never known before over evil spirits.

In some places of the world, obedience to the Lord results in imprisonment. This was Peter's experience. In answer to prayer, the Lord miraculously delivered him. This was so dramatic Peter first thought it was a dream. The praying Christians thought he was an angel. Soon they discovered the Lord's deliverance was real. That deliverance probably saved Peter's life.

In exile on the island of Patmos, John was spending the Lord's Day in fellowship with God. During this time of fellowship in the Spirit, the revelation of Jesus Christ came to John to "show his servants what must soon take place" (Rev. 1:1). This message has challenged and encouraged churches from John's day to now.

Do you sense, as you read Scripture, God became real and personal to people? Do you see their relationships with God were practical? Was He also real and personal to Noah? to Abraham? to Moses? to Isaiah? Yes! Has God changed? No! What was true in the Old Testament also occurred during the time of Jesus' life and ministry. It was the same after the coming of the Holy Spirit at Pentecost. Your life can also reflect a real, personal, and practical relationship as you respond to God's work in your life.

2 **Briefly describe an experience in your life when God was real, personal, and practical in His relationship with you.**

> Everytime I realize that He always walks
> beside me, sustaining me through his mercy,
> love & grace each day.

Love must be real and personal. A person cannot love without someone to love. A love relationship with God takes place between two persons. A relationship with God is real and personal. This has always been His desire. His efforts are expended to bring this desire to reality. God is a Person pouring His life into yours. Christianity is a personal, practical, progressive relationship with Almighty God.

If for some reason you cannot think of a time when your relationship with God was real, personal, and practical, spend time evaluating your relationship with Him. Go to the Lord in prayer and ask Him to reveal the true nature of your walk with Him. Ask Him to bring you into that kind of relationship. If you realize you have never entered a saving relationship with God, turn to the activity on page 8 for help in settling that most important issue now.

God's Presence and Work in Your Life Are Practical

Some people say to me, "Henry, what you are suggesting about doing God's will is not practical in our day." I always differ with them. God is an extremely realistic God. He was in Scripture. He is the same today. When He provided manna, quail, and water for the children of Israel, He was being helpful. When Jesus fed five thousand people, He was being practical. The God I see revealed in Scripture is real, personal, and practical. You can trust God to be practical and real as He relates to you too.

God's constant presence is the most practical part of your life and ministry. Unfortunately, we often assign God a limited role in our lives. Then we call on Him whenever

God's constant presence is the most practical part of your life and ministry.

we need help. That is the exact opposite of what we find in God's Word. He is the One who is working in our world. He invites you to relate to Him so He will accomplish His work through you. His plan for the advancement of the kingdom depends on His working in real and practical ways through His relationships with His people.

Knowing and experiencing God through a real and personal relationship was practical in the Scriptures. Be patient as we work together. I believe you will find that this kind of walk with God will be exceedingly helpful to you. God can make a significant difference in your relationships in your family, in your church, and with other people. You can encounter God in such a way you know you are experiencing Him.

3 **Can you describe your relationship with God as real, personal, and practical?** ☑ **Yes** ❑ **No Why or why not?** _____
I pray this o must Remember to seek it with all my heart.

4 **Fill in the blank to complete the second reality of experiencing God. Make it personal.**
Reality 1: God is always at work around me.
Reality 2: God _pursues_ a continuing _love_ _Relationship_ with me that is _real_ and _personal_.

5 **Review your Scripture-memory verses and be prepared to recite them to a partner in your small-group session this week.**

6 **If you have not taken time to walk with God and write about the experience in day 3, try to do so before your small-group session.**

SUMMARY STATEMENTS

The relationship God wants to have with me will be real and personal.

God's plan for the advancement of the kingdom depends on His working in real and practical ways through His relationships with His people.

Review today's lesson. Pray and ask God to identify one or more statements or Scriptures He wants you to understand, learn, or practice. Underline them. Then respond to the following.

What was the most meaningful statement or Scripture you read today?	Reword the statement or Scripture into a prayer of response to God.	What does God want you to do in response to today's study?

1. Carrie is now doing well. She graduated from seminary, married, has two beautiful children, and serves with her husband as a church planter in Germany.
2. Rhea F. Miller, "I'd Rather Have Jesus," © Copyright 1922. Renewal 1950. Assigned to Chancel Music, Inc. International copyright secured. All rights reserved. Used by permission.

GOD PURSUES A LOVE RELATIONSHIP

DVD Message Notes

1. Christianity is not a religion; it's a relationship.
2. God never speaks without a purpose.
3. God is a God who pursues.
4. We don't have quiet times so we can grow to love God. We have quiet times because we love God.
5. When we obey God, it says, "I love You."

Your Notes

_____

_____

_____

_____

_____

_____

_____

_____

_____

_____

_____

_____

Unit Review

Which of the following ought to be the primary influence in shaping your life? Why (p. 57)?

❑ a. My past   ❑ b. My future

_____

_____

Who takes the initiative in establishing a love relationship between you and God (p. 61)?

❑ a. I do.
❑ b. My pastor does.
❑ c. God does.

Fill in the blanks to complete the second reality of experiencing God.

God _____ a continuing _____ relationship with you that is _____ and _____.

Check your answers, using the pages cited in parentheses.

Scriptures Referenced

Hosea 1:2-3
Hosea 3:1
Romans 3:11

Testimony

Jim and Kaye Johns

Sharing Time

• Things in which you are investing your life, time, and resources and the adjustments God wants you to make (activities 7–8, pp. 58–59)
• Reasons you know God loves you (activity 3, p. 62)
• An experience when God was real, personal, or practical in His relationship to you (activity 2, p. 65)
• One of the most meaningful statements or Scriptures from this unit's lessons and your prayer response to God. Choose one from pages 55, 59, 63, and 66.

For Makeup or Review

Audio and video downloads are available at *www.lifeway.com*.

UNIT

4

"WHOEVER HAS MY COMMANDS
AND OBEYS THEM, HE IS THE ONE
WHO LOVES ME. HE WHO LOVES
ME WILL BE LOVED BY MY FATHER,
AND I TOO WILL LOVE HIM AND
SHOW MYSELF TO HIM."

JOHN 14:21

Love and God's Invitation

GOD IS PROVIDER

When the church I led in Canada started its first mission, we called Jack Conner as our mission pastor. However, we had no money for moving expenses and no funds for his salary. Jack had three children in school, so we felt we ought to pay him at least a modest salary to provide for his family. We prayed that God would provide for his moving expenses and salary since our church had no funds to pay him ourselves. I had never guided a church to do that before. We had stepped out in faith, believing God wanted Jack to pastor our mission in Prince Albert. Except for a few people in California, I didn't know anybody who could help us financially. I began to ask myself, *How in the world will God make this provision?* Then it dawned on me that as long as God knew where I was, He could cause anybody in the world to know where I was. As long as He knew our situation, He could place our need on the heart of anybody He chose.

Jack started his move of faith to Canada, convinced that God had called him. I then received a letter from a church in Fayetteville, Arkansas, that read, "God has laid it on our heart to send 1 percent of our mission giving to Saskatchewan missions. We are sending a check to use however you choose." I did not know how they got involved with us at that time, but a check arrived for $1,100.

One day I received a phone call from someone who heard about what we were doing and wanted to send regular financial support. The person's pledge completed the amount of money we needed for Jack's monthly salary. Just as I got off the phone, Jack pulled into our driveway.

I asked, "Jack, what did it cost to move you?"

He said, "Well, Henry, as best I can tell, it cost me $1,100."

We took a step of faith by believing that the God who knows where we are is the God who can touch people anywhere and cause them to know where we are and what we need. We made the adjustments and were obedient. We believed that the God who called Jack also said, "I AM Provider." As we obeyed, God demonstrated Himself to be our Provider. In an extremely practical way, that experience led us to a deeper love relationship with our all-sufficient God.

Know God

I KNOW GOD MORE
INTIMATELY AS HE
REVEALS HIMSELF
TO ME THROUGH
MY EXPERIENCES
WITH HIM.

This unit continues to focus on your love relationship with God. You will find that the call to a relationship is also a call to be on mission with Him. If you want to know God's will, you must respond to His invitation to love Him wholeheartedly. God works through those He loves in order to carry out His Kingdom purposes in the world. During this unit we will look at the way God invites you to become involved with Him in His work.

Knowing God by Experience

You will never be satisfied merely to know *about* God. Knowing God comes only through experience as He reveals Himself to you. When Moses was at the burning bush, he asked God, "Suppose I go to the Israelites and say to them, 'The God of your fathers has sent me to you,' and they ask me, 'What is his name?' Then what shall I tell them?" (Ex. 3:13).

God responded, "I AM WHO I AM. This is what you are to say to the Israelites: 'I AM has sent me to you' " (Ex. 3:14). When God said, "I AM WHO I AM," He was saying, "I AM the eternal One. I will be what I will be." He was saying, "I am everything you will need." Just fill in the blank for your particular situation: "I am …" During the next 40 years Moses came to know God experientially as Jehovah or Yahweh, the great I AM.

In the Bible God took the initiative to reveal Himself to people by experience. Frequently, when God revealed Himself to individuals, He disclosed a new name to them or described Himself in a new way. To a Hebrew, a person's name represented his character and described his nature. This is why in the Bible we frequently see new names or titles for God following an event in which someone experienced God. To know God by name required a personal experience of His presence.

Biblical names, titles, and descriptions of God therefore identify ways Bible characters personally came to know God. The Scriptures are a record of God's revelation of Himself to people. Each name for God is a part of that revelation.

For example, Joshua and the Israelites were fighting the Amalekites. Moses was overseeing the battle from a nearby mountain. While he held his hands up to God, the Israelites were victorious. When he wearily lowered his hands, they began to lose. God defeated the Amalekites through Israel that day. Moses built an altar and gave it the name "The LORD is my Banner." A banner is the standard that goes in front of an army to indicate whom it represents. "The LORD is my Banner" says we are God's people; He is our God. Moses' uplifted hands gave constant glory to God, indicating the battle was His and Israel belonged to Him. Israel came to know God in a deeper way as they realized anew, "We are God's people; the Lord is our Banner." (See Ex. 17:8-15.)

1 **For another example read Genesis 22:1-18 and answer the following.**
a. What did God ask Abraham to do (v. 2)? take your son, Isaac, to Mt. Moriah & sacrifice him there

b. What do you think verse 8 indicates about Abraham? He would obey God.

c. What did God do for Abraham (v. 13)? _He provided an alternate sacrifice_

d. What name did Abraham give the place (v. 14)? _The Lord will provide._

e. Why did God promise to bless Abraham (vv. 15-18)? _Because Abraham did not withhold anything from God_

God was in the process of developing Abraham's character to be the father of a nation. He put Abraham's faith and obedience to the test, bringing Abraham to a crisis of belief. Abraham had faith that the Lord would provide (see v. 8). He adjusted his life to act on his belief that God was Provider. He obeyed God. When God provided a ram, Abraham came to an intimate knowledge of God by experiencing God as his Provider.

2 **Look at the seven realities on the inside back cover. How does Abraham's experience of God follow that sequence?** _He obeyed & he experienced God in a new and personal way._

At the beginning of this unit, you read how my church and Jack Conner came to know God as Provider. God revealed Himself to us through our experience of Him at work in our lives.

As a pastor of college students, I regularly called the students in and talked with them. I knew they were in a period of rapid change in their lives, and I wanted to help them as they made major life decisions. A wonderful young woman who was studying nursing came to my office. I had been praying for her and God's work in her life. We talked about her alcoholic father. We discussed her decision to continue in nursing. Then I looked at her and said, "I want you to know that God has laid on my heart to pray for a husband for you."

She asked, "Are you serious?"

I said, "I *am* serious. Because you have had an alcoholic father and have experienced so much turmoil and heartache, I believe God wants to give you a wonderful man to love you for who you are. I want you to know that, beginning today, I am praying that God will give you a wonderful, loving husband."

The young woman wept. She and I began to pray that God would provide her a life partner. About three months later, God brought into our church a young man who was an engineering student. The two fell in love, and I performed their wedding ceremony. They now have two children and are faithfully and joyfully serving their Lord.

How did this college student know God could provide a husband? She claimed who God was and then watched and prayed as God acted toward her in that way. She was willing to receive the one God gave her. She was prepared to respond when God revealed His choice to her. Then she came to know God as the Provider of partners.

3 **Describe an event through which you know you experienced God at work in your life.** _I really believe He has provided this life in Jordan for us._

What name could you use to describe the God you experienced? _The God who sees me & the God who provides._

4 **Read the following list of names, titles, and descriptions of God. Check those that describe God in ways you have personally experienced Him.**

❑ My Advocate (Job 16:19)
❑ Comforter in sorrow (Jer. 8:18)
❑ Wonderful Counselor (Isa. 9:6)
☑ My strong Deliverer (Ps. 140:7)
❑ Our Father (Isa. 64:8)
❑ A sure Foundation (Isa. 28:16)
❑ God Almighty (Gen. 17:1)
☑ God who avenges me (Ps. 18:47)
❑ Our Guide (Ps. 48:14)
☑ Our Help (Ps. 33:20)
❑ Great High Priest (Heb. 4:14)
❑ My Hope (Ps. 71:5)
❑ Righteous Judge (2 Tim. 4:8)
❑ Our Leader (2 Chron. 13:12)
☑ Light of life (John 8:12)
❑ Lord of the harvest (Matt. 9:38)
☑ The Most Holy (Dan. 9:24)
❑ Prince of Peace (Isa. 9:6)
☑ Refuge and Strength (Ps. 46:1)
☑ My Savior (Ps. 42:5)
☑ Sovereign Lord (Luke 2:29)
❑ My Support (2 Sam. 22:19)

❑ Bread of life (John 6:35)
☑ My Confidence (Ps. 71:5)
❑ Defender of widows (Ps. 68:5)
☑ Faithful and True (Rev. 19:11)
❑ A consuming Fire (Deut. 4:24)
❑ My Friend (Job 16:20)
☑ God of all comfort (2 Cor. 1:3)
☑ God who saves me (Ps. 51:14)
❑ Head of the church (Eph. 5:23)
☑ My Hiding Place (Ps. 32:7)
❑ Holy One among you (Hos. 11:9)
❑ Jealous (Ex. 34:14)
❑ King of kings (1 Tim. 6:15)
❑ Your Life (Col. 3:4)
❑ Lord of lords (1 Tim. 6:15)
☑ Mediator (1 Tim. 2:5)
❑ Our Peace (Eph. 2:14)
☑ My Redeemer (Ps. 19:14)
☑ My Salvation (Ex. 15:2)
☑ The Good Shepherd (John 10:11)
☑ My Stronghold (Ps. 18:2)
❑ Good Teacher (Mark 10:17)

SUMMARY STATEMENTS

Knowing God comes only through experience as He reveals Himself to me.

I know God more intimately as He reveals Himself to me through my experiences with Him.

Did you see that you have come to know God through experience? Could you check any of the names and not think of an experience in which God acted that way in your life? For instance, you could not have known God as Comforter in sorrow unless you had *experienced* His comfort during a time of sorrow. You come to know God when He reveals Himself to you. You come to know Him as you experience Him. That is why we have titled this course *Experiencing God.* You come to know God more intimately as He reveals Himself to you through your experiences with Him.

5 **Write your Scripture-memory verse for this unit in the margin above and review your verses from other units.**

Whoever has my commands & obeys them is the one who loves me. He who loves me will be loved by my

Review today's lesson. Pray and ask God to identify one or more statements or Scriptures He father, **wants you to understand, learn, or practice. Underline them. Then respond to the following.** and I, too, will love him and draw myself to him.

What was the most meaningful statement or Scripture you read today?	Reword the statement or Scripture into a prayer of response to God.	What does God want you to do in response to today's study?

Worship God

Yesterday you learned that you come to know God by experience at His initiative. You learned that a Hebrew name described a person's character or nature. The name was closely associated with the person and his presence. Thus, to call on someone's name was to seek his presence. God's name is majestic and worthy of our praise. David wrote about the majesty of God's name in **Psalm 8:1**. Acknowledging God's name amounts to recognizing who God is. Calling on His name indicates that you are seeking His presence. Praising His name is praising *Him*.

Seeing God's names in Scripture can call you to worship Him. To worship is to reverence and honor God, to acknowledge Him as worthy of your praise. Spend this day worshiping God through His names. The psalms are rich in their instructions to direct your worship toward God through His names.

> TO WORSHIP IS TO REVERENCE AND HONOR GOD, TO ACKNOWLEDGE HIM AS WORTHY OF YOUR PRAISE.

O Lord, our Lord, how excellent is thy name in all the Earth!

1 **Read the Scriptures below and on the next page. Circle or underline words or phrases that describe ways you can direct your worship toward God through His names. I've underlined one for you.**

"Save us, O Lord our God,
and gather us from the nations,
that we may give thanks to your holy name
and glory in your praise" (Ps. 106:47).

"All the nations you have made
will come and worship before you, O Lord;
they will bring glory to your name" (Ps. 86:9).

"I will praise you forever for what you have done;
in your name I will hope, for your name is
good" (Ps. 52:9).

"Those who know your name will trust in you,
for you, Lord, have never forsaken those
who seek you" (Ps. 9:10).

"Let all who take refuge in you be glad;
let them ever sing for joy.
Spread your protection over them,
that those who love your name may
rejoice in you" (Ps. 5:11).

"In God we make our boast all day long,
and we will praise your name forever"
(Ps. 44:8).

"Blessed are those who have learned
to acclaim you,
who walk in the light of your presence,
O Lord.
They rejoice in your name all day long;
they exult in your righteousness"
(Ps. 89:15-16).

O Lord, our Lord,
how majestic is your name in all the earth!
(Ps. 8:1)

"Sing unto the Lord, bless his name"
(Ps. 96:2, KJV).

"Revive us, and we will call on your name"
(Ps. 80:18).

"I will declare your name to my brothers"
(Ps. 22:22).

"Give me an undivided heart,
that I may fear your name" (Ps. 86:11).

"Thus will I bless thee while I live:
I will lift up my hands in thy name"
(Ps. 63:4, KJV).

give thanks to ...
bring glory to ...
hope in ...
trust in ...
love
praise
rejoice in ...
proclaim ...
sing to
call on ...
declare ...
fear ...
lift up your hands to ...
His Name!

Ways to Worship God

- Bless His name
- Glory in His name
- Rejoice in His name
- Call on His name
- Hope in His name
- Remember the name
- Declare His name
- Know His name
- Seek His name
- Fear His name
- Lift up hands in His name
- Sing praise to His name
- Give thanks to His name
- Love His name
- Sing to His name
- Glorify His name
- Praise His name
- Trust in His name

"Glory in his holy name;
    let the hearts of those who seek the
    LORD rejoice" (Ps. 105:3).

"In him our hearts rejoice,
    for we trust in his holy name"
(Ps. 33:21).

"In the night I remember your name, O LORD,
    and I will keep your law" (Ps. 119:55).

"Cover their faces with shame
    so that men will seek your name, O LORD"
    (Ps. 83:16).

"I will give thanks to the LORD because of
    his righteousness
    and will sing praise to the name of the
    LORD Most High" (Ps. 7:17).

"All the earth bows down to you;
    they sing praise to you,
    they sing praise to your name" (Ps. 66:4).

2 **Use these ways to worship God. Turn to "Names, Titles, and Descriptions of God" on page 268. Spend the remainder of your study time today in worship. The names direct your attention to Him, who He is, and what He does. Praise Him for who He is. Thank Him for what He has done. Glorify Him. Love and adore Him. Seek Him. Trust Him. Sing to Him. Take as much time as you like for this period of worship. Make this a meaningful time to experience your love relationship with the Lord.**

DAY 3

IF I LOVE HIM,
I WILL OBEY HIM!

John 14:21

"Whoever has my commands and obeys them, he is the one who loves me. He who loves me will be loved by my Father, and I too will love him and show myself to him."

Love God

God takes the initiative to pursue a love relationship with you. This love relationship is not a one-sided affair. He wants you to know Him, worship Him, and love Him.

1 **Read John 14:21 in the margin and answer these questions.**
a. Who is the one who loves Jesus? What does he have and do? _whoever has Christs commandments o obey them._

b. How does the Father respond to the one who loves Jesus? _He loves us._

c. What two things will Jesus do for the one who loves Him? _love us and show Himself to us._

Jesus said, "If you love me, you will obey what I command" (John 14:15). When you obey Jesus, you demonstrate that you love Him and trust Him. The Father loves those who love His Son. For those who love Him, Jesus said He would love them and show Himself to them. Obedience is the outward expression of your love for God. The reward for your obedience and love is that Jesus will show Himself to you. Jesus set an example for you in His life. He said, "The world must learn that I love the Father and that I do exactly what my Father has commanded me" (John 14:31). Jesus obeyed every command of the Father. He demonstrated His love for the Father by obedience.

2 **How can you demonstrate your love for God?** _obeying him_

A love relationship with God requires that you demonstrate your love by obedience. If you love Him, you will obey Him. This is not just following the letter of the law but following the spirit of the command as well. If you have an obedience problem, you have a love problem. Focus your attention on God's love.

God's Nature

God's nature is love. He can never function contrary to His nature. Never in your life will God express His will toward you except as an expression of His perfect love. He can't! He can never give you second best. His nature will not let Him. He will bring discipline, judgment, and wrath on those who continue in sin and rebellion. His disciplines, however, are always based on love (see **Heb. 12:6**). Because God's nature is love, the way He expresses Himself to you is always best. Two verses describe His love toward us: "God so loved the world that he gave his one and only Son" (John 3:16) and "This is how we know what love is: Jesus Christ laid down his life for us" (1 John 3:16).

"God is love" (1 John 4:16). Your total trust in God's love is crucial. This has been a powerful influence in my life. I never look at circumstances without seeing them against the backdrop of the cross. My relationship with God determines everything I do.

3 **Fill in the two blanks.**
God is _love_. His will is always _perfect_.

Your relationship with God right now reveals what you believe about Him. It is spiritually impossible for you to truly believe one way and practice another. If you really believe God is love, you will also accept the fact that His will is always best. By nature God is omniscient—all-knowing. He has all knowledge—past, present, and future. Nothing is outside His knowledge. Whenever God expresses Himself to you, therefore, His directions are always trustworthy.

Have you ever asked God to give you several alternatives so you could choose the best one for you? How many options does God have to give you for you to have the right one? One! God always gets it right the first time!

4 **Fill in the two blanks.**
God is all-_seeing_. His directions are always _right_.

Whenever God gives you a directive, it is always right. God's will is always best. You never have to question whether His will is best or right. It always is. This is true because He loves you and knows the future. Because He loves you perfectly, you can completely trust Him and obey Him.

God is omnipotent—all-powerful. He created the world from nothing. He will accomplish anything He purposes to do. If He asks you to do something, He Himself will enable you to do it. We will look at this fact more closely in day 5.

5 **Fill in the two blanks.**
God is all-_powerful_. He can _enable_ me to do His will.

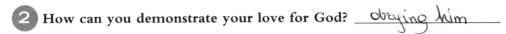

If you have an obedience problem, you have a love problem.

Hebrews 12:6
"The Lord disciplines those he loves, and he punishes everyone he accepts as a son."

↳ the prodigal son

75

6 Match the fact about God's nature on the left with the correct application statement on the right. Write the correct letters in the blanks.

<u>C</u> 1. God is love.   a. God's directions are right.
<u>A</u> 2. God is all-knowing.   b. God can enable me to do His will.
<u>B</u> 3. God is all-powerful.   c. God's will is best.

When your life is in the middle of God's activity, He will rearrange your thinking. God's ways and thoughts are so different from yours and mine they will often sound wrong or impossible. You need a readiness to believe God and trust Him completely. You must believe that what He is doing is best for you. Don't try to second-guess Him. Let Him be God. The answers are 1–c, 2–a, 3–b.

God will start to make Himself known to you simply as He would to a child. As you respond to Him in childlike trust, a whole new way of looking at life will begin to unfold for you. Your life will be fulfilling. You will never sense an emptiness or a lack of purpose in your life. God always fills your life with Himself. When you have Him, you have God at your side.

God's Commands

7 When you hear words like *commands, judgments, statutes,* and *laws,* is your first impression negative or positive? ❑ Negative ❑ Positive

God's commands are expressions of His love nature. In Deuteronomy 10:12-13 God declares that His commands are for our good: "What does the LORD your God ask of you but to fear the LORD your God, to walk in all his ways, to love him, to serve the LORD your God with all your heart and with all your soul, and to observe the LORD's commands and decrees that I am giving you today for your own good?"

8 Read Deuteronomy 32:46-47 in the margin. How important are God's words to you? _they are your life_

The foundation of these passages is the love relationship. When you come to know God by experience, you will be convinced of His love. When you are assured of His love, you can believe Him and trust Him. When you trust Him, you will obey Him. Scripture indicates, "This is love for God: to obey his commands. And his commands are not burdensome" (1 John 5:3).

God loves you deeply and profoundly. Because He loves you, He has given you guidelines for living so you will not miss the full dimensions of the love relationship. Life also has some land mines that can destroy you or harm your life. God does not want to see you miss His best, and He does not want your life destroyed by foolish choices.

Suppose you had to cross a field full of land mines, and a person who knew exactly where each one was buried offered to take you through it. Would you say to him, "I don't want you to tell me what to do. I have free will! I don't want you to impose your ways on me"?

I don't know about you, but I would stay as close to that person as I could. I certainly would not wander off. His directions to me would preserve my life. He would say, "Don't go that way, because that way will kill you. Go this way, and you will live."

That is the purpose of God's commands. He wants you to receive life and have it abundantly. When the Lord gives you a command, He is trying to protect and preserve

Deuteronomy 32:46-47

"He said to them, 'Take to heart all the words I have solemnly declared to you this day, so that you may command your children to obey carefully all the words of this law. They are not just idle words for you—they are your life. By them you will live long in the land you are crossing the Jordan to possess.'"

the best He has for you. He does not want you to lose it. When God gives a command, He is not restricting you. He is freeing you.

9 **Read Deuteronomy 6:20-25 below. Then underline or describe the purpose of God's commandments, decrees, stipulations, and laws.**

"In the future, when your son asks you, 'What is the meaning of the stipulations, decrees and laws the LORD our God has commanded you?' tell him: … 'The LORD commanded us to obey all these decrees and to fear the LORD our God, so that we might always prosper and be kept alive, as is the case today. And if we are careful to obey all this law before the LORD our God, as he has commanded us, that will be our righteousness' " (Deut. 6:20-25).

to prosper & live, to be one righteousness

God has given His commands so you can prosper and live life to its fullest measure. Let me give you an example. Suppose the Lord says, "Let me tell you where a beautiful, wonderful expression of love is. I will provide you with a spouse. Your relationship with this person will bring out the best in you. It will give you an opportunity to experience some of the deepest and most meaningful expressions of human love. That individual will release some wonderful things in you, affirm some things in you, and strengthen you when you lose heart. That person will love you, believe in you, and trust you. From that relationship I will give you children who will sit on your knee and say, 'Daddy, I love you.' "

But God also says, "Do not commit adultery" (Matt. 5:27). Is that command to limit or restrict you? No! It is to protect and free you to experience love at its human best. What happens if you break the command and commit adultery? The love relationship is ruptured between husband and wife. Trust is gone. Hurt sets in. Guilt and bitterness creep in. Even the children begin to respond differently. Scars severely limit the future dimensions of love you could have experienced together.

God's commands are designed to guide you to life's best. You will not obey Him, however, if you do not believe Him and trust Him. You will not believe Him if you do not love Him. You cannot love Him unless you know Him. But if you really come to know God as He reveals Himself to you, you will love Him. If you love Him, you will believe and trust Him. If you believe and trust Him, you will obey Him.

God is love. Because of His love, His will for you is always best. He is all-knowing, so His directions are always right. He has given His commands so you can prosper and live life to its fullest measure. If you love Him, you will obey Him!

Know Him
↓
Love Him
↓
Believe Him
↓
Trust Him
↓
Obey Him

SUMMARY STATEMENTS

Obedience is the outward expression of my love for God. ✔

If I have an obedience problem, I have a love problem.

God is love. His will is always best. ✔

God is all-knowing. His directions are always right. ✔

God is all-powerful. He can enable me to do His will. ✔

When God gives a commandment, He is not restricting me. He is freeing me. ✔

Review today's lesson. Pray and ask God to identify one or more statements or Scriptures He wants you to understand, learn, or practice. Underline them. Then respond to the following.

What was the most meaningful statement or Scripture you read today?	Reword the statement or Scripture into a prayer of response to God.	What does God want you to do in response to today's study?
When you are assured of His love, you can believe Him & trust Him.		

"I'm a Pastor Once Again"

I was attending a large convention meeting with my wife and my son Richard. Suddenly a man approached me and grabbed my hand. Fighting back his emotion, he explained that several years before, God had clearly called him to be a pastor. He had served in a church but had suffered deep hurts from vicious attacks by some of its members. He had resigned from the church, vowing never to serve in a church again. He obtained a good job in a new company and was soon a vice-president earning a large salary. For several years this man forsook his calling and immersed himself in his lucrative career.

Then the church he attended began studying *Experiencing God.* Through that course God reminded the bitter man that His love for him had never changed; neither had His call on his life. With tears streaming down his face, the man choked out, "I'm a pastor once again!" Bitter circumstances had taken this dear man's eyes off the love of his Lord, but as he returned to that love relationship, God enabled him to overcome the difficulties he had faced in life.

DAY 4

God Invites You to Join Him

WHEN YOU SEE THE FATHER AT WORK AROUND YOU, THAT IS YOUR INVITATION TO ADJUST YOUR LIFE TO HIM AND JOIN HIM IN THAT WORK.

The Bible is the record of God's activity in the world. In it He reveals Himself (His nature), His purposes and plans, and His ways. The Bible is not primarily a book about individuals and their relationships with God, such as Abraham, Moses, and Paul. Rather, the Bible focuses on the activity of God and His relationships with individuals.

1 **Review reality 3 of experiencing God by filling in the blanks with the correct words. If you need help, look on the inside back cover.**

Reality 3: God invites you to become ___involved___
with Him in His ___work___ .

REALITY 3

INVITATION

God Works Through People

The Bible reveals that God has always been involved in the world. He has never been absent from it or from what is taking place in history. When we read the Bible, we are reading God's redemptive activity in our world. We see that He chooses to take the initiative and involve His people with Him. He chooses to work *through* them to accomplish His purposes.
- When God was about to judge the world, He came to Noah. He was going to do an awesome thing, and He was going to accomplish it through Noah.
- When God was going to build a nation for Himself, He came to Abraham. God was going to carry out His will through Abraham.
- When God heard the cry of the children of Israel and decided to deliver them, He appeared to Moses. God came to Moses because of His purpose. He planned to deliver the Israelites through Moses.

Both the Old and New Testaments confirm that God works through people. When God's fullness of time had come to redeem a lost world through His Son, He gave 12 men to Jesus to prepare them to accomplish His purposes.

When God is about to do something, He takes the initiative and comes to one or more of His servants to let them know what He is about to do. He invites them to adjust their lives to Him so He will accomplish His work through them. The prophet Amos stated that:

> The Sovereign LORD does nothing
> without revealing his plan to his servants the prophets (Amos 3:7).

2 **Mark the following statements _T_ (true) or _F_ (false).**

   F a. God created the world and then abandoned it to function on its own.

   T b. God is not absent. He is actively at work in the world.

   F c. People do God's work by deciding what they think would be good to do and then doing it.

   T d. God involves people in His work.

   T e. God always takes the initiative to involve people in His work.

Answers: Statements b, d, and e are true. The others are false.

God's Revelation Is Your Invitation

You may be asking, *How does God invite me to be involved with Him?* Let's review Jesus' example from **John 5:17,19-20**. (See unit 1, p. 16.)

Jesus' Example

1. The Father has been working right up until now.
2. Now the Father has Me working.
3. I do nothing on My own initiative.
4. I watch to see what the Father is doing.
5. I do what I see the Father doing.
6. The Father loves Me.
7. He shows Me everything He is doing.

3 **Read the verses in the margin. How did Jesus know what to do in His Father's work?** _He saw what God was doing._

How did Jesus respond? _He did it, too._

To experience God personally, remember God has been at work in our world from the beginning, and He is still at work. Jesus lived His life with this awareness. He announced He had come not to do His own will but the will of the Father who had sent Him (see John 4:34; 5:30; 6:38; 8:29; 17:4). To know the Father's will, Jesus said He watched to see what the Father was doing. Then Jesus joined Him in that work.

4 **In the box "Jesus' Example," circle the key word in statement 4 that tells what Jesus did to recognize the Father's invitation to join Him.**

God always takes the initiative to involve people in His work.

———

John 5:17,19-20

"My Father is always at his work to this very day, and I, too, am working. I tell you the truth, the Son can do nothing by himself; he can do only what he sees his Father doing, because whatever the Father does the Son also does. For the Father loves the Son and shows him all he does."

The Father loved the Son and took the initiative to come to Him and reveal what He (the Father) was doing. The Son was alert for the Father's activity around Him so He could unite His life with what the Father was doing.

As God's obedient child, you are in a love relationship with Him. Because He loves you and wants to involve you in His work, He will show you where He is working so you can join Him. The key word in statement 4 is *watch*. Jesus watched to see where the Father was at work. Then He did what He saw the Father doing. For Jesus the revelation of where the Father was working was His invitation to join the activity. When you see the Father at work around you, that is your invitation to adjust your life to Him and join Him in that work.

Is it possible for God to be working around you without your seeing it? Yes. Elisha and his servant were in the city of Dothan surrounded by an enemy army. The servant was terrified, but Elisha remained calm. "Elisha prayed, 'O Lord, open his eyes so he may see.' Then the Lord opened the servant's eyes, and he looked and saw the hills full of horses and chariots of fire all around Elisha" (2 Kings 6:17). Only when the Lord opened the servant's eyes did he see God's activity all around him.

Jesus wept over Jerusalem and its leaders as He prophesied the destruction that would take place in A.D. 70. He said, "If you, even you, had only known on this day what would bring you peace—but now it is hidden from your eyes" (Luke 19:42). God was in their midst performing wonderful signs and miracles; yet they did not recognize Him.

Two factors are important for you to recognize God's activity around you.
1. You must live in an intimate love relationship with God.
2. God must take the initiative to open your spiritual eyes so you can see what He is doing.

5 **Fill in the blank:**
God's revelation to me of His activity is my *invitation*
to join Him.

6 **What are two factors important to your recognizing God's activity around you?**
1. Having a love relationship with God.
2. Having your spiritual eyes open.

Unless God allows you to see where He is working, you will not recognize it. When God reveals to you what He is doing around you, that is your invitation to join Him. Recognizing God's activity depends on your love relationship with Him and His taking the initiative to open your spiritual eyes to see His activity.

Working Where God Is at Work

Our church sensed God wanted us to start new churches all across central and western Canada. Hundreds of towns and villages needed a church.

7 **If you were in that situation, how would you decide which towns to choose?** _____
_____

Some churches would start with a population study or a survey. Then they would tabulate the results and apply human logic to decide where the most promising, productive places might be. Instead, we tried to find out what God was already doing around us. We believed He would show us where He was at work, and that revelation would be our invitation to join Him. We began praying and watching to see what God would do next to answer our prayers.

Allan was a small town 40 miles from Saskatoon that had never had a Protestant church. It desperately needed one. One of our members felt led to conduct a Vacation Bible School for the children in Allan. We said, "Let's find out if God is at work here." At the end of the week of Vacation Bible School, we held a parents night. We said to the group, "We believe God may want us to establish a church in this town. If any of you would like to begin a regular Bible-study group and be a part of a new church, would you come forward?"

From the back of the hall came a woman who was weeping. She said, "I have prayed for 30 years that a church would be started in this town, and you are the first people to respond."

Right behind her came an elderly man. Deeply moved, he was also weeping. He said, "For years I was active in a church. Then I turned to alcohol. Four and a half years ago I came back to the Lord. I promised God then that I would pray four or five hours every day until God brought a church to our town. You are the first people to respond."

We didn't have to take a survey. God had just shown us where He was at work! That was our invitation to join Him. We went back and joyfully shared with our church what God was doing. The congregation immediately voted to start a new church in Allan. That congregation eventually helped establish several other congregations in surrounding towns.

God hasn't told us to go and do what we can. He has instructed us that He is already at work bringing a lost world to Himself. If we will adjust our lives to Him in a love relationship, He will show us where He is at work. That revelation is His invitation for us to become involved in what He is doing. Then when we join Him, He completes His work through us.

SUMMARY STATEMENTS

God is at work in the world.

God takes the initiative to involve me in His work.

God must take the initiative to open my spiritual eyes so that I can see what He is doing.

When I see the Father at work around me, that is my invitation to adjust my life to Him and join Him in that work.

God's revelation is my invitation to join Him.

Review today's lesson. Pray and ask God to identify one or more statements or Scriptures He wants you to understand, learn, or practice. Underline them. Then respond to the following.

What was the most meaningful statement or Scripture you read today?	Reword the statement or Scripture into a prayer of response to God.	What does God want you to do in response to today's study?

god - none of this hits home with me. Am I selfish that I'm not "on fire" for you? I'm trying to be a good mom, but I think I might be messing my kids up more than helping. I don't think "doing stuff" for you proves I love you. Learning to love you comes first.

Knowing Where God Is at Work

WHAT GOD INITIATES, HE COMPLETES.

Sometimes God tries to get our attention by revealing where He is at work. We see it, but we do not immediately identify it as His activity. We say to ourselves, *I don't know whether God wants me to get involved here. I had better pray about it.* By the time we pray, the opportunity to join God is gone. A tender, sensitive heart will be ready to respond to God at the slightest prompting. God makes your heart tender and sensitive in the love relationship so you are in tune with what is on His heart for the circumstances around you.

If you are going to join God in His work, you need to know where He is working. The Scriptures identify things only God can do. You need to learn to identify these. Then when something happens around you that only God can do, you will recognize it is God's activity. This does not deny God's initiative. Unless God opens your spiritual eyes, you will not know He is the One at work. He takes the initiative to open your eyes.

Things Only God Can Do

1 **At the beginning of unit 2, I gave an illustration of something only God can do. Review "College Campus Bible Studies" on page 31 and write something only God can do.** Only God can reveal to us where He is already at work.

The Scriptures say no one can come to Christ unless the Father draws him (see John 6:44). No one seeks God or pursues spiritual things unless the Spirit of God is at work in his life. Suppose a neighbor, a friend, or one of your children begins to inquire about spiritual things. You do not have to question whether that is God drawing him or her. He is the only One who can do that. People do not seek God unless He is at work in their lives.

For example, as Jesus passed through a crowd, He always looked for where the Father was at work. The crowd was not the harvest field. The harvest field was within that crowd. Jesus saw Zacchaeus in a tree. Jesus may have said to Himself, Nobody can seek Me with that kind of earnestness unless My Father is at work in his heart. So Jesus pulled away from the crowd and said, "Zacchaeus, come down immediately. I must stay at your house today" (Luke 19:5). What happened? Salvation came to that household that day. Jesus always looked for the activity of the Father and joined Him. Salvation came as a result of Jesus' joining His life to the Father's activity.

2 **Read the following Scriptures and answer the questions that follow.**

> "If you love me, you will obey what I command. And I will ask the Father, and he will give you another Counselor to be with you forever—the Spirit of truth. … You know him, for he lives with you and will be in you" (John 14:15–17).

If you love and obey Christ, whom will the Father give you? List two of His names. Holy Spirit, Counselor, Spirit of truth

Where will this Person live? _with you & in you_

"The Counselor, the Holy Spirit, whom the Father will send in my name, will teach you all things and will remind you of everything I have said to you" (John 14:26).

What are two things the Holy Spirit will do for Jesus' disciples? _teach them all things & help them Remember what Jesus taught_

"When he comes, he will convict the world of guilt in regard to sin and righteousness and judgment" (John 16:8).

What are three things the Holy Spirit does? _convict the world of sin, of righteousness & of judgment_

When you become a Christian, you enter a love relationship with Jesus Christ—God Himself. At that point the Counselor, the Spirit of truth, takes up residence in your life. He is always present to teach you. The Holy Spirit also convicts people of guilt for their sin. He convicts the world of righteousness and judgment. Here's a list of some things only God can do.

Things Only God Can Do

1. Draws people to Himself ✔
2. Causes people to seek Him ✔
3. Reveals spiritual truth ✔
4. Convicts the world of guilt about sin ✔
5. Convicts the world of righteousness ✔
6. Convicts the world of judgment ✔

When you see one of these things happening, you know God is at work. He is at work when you see someone coming to Christ, asking about spiritual matters, beginning to understand spiritual truth, experiencing conviction of sin, being convinced of Christ's righteousness, or being convinced of judgment.

Watching for God's Activity

Jim had worked hard to become the CEO of his company. For years he had focused on climbing the corporate ladder, paying whatever price was necessary to get to the top. God began to convict Jim that he had never asked God why He had placed him in his influential position. Jim prayed and asked God to open his eyes to what He was doing in the company. That week someone on his staff began talking about the Bible. When Jim answered the questions, the employee asked him how he knew so much about the Bible. He asked Jim what he could do to know the Bible the way Jim did.

3 **Suppose you were in Jim's place. How would you find out what to do next?** _I would probably start a Bible study w/o praying - but this is easy answer in the context of the course._

God is at work in Ali & Jona. Praise the Lord!

Pray and watch to see what God does next.

Pray and watch to see what God does next. Only the Father knows what He has purposed, and He knows the best way to accomplish His will. He knows why He brought these individuals together in this company and why He gave Jim the burden to bring them together. After you pray, get off your knees and watch to see what God does next. For Jim, it might be to lead a Bible study for interested employees on Wednesdays during the lunch hour. Jim would watch to see what people said when they participated. Suppose someone in the plant comes to Jim and says, "My family is really having a hard time financially. I am having an especially tough time with my teenager."

Make the connection. Jim had just prayed, "God, show me where You are at work." He needs to make the connection between his prayers and what happens next. If you do not connect what happens next, you may miss God's answer to your prayer. Always connect what happens next. Then what should Jim do?

Find out what God is already doing by asking probing questions. Ask the kind of questions that will reveal what is happening in that person's life to find out what God is doing:

Probing Questions

- How can I pray for you?
- Do you want to talk?
- What do you see as the greatest challenge in your life?
- What is the most significant thing happening in your life now?
- Would you tell me what God is doing in your life?
- What is God bringing to the surface in your life?
- What particular burden has God given you?

Listen. The person responds, "I really don't have a relationship with God. But since having this problem with my teenager, I sure have been thinking about it." Or "When I was a kid, I used to go to Sunday School. My mom and dad made me go. I got away from it, but our financial problems have really caused me to think about this." Those statements sound as if God is at work in the person's life. He may be drawing the person to Himself, causing the person to seek God, or bringing conviction of sin.

4 **What are some actions described in the previous paragraphs that will help you see whether God is at work in a situation?**

_____

_____

5 **Look again at the box "Things Only God Can Do" on page 83. What would you watch for as you look for God's activity in the lives of people around you? List at least three.**

I would watch for someone who _____

_____

6 **List in the margin the names of people around you who are experiencing God's activity in their lives.**

When you want to know what God is doing around you, pray. Watch to see what happens next. Make the connection between your prayer and what follows. Find out what God is doing by asking probing questions. Then listen. Be ready to make the adjustments required to join God in what He is already doing.

A man visited our church by accident and saw in the bulletin statements requesting prayer for our missions in Kyle, Prince Albert, Love, Regina, Blaine Lake, and other locations. He asked what the requests meant. I explained that our church had made a commitment: if God showed us where someone desired a Bible study or a church, we would respond. He asked, "You mean if I asked you to come and help us start a church in our town, you would come?" I told him we would, and he started to cry. He was a construction worker in Leroy, 75 miles east of us. He said he had been pleading with people to start a church in Leroy for 24 years. Nobody had wanted to help. He asked if we would come. We established a church in Leroy and bought two lots on the main street. This man was so excited he bought a school building and moved it to the site. He now serves as a lay pastor.

As a church we were already conditioned to recognize things only God can do. When He let us see where He was working, we immediately realized that was our invitation to join Him. Frequently, the reason we do not join God is because we are not committed to join Him. We want God to bless us, not to work through us. As a church, do not look for ways God is going to bless you. Look for ways God is going to reveal Himself by working through you and beyond you to accomplish His purposes. God's work in you will bring a blessing to you and others, but the blessing is a by-product of your obedience and experience of God at work in your midst.

Who can tell what a stranger's visit can mean in your church? Ask questions about what God is doing where that person is. Then you will know how to adjust your life to be an instrument of God so He can accomplish His work through you. When you start to see God moving, adjust your life and respond.

7 Has this illustration given you any ideas about how you can begin to watch for God's activity around you? in your family? in your work? in your church? Write any ideas you have in the margin.

The impressions you wrote down may be from God Himself. He may be inviting you to look for His activity. Don't miss the opportunity. Pray and watch to see what happens next.

When God Speaks

We have spent two days focusing on God's invitation for you to become involved with Him in His work. Be aware of two points about God's invitation for you to join Him.

1. *God speaks when He is about to accomplish His purposes.* All Scripture shows that when God reveals to you what He is doing, that is the time to respond. Although the completion of God's work may be a long time away—for example, Abram's son was born 25 years after God's promise—the time God comes to you is the time for your response. That is when you need to adjust your life to Him. You may need to prepare for what He is going to do through you.

2. *What God initiates, He completes.* Isaiah confirmed this truth when God said,

> What I have said, that will I bring about;
> what I have planned, that will I do" (Isa. 46:11).

If God showed us where someone desired a Bible study or a church, we would respond.

We are busy wanting God to bless us instead of seeking for opportunities for Him to work through us.

God speaks when He is about to accomplish His purposes.

Earlier he warned God's people,

> The LORD Almighty has sworn,
> "Surely, as I have planned, so it will be,
>   and as I have purposed, so it will stand."
> For the LORD Almighty has purposed, and who can thwart him?
>   His hand is stretched out, and who can turn it back?
> (Isa. 14:24,27).

God says that if He lets His people know what He is about to do, it is as good as done—He Himself will bring it to pass (also see 1 Kings 8:56; Phil. 1:6).

When God speaks, He guarantees it will happen. This holds enormous implications for individual believers, churches, and denominations. When we come to God to know what He is about to do where we are, we also have the assurance that what God indicates He is about to do will certainly occur.

8 **Do you agree or disagree with the following statement? What God initiates, He always completes.   ❏ Agree   ❏ Disagree   What is the reason for your response?** _We have the testimony & witness of Jesus Christ risen from the dead. Our God will compt fulfill His work._

If you disagreed with the statement, be sure you always base your understanding of God on Scripture, not on personal opinion or experience alone. Throughout history, people have said they had a word from the Lord, but then it did not come to pass. Do not look to these kinds of experiences to determine your understanding of God.

I must add a strong word of caution for spiritual leaders: if you ever indicate to God's people that you have a word from the Lord, you are obligated to follow through with what God said until He brings it to pass. God declared that anyone who says, "I have a word from the Lord" that does not come to pass is a false prophet (see Deut. 18:18–22; Jer. 28:9; Ezek. 12:24–25). A true prophet of God is someone who has a word from the Lord that comes to pass. God's nature demands it! Whatever God says inevitably occurs.

9 **Review your Scripture-memory verses and be prepared to recite them to a partner in your small-group session this week.**

SUMMARY STATEMENTS

A tender, sensitive heart will be ready to respond to God at the slightest prompting.

Pray and watch to see what God does next.

Make the connection. Ask probing questions. Listen.

God speaks when He is about to accomplish His purposes.

What God initiates, He completes.

Review today's lesson. Pray and ask God to identify one or more statements or Scriptures He wants you to understand, learn, or practice. Underline them. Then respond to the following.

What was the most meaningful statement or Scripture you read today?	Reword the statement or Scripture into a prayer of response to God.	What does God want you to do in response to today's study?

LOVE AND GOD'S INVITATION

DVD Message Notes

1. One of the most beautiful things about our relationship with God is that He invites us to become involved with Him.
2. Don't ever underestimate what God can make of you.
3. Hear Jesus say, "Come follow Me, and I will make you to become."
4. "If you love Me, then anything I say, you need to immediately practice in your life."
5. God never give suggestions. He gives commands.
6. It is not a minor matter when God speaks to you. It is both life and death.
7. Most of the commandments of God are positive.
8. Do you want to experience the ever-expanding, measureless love of God? Then whenever Christ gives you a directive, do it!
9. Every word from God is your life.

Your Notes

_____

_____

_____

_____

_____

_____

_____

Unit Review

Match the fact about God's nature on the left with the correct application statement on the right. Write the correct letters in the blanks (activity 6, p. 76).

___ 1. God is love.
___ 2. God is all-knowing.
___ 3. God is all-powerful.

a. God's directions are right.
b. God can enable me to do His will.
c. God's will is best.

Fill in the blanks in the third reality of experiencing God (activity 1, p. 78).

God invites you to become _____
with Him in His _____ .

List at least three things only God can do (p. 83).

_____

_____

_____

Check your answers, using the pages cited in parentheses.

Scriptures Referenced

Mark 1:17
John 14:15
Deuteronomy 30:19-20
John 6:63
John 13:34
John 14:21
John 14:23
John 14:24

Testimony

Lonnie Riley

Sharing Time

- An event through which you have come to know God by experience and the name that describes Him (activity 3, p. 71)
- (Move to quads.) What you thought, felt, or experienced during worship on day 2 (activity 2, p. 74)
- Ideas for recognizing God's activity around you (activity 7, p. 85)
- One of the most meaningful statements or Scriptures from this unit's lessons and your prayer responses to God. Choose one from pages 72, 77, 81, and 86.

For Makeup or Review

Audio and video downloads are available at *www.lifeway.com*.

UNIT S

EXPERIENCING GOD

VERSE TO MEMORIZE

"HE WHO BELONGS TO GOD
HEARS WHAT GOD SAYS. THE
REASON YOU DO NOT HEAR
IS THAT YOU DO NOT BELONG
TO GOD."

JOHN 8:47

God Speaks, Part I

GOD'S ACTIVITY IN AFRICA

I had the privilege of ministering to missionary personnel in Africa. During the week I met a wonderful African-American missionary serving in Zambia. He told me of the millions of AIDS orphans in Africa and of the terrible suffering they endured. He shared his burden for African-American churches in the United States to minister to this enormous need. As the missionary shared, the Holy Spirit impressed on me that I was to be a part of God's activity for this need. I told the missionary that I was deeply moved by what he had said and that I would be glad to help in any way I could. I explained that I did not have many contacts in African-American churches. Nevertheless, I would be praying, and I would respond to whatever God directed me to do next.

I had been home for about two days when the phone rang. The call was from one of a leading African-American pastor in America. He said he was hosting one of the largest gatherings of African-American church leaders and wanted me to speak to them. I instantly recognized that God was giving me my next set of instructions.

Not long after that, I received another unusual invitation. This time it was to speak to a group of ambassadors from Africa at the United Nations. After I shared with them about being spiritual leaders in their homelands, they gave me their business cards and asked me to visit their countries. Since that time, God has steadily revealed to me His great love for the people of Africa and for the millions of people who suffer there daily. As I responded to the request of one missionary, I had no idea God had so much He wanted to do through my life. Every conversation with God has limitless possibilities attached to it, because He "is able to do immeasurably more than all we ask or imagine, according to his power that is at work within us" (Eph. 3:20).

God Speaks in Different Ways

IF A CHRISTIAN
DOES NOT KNOW
WHEN GOD IS
SPEAKING, HE IS
IN TROUBLE AT
THE HEART OF HIS
CHRISTIAN LIFE.

REALITY 4

GOD SPEAKS

That God spoke
is the most
important
factor, not
how He spoke.

A critical requirement for understanding and experiencing God is clearly knowing when He is speaking. If Christians do not know when God is speaking, they are in trouble at the heart of their Christian lives. In this unit we will discover ways God speaks through the Holy Spirit to reveal Himself, His purposes, and His ways. We will also examine ways God speaks through the Bible, prayer, circumstances, and the church or other believers.

God Spoke in the Old Testament

"In the past God spoke to our forefathers through the prophets at many times and in various ways" (Heb. 1:1). A truth that is evident throughout the Bible is that God speaks to His people. In the Old Testament God spoke in many different ways. He spoke through—

- angels (see Gen. 16);
- visions (see Gen. 15);
- dreams (see Gen. 28:10-19);
- the use of the Urim and Thummim (see Ex. 28:30);
- symbolic actions (see Jer. 18:1-10);
- a gentle whisper (see 1 Kings 19:12);
- miraculous signs (see Ex. 8:20-25);
- other ways.

How God spoke in the Old Testament is not the most important factor. *That* He spoke is the crucial point. Those He spoke to knew He was God, and they understood what He was saying.

1 **Which of the following is most important?**
☐ a. How God spoke   ☐ b. That God spoke

2 **When God spoke to a person in the Old Testament, what two things did the person know?**
a. _____
b. _____

That God spoke to people is far more important than *how* He spoke. When He spoke, the person knew God was speaking, and he understood what God was saying. Four important truths characterize each instance when God spoke in the Old Testament. The burning-bush experience of Moses in Exodus 3 illustrates these truths.

1. When God spoke, the experience was usually unique to that individual. For instance, Moses had no precedent for a burning-bush experience. He could not say, "Oh, this is my burning-bush experience. My fathers, Abraham, Isaac, and Jacob, had theirs, and this is mine." There were no other times when God spoke this way. God's speaking is unique because He wants our experience with Him and His voice to be personal to us. He wants us to look to Him in a relationship rather than depend on a method or a technique. If Moses had been around today, he would have been tempted to write a book titled *My Burning-Bush Experience.* Then people would search all over the countryside for *their* burning bush. God spoke to Moses in a way that was unique to him. The key is not *how* God spoke but *that* He spoke. That has not changed. He still speaks to His people in unique ways today.

3 **What is the first important truth about the way God spoke to individuals in the Old Testament?**

_____

2. *When God spoke, the person was sure God was speaking.* Because God communicated to Moses in a unique way, Moses had to be certain it was God. Scripture testifies that Moses had no question that his encounter was with God—the "I AM THAT I AM" (Ex. 3:14). He trusted God, obeyed Him, and experienced Him acting just as He said He would. Could Moses logically prove to someone else he had heard from God in a burning bush? No, all Moses could do was testify to his encounter with God. Only God could cause His people to know that the word He gave Moses was a message from the God of their fathers.

When someone like Gideon lacked assurance, God was gracious to reveal Himself even more clearly. When Gideon first asked for a sign, he prepared a sacrifice. Then "the angel of the Lord touched the meat and the unleavened bread. Fire flared from the rock, consuming the meat and the bread. And the angel of the Lord disappeared. When Gideon realized it was the angel of the Lord, he exclaimed, 'Ah, Sovereign Lord! I have seen the angel of the Lord face to face!' " (Judg. 6:21-22). Gideon was sure God had spoken.

4 **What is the second truth about the way God spoke in the Old Testament?**

_____

3. *When God spoke, the person knew what God said.* Moses knew what God was telling him to do. He knew how God wanted to work through him. That is why Moses raised so many objections. He understood exactly what God was expecting. This was true for Moses, and it was true for Noah, Abraham, Joseph, David, Daniel, and others.

5 **What is the third truth about the way God spoke in the Old Testament?**

_____

4. *When God spoke, that was an encounter with God.* Moses would have been foolish to say, "This has been a wonderful experience with this burning bush. I hope this leads me to an encounter with God!" His experience *was* the encounter with God! When God reveals truth to you, by whatever means, that is a divine encounter. That is an experience of His presence in your life. God is the only One who can cause you to experience His presence.

6 **What is the fourth truth about the way God spoke in the Old Testament?**

_____

7 Using the hints below, see if you can write the four truths about the way God spoke in the Old Testament.

Unique: _____

Sure: _____

What: _____

Encounter: _____

This pattern of God's speaking is found throughout the Old Testament. The *methods* He used to speak differed from person to person. The important points are:

- God uniquely spoke to His people.
- They knew it was God.
- They understood what He said.
- When God spoke, that was an encounter with God.

When God speaks to you by the Holy Spirit through the Bible, prayer, circumstances, and the church, you will know it is God, and you will understand what He is saying. When God speaks to you, that is an encounter with God.

A Wrong Pattern

I hear many people say something like this: "Lord, I really want to know Your will. Stop me if I am wrong and bless me if I am right" or "Lord, I will proceed in this direction. Close the door if it is not Your will." This approach isn't found in Scripture.

Don't let experience alone guide your life. Don't allow yourself to be led by tradition, a method, or a formula. Often people trust these ways because they appear easier than cultivating an intimate walk with God. People do as they please and put the whole burden of responsibility on God. If they are wrong, He must intervene and stop them. If they make a mistake, they blame Him. God is not obligated to stop you from making a mistake!

If you want to know the will and voice of God, you must devote time and effort to cultivate a love relationship with Him. That is what He wants!

If you want to know the will and voice of God, you must devote time and effort to cultivate a love relationship with Him.

8 Which of the following is the scriptural pattern for knowing God's will? Check one.

❑ a. Look for open and closed doors and go through the open ones.

❑ b. Ask God to stop you if you are wrong and then proceed to carry out your plan..

❑ c. Wait until you hear a clear word from God.

God's Word is our guide. The pattern in Scripture is that God always gives a direction on the front end. He may not tell you all you want to know at the beginning, but He will tell you what you need to know to make necessary adjustments and take the first step of obedience. Wait until the Master gives you instructions. If you start doing before you have a direction from God, more than likely you will be wrong. One of the most difficult things for Christians to do is to wait on the Lord. However, waiting reflects our absolute dependence on God.

Does God Give Specific Directions?

A common teaching today claims that God does not give you clear instructions. Instead, He merely sets your life in motion, and you try to figure out the directions, using your God-given mind. For these people, freedom to choose is the highest good. This implies that a Christian always thinks correctly and according to God's will. It doesn't take into account that the old nature constantly battles with the spiritual nature (see Rom. 7). Our ways are not God's ways (see Isa. 55:8). Only God can give you the kind of specific directions to accomplish His purposes *in His ways*. From God's perspective, doing His will is the highest good and results in the greatest joy.

After God spoke to Noah about building an ark, Noah knew its size, the type of materials to use, and the way to put it together. When God spoke to Moses about building the tabernacle, He was extremely specific about the details. When God walked on the earth in the Person of Jesus Christ, He gave specific directions to His disciples—where to go, what to do, how to respond, and what to say.

What about when God called Abraham (Abram) and said, "Go to the land I will show you" (Gen. 12:1)? That was not very specific. That required faith. But God did say, "I will show you." God always gives you enough specific directions to do what He wants you to do *now*. When you need more directions, He gives you more in His timing. God later told Abraham about the son to be born to him, the number of his descendants, the territory they would inhabit, and that they would go into bondage and eventually be delivered.

The Holy Spirit gives clear directions today. Because God is personal, He wants to be intimately involved in your life. Therefore, He will give you clear guidance for living. You may say, "That has not been my experience." Base your understanding of God on Scripture, not on your personal experience or lack of it.

9 **Underline the suggestions in the following paragraph that will help you look to God for direction in your life.**

If you do not have clear instructions from God in a matter, pray and wait. Learn patience. Depend on God's timing, which is always right and best. Don't get in a hurry. He may withhold directions to cause you to seek Him more intently. Don't try to skip over the relationship to start doing something. God is more interested in a love relationship with you than He is in what you can do for Him. If God is having you wait, He may want to develop a deeper relationship with you before He gives you your next assignment. He may have you wait because the timing is not yet right.

10 **In your own words summarize the directions you underlined.**

_____
_____
_____
_____

11 **Write your Scripture-memory verse for this unit on the following lines and review your verses from other units. Remember, you may select a different verse or translation if you want to.**

_____
_____
_____

Isaiah 55:8

" 'My thoughts are not your thoughts, neither are your ways my ways,' declares the LORD."

SUMMARY STATEMENTS

If I do not know when God is speaking, I am in trouble at the heart of my Christian life.

God speaks to His people.

That God spoke to people is far more important than *how* He spoke.

When God spoke, it was usually unique to that individual.

When God spoke, the person was sure it was God.

When God spoke, the person knew what God said.

When God spoke, that was an encounter with God.

If I do not have clear instructions from God in a matter, I will pray and wait. I will not try to bypass the love relationship.

Review today's lesson. Pray and ask God to identify one or more statements or Scriptures He wants you to understand, learn, or practice. Underline them. Then respond to the following.

What was the most meaningful statement or Scripture you read today?

_____
_____
_____
_____
_____
_____

Reword the statement or Scripture into a prayer of response to God.

_____
_____
_____
_____
_____
_____

What does God want you to do in response to today's study?

_____
_____
_____
_____
_____
_____

DAY 2

WHEN I UNDER-STAND SPIRITUAL TRUTH, IT IS BE-CAUSE THE HOLY SPIRIT IS WORKING IN MY LIFE.

When the disciples heard Jesus, they heard God.

God Speaks by the Holy Spirit

Hebrews 1:1-2 declares, "In the past God spoke to our forefathers through the prophets at many times and in various ways, but in these last days he has spoken to us by his Son."

God Spoke in the Gospels

In the Gospels God spoke through His Son, Jesus. The Gospel of John begins, "In the beginning was the Word, and the Word was with God, and the Word was God.–The Word became flesh and made his dwelling among us" (John 1:1,14). God became flesh in the Person of Jesus Christ (also see 1 John 1:1-4).

The disciples would have been foolish to say, "It's wonderful knowing You, Jesus; but we would really like to know the Father." When Philip said, "Lord, show us the Father and that will be enough for us" (John 14:8), Jesus responded, "Don't you know me, Philip, even after I have been among you such a long time? Anyone who has seen me has seen the Father. How can you say, 'Show us the Father'? Don't you believe that I am in the Father, and that the Father is in me? The words I say to you are not just my own. Rather, it is the Father, living in me, who is doing his work" (John 14:9-10). When Jesus spoke, the Father was speaking through Him. When Jesus did a miracle, the Father was doing His work through Jesus.

Just as surely as Moses was face-to-face with God at the burning bush, the disciples were face-to-face with God in a personal relationship with Jesus. Their encounter with Jesus *was* an encounter with God. To hear from Jesus *was* to hear from God.

1 **Write a summary statement of the way God spoke during Jesus' life.**

_____

In the Gospel accounts God was in Christ Jesus. God spoke by Jesus. When the disciples heard Jesus, they heard God. When Jesus spoke, that was an encounter with God.

God Speaks Today

When we move from the Gospels to Acts and to the present, we often change our mind-set. We live as if God quit speaking personally to His people. We fail to realize that an encounter with the Holy Spirit, who lives within us, *is* an encounter with God. God clearly spoke to His people in Acts. He speaks to us today. From Acts to the present, God has been speaking to His people by the Holy Spirit.

The Holy Spirit takes up residence in someone's life when that person becomes a Christian: "You yourselves are God's temple and … God's Spirit lives in you" (1 Cor. 3:16). "Your body is a temple of the Holy Spirit, who is in you, whom you have received from God" (1 Cor. 6:19). Because the Spirit is always present in a believer, He can speak to you clearly at any time. We have already learned that God speaks to His people. Here are some of the key ideas we examined.

- In the Old Testament God spoke in many different ways.
- In the Gospels God spoke through His Son.
- God spoke in Acts and speaks in the present by the Holy Spirit.
- God speaks by the Holy Spirit through the Bible, prayer, circumstances, and the church to reveal Himself, His purposes, and His ways. (We will study reality 4 in the coming days.)
- Knowing God's voice comes from an intimate love relationship with God.
- God speaks when He has a purpose in mind for your life.
- The moment God speaks to you is the time He wants you to respond to Him.
- The moment God speaks to you is God's timing.

2 **Based on these truths, answer the following questions.**

a. How did God speak in the Old Testament? _____

_____

b. How did God speak in the Gospels? _____

_____

c. How did God speak in Acts and in the present? _____

_____

d. How do you know God's voice? _____

_____

e. How do you know God's timing? _____

_____

Let's review several other things you learned in earlier units about ways God speaks through the Holy Spirit.

- Because of sin "there is no one who understands, no one who seeks God. All have turned away, they have together become worthless; there is no one who does good, not even one" (Rom. 3:11-12).
- The Holy Spirit is the "Spirit of truth" (John 14:17; 15:26; 16:13).
- Spiritual truths can be revealed only by God:" 'No eye has seen, no ear has heard, no mind has conceived what God has prepared for those who love him'—but God has revealed it to us by his Spirit. The Spirit searches all things, even the deep things of God. … No one knows the thoughts of God except the Spirit

An encounter
with the Holy
Spirit is an
encounter
with God.

Truth is never
discovered;
truth is revealed.

of God. We have not received the spirit of the world but the Spirit who is from God, that we may understand what God has freely given us" (1 Cor. 2:9-12).
- Jesus said the Holy Spirit would "teach you all things and will remind you of everything I have said to you" (John 14:26).
- The Holy Spirit will testify about Jesus (see John 15:26).
- "He will guide you into all truth. He will not speak on his own; he will speak only what he hears, and he will tell you what is yet to come. He will bring glory to me by taking from what is mine and making it known to you" (John 16:13-14).

Encountering God

When God spoke to Moses and others in the Old Testament, those events *were* encounters with God. An encounter with Jesus *was* an encounter with God for the disciples. In the same way, your encounter with the Holy Spirit *is* an encounter with God for you.

Because you have the Holy Spirit, He guides you into all truth and teaches you all things. You understand spiritual truth because the Holy Spirit works in your life. You cannot understand God's Word unless the Spirit of God teaches you. When you read the Word, the Author Himself is present to instruct you. Truth is never *discovered;* truth is *revealed.* When the Holy Spirit reveals truth to you, He is not leading you to an encounter with God. That *is* an encounter with God!

3 **Has God been speaking to you during your study of this course?**
❑ **Yes** ❑ **No** **Review each day's final activity in units 1–4.**
- Read the statements or Scriptures God called to your attention.
- Read and pray again your prayer responses.
- Review the things you sensed God wanted you to do in response to the lessons.

4 **Briefly summarize what you sense God has said to you so far in the course. Focus on general themes or directions rather than specific details. If you don't sense God has spoken clearly, you don't need to make something up. Just leave the lines blank for now.**

_____
_____
_____
_____

5 **Have you responded to what God has called to your attention? How would you describe your response to His leading thus far?**

_____
_____

6 **What do you sense is your greatest spiritual challenge now?**

_____

7 **Without looking, try to quote the first four realities of experiencing God. Use these hints: work, relationship, invitation, speaks. Check yourself, using the inside back cover, or quote them to another person and ask him or her to check your answers.**

Respond Immediately

When God spoke to Moses, what Moses did next was crucial. After Jesus spoke to the disciples, what they did next was paramount. What you do immediately after the Spirit of God speaks to you through His Word is critical. Our problem is that when the Spirit of God speaks to us, we want to debate. Moses engaged in a long discussion with God (see Ex. 3:11–4:13), and it limited him for the rest of his life. After that discussion Moses had to speak to the people through his brother, Aaron (see Ex. 4:14-16).

Regularly review what you sense God has been saying to you. If God speaks and you hear but do not respond, a time could come when you do not hear His voice. Disobedience can lead to a "famine of hearing the words of the Lord" (Amos 8:11-12).

The Gospels indicate that when Jesus invited Peter, Andrew, James, and John to abandon their fishing careers and follow Him, they did so immediately (see Mark 1:16-20). Strive to be like the disciples and instantly obey every word from God.

In Luke 8:5-15 Jesus told the parable of the sower and the seeds. The seed that fell on good soil represented someone who heard God's word, retained it, and produced fruit. Then Jesus said, "Consider carefully how you listen. Whoever has will be given more; whoever does not have, even what he thinks he has will be taken from him" (Luke 8:18). If you hear God's Word and do not apply it to produce fruit in your life, even what you think you have will be taken away. Be careful how you listen to God! Make up your mind now that when the Spirit of God speaks to you, you will do whatever He says.

SUMMARY STATEMENTS

An encounter with the Holy Spirit is an encounter with God.

I understand spiritual truth because the Holy Spirit is working in my life.

When I come to God's Word, the Author Himself is present to instruct me.

Truth is never discovered; truth is revealed.

Review today's lesson. Pray and ask God to identify one or more statements or Scriptures He wants you to understand, learn, or practice. Underline them. Then respond to the following.

What was the most meaningful statement or Scripture you read today?

Reword the statement or Scripture into a prayer of response to God.

What does God want you to do in response to today's study?

A Lawyer Learns to Hear God's Voice

God has given me a wonderful opportunity to lead a Bible study for several hundred men and women in the workplace. We meet monthly from 6:30 to 7:30 a.m. One lawyer drives nearly every month from Macon to south Atlanta. I became his friend and followed his deep desire to know God's clear will, especially in cases he was handling. He had a very sensitive case of a prisoner who was incarcerated for life. She became a Christian and desired to gain parole so that she could help others know Christ as she knew Him. It seemed impossible, but the more the lawyer learned how God guides His children, the more he trusted God and obeyed what God told him to do. Over a long period of time his client was not only paroled but also remarried the father of her 11-year-old son, and they are living happily and faithfully to this day. The Christian lawyer rejoices that he knows how and when God speaks and what happens when he obeys.

DAY 3

GOD'S REVELATIONS ARE DESIGNED TO BRING YOU INTO A LOVE RELATIONSHIP WITH HIM.

God Reveals

God speaks to His people. When He speaks, what does He reveal? Throughout the Scriptures when God speaks, His desire is to reveal something about Himself, His purposes, or His ways. God's revelations are designed to bring you into an increasingly deeper and profound love relationship with Him.

God Reveals Himself

When God speaks by the Holy Spirit, He often reveals something about Himself. He reveals His name, His nature, and His character.

1 **Read these Scriptures. After each one, write what God revealed about Himself.**

"When Abram was ninety-nine years old, the LORD appeared to him and said, "I am God Almighty" (Gen. 17:1). *He is Almighty*

"The LORD said to Moses, 'Speak to the entire assembly of Israel and say to them: "Be holy because I, the LORD your God, am holy" ' " (Lev. 19:1-2). *Holy*

" 'I the LORD do not change. ... Ever since the time of your forefathers you have turned away from my decrees and have not kept them. Return to me, and I will return to you,' says the LORD Almighty." (Mal. 3:6-7). *Faithful, Unchanging*

"Jesus said to the Jews, 'I am the living bread that came down from heaven. If anyone eats of this bread, he will live forever' " (John 6:51). *Our Strength, Our Eternal Life*

God revealed Himself to Abram by His name—God Almighty. To Moses He revealed His holy nature. God spoke through Malachi to Israel to reveal that He is unchanging and forgiving. Jesus revealed Himself as Living Bread and the source of eternal life.

God speaks when He wants to involve a person in His work. He reveals His character to help the person respond in faith. The person can better obey God's instructions when he believes God is who He says He is and when he believes God can do what He says He will do.

2 **Stop for a minute and meditate on why God revealed Himself as He did to the people in the previous Scriptures. When you think you have an idea of why each revelation was given, continue reading.**

• Ninety-nine-year-old Abram needed to know God was almighty (all-powerful, able to do anything) so He could believe God could give Him a son in his old age.

- Through Moses God said He was holy. His people had to believe He was holy so they would respond by being holy themselves.
- Through Malachi God revealed His forgiving nature so the people could believe they would be forgiven if they would return to God.
- Jesus revealed that He was the source of eternal life so people could believe, respond to Him, and receive life.

3 **Why does God reveal Himself—His name, His nature, and His character?**

to help a person Respond in faith.

God reveals Himself to increase faith that leads to action. Listen attentively to what God reveals to you about Himself. What He shows you will be critical when you come to a crisis of belief.

- You will have to **believe** God is who He says He is.
- You will have to **believe** God can do what He says He will do.
- You will have to **adjust** your thinking in light of this belief.
- Trusting that God will demonstrate Himself to be who He says He is, you then **obey** Him.
- When you **obey,** God does His work through you and demonstrates that He is who He says He is.
- Then you will **know** God by experience.
- You will **know** God is who He says He is.

When did Abram know God was almighty? He knew it in his mind as soon as God said it. However, he came to know God to be almighty by experience when God did something in his life that only God could do. When God gave Abraham (100 years old) and Sarah (90 years old) a son, Abraham _knew_ God was God Almighty.

4 **When God speaks by the Holy Spirit, what is one thing He reveals?**
God speaks by the Holy Spirit to reveal _His nature_, His purposes, and His ways.

God Reveals His Purposes

God reveals His purposes so you will know what _He_ plans to do. If you are to join Him, you need to know what God is going to do. What you plan to do for God is not important. What He plans to do where you are is critical. God always speaks with a purpose in mind. This point should be a review for you (see pp. 38–41).

When God came to Noah, He did not ask, "What do you want to do for Me?" He revealed what He was going to do. It really did not matter what Noah had planned to do for God. It was far more important to know what _God_ was about to do. He was about to destroy the world, and He wanted to work through Noah to accomplish _His_ purposes of saving a remnant of people and animals to repopulate the earth.

Similarly, God came to Abram and spoke to him because He had a purpose in mind. He was preparing to build a nation for Himself. God intended to accomplish _His_ purposes through Abram.

When God prepared to destroy Sodom and Gomorrah, He did not ask Abraham what he wanted to do or was planning to do for Him. But knowing what _God_ was about to do was crucial for Abraham. God revealed His purposes.

God reveals
Himself to
increase faith
that leads
to action.

God reveals
His purposes
so you will
know what He
plans to do.

This sequence is seen throughout the entire Bible in the lives of the judges, David, the prophets, the disciples, and Paul. When God was about to do something, He took the initiative to come to His servants (see **Amos 3:7**). He spoke to reveal His purposes and plans. Then He involved His people and accomplished His purposes through them.

In contrast, today we often set about to dream up what we want to do for God. Then we make long-range plans based on priorities of *our* choosing. What is important is what *God* plans to do where we are and how He wants to accomplish it through us. Notice what the psalmist said about our plans and purposes:

> The LORD foils the plans of the nations;
>   he thwarts the purposes of the peoples.
> But the plans of the LORD stand firm forever,
>   the purposes of his heart through all generations (Ps. 33:10-11).

5 **Read Proverbs 19:21 in the margin and Psalm 33:10-11 above. Why does God reveal His purposes?** _do His children know what He is going to do._

6 **Based on Psalm 33:10-11, answer the following questions.**
a. What does the Lord do to the plans of the nations? _foils_

b. What does the Lord do to the purposes of the peoples? _thwarts_

c. What happens to the Lord's plans and purposes? _nothing_

Do you see why you need to know God's plans and purposes? If your plans and purposes are not God's, you will not experience God working through you. God reveals His purposes so you will know what He plans to do. Then you can join Him. His plans and purposes will stand. They will be accomplished. The Lord foils and thwarts the intent of the nations and the purposes of the peoples.

Planning is a good thing to do if it is motivated and guided by God. But often our plans reflect our own priorities and understanding. We can trust more in our plans and in our reasoning abilities than in God. We may be able to achieve all of our goals and yet be far from God's will. Planning is a tool God may lead you to use, but it must never become a substitute for trusting Him. Your relationship with God is far more important to Him than any planning you will do. The biggest problem with planning is that we often plan and carry out things in our own wisdom that only God has a right to determine. We cannot know the when, where, or how of God's will until He tells us. Just because we accomplished our plans does not mean we are pleasing to God.

God wants us to follow *Him* daily, not just follow a plan. If we try to spell out all the details of His will in a planning session, we tend to think, *Now that we know where we are going and how to get there, we can get the job done.* Then we forget about the need for a daily, intimate relationship with God. We may set about to accomplish our plans and forget the relationship. Or God may try to lead us to do a new thing, but we reject it because it is not in our long-range plan! God created us for an eternal love relationship. Life is our opportunity to experience Him at work.

It isn't wrong to plan. Just be careful not to plan more than God intends for you to do. Let God interrupt or redirect your plans anytime He wants. Remain in a close relationship with Him so you can always hear His voice when He speaks to you.

7 **When God speaks by the Holy Spirit, what are two things He reveals?**
God speaks by the Holy Spirit to reveal ___*purpose*___,
His ___*plan*___, and His ways.

God Reveals His Ways

Even the casual or uninformed reader of the Bible can see God's ways and plans are radically different from people's. God uses *Kingdom* methods to accomplish *Kingdom* purposes. God reveals His ways to us because they are the only means to accomplish His purposes. We must do God's work God's way.

God's goal is to reveal Himself to people to draw them into a love relationship with Himself. His ways are redemptive. He acts in a way that reveals Himself and His love. He does not simply wait around to help us achieve our goals for Him even if we promise Him all the glory when we are successful. He seeks to accomplish His own goals through us—in His way. God said,

> My thoughts are not your thoughts,
> neither are your ways my ways (Isa. 55:8).

God does not work in man's ways. We will not accomplish God's work in our own ways. This is one of the basic sin problems people face:

> We all, like sheep, have gone astray,
> each of us has turned to his own way (Isa. 53:6).

8 **Why does God reveal His ways?** *His ways are the only way we can accomplish god's purpose.*

Our methods may seem attractive to us. We may even achieve moderate success with them. When we try to do God's work in our ways, however, we will never see His mighty power in what we do. With God, *what* you do is not the only important thing. God is also concerned with *how* you do something. God reveals His ways because that is the only means to accomplish His purposes. When God accomplishes His purposes in His ways through us, people will come to know God. They will recognize that what has happened can be explained only by God. He will receive all the glory!

Jesus taught His disciples Kingdom methods. When He asked the disciples to feed the multitudes, they responded, "Send them home!" Jesus, using *Kingdom* methods, had them sit down, fed them, and had baskets full of leftovers. What a contrast! The disciples would have sent the people home empty and hungry, but God displayed to a watching world His love, His nature, and His power. This kind of display would draw people to Himself through His Son Jesus. The disciples witnessed this kind of mighty display many times as Jesus taught them to function according to *Kingdom* principles to do *Kingdom* work. As a result, they experienced Kingdom power and Kingdom results. God's purposes, accomplished in His ways, bring glory to Him. You must learn to do Kingdom work in Kingdom ways.

9 **When God speaks by the Holy Spirit, what are three things He reveals?**
God speaks by the Holy Spirit to reveal ___*person*___,
His ___*plan*___, and His ___*purpose*___.

God reveals His ways to us because they are the only means to accomplish His purposes.

Using Kingdom methods, Jesus fed five thousand.

10 **Match the things God reveals with the correct reasons. Write the correct letters in the blanks.**

God reveals...	Because ...
_C_ 1. Himself	a. He wants me to know how to accomplish things only He can do.
_B_ 2. His purposes	b. He wants me to know what He is about to do so I can join Him.
_A_ 3. His ways	c. He wants me to have faith to believe He can do what He says.

#10 answers: 1-c, 2-b, 3-a

When I was first learning how to walk with God, I depended too much on other people. I would regularly ask others, "Do you think this is really God? Here is what I think. What do you think?" I would depend on others rather than on my relationship with God.

Finally I had to say, "I am going to go to the Lord to clarify what I think He is saying to me. Then I am going to proceed and watch to see how God affirms it." I began that process over a period of time in many areas of my life. My love relationship with God became all-important. I began to discover a clear, personal way God was making known His ways to me.

Tomorrow we will look at ways God speaks through His Word. In future lessons we will look at ways God speaks through prayer, circumstances, and the church to confirm His will to us.

11 **Practice quoting your Scripture-memory verses aloud.**

SUMMARY STATEMENTS

God's revelations are designed to bring me into a love relationship with Him.

God reveals Himself to increase my faith.

God reveals His purposes so that I will do *His* work.

God reveals His ways so that I can accomplish His purposes.

Review today's lesson. Pray and ask God to identify one or more statements or Scriptures He wants you to understand, learn, or practice. Underline them. Then respond to the following.

What was the most meaningful statement or Scripture you read today?	Reword the statement or Scripture into a prayer of response to God.	What does God want you to do in response to today's study?

God Speaks Through the Bible

God speaks to you by the Holy Spirit to reveal Himself, His purposes, and His ways. Perhaps the questions people ask most about God's speaking are:
- How does God speak to me?
- How can I know when God is speaking?
- How can God be more real and personal to me?

God speaks uniquely to individuals, and He does it in any way He pleases. As you walk in an intimate love relationship with God, you will come to recognize His voice. You will grow to know when God is communicating with you.

Jesus compared His relationship with His followers to a shepherd's relationship with his sheep: "The man who enters by the gate is the shepherd of his sheep. ... The sheep listen to his voice. ... His sheep follow him because they know his voice" (John 10:2-4). In this way, when God speaks to you, you will recognize His voice and follow Him.

God speaks through a variety of means. Today God primarily speaks by the Holy Spirit through the Bible, prayer, circumstances, and the church. These four ways are difficult to separate. God uses prayer and the Bible together. Often circumstances and the church, or other believers, will help confirm what God is saying to you. Frequently, God uses circumstances and the church to help you know His timing. We will talk more about that in the next unit. Today let's look at ways God speaks through the Bible. Tomorrow we will look at God's speaking to us through prayer.

> WHEN THE SPIRIT DIRECTS MY ATTENTION TO A TRUTH, I WRITE IT DOWN, MEDITATE ON IT, AND ADJUST MY LIFE TO IT. I ALERT MYSELF TO WATCH FOR WAYS GOD MAY BE THAT WAY IN MY LIFE DURING THE DAY.

1 **Mark the following statements *T* (true) or *F* (false).**
____ a. God speaks to individuals in unique ways.
____ b. God reveals His greatest truths through dreams and visions.
____ c. When rightly related to God, His people will hear and recognize His voice.
____ d. God frequently speaks by the Holy Spirit through the Bible and prayer.

God is sovereign. He can do whatever He chooses. With Scripture as our guide, we know God speaks in unique ways to individuals. His people will hear and recognize His voice. Today He primarily speaks by the Holy Spirit through the Bible, prayer, circumstances, and the church. Only statement b is false. The others are true.

The Spirit of Truth

The Bible is God's Word. It describes God's complete revelation of Himself to humanity. God speaks to you through the Bible. As you have already learned, however, a person cannot understand spiritual truth unless the Spirit of God reveals it. The Holy Spirit is "the Spirit of truth" (John 14:17). The following diagram should help you visualize how the Holy Spirit speaks to you through God's Word.

GOD SPEAKS

THROUGH

THE BIBLE

This is a diagram of an encounter with God. When the Holy Spirit reveals a spiritual truth from God's Word, He is personally applying it to your life. That is an encounter with God. This is the sequence:

1. You read God's Word—the Bible.
2. The Spirit of truth takes God's Word and reveals truth.
3. You adjust your life to God's truth.
4. You obey God.
5. God works in and through you to accomplish His purposes.

2 **Using the description and the diagram, summarize the way God speaks through the Bible.** _____

_____

_____

3 **Write the following key words in the correct sequence:**
adjust, reveals, obey, read.
1. I _____ God's Word—the Bible.
2. The Spirit of truth takes God's Word and _____ truth.
3. I _____ my life to God's truth.
4. I _____ God.
5. God works in and through me to accomplish His purposes.

The Spirit uses God's Word (the sword of the Spirit; see Eph. 6:17) to reveal God and His purposes. The Spirit uses God's Word to instruct us in the ways of God. We cannot understand God's truths on our own. Unaided by the Spirit of God, it will appear to be foolishness to us. Aided by the Spirit, we can understand all things (see **1 Cor. 2:14-15**).

4 **God has probably used a particular Scripture verse to speak to you at some time during this course. Look back through units 1–5 and find one passage of Scripture God seems to have called to your attention.**
a. What is the reference? _John 15:5   I am the vine; you are the_

branches If a man remains in me and I in him, he

will bear much fruit; apart from me, you can do
nothing.

1 Corinthians
2:14-15

"The man without the Spirit does not accept the things that come from the Spirit of God, for they are foolishness to him, and he cannot understand them, because they are spiritually discerned. The spiritual man makes judgments about all things."

b. What does that verse reveal to you about God, His purposes, or His ways?

_____

Meditate on this verse and pray. Ask God to continue speaking to you about the truth in this passage. Keep in mind He is more interested in what you become than in what you do.

c. What does God want to do or be in and through your life? _____

_____

d. What adjustments would you have to make to align your life with this truth—
• in your personal life? _____
• in your family life? _____
• in your church life? _____
• in your work life? _____

e. Write a prayer in the margin of response to God about this truth and its application to your life.

f. Since you first came to understand this truth, has God done anything in your life that required you to apply the truth or share it with someone else?
❑ Yes ❑ No If so, what? _____

Understanding spiritual truth does not lead you *to* an encounter with God; it *is* the encounter with God. You cannot understand God's purposes and ways unless the Spirit of God teaches you. If God has revealed spiritual truth to you through this passage of Scripture, you have encountered God Himself working in you!

Responding to Truth

I always approach the Scriptures with excited anticipation. The Spirit of God knows the mind of God. Because He knows what God wants to do in my life, He begins to open my understanding about God, His purposes, and His ways. I take that work seriously. Therefore, when God reveals truth to me in His Word, I write down the passage of Scripture. Then I meditate on the passage, immersing myself in its meaning. I adjust my life to the truth and thus to God. I agree with God and take any actions necessary to allow God to work in the way He has revealed. Finally, I watch for ways God may use that truth in my life during the day.

You may want to follow the same process as God reveals truth to you. When God leads you to a fresh understanding of Himself or His ways through Scripture, respond to His revelation in these ways.

1. Write down the verse or verses in a spiritual journal or diary.
2. Meditate on the verse.
3. Study the verse to immerse yourself in its meaning. What is God revealing about Himself, His purposes, or His ways?
4. Identify adjustments you need to make in your personal life, your family, your church, and your work so God will work this way with you.
5. Write a prayer response to God.
6. Make the necessary adjustments to God.
7. Watch to see how God may use that truth in your life during the day.

> Understanding spiritual truth does not lead you *to* an encounter with God; it *is* the encounter with God.

Here is an example of the way God may use His Word to speak to you. Suppose you are reading Psalm 37. Although you have read this psalm many times before, you come to verse 21 and read, "The wicked borrow and do not repay." You are drawn back to that verse. You read it again. Then you remember a debt you have failed to repay. You realize this Scripture applies to you. You immediately take action and repay your debt.

The Holy Spirit has just spoken to you through that verse. You have encountered truth. Now you understand that those who borrow and do not repay are sinning in God's sight. The Holy Spirit has called your attention to a specific instance in which this verse applies to you. He is convicting you of sin. He is the only One who can do that. God has spoken to you by the working of the Holy Spirit and through His Word. God wants you to have no hindrances to a love relationship with Him in your life.

5 **If you were in this situation, what should you do next? Following the sequence in the diagram on page 104, what do you do after the Holy Spirit reveals an understanding of truth to you?** _____
_____

Once God has spoken to you through His Word, your response is crucial. You must adjust your life to the truth. In this case the adjustment is this:
- You must *agree* with the truth: those who borrow and do not repay are morally wicked in God's sight.
- You must *agree* that the truth applies to you in the particular instance God has brought to your memory. This is confession of sin. You *agree* with God about your sin.

In this way you have adjusted your understanding about borrowing and repaying to agree with God's will in this matter. To agree with God, you must change your understanding to comply with His. This requires an adjustment. Is that all you must do? No!

Agreeing with God in confession is not enough. Until you repay the debt, you have not repented of your sinful ways. This is where obedience comes in. You obey God's will by repaying the debt and making any necessary amends. After you respond, you are free to experience a more complete relationship with God. Always connect a revealed truth with your understanding of God and your relationship with Him.

SUMMARY STATEMENTS

God speaks uniquely to individuals, and He does it in any way He pleases.

When God speaks to me, I will recognize His voice and follow Him.

I cannot understand spiritual truth unless the Spirit of God reveals it.

God is more interested in what I become than in what I do.

Review today's lesson. Pray and ask God to identify one or more statements or Scriptures He wants you to understand, learn, or practice. Underline them. Then respond to the following.

What was the most meaningful statement or Scripture you read today?

Reword the statement or Scripture into a prayer of response to God.

What does God want you to do in response to today's study?

God Speaks Through Prayer

If you are not keeping a spiritual journal[1] or diary, you need to. When the Creator of the universe tells you something in your quiet time, record it before you forget it. Then write your prayer response. I record the verse of Scripture through which God speaks to me and what He has said to me about Himself from that verse. I write down the prayer response I am making so I have a record of the encounter with God, what He said, and the way I responded to Him. I also write what I need to do to adjust my life to God so I can begin to experience Him relating to me this way.

Truth Is a Person

Truth is not just a concept to study. Truth is a Person. Jesus did not say, "I will teach you the truth." He said, "I am … the truth" (John 14:6).

When God gives you eternal life, He gives you Himself (see John 17:3). His Holy Spirit, who lives in you, reveals truth. When the Holy Spirit reveals truth, He is not teaching you a concept to consider. He is leading you to a relationship with a Person. *He* is your life! When God gives you eternal life, He gives you a Person. When you became a Christian, Jesus didn't give you a *thing;* He gave you Himself.

1 **Fill in the blanks with the correct words from the previous paragraphs.**
   a. Truth is not just a _____ to study.
   b. Truth is a _____
   c. The Holy Spirit reveals _____.
   d. The Holy Spirit is leading you to a _____ with a Person.

Here is the way I try to live my relationship with God.
   • God creates in me the desire to participate in His mission to reconcile a lost world to Himself.
   • I come to God seeking to know His will.
   • When God reveals a truth to me, I know He is alerting me to what He is doing in my life.

Prayer Is a Relationship to a Person

Prayer is two-way fellowship and communication with God. You speak to God, and He speaks to you. Prayer is not a one-way conversation in which you merely list everything you want God to do. Your personal prayer life may primarily be one-way communication—you talking to God—but prayer is more than that. Prayer includes listening. In fact, what God says in prayer is far more important than what you say. God already knows what you are going to say. You, however, do not know what God is thinking.

Prayer is a relationship, not just a religious activity. Its purpose is to adjust you to God, not to align God with your thinking. God doesn't need your prayers, but He wants you to pray because of what God wants to do in and through your life as you

---

PRAYER IS A RELATIONSHIP, NOT JUST A RELIGIOUS ACTIVITY.

"I am the truth." —Jesus

John 17:3
"This is eternal life: that they may know you, the only true God, and Jesus Christ, whom you have sent."

What God says in prayer is far more important than what you say.

GOD SPEAKS

THROUGH

PRAYER

pray. God speaks to His people by the Holy Spirit through prayer. This diagram shows the way God speaks through prayer.

When the Holy Spirit reveals a spiritual truth to you in prayer, He is present and actively working in your life. Genuine prayer does not lead *to* an encounter with God. It *is* an encounter with God. What happens as you seek God's will in prayer?

2 As you read the following list, underline or circle a key word or phrase in each statement.

    1. God takes the initiative by causing you to want or need to pray.
    2. The Holy Spirit takes the Word of God and reveals to you the will of God.
    3. In the Spirit you pray in agreement with God's will.
    4. You adjust your life to the truth (to God).
    5. You look and listen for confirmation or further direction from the Bible, circumstances, and the church (other believers).
    6. You obey.
    7. God works in you and through you to accomplish His purposes.
    8. You experience God just as the Spirit revealed in your prayer.

Praying in the Spirit

The Spirit of God uses the Word of God when you pray. When I pray about something, Scripture often comes to my mind. I don't see that as a distraction. Instead, God uses it to guide me. As I pray about a particular matter, the Spirit of God takes the Word of God and applies it to my heart and mind to reveal the truth. I immediately stop praying and open God's Word to the passage I believe the Spirit brought to my mind. I assume God wants to give me specific direction through the Scripture He led me to. Sometimes as I pray, the Spirit places a particular person on my heart. I assume God is alerting me, through prayer, to someone He wants to minister to through me. After I pray, I look for ways God leads me to minister to that person.

3 Read Romans 8:26-27 in the right margin and answer these questions.

a. Why do we need the Holy Spirit's help when we pray (v. 26)?

_____

b. What advantage does the Holy Spirit have that we do not have (v. 27)?

_____

c. What does the Holy Spirit do for us? _____

_____

We are weak and do not know how we ought to pray. The Holy Spirit has an advantage over us: He already knows God's will—He is God. When He prays for us, He is interceding in agreement with God's will. He then helps us know God's will as we pray.

For his sixth birthday my oldest son, Richard, was old enough to have a bicycle. I bought a blue Schwinn and hid it in the garage. Then I had a task—to convince Richard that he needed a blue Schwinn bike. At first Richard was interested only in small toys that would have quickly broken. I sought to elevate his desires until he wanted something of quality and durability. We worked with him for a while, and he eventually decided that he really wanted a blue Schwinn bike for his birthday. Do you know what Richard got? The bike was already in the garage. I just had to convince him to ask for it. He asked for it, and he got it!

What happens when you pray? The Holy Spirit knows what God has "in the garage" for you! It is already there. The Holy Spirit's task is to convince you to want it—to get you to ask for it. What will happen when you ask for things God already wants to give or do? You will always receive it. Why? Because you have asked *according to His will*. When God answers your prayer, He gets the glory, and your faith is increased.

How do you know what the Holy Spirit is saying? I cannot give you a formula, but you will know His voice when He speaks (see **John 10:4**). You must decide, however, that you want only His will. You must dismiss any selfish or fleshly desires of your own. Then as you start to pray, the Spirit of God touches your heart and leads you to pray God's will (see **Phil. 2:13**). When you pray, anticipate that the Holy Spirit already knows what God has ready for your life. He does not guide you on His own initiative; He tells you only what He hears from the Father (see **John 16:13**). He guides you as you pray.

When I pray and read God's Word, I always write down what God says to me and what He leads me to pray. As I begin to see what God is telling me about Himself, His purposes, and His ways, I often see a pattern develop. As I watch the direction the Spirit is leading me to pray, I get a clear indication of what God is saying to me. This process calls for spiritual concentration!

You may be asking, How do I know the directions I am praying are the Spirit's leading and not my own selfish desires? Do you remember what George Müller said he does first in seeking God's directions?

 Look back at item 1 on page 40. What did Müller do in the beginning?

_____

First, deny self. In all honesty with yourself and before God, come to the place where you are certain your only desire is to know God's will. Then check to see what the Holy Spirit is saying in other ways. Ask yourself:

- What is He saying to me in His Word and in prayer? Do they agree?
- Is He confirming it through circumstances?
- Is He confirming it through the counsel of other believers?

Romans 8:26-27

[26] "The Spirit helps us in our weakness. We do not know what we ought to pray for, but the Spirit himself intercedes for us with groans that words cannot express. [27] And he who searches our hearts knows the mind of the Spirit, because the Spirit intercedes for the saints in accordance with God's will."

John 10:4

"When he has brought out all his own, he goes on ahead of them, and his sheep follow him because they know his voice."

Philippians 2:13

"It is God who works in you to will and to act according to his good purpose."

John 16:13

"He will not speak on his own; he will speak only what he hears, and he will tell you what is yet to come."

Watch for God to use the written Word to confirm or correct what you sense in prayer.

SUMMARY STATEMENTS

When the God of the universe tells me something in my quiet time, I should write it down before I forget it.

Truth is a Person.

Prayer is two-way communication with God.

Prayer is a relationship, not just a religious activity.

I need to make sure that my only desire is to know God's will.

God will never lead you to do something that contradicts His written Word. If what you sense in prayer runs contrary to Scripture, it is wrong. For instance, God will never lead you to commit adultery. He is always opposed to that. Watch for God to use the written Word to confirm or correct what you sense in prayer. However, don't play games with God. Don't just look for a Scripture that seems to say what you want to do and then claim it is God's will. That is dangerous.

5 **Write the following key words in the correct sequence:** *purposes, adjust, confirmation, Word, initiative, experience, agreement, obey.* **If you need help, look at the list below the diagram on page 108.**

1. God takes the _____ by causing me to want or need to pray.
2. The Holy Spirit takes the _____ of God and reveals to me the will of God.
3. In the Spirit I pray in _____ with God's will.
4. I _____ my life to the truth.
5. I look and listen for _____ or further direction from the Bible, circumstances, and the church (other believers).
6. I _____.
7. God works in me and through me to accomplish His _____.
8. I _____ Him just as the Spirit revealed as I prayed.

6 **Has God spoken to you by the Holy Spirit through prayer during this course?** ❑ Yes ❑ No **If so, describe what you sensed He was saying in one of the times He has spoken. If you do not think He has spoken, ask Him to reveal the reason to you.** _____
_____
_____

7 **Has God given you any confirmation through the Bible, circumstances, or the church (other believers)?** ❑ Yes ❑ No **If so, what did you sense He was saying?** _____
_____

8 **Review your Scripture-memory verses and be prepared to recite them to a partner in your small-group session this week.**

Review today's lesson. Pray and ask God to identify one or more statements or Scriptures He wants you to understand, learn, or practice. Underline them. Then respond to the following.

What was the most meaningful statement or Scripture you read today?	Reword the statement or Scripture into a prayer of response to God.	What does God want you to do in response to today's study?

GOD SPEAKS, PART I

DVD Message Notes

1. Scripture has to be your guide for knowing when God is speaking.
2. God speaks in unique ways to individuals.
3. God doesn't want us to trust in a formula.
4. When God spoke, people knew it was God, and they knew what God was saying.
5. The Holy Spirit prepares us for things to come.
6. Prayer is a conversation. It's us in communion with Him in a conversation.
7. God, would You raise the level of my prayer to a point where it would be pleasing to You?
8. When you pray, you've got to practice spiritual concentration. Watch to see what happens next.

Your Notes

_____

_____

_____

Unit Review

Using the hints below, write the other three important factors in the way God spoke to individuals in the Old Testament (activities 3–6, p. 91).
1. When God spoke, it was usually unique to that individual.
2. Sure: _____
3. What: _____
4. Encounter: _____

When God speaks by the Holy Spirit, what are three things He reveals (activity 9, p. 101)?
God speaks by the Holy Spirit to reveal _____,
His _____, and His _____.

Match the things God reveals with the correct reasons. Write the correct letters in the blanks (activity 10, p. 102).

God reveals …	Because …
____ 1. Himself	a He wants me to know how to accomplish things only He can do.
____ 2. His purposes	b. He wants me to know what He is about to do so I can join Him.
____ 3. His ways	c. He wants me to have faith to believe He can do what He says.

Check your answers, using the pages cited in parentheses.

Scriptures Referenced

Judges 6
John 16:7
John 14:16-18
1 Corinthians 2:9-12
Proverbs 10:1
Mark 8:38
Jeremiah 33:3
Ephesians 3:20

Testimony

Sheri Stallings

Sharing Time

- What God has been saying in this course (activity 3, p. 96)
- What God has said through the Bible (activity 4, p. 104)
- What God has said through prayer (activity 6, p. 110)
- One of the most meaningful statements or Scriptures from this unit's lessons and your prayer responses to God. Choose one from pages 94, 97, 102, 106, and 110.

For Makeup or Review

Audio and video downloads are available at *www.lifeway.com*.

UNIT 6

VERSE TO MEMORIZE

"JESUS GAVE THEM THIS ANSWER:
'I TELL YOU THE TRUTH, THE SON
CAN DO NOTHING BY HIMSELF;
HE CAN DO ONLY WHAT HE SEES
HIS FATHER DOING, BECAUSE
WHATEVER THE FATHER DOES
THE SON ALSO DOES.'"

JOHN 5:19

God Speaks, Part 2

PLEASE CANCEL MY REQUEST!

Have you ever prayed for one thing and received another? I have. When that happened to me, some dear soul would inevitably say, "God is trying to get you to persist. Keep praying until you receive what you are asking for." I kept asking God for one thing, but I kept receiving something else.

During one of these experiences I started reading from Mark 2, which tells the account of the four men who brought their crippled friend to Jesus to be healed. Because of the large crowd they opened a hole in the roof of the house and let the man down in front of Jesus. Jesus said, "Son, your sins are forgiven" (Mark 2:5).

I started to read on, but I sensed the Spirit of God saying, "Henry, did you see that?" I went back and meditated on that Scripture. Under the Holy Spirit's guiding, teaching ministry I discovered a wonderful truth: the four men asked Jesus to physically heal the man, but Jesus forgave the man's sins. They asked for one thing, and Jesus gave another! This man and his friends asked for a temporary gift, but Jesus wanted to make the man a child of God for eternity so he could inherit everything!

I found myself weeping before God and saying, "O God, if I ever ask You for one thing and You have more to give me than I am asking, please cancel my request!"

What Happens When You Pray?

ONLY THE SPIRIT OF GOD KNOWS WHAT GOD IS DOING OR PURPOSING IN MY LIFE.

1 Corinthians 2:10-12

"The Spirit searches all things, even the deep things of God. For who among men knows the thoughts of a man except the man's spirit within him? In the same way no one knows the thoughts of God except the Spirit of God. We have not received the spirit of the world but the Spirit who is from God, that we may understand what God has freely given us."

You must decide whether you will do what you want and ask God to bless it or go to work where He is working.

If I start asking God for one thing and something different happens, I always respond to what begins happening. I have found God always has far more to give me than I can even ask or think. Paul wrote, "Now to him who is able to do immeasurably more than all we ask or imagine, according to his power that is at work within us, to him be glory in the church and in Christ Jesus throughout all generations, for ever and ever!" (Eph. 3:20-21).

You can't imagine a prayer that comes close to what God wants to give you. Only the Spirit of God knows what God is doing or purposing in your life. Let God give you all He wants to bestow (see 1 Cor. 2:10-12).

1 Are you experiencing what God intends for you, or are you experiencing only what you have asked for? _____
What is the evidence? _____
_____

2 Who alone can guide you into the center of God's will? _____

3 Suppose you want to start a mission church in a particular area of town. You have taken a survey to identify needs. You have made long-range plans. You have asked God to bless and guide your work. Then God begins to bring to your church a group of ethnic people to whom you did not intend to minister. What would you do?
❏ a. I would not be diverted from starting the mission church we had planned.
❏ b. I would add the ethnic group to our future plans.
❏ c. I would start asking God questions to learn whether we should start an ethnic mission church instead of or in addition to the other one.
❏ d. Other _____

In this situation I would immediately go before God to clarify what He is saying. If I have been working and praying in one direction and I see God working in a different way, I adjust my life to what God is doing. You must decide whether you will do what you want and ask God to bless it or go to work where He is working.

We started a special emphasis to reach university students in Vancouver. We began with 30 students in the fall. By the end of the spring semester, about 250 were attending. Two-thirds of these were international students. We could have said, "We didn't plan for a ministry to internationals. Please go somewhere else, and may God bless you." Of course, we didn't do that. We adjusted our plans to what God was doing around us.

Spiritual Concentration

Our problem is that when we pray, we usually don't relate to our prayers anything that subsequently happens. After you pray, practice spiritual concentration. When you pray in a particular direction, immediately anticipate God's activity in answer to your prayer. Throughout Scripture when God's people prayed, He responded.

Here's what happens if you pray and then forget about what you prayed about. Things start to happen during the day that are unusual. Seeing them as distractions, you try to ignore them and fail to connect them with what you prayed about earlier.

When I pray, I immediately begin to watch for what happens next. I prepare to make adjustments to what happens in my life. When I pray, the idea that God is not going to answer never crosses my mind. Expect God to answer your prayers, but stick around for the answer. His timing is always right and best.

4 **Have you ever persistently prayed for something and not received it or received something different?** ❑ **Yes** ❑ **No** **Briefly describe one or more experiences.** _____

_____

_____

5 **Are you currently praying for anything God is not granting?** ❑ **Yes** ❑ **No** **If so, what are you praying for?** _____

_____

6 **If you answered yes to 5, pause and ask God to help you understand what He is doing in your life. Then watch to see what happens next or pay attention to what He begins to reveal to you through His Word.**

The Silences of God

I went through a lengthy time when God was silent. You have probably had that experience too. I had been praying for many days, but God seemed to be totally silent. I sensed heaven was shut up, and I didn't understand what was happening. Some people had told me that if God does not hear my prayer, I have sin in my life, but I had repented of and confessed all known sin. I could not understand God's silence.

Do you remember a biblical person who had a problem like this? Job did. His counselors told him all his problems were caused by sin, while Job claimed he and God were on proper terms. Job did not know all God was doing during that time, but his counselors were wrong. God had another reason for His silence.

7 **If you have experienced silences of God, briefly describe one such time.**

_____

_____

All I knew to do was to go back to God, believing that the God who was in a love relationship with me would let me know what was happening in my life when and if I needed to know. So I prayed, "Heavenly Father, I don't understand this silence. You are going to have to tell me what You are doing in my life." He did—from His Word. This became one of the most meaningful experiences in my life.

I did not frantically search for an answer but continued my daily reading of God's Word. I was convinced that as I regularly read the Word of God, the Spirit of God—who knew the mind of God for me—was in the process of helping me understand what God was doing in my life. God will let you know what He is doing in your life when and if you need to know.

One morning I was reading the account of the death of Lazarus (see John 11:1–45). John reported that Jesus loved Lazarus, Mary, and Martha. Although Jesus received

God will let you know what He is doing in your life when and if you need to know.

word that His good friend was sick and at the point of death, He delayed going until Lazarus died. In other words, Mary and Martha asked Jesus to come help their brother when he was sick, and Jesus was silent. All the way through Lazarus's final sickness and death, Jesus did not answer. They received no response from the One who said He loved Lazarus. Jesus even said He loved Mary and Martha. Yet He did nothing.

Lazarus died, and Mary and Martha went through the funeral process, preparing his body, putting him in the grave, and covering it with a stone. Still, God's silence continued. Finally, Jesus said to His disciples, "Let's go."

When Jesus arrived, Lazarus had been dead four days. Martha said to Jesus, "Lord, if you had been here, my brother would not have died" (v. 32). Then the Spirit of God began to help me understand something. It seemed to me as if Jesus said to Mary and Martha: "You are exactly right. If I had come when you asked, your brother would not have died. You know I could have healed him, because you have seen Me heal people many times before. If I had come when you asked Me to, I would have healed him. But you would have never known any more about Me than you already understood. I knew you were ready for a greater revelation of Me than you had known before. I wanted you to experience that I am the Resurrection and the Life. My refusal and My silence were not rejection. They were opportunities for Me to disclose to you more of Me than you had ever known."

When that truth dawned on me, I almost jumped out of my chair. I said, "That's what's happening in my life! God's silence means He is ready to bring into my life a greater revelation of Himself than I have ever known." I immediately changed my whole attitude toward God. With great anticipation I began to watch for what God was going to teach me about Himself. Then some things happened that I might never have responded to without that readiness and anticipation.

 What are two possible reasons for God's silence when you pray?

_____

_____

Now when I pray and God is silent, I still pray through my sin checklist. Sometimes God's silences are caused by sin in my life. If unconfessed sin is in my life, I confess it and make it right. If God is still silent after that, I get ready for a new experience with Him I have never previously experienced. Sometimes God is silent as He prepares to bring you to a deeper understanding of Himself. Sometimes His silence is designed to bring me into a state of absolute dependence on and trust in God. Whenever God is silent, continue doing the last thing God told you and watch and wait for a fresh encounter with Him.

You can respond to God's silence in two ways. You can become frustrated, feel guilty, or be impatient. Or you can expect that God is about to bring you to a deeper knowledge of Himself. These responses are as different as night and day.

Do you know what set me free? Truth. Truth is a *Person* who is actively involved in my life. The moment I understood what God might be doing, I adjusted my life to Him. I put away my discouragement and guilt. I quit feeling that maybe I was of no use to God and He wasn't listening to me. I made the major adjustment in my life to an attitude of expectation, faith, and trust. The moment I did, God began to show me how I could respond to Him in such a way that I would know Him on a deeper level.

9 **Start memorizing your Scripture-memory verse for this unit and review your verses from other units. Remember, you may select a different verse and translation if you want to.**

SUMMARY STATEMENTS

O God, if I ever give You a request and You have more to give me than I am asking, cancel my request.

Only the Spirit of God knows what God is doing or purposing in my life.

God will let me know what He is doing in my life when and if I need to know.

Sometimes God's silences are caused by sin.

Sometimes God is silent as He prepares to bring me to a deeper understanding of Himself.

Review today's lesson. Pray and ask God to identify one or more statements or Scriptures He wants you to understand, learn, or practice. Underline them. Then respond to the following.

What was the most meaningful statement or Scripture you read today?

_____
_____
_____
_____
_____
_____

Reword the statement or Scripture into a prayer of response to God.

_____
_____
_____
_____
_____
_____

What does God want you to do in response to today's study?

_____
_____
_____
_____
_____
_____

God Speaks Through Circumstances

DAY 2

TO UNDERSTAND YOUR BAD OR DIFFICULT CIRCUMSTANCES, GOD'S PERSPECTIVE IS VITAL.

John 5:17

"Jesus said to them, 'My Father is always at his work to this very day, and I, too, am working.'"

The Holy Spirit uses the Bible, prayer, circumstances, and God's people to speak to us—to show us the Father's will. This third means—circumstances—is illustrated in the way Jesus knew what the Father wanted Him to do. This is how Jesus knew the Father's will for His life and daily activity. Jesus described the process in John 5:17, 19-20.

1 Verse 19 is your memory verse for this unit. Try to recite it now.

Jesus said He did not take the initiative in doing anything for the Father (see v. 19). Only the Father has the right to initiate a divine work. The Father had been working right up until Jesus' time on earth, and He was still working (see **v. 17**). The Father would let the Son know what He was doing (see v. 20). When the Son saw the Father's activity, that was the Father's invitation for the Son to join Him.

2 We have already looked at Jesus' example twice. To review, see if you can fill in the blanks in the following sequence, using the key words below. Then check your answers on page 16.

working everything watch Father doing initiative loves nothing

The _____ has been working right up until now.

Now God has Me _____.

I do nothing on My own _____.

I _____ to see what the Father is doing.

I do what I see the Father is already _____.

You see, the Father _____ Me.

He shows Me _____ that He Himself is doing.

God used circumstances to reveal to Jesus what He was to do. The circumstances were the things Jesus saw the Father doing. Only the Father can do certain things.

> Jesus did not have to guess what to do. Jesus did not have to dream up what He could do for the Father.

3 **Turn to page 83 and review the list of things only God can do.**

Jesus always looked for where the Father was at work; then He joined Him. The Father loved the Son and showed Him everything He was doing. Jesus did not have to guess what to do. Jesus did not have to dream up what He could do for the Father. He watched to see what the Father was doing around His life, and Jesus immediately adjusted His life to His Father's activity around Him. The Father then accomplished *His* purposes through Jesus.

This is exactly what Jesus wants us to do through *His* lordship in our lives. We see what *He* is doing; then we adjust our lives, our plans, and our goals to *Him*. We are to place our lives at His disposal—where *He* is working—so He will accomplish *His* purposes through us.

4 **See if you can state the seven realities in your own words. Use the key words below as hints and check each reality as you say it. After you finish, check your work on the inside back cover.**

❑ Reality 1—work   ❑ Reality 4—speaks   ❑ Reality 6—adjust
❑ Reality 2—relationship   ❑ Reality 5—crisis   ❑ Reality 7—obey
❑ Reality 3—invitation

God's Perspective Is Vital

Jesus' example is a positive way God speaks through circumstances. Sometimes circumstances appear to be negative. Maybe you have found yourself in the middle of a difficult circumstance and you asked God, "Why is this happening to me?" You are not alone. Job had an experience like that. He did not know what was happening when everything he owned was destroyed, when his children were killed, and when he developed excruciating sores all over his body (see Job 1—2). Job wrestled with understanding his circumstances. They certainly appeared bad! He did not know what was happening from God's perspective (see Job 1:6-12; 2:1-7). Neither did He know the last chapter of the story (see Job 42:12-17), in which God would restore his property, his family, and his health.

Job's friends, thinking they had God's perspective, told Job to confess his sin. Job could not find any unrighteousness in his life to confess. If you didn't have that last chapter and didn't know God's perspective, whose side do you think you would be on—God's or Job's? You would probably be with Job, saying, "I want to ask God what's going on. Why is He allowing this to happen?" You would think God was being cruel to Job.

To understand your painful or difficult circumstances, God's perspective is vital. When you face hardships or confusing situations, they can overwhelm you. When you look at God from the middle of your circumstances, you will always have a distorted understanding of Him. For instance, you might say, "God doesn't love me" or "God isn't fair." Both of those statements about God are completely false.

5 **Have you ever been in the middle of a tragic or confusing circumstance in which, in your prayers, you accused God of things you knew were not really true of Him?** ❑ **Yes** ❑ **No** **If so, describe one of those circumstances in the margin.**

Perhaps you began to question God's love or His wisdom. Maybe you were afraid to say He was wrong, but you said, "God, You misled me in letting me believe this was the right thing to do. Why didn't You stop me? If I had known things were going to turn out like this, ..."You can get into spiritual difficulty if you look at God from the middle of circumstances.

What should you do? First, go to God and ask Him to show you His perspective on your circumstances. Look *back* at your circumstances from the heart of God. When you face confusing events, the Spirit of God will take the Word of God and help you understand your circumstances from God's perspective. He will reveal to you the truth of your situation.

At the beginning of unit 3 I told you about our daughter Carrie's bout with cancer, a challenging situation for our whole family. The doctors prepared us for six to eight months of intense chemotherapy, plus radiation treatments. We knew God loved us, so we went to Him in prayer and asked for understanding of what He was doing or was going to do in our lives. We wanted to be rightly adjusted to Him through this time. We prayed, "What are You purposing to do in this experience that we need to adjust ourselves to?"

As we prayed, a Scripture promise came that we believed was from God. Not only did we receive the promise, but we also received letters and calls from many people who quoted this same Scripture promise to us, sensing this verse was from God for our circumstance. The verse reads, "This sickness will not end in death. No, it is for God's glory so that God's Son may be glorified through it" (John 11:4). While it would have been natural for us to claim this verse for our daughter, we sensed God was giving us this Scripture as His word for our circumstances. Our sense that God was speaking to us grew stronger as the Bible, prayer, and other believers' testimonies began to agree. We then adjusted our lives to the truth and began to watch for ways God would use this situation for His glory.

During this time people from many places in Canada, Europe, and the United States prayed for Carrie. Individuals, college-student groups, and churches called to tell us of their prayers. One thing surfaced in conversations with these people. Many said something like this: "Our prayer ministry had become so dry and cold, and we hadn't seen any special answers to prayer in a long time. But when we heard about Carrie, we put her on our prayer list."

After three months of treatments, the doctors ran more tests. They said, "We don't understand this, but all the tests are negative. We cannot find any trace of cancer." I immediately communicated this answer to prayer with those who had committed to pray for Carrie. In instance after instance people said God used this answer to prayer to renew their prayer lives. Church prayer ministries were revitalized. Student prayer groups found new life.

Then I began to see what God had in mind for this circumstance: through this experience God was glorified in the eyes of His people. Many people sensed a fresh call to prayer. They personally began to experience anew the presence of Truth—Truth as a Person. Some of Carrie's closest friends began to pray fervently. Some students even became Christians after observing what God had done in and through Carrie. God indeed brought glory to Himself through this sickness.

Do you see what happened? We faced a trying situation. We could have looked back at God from the middle of our circumstances and developed a distorted understanding of God. Instead, we went directly to Him and sought His perspective. The Holy Spirit took God's Word and revealed to us God's perspective on the end result of that circumstance. We believed God and adjusted our lives to Him and to what He was doing. Then we went through the circumstance looking for ways His purposes would be accomplished in ways that would bring Him glory. So when the answer to prayer came, I immediately knew that my job was to give God the glory to everyone I could tell. In the process we came to know God in a new way because of the compassion

Go to God and ask Him to show you His perspective on your circumstances.

He showed us by revealing His perspective on our situation. Let me summarize how you can respond when circumstances are difficult or confusing.

6 **As you read this list circle a key word or phrase in each statement.**

When Circumstances Are Confusing

1. Settle in your mind that God has forever demonstrated His unfailing love for you on the cross. That love will never change.
2. Do not try to understand what God is like from the middle of your circumstances.
3. Go to God and ask Him to help you see His perspective on your situation.
4. Wait on the Holy Spirit. He may take God's Word and help you understand your circumstances.
5. Adjust your life to God and to what you see Him doing in your circumstances.
6. Do all He tells you to do.
7. Experience God working in and through you to accomplish His purposes.

7 **In your own words summarize what you need to do when you find yourself in confusing or difficult circumstances.** _____
_____
_____
_____
_____
_____

Remember God is sovereign. You may face a situation like the one Job experienced in which God does not tell you what He is doing. In those instances acknowledge God's love and sovereignty and trust His sustaining grace to see you through the situation.

Review today's lesson. Pray and ask God to identify one or more statements or Scriptures He wants you to understand, learn, or practice. Underline them. Then respond to the following.

What was the most meaningful statement or Scripture you read today?
_____
_____
_____
_____
_____

Reword the statement or Scripture into a prayer of response to God.
_____
_____
_____
_____
_____

What does God want you to do in response to today's study?
_____
_____
_____
_____
_____

The Truth of Your Circumstance

You cannot know the truth of your circumstance until you have heard from God. In Exodus 5–6 Moses did as God instructed and asked Pharaoh to let Israel go. Pharaoh refused and multiplied the hardship for the Israelites. Then the people turned to Moses and criticized him for causing them so much trouble.

> YOU CANNOT KNOW THE TRUTH OF YOUR CIRCUMSTANCE UNTIL YOU HAVE HEARD FROM GOD.

1 **What would you have done if you had been in Moses' place? Check one or more responses.**
- ❑ a. I would have become angry at Israel and gone back to tending sheep.
- ❑ b. I would have become bitter at God and told Him to get somebody else to do the job.
- ❑ c. I would have concluded I had misunderstood God's will.
- ❑ d. I would have patiently gone back to God and asked Him to give me His perspective on this difficult circumstance.

Moses' story really encourages me. The first three responses above are more like the ways we usually respond. If you haven't read Exodus 5–6, you may have the idea from what I have said that Moses picked response d. He didn't! He blamed God and accused Him of failing to do what He had promised. Moses said, "O Lord, why have you brought trouble upon this people? Is this why you sent me? Ever since I went to Pharaoh to speak in your name, he has brought trouble upon this people, and you have not rescued your people at all" (Ex. 5:22-23). Moses was so discouraged he was ready to quit (see Ex. 6:12).

I'm glad God is patient with us! He took time to reveal His perspective to Moses. God explained He wanted Pharaoh to resist so the people could see God's mighty hand of deliverance. He wanted the people to know Him by experience as the great I AM. Learn from Moses' example. When you face confusing circumstances, don't blame God. Don't give up following Him. Go to God. Ask Him to reveal the truth of your circumstances. Ask Him to show you His perspective. Then wait on the Lord.

Radically orient your life to God. The most difficult thing you will ever have to do is deny self, take up God's will, and follow Him. The most challenging part of your relationship with God is being God-centered. If you recorded a day in your life, you might find that your prayers, your attitudes, your thoughts, and your actions are intensely self-centered. You may not see things from God's perspective; rather, you may try to explain to God what your perspective is. When He becomes the Lord of your life, He alone has the right to be: the Focus of your life; the Initiator in your life; the Director of your life. That is what it means for Him to be Lord.

Hearing from Truth

When the Holy Spirit talks to you, He reveals Truth. He communicates with you about a Person—about Jesus. Truth is a Person (see John 14:6)!

The disciples were in a boat during a storm, while Jesus slept at the back. If you had gone to those disciples in the middle of that tempest and asked them, "What is the truth of this situation?" what would they have said? "We perish!" Was that the

John 14:6

"I am … the truth."

Don't evaluate your situation until you have heard from Jesus. He is Truth.

SUMMARY STATEMENTS

Never determine the truth of a situation by looking at the circumstances.

truth? No, Truth was asleep at the back of the boat. Truth is a Person. In a moment Truth Himself would stand up and calm the storm. Then they knew the Truth of their circumstance. Truth is a Person who is always present in your life. You cannot know the truth of your circumstance until you have heard from God. He is Truth! Truth is present and active in your life!

2 **Read Luke 7:11-17 in the margin and answer the following questions.**
  a. Suppose you were attending this funeral. Before Jesus came, how do you think the **widow of Nain** would have responded to this question: "What is the truth of this situation?" She would have said … _____
_____

  b. When Truth (Jesus) was present, what difference did He make? _____
_____

  c. When Truth (Jesus) revealed Himself to that crowd, how did they respond?
_____

If you had asked the widow in her only son's funeral procession, "What's the truth of this situation?" she might have replied, "My husband died several years ago. I had one son, and I anticipated that we would spend wonderful days together. He would care for me, and we would have fellowship together. Now my son is dead, and I must live the rest of my life without anyone to care for me." Was that the truth?

No, Truth was standing in front of her! When Truth reached out, touched her son, and restored him, everything changed. You never know the truth of any situation until you have heard from Jesus. When Jesus revealed Himself in this circumstance, the people "were all filled with awe and praised God. 'A great prophet has appeared among us,' they said. 'God has come to help his people.' This news about Jesus spread throughout Judea and the surrounding country" (Luke 7:16-17). Never determine the truth of a situation only by looking at the circumstances. Don't evaluate your situation until you have heard from Jesus. He is Truth.

3 **In your Bible read John 6:1-15 and answer the following questions.**
  a. **Five thousand hungry people** came to Jesus. He wanted to feed them. If you had asked the disciples what the truth of the situation was, how do you think they would have responded? _____
_____

  b. Why did Jesus ask Philip where they could buy bread (vv. 5-6)?
_____

  c. When Truth (Jesus) was present, what difference did He make?
_____

  d. When Truth (Jesus) revealed Himself to the crowd, how did they respond (v. 14)?
_____

I wonder whether God ever tests our faith as He did Philip's. Does He say, "Feed the multitudes," and our church responds, "Our budget can't do it"? If you had asked the disciples about the truth of that situation, they might have said, "We can't do it. Lord, the truth is that this situation is impossible." Was that correct? No. We know the other half of the story. Wouldn't we be better off if we trusted God with the other half of the story in our lives? Truth Himself fed five thousand men, plus their families, and had 12 baskets full of leftovers!

Suppose God says to your church, "Take the gospel to the whole world," and the church says, "We can't. We're too small." Truth stands in the middle of that church, as the Head of that church, to say, "Believe Me. I will never give you an order without releasing My power to enable it to happen. Trust Me and obey Me, and it will happen."

> I cannot know the truth of my circumstance until I have heard from God.

> The Holy Spirit takes God's Word and reveals God's perspective on the circumstance.

Review today's lesson. Pray and ask God to identify one or more statements or Scriptures He wants you to understand, learn, or practice. Underline them. Then respond to the following.

What was the most meaningful statement or Scripture you read today?	Reword the statement or Scripture into a prayer of response to God.	What does God want you to do in response to today's study?
_____	_____	_____
_____	_____	_____
_____	_____	_____
_____	_____	_____
_____	_____	_____
_____	_____	_____

Spiritual Markers

DAY 4

The diagrams I used for circumstances (pp. 119–20) may imply that the circumstance is a bad situation. That is not always the case. Sometimes the circumstance is a decision-making situation. In a decision-making time your greatest difficulty may not be choosing between good and bad but choosing between good and best. You may have several options that appear to be equally attractive. At a time like this, begin by saying with all your heart, "Lord, whatever I know to be Your will, I will do it. Regardless of the cost and regardless of the adjustment, I commit myself ahead of time to follow Your will. Lord, no matter what that will looks like, I will do it!"

If you cannot say that when you begin to seek God's will, you do not mean "Thy will be done" (Matt. 6:10, KJV). Instead, you mean "Thy will be done as long as it does not conflict with my will." Two words in a Christian's language cannot go together: "No, Lord." If you say no to God, He is not your Lord. If He really is your Lord, your answer must always be yes, Lord. In decision making, always begin at this point. Do not proceed until you can honestly say, "Whatever You want of me, Lord, I will do it."

> WHEN GOD GETS READY FOR YOU TO TAKE A NEW STEP OR DIRECTION IN HIS ACTIVITY, IT WILL ALWAYS BE IN SEQUENCE WITH WHAT HE HAS ALREADY BEEN DOING IN YOUR LIFE.

> "YES, LORD!"

Physical Markers of Spiritual Encounters

When Israel crossed the Jordan River into the promised land, God gave Joshua the following instructions: "Choose twelve men from among the people, one from each tribe, and

tell them to take up twelve stones from the middle of the Jordan from right where the priests stood and to carry them over with you and put them down at the place where you stay tonight" (Josh. 4:2-3). These stones were to serve as a sign to the Israelites. Joshua explained, "In the future, when your children ask you, 'What do these stones mean?' tell them that the flow of the Jordan was cut off before the ark of the covenant of the Lord. When it crossed the Jordan, the waters of the Jordan were cut off. These stones are to be a memorial to the people of Israel forever" (Josh. 4:6-7). The stones were to remind the people of a mighty act of God on their behalf. On many other occasions people built altars or set up stones as a reminder of significant encounters with God.

1 **Select one of the following persons you would like to study. Check the box beside the person you chose. Read about his encounter with God. Then answer the questions that follow.**

☐ Moses—Exodus 17:8-16 or 24:1-11   ☐ Noah—Genesis 6–8
☐ Abram—Genesis 12:1-8 or 13:1-18   ☐ Joshua—Joshua 3:5–4:9
☐ Isaac—Genesis 26:17-25   ☐ Gideon—Judges 6:11-24
☐ Jacob—Genesis 28:10-22; 35:1-7   ☐ Samuel—1 Samuel 7:1-13

Briefly describe the encounter between this person and God. What did God do? _____

_____

Why do you think the person built an altar or set up a stone marker?

_____

What, if any, special names of God or of the stone/altar does the text give?

_____

Often people in the Old Testament set up stone markers or altars as reminders of their encounters with God. Places like Bethel *(house of God)* and Rehoboth *(room)* became reminders of God's great activity in the midst of His people. Moses named an altar *The Lord is my Banner*, and Samuel called a stone *Ebenezer*, saying, "Thus far has the Lord helped us" (1 Sam. 7:12). These altars and stones became physical markers of great spiritual encounters with God. They provided opportunities for people to teach their children about God's activity on behalf of His people.

Seeing God's Perspective

God works in sequence to accomplish His divine purposes. What He did in the past was accomplished with a Kingdom purpose in mind. What He is doing in the present is in sequence with the past and with the same Kingdom purpose. Every act of God builds on the past, with a view toward the future.

When God called Abraham (see Gen. 12), He began to develop a people for Himself. When He came to Isaac, Isaac saw God's perspective when God reminded him of His relationship with Isaac's father, Abraham (see Gen. 26:24). To Jacob God identified Himself as the God of Abraham and Isaac (see Gen. 28:13). When God encountered Moses, He helped Moses see His perspective on what He was doing through history. He said He was the God of Abraham, Isaac, and Jacob (see Ex. 3:6-10). At each new step in His divine plan, God involved a person. Often in the call God rehearsed His previous activity so the individual could see God's perspective on what was happening at that moment.

Throughout Deuteronomy **Moses** reviewed all God had done for Israel. God was preparing to move the people into the promised land, and He wanted His people to have the perspective of history as they took this new step. In Deuteronomy 29 Moses briefly summarized the nation's history. At this time of covenant renewal, Moses wanted to remind the people to be faithful in following God. They were getting ready to change leaders (from Moses to Joshua) and move into the promised land. They needed to see this new direction from God's perspective. Israel needed to see the new direction was in line with all God had done previously.

In the diagram on the inside back cover, God's purposes are illustrated by the arrow at the top of the diagram.

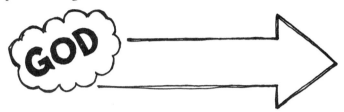

❷ **Look at the perspective God gave Moses when He called him into service at the burning bush in Exodus 3. On the lines that follow, write:**
- *past* **beside items that speak of God's past activity with His people;**
- *present* **beside items that speak of what God was doing at the time He spoke to Moses;**
- *future* **beside items that speak of what God was going to do.**

_____ a. "I am the God of your father, the God of Abraham, the God of Isaac and the God of Jacob" (v. 6).

_____ b. "I have indeed seen the misery of my people in Egypt. I have heard them crying out because of their slave drivers" (v. 7).

_____ c. "I am concerned about their suffering. So I have come down to rescue them from the hand of the Egyptians" (vv. 7–8).

_____ d. "So now, go. I am sending you to Pharaoh to bring my people the Israelites out of Egypt" (v. 10).

_____ e. "I will be with you. And this will be the sign to you that it is I who have sent you: When you have brought the people out of Egypt, you will worship God on this mountain" (v. 12).

_____ f. "I have promised to bring you up out of your misery in Egypt into the land of the Canaanites … —a land flowing with milk and honey" (v. 17).

_____ g. "I will make the Egyptians favorably disposed toward this people, so that when you leave you will not go empty-handed. … And so you will plunder the Egyptians" (vv. 21–22).

#2 answers: Items a, b, and f are past. Items c and d are present. Items e and g are future.

Do you see what God was doing with Moses? He was helping him see his call from God's perspective.
- God had been working with Abraham, Isaac, Jacob, and even Moses' father to build a nation.
- God had promised Abraham He would bring the people out of bondage and give them the promised land.
- God had been watching over them in Egypt.
- Now He was responding to their suffering.

Israel needed to see the new direction was in line with all God had done previously.

• God had chosen to involve Moses in His divine purpose for Israel. He was going to use Moses to deliver the Israelites from Egypt and plunder the Egyptians at the same time.
• After Moses obeyed, God would bring them to this very mountain to worship. This worship service on the mountain would be Moses' sign God had sent him.

God wants to involve you in His purposes. God has been working in the world all along (see John 5:17). He was accomplishing His purposes for your life prior to your birth, and He has been active in your life since you were born. God said to Jeremiah the prophet, "Before I formed you in the womb I knew you, before you were born I set you apart; I appointed you as a prophet to the nations" (Jer. 1:5). When God is ready for you to take a new step or direction in His activity, it will always be in sequence with what He has already been doing in your life. He does not go off on tangents or take meaningless detours. He builds your character in an orderly fashion with a divine purpose in mind.

A Spiritual Inventory

I have found it helpful to identify spiritual markers in my life. Each time I have encountered God's call or directions for my life, I have mentally built a spiritual marker at that point. A spiritual marker identifies a time of transition, decision, or direction when I clearly know God has guided me. Over time I can look back at these spiritual markers and see how God has faithfully directed my life according to His divine purpose.

When I face a decision about God's direction, I review those spiritual markers. I don't take the next step without the context of God's full activity in my life. This helps me see God's perspective for my past and present. Then I examine the options before me, looking to see which direction is most consistent with what God has been doing in my life. Often one of these opportunities will be right in line with what God has already been doing. If none of the directions seem consistent, I continue to pray and wait on the Lord's guidance. When circumstances do not align with what God is saying in the Bible and in prayer, I assume the timing may be wrong. I then wait for God to reveal His timing.

3 **In your own words write a definition of *spiritual marker*.** _____

_____

4 **Using the previous paragraph, describe in your own words how you could use spiritual markers to help you discern God's direction at a time of decision.** _____

_____
_____
_____
_____
_____

5 **Why do you think spiritual markers are helpful? What do they help you do?** _____

_____

When I was approached about taking a position with my denomination to direct its emphasis on prayer and spiritual awakening, I had never had such a job. Only God

A spiritual marker identifies a time of transition, decision, or direction when I clearly know God has guided me.

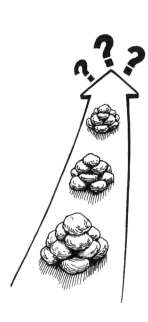

could reveal whether this was part of His divine purpose. I recalled the spiritual markers in my life to see this decision from God's perspective.

My heritage goes back to England, where a number of my family were graduates of Spurgeon's College at a time when Charles Spurgeon was trying to win England to Christ. I grew up in a town in Canada where an evangelical witness of Christ was desperately needed. My father served as a lay pastor to help start a mission church in that town. In my teen years I began to sense a deep burden for communities all across Canada that did not have an evangelical church. In 1958 when I was in seminary, God assured me He loved my nation enough to want to bring a great movement of His Spirit across our land. When I accepted God's call to go to Saskatoon as a pastor, God used the prospect of a spiritual awakening there to affirm my call. While I was in Saskatoon, a spiritual awakening started in that city and spread across Canada in the early 1970s.

In 1988 a man called me and said, "Henry, for more than two years we have prayed about filling a position in prayer for spiritual awakening. Would you consider coming and directing our denomination in the area of spiritual awakening?"

As I reviewed God's activity in my life (my spiritual markers), I saw that an emphasis on spiritual awakening was an important element throughout my ministry. I said, "You could have asked me to do anything else in the world, and I would not have considered leaving what I am doing, but spiritual awakening has been a deep current that has run through my life since the time I was a teenager." After much prayer and confirmation in the Word and by other believers, I accepted the position. God didn't shift me; He focused me on something He had already been doing through the course of my life.

6 **Prepare a spiritual inventory of your life and identify your spiritual markers. These may begin with your heritage, your salvation experience, and times you made significant decisions about your future. What are some times of transition, decision, or direction in your life when you clearly knew that God guided you? Using a separate sheet of paper, your spiritual journal, or a notebook, start preparing a list. If God used specific Scriptures to speak during those times, record the Scriptures. Don't think it has to be comprehensive. Add to it as you continue to reflect and pray about God's activity in your life.**

You will have an opportunity to share some of your spiritual markers in this week's small-group session.

SUMMARY STATEMENTS

In a decision-making time my greatest difficulty may not be choosing between good and bad but choosing between good and best.

Two words in a Christian's language cannot go together: "No, Lord."

God works in sequence to accomplish His divine purposes.

When God gets ready for me to take a new step or direction in His activity, it will be in sequence with what He has already been doing in my life.

A spiritual marker identifies a time of transition, decision, or direction when I clearly know that God has guided me.

Review today's lesson. Pray and ask God to identify one or more statements or Scriptures He wants you to understand, learn, or practice. Underline them. Then respond to the following.

What was the most meaningful statement or Scripture you read today?	Reword the statement or Scripture into a prayer of response to God.	What does God want you to do in response to today's study?

God Speaks Through the Church

AS I FUNCTION IN RELATIONSHIP TO THE CHURCH, I DEPEND ON OTHERS IN THE CHURCH TO HELP ME UNDERSTAND GOD'S WILL.

The Holy Spirit speaks to us through God's people, the local church. Later in this course we will devote a whole unit to ways a church hears and understands God's will. Today we will look at some ways you can understand God's will through the church.

1 **Let's review for a moment. Answer the following questions.**

a. How did God speak in the Old Testament? _____

_____

b. How did God speak in the Gospels? _____

_____

c. How does God speak from Acts to the present? _____

_____

d. What are four ways the Holy Spirit speaks? _____

_____

The Body of Christ

One problem many churches face today is they have so emphasized the doctrine of the priesthood of believers they have lost their sense of corporate identity. What does that mean in simple words? Christians think their walk with God is independent of anyone else and they are not accountable to the church. It is true Christians have direct access to God through Christ. However, God created the church as His redemptive agent in the world. He has a purpose for the church. God places every member in a church to accomplish His redemptive purposes through that congregation.

A church is a body—the body of Christ (see 1 Cor. 12:27). Jesus Christ is the Head of every local church (see **Eph. 4:15**), and God places every member in the body as it pleases Him (see 1 Cor. 12:18). The Holy Spirit manifests Himself to every person for the common good (see 1 Cor. 12:7). The Father fits together the whole body (see Eph. 5:16), and the Holy Spirit enables and equips members to function where the Father has placed them in the body. The body builds itself up until every member experiences the fullness of Christ (see Eph. 4:13). God made us mutually interdependent. We need one another. What one lacks, others in the body can supply.

What God is doing in and through the body is essential to my knowing how to respond to Him. When I see Him working in my church, I immediately adjust and put my life in that place too. In the church I let God use me in any way He chooses to complete His work in other members. This was Paul's goal when he said, "We proclaim him, admonishing and teaching everyone with all wisdom, so that we may present everyone perfect in Christ" (Col. 1:28). Paul constantly asked believers to become vitally involved with his life and ministry. The effectiveness of Paul's ministry rested on them (see Eph. 6:19; Col. 4:3; 2 Thess. 3:1-2).

Ephesians 4:15-16

"Speaking the truth in love, we will in all things grow up into him who is the Head, that is, Christ. From him the whole body, joined and held together by every supporting ligament, grows and builds itself up in love, as each part does its work."

2 **Read 1 Corinthians 12:7–31 and answer the following questions.**

   a. Paul addressed the Christians of a local church in the city of Corinth. What is a local church (v. 27)? _____

   b. Circle the picture in the margin that best illustrates a church (v. 12).

   c. What does verse 25 say should be true of the church? Does this describe your church? _____
_____

   d. Based on verses 14–24, mark the following statements *T* (true) or *F* (false). Rewrite the false statements on the lines to state them correctly.
   ___ (1) The body consists of one part. _____
   ___ (2) The foot is still a part of the body even though it is not a hand.
_____
   ___ (3) The ear is not part of the body because it is not an eye.
_____
   ___ (4) Members of the body decide how they should be arranged.
_____
   ___ (5) All members need every other member of the body. _____
_____

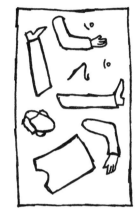

A local church is the *body of Christ* (2–a). All believers worldwide are united in the kingdom of God under the rule of the King! But the local church is to function like a body. It is not *part* of a body. It *is* a body. In 2–b the picture on the top may better represent the way some churches function. However, God has always intended for the church to function as a unit, not as individual parts. (2–c) A church should not be divided. If your church is fragmented, it is unhealthy. The Great Physician, Christ Himself, can heal the body if your church will let Him. In 2–d statements 1, 3, and 4 are false. The others are true.

Apart from the body you cannot fully know God's will for relating to God's people. Without the eye the hand does not know where to touch. Without the ear the rest of the body may not know when or how to respond. Every member needs to listen to what the other members say. If the members are not talking about what they sense God is doing in their midst, the whole body will be disoriented to God.

Allow God to Speak Through the Church

As I function in relationship to the church, I depend on others in the congregation to help me understand God's will. Let me illustrate this for you. Then in unit 10 we will spend more time studying the way members function as part of a body.

While I was in seminary, I was involved in a local church. The first year I taught teenage boys, and I did so with a willing heart. The next year I was asked to be the music and education director. I had never done either job in my life. I had sung in a choir, but I had never led congregational music. I knew nothing about directing the educational program of a church. Here is the way I approached this decision.

The people of God at this church needed a leader. As they prayed, they sensed God had purposely put me there to meet that need. I also saw the need and realized God wanted to use me to meet it. As a servant of Jesus Christ, I did not have the option to say no. I believed the Head—Jesus Christ—could speak through the rest of the body to guide me to know how I should function in their midst. I said I would do my best.

Apart from the body you cannot fully know God's will for relating to God's people.

SUMMARY
STATEMENTS

A church is a body—
the body of Christ!

Jesus Christ is the Head
of a local church.

God places every member in
the body as it pleases Him.

God made us mutually
interdependent. We need
one another.

Apart from the body I cannot
fully know God's will for my
relationship to the body.

Every member needs to
listen to what the other
members say.

As I function in relationship
to the church, I depend on
others in the church to help
me understand God's will.

For two years I served as the music and education director. Then the church voted to call me to be their pastor. I hadn't preached three sermons in my life. I had not gone to seminary because I felt called to be a pastor, but I had gone because I felt called by God into a relationship with Him for whatever He had in mind. I sensed I needed theological training so I would have tools for God to work with. I didn't say, "I am going into foreign missions or home missions." I didn't confine myself to music or education or preaching. I said, "Lord, whatever You direct me to do in relation to Your body, that is what I will do. I am Your servant for Your purposes." I agreed to be the church's pastor.

In the church a need does not constitute the call. A need, however, is not to be ignored. Don't be afraid to let the body of believers assist you in knowing God's will. Also keep in mind that one individual is not the church. In the final analysis you must take all the counsel of people and go to God for clear direction. You will find that a number of things will begin to line up. When what you hear from the Bible, prayer, circumstances, and the church says the same thing, you can proceed with confidence.

You may say, "Henry, you don't know my church. I can't depend on them to help me know God's will." Be careful. When you say that, you have said more about what you believe about God than what you believe about your church. You are saying, "Henry, not even God can work through these people. He is not powerful enough." I don't think you believe that in your mind, but what you do says more about what you believe about God than what you say. This is the point where we need to focus on the crisis of belief. When God speaks, you have to decide what you really believe about God and act on it.

3 **Write your Scripture-memory verse (John 5:19) on the following lines.**

_____
_____
_____
_____
_____
_____

4 **Review your other Scripture-memory verses and be prepared to recite them to a partner in your small-group session this week.**

5 **If you have not completed your list of spiritual markers (day 4), try to finish it before your group session this week. Bring the paper or notebook with you to the session.**

Review today's lesson. Pray and ask God to identify one or more statements or Scriptures He wants you to understand, learn, or practice. Underline them. Then respond to the following.

What was the most meaningful statement or Scripture you read today?	Reword the statement or Scripture into a prayer of response to God.	What does God want you to do in response to today's study?

GOD SPEAKS, PART 2

DVD Message Notes

1. How can I know when God is speaking? It's not a formula. You just have to spend time with Him.
2. If you can't distinguish between God's voice and Satan's voice, you are in incredible jeopardy.
3. There are no shortcuts to knowing God intimately. You have to spend time with Him.
4. A circumstance is an event in your life through which God chooses to speak.
5. Not all circumstances have significance.
6. If you have the spiritual eyes to see, you'll recognize that God is involved in this.
7. It may be that God loves you so much, He refuses to allow your life to remain in bondage to your fear.
8. God will never introduce anything into your life that is a substitute for Him.
9. Just because a door seems closed to you does not mean it is closed to God.
10. Ask God to help you understand what part of the body He's placed you in.

Your Notes

Unit Review

Write the first four realities of experiencing God in your own words.

1. Work: _____

2. Relationship: _____
   _____

3. Invitation: _____
   _____

4. Speaks: _____
   _____
   _____

Check your answers on the inside back cover.

Scriptures Referenced

Joshua 6
1 Corinthians 12:12–31

Testimony

Boon Vongsurith

Sharing Time

• One of the most meaningful statements or Scriptures from this unit's lessons and your prayer response to God. Choose one from pages 117, 120, 123, 127, and 130.
• Spiritual markers in your life (activity 6, p. 127).

For Makeup or Review

Audio and video downloads are available at *www.lifeway.com*.

UNIT 7

VERSE TO MEMORIZE

"WITHOUT FAITH IT IS IMPOS-
SIBLE TO PLEASE GOD, BECAUSE
ANYONE WHO COMES TO HIM
MUST BELIEVE THAT HE EXISTS
AND THAT HE REWARDS THOSE
WHO EARNESTLY SEEK HIM."

HEBREWS 11:6

The Crisis of Belief

A FAITH BUDGET FOR OUR CHURCH

One year the members of our finance committee said, "Pastor, you have taught us to walk by faith in every area in the life of our church except the budget." I asked them to explain. They said, "We develop the budget on the basis of what we believe we can do. It does not reflect that we expect God to do anything."

"Then how do you feel we ought to produce the budget?" I asked.

They said, "First, we ought to determine all God wants to do through us in the coming year. Second, we need to estimate what that will cost. Then we need to divide the budget revenue into three categories: (1) what we plan to do through our own giving, (2) what others have promised to do to help us, and (3) what we must depend on God to do."

As a church we prayed and decided God wanted us to use this approach to budgeting. We did not try to dream our own dreams for God. We had to be absolutely sure God was leading us to do the things we put in the budget. Then we listed what that would cost. We estimated what we thought our people would give and what others (the mission board, partnership churches, and individuals) had said they would contribute. The difference between what we could reasonably expect to receive and the total was what we asked God to provide.

The big question was, What would our operating budget be? By faith we adopted the grand total as our operating budget. At this point we reached a crisis of belief. Did we really believe the God who had led us to do these things would really provide the resources to bring them to pass? Anytime God leads you to do something that has God-sized dimensions, you will face a crisis of belief. At that point what you do next reveals what you believe about God.

That year we set our budget at more than twice the amount we would normally have planned. Yet at year end God had exceeded even that amount by providing us with revenue we could not have anticipated. God taught our church a lesson in faith that radically changed us all.

A Turning Point

WHEN GOD TELLS
ME WHAT HE WANTS
TO DO THROUGH ME,
I WILL FACE A CRISIS
OF BELIEF.

REALITY 5

CRISIS OF BELIEF

The way you
live your life is
a testimony
of what
you believe
about God.

This unit focuses on a major turning point in following God's will. When God invites you to join Him in His work, He has a God-sized assignment for you. You will quickly realize you cannot do what He is asking on your own. If God doesn't help you, you will fail. This is the crisis of belief when you must decide whether to believe God for what He wants to do through you. At this point many people decide not to follow what they sense God is leading them to do. Then they wonder why they do not experience God's presence and activity the way other Christians do. Let's review in order to see the relationship between the crisis of belief and what you have already studied.

1 **We have been studying seven realities of the sequence in which God works with His people. Using the following hints, see if you can write the first four realities in your own words. Then check yourself by referring to the inside back cover of your book.**
Reality 1—God's work: _____
Reality 2—relationship: _____
_____
Reality 3—invites: _____
_____
Reality 4—speaks: _____
_____
_____

2 **Now see if you can fill in the blanks in the fifth reality. You can peek if you need to.**
Reality 5: God's invitation for you to work with Him always leads you to a
_____ of _____ that requires
_____ and _____.

The word *crisis* comes from a Greek word that means *decision* or *judgment*. A crisis of belief is not a calamity in your life but a turning point where you must make a decision. You must decide what you truly believe about God. The way you respond at this turning point will determine whether you become involved with God in something God-sized that only He can do or whether you will continue to go your own way and miss what He has purposed for your life. This is not a one-time experience. It is a regular occurrence. The way you live your life is a testimony of what you believe about God.

3 **You read about our church-budgeting process (p. 133). In that experience what was the crisis of belief? Check your response.**
❏ a. When the committee decided to change the way we developed the budget
❏ b. When the church had to decide what God was leading us to do in the coming year
❏ c. When the committee had to decide whether to recommend the grand total as the operating budget or what it knew the church could do

In a sense every one of these choices could have been checked. In each case we had to decide what we believed about God. The greatest crisis came, however, when we decided to operate on the grand total rather than what we knew we could do. Operating on our projected revenue would not require much faith. We were sure we could do that. But operating on a budget incorporating everything God had told us to do required faith. We could not see any way to get that much money unless God provided it. Do you see the turning point—the crisis of belief? We could have decided on the lesser amount, met our budget, and never known anything more about God. People in the community watching our church would have seen merely what people could do. They would not have seen God at work.

Another crisis of belief came in the middle of our church's building program. We had a unique **opportunity to buy a building** on Main Street in Allan, Saskatchewan, Canada, for use as a church building for our mission. Len Koster, our mission pastor, talked with the owner, who said, "I bought this for $15,000, and I put $7,000 into it. But we will sell this building to you and the property on Main Street for $15,000." He asked us for $9,000 down and said he would give us a loan of $6,000 at 8 percent interest.

Len said, "Give us two weeks, and we will get back to you."

We were a small group of people ourselves, and we were already sponsoring four missions. At that point we were $100,000 short in our own building program. God had called us to start the mission, but we didn't have nine cents, let alone $9,000. We asked the church family, "What do you suppose God wants us to do?"

With one heart the church said, "Let's earnestly pray that God will provide for our mission." We began to pray. We decided that any unexpected money that came in during the next two weeks would be God's provision for Allan in answer to our prayer.

Almost a week later I received a phone call from a church in Halfway, Texas. The caller said, "Someone came by our church and told us that you are doing mission work. Would you describe it to us over the phone?" I did. He said, "We are thinking of sending you $5,000 and then $200 a month for two years to support a mission pastor. Do you know where that might be used?"

"Oh, yes," I said. "We would use it in Allan. We have been praying for Allan."

The next day another pastor called and said, "Someone has told our church about the mission work you are doing. A woman in our church whose husband was an evangelist would like to give $1,000 to mission work. Do you know a place that could use the money?"

I said, "Oh, yes! We are praying for our mission in Allan." Now we had $6,000 for the building and $200 for a pastor. We kept praying. At the end of the two weeks we were short $3,000. Len went back to see the owner.

Before Len could say anything, this man said, "By the way, since you were last here, I've been thinking about income tax. It would be much better for me if you put $6,000 down, and I will carry the $9,000 at 8 percent. How would that be?"

"Oh," Len said. "That is exactly what I was going to suggest." We got the clear deed to the property and built that church. That church has since bought other property, built another building, and sponsored several other missions.

If we had looked at what we had in the bank, would we have proceeded? Not at all. If we had looked at all of the circumstances, would we have moved forward? No. But what you believe about God will determine what you do. When God tells you what He wants to do through you, you will face a crisis of belief. What you do next reveals what you believe.

When God tells you what He wants to do through you, you will face a crisis of belief.

4 In your own words define *crisis of belief.* **Write in the margin.**

5 **Read each passage of Scripture and describe the crisis of belief.**

Joshua 6:1-5: _____

_____

Judges 6:33; 7:1-8: _____

_____

1 Chronicles 14:8-16: _____

_____

Matthew 17:24-27: _____

_____

6 **Have you or your church ever faced a crisis of belief when you sensed God wanted you to do something beyond what you could do?**
❑ Yes   ❑ No   **If so, briefly describe one situation and how you or your church responded.** _____

_____

_____

7 **What did your response demonstrate about your belief in God? Did it reveal faith or a lack of faith?** _____

Would you tell an army to follow you in walking around a city expecting the walls to fall down when you blew some trumpets? That was a crisis of belief for Joshua and for all Israel. They had to decide if they believed God could do what He said. Though they had just seen God dam up the Jordan River for them to cross, this next step required faith. In fact, every assignment God gave Israel required a new measure of faith.

Gideon must have struggled with his crisis. Joint forces of the Midianites, Amalekites, and other eastern peoples were prepared to attack his people. Gideon started with 32,000 men, but God had Gideon send 31,700 of them home. He was going to give victory with only 300 soldiers. Do you see what a difference it made from God's perspective? When the battle was won, everyone knew God did it!

David, a faithful servant of the Lord, refused to rely on human wisdom for guidance. He asked for God's direction. Even though God said He would give David victory over the Philistines, was this a crisis of belief for David? Yes! David still had to decide what he believed about God, and he had to trust God to do what He said He would do.

An important characteristic of David's walk with the Lord is that he stayed in a close relationship with God. He didn't rely on yesterday's guidance for today, and he didn't use human wisdom to decide whether to attack this second time. This is a good example of how God wants you to depend on Him—through an ongoing relationship with Him, not a method or a program. What worked yesterday or in another church may not be what God wants to use today. Only He has a right to tell you what to do next.

Peter was a fisherman. Never before had he found coins in the mouth of a fish. Great faith was required to go and catch one fish to find the exact amount of money needed to pay their taxes. When he acted in faith, God provided.

As we continue our study of the crisis of belief, we will examine four truths.

8 In the following list underline a key word or phrase in each truth.

The Crisis of Belief

1. An encounter with God requires faith.
2. Encounters with God are God-sized.
3. What you do in response to God's revelation (invitation) reveals what you believe about God.
4. True faith requires action.

9 Write your Scripture-memory verse for this unit on the following lines and review your verses from previous units.

_____
_____
_____
_____

Review today's lesson. Pray and ask God to identify one or more statements or Scriptures He wants you to understand, learn, or practice. Underline them. Then respond to the following.

What was the most meaningful statement or Scripture you read today?

_____
_____
_____
_____

Reword the statement or Scripture into a prayer of response to God.

_____
_____
_____
_____

What does God want you to do in response to today's study?

_____
_____
_____
_____

AIDS RESEARCHER CALLED TO UGANDA

We were leading a weekend conference for couples in Ridgecrest, North Carolina. Many individuals wanted to speak with me, for God had touched their lives with truth. One man shared, "Henry, when you were speaking, God reminded me of a time when I was a boy. He asked me to get a medical degree, go to a part of the world that needed medical care, and share the gospel as I practiced medicine. I got my medical degree, did postdoctoral work on the immune system, and specialized in AIDS. I am now a research professor at a highly respected medical-research university. What should I do?" I replied, "Because God reminded you of a vow you made to Him, I have only two words for you—obey immediately!" He replied, "I thought you would say that." We talked and prayed together, and I did not hear from him for a year.

Then one day a friend told me, "At a recent international-missionary commissioning service, a wonderful couple was appointed as career missionaries. The husband has been a research professor where the national AIDS research is housed. They've been appointed to Uganda." I knew who it was! Facing a crisis of belief, this doctor had said, "Yes, Lord!" and was on his way to doing God's will. He now has a wonderful, growing ministry in Africa.

DAY 2

Encounters with God Require Faith

FAITH IS
CONFIDENCE THAT
WHAT GOD HAS
PROMISED OR SAID
WILL COME TO PASS.

When God speaks, your response requires faith. Throughout Scripture when God revealed Himself, His purposes, and His ways, the response to Him required faith.

1 **Read the following Scriptures and respond to the questions.**

a. "Faith is being sure of what we hope for and certain of what we do not see" (Heb. 11:1). What is faith? _____

_____

b. "We live by faith, not by sight" (2 Cor. 5:7). What is the opposite of faith?

_____

c. "A prophet who presumes to speak in my name anything I have not commanded him to say ... must be put to death. If what a prophet proclaims in the name of the Lord does not take place or come true, that is a message the Lord has not spoken. That prophet has spoken presumptu-ously" (Deut. 18:20,22). How important is it for your faith to be in God and what He says rather than in what you or someone else declares ought to happen? _____

d. Jesus said, "Anyone who has faith in me will do what I have been doing. He will do even greater things than these, because I am going to the Father" (John 14:12). What is the potential of faith? _____

_____

e. "I tell you the truth, if you have faith as small as a mustard seed, you can say to this mountain, 'Move from here to there' and it will move. Nothing will be impossible for you" (Matt. 17:20-21). How much faith is required for God to do through you what is humanly impossible? _____

_____

f. Paul said, "My message and my preaching were not with wise and persua-sive words, but with a demonstration of the Spirit's power, so that your faith might not rest on men's wisdom, but on God's power" (1 Cor. 2:4-5). On what should we base our faith? _____
On what should we not base our faith? _____

g. "If you do not stand firm in your faith, you will not stand at all" (Isa. 7:9). What is one danger of a lack of faith? _____

Faith is confidence that what God promised or said will come to pass. Sight is the opposite of faith. If you can clearly see how something can be accomplished, more than likely, faith is not required. Remember the illustration about our church budget? If we had chosen to operate on what we knew we could do, faith would not have been necessary. Faith was believing that the God who called us to the assignments was the One who would provide for their accomplishment.

Your faith does not rest on a concept or an idea. Faith must be in a Person—God Himself. Faith is not drawing up a grandiose idea and then asking God to make it come to pass. If you or someone else decides something would be good to do and then leads people to "believe" or "have faith," you are in a dangerous position. Faith is valid only in God and in what He says He is purposing to do. If what you want to happen is from you and not from God, you must depend on your own resources to bring it about. Before you call yourself, your family, or your church to exercise faith, be sure you have heard a word from God.

With only mustard-seed-size faith in God, anything is possible. Jesus said His followers would do greater things than He had done. Our faith, however, must be based on God's power and not on human wisdom. Without firm faith you will stumble and fall.

> Faith is valid only in God and in what He says He is purposing to do.

Something Only God Can Do

Moses could not deliver the children of Israel from Pharaoh's army, cross the Red Sea on dry land, produce water from a rock, or provide bread and meat for food. Moses had to have faith that the God who called him would do what He said He would do. Joshua could not take the Israelites across the Jordan River on dry land, bring down walled cities, defeat enemies, or make the sun stand still. Only God could accomplish these things. Joshua had to have faith in God.

In the New Testament this was also true for the disciples. On their own they could not feed the multitudes, heal the sick, calm a storm, or raise the dead. Only God could do these things. But God called servants to let Him do those things through them.

When God lets you know what He wants to do through you, it will be something only He can do. What you believe about Him will determine what you do next. If you have faith in the God who called you, you will obey Him, and He will bring to pass what He purposed to do. If you lack faith, you will not do what He asks. That is disobedience. Jesus asked those around Him, "Why do you call me, 'Lord, Lord,' and do not do what I say?" (Luke 6:46). He frequently rebuked His disciples for their unbelief. Their lack of faith revealed they did not know who He was. Thus, they did not know what He could do.

2 Answer the following questions.
a. What is one thing God wanted to do through Moses that only God could do?

_____

b. What is one thing Jesus wanted to do through the disciples that only God could do? _____

c. When God asks someone to join Him in doing something only He can do, what is required for the person to respond? _____

d If the person disobeys, what does that indicate? _____

e. If the person obeys, what does that demonstrate? _____

f. Hebrews 11:6, tells why faith is important. Circle the correct word in parentheses: "Without faith it is (possible   impossible) to please God."

Obedience indicates faith in God.

Mark 10:27

"Jesus looked at them and said, 'With man this is impossible, but not with God; all things are possible with God.' "

Faith was required of Moses and the disciples. When God calls a person to join Him in a God-sized task, faith is always required. Obedience indicates faith in God. Disobedience often reveals a lack of faith. Without faith a person cannot please God. Without faith a church cannot please God.

We face the same crisis Bible characters dealt with. When God speaks, what He asks of us requires faith. Our major problem, however, is self-centeredness. We assume we have to accomplish the assignment in our own strength and with our current resources. We think, *I can't do that. That is impossible.*

We forget that when God speaks, He always reveals what *He* is going to do—not what He wants us to do for Him. We join Him so He can do His work through us. We don't have to be able to accomplish the task with our limited ability or resources. With faith we can confidently proceed to obey Him because we know *He* is going to bring to pass what *He* purposes. Jesus indicated that what is impossible with man is possible with God (see **Mark 10:27**). The Scriptures continually bear witness that this is true.

The church I pastored sensed we needed God to use us to reach people for Christ throughout our province. The province contained more than two hundred cities, towns, and villages. This meant we would have to start new churches. To do that, we felt God was leading us to call **Len Koster** to become our minister of mission outreach. He would equip the church to start churches.

For 14 years Len had pastored small churches. Len was so committed to the Lord that he worked as a service-station attendant for 14 years in order to pastor bivocationally. Without a part-time pastor these churches would have had no pastor at all. In that time Len and his wife, Ruth, had saved seven thousand dollars, hoping one day they would have enough money to buy their own home. When Len felt absolutely convinced he ought to come help us start churches, I said, "Len, we have no money to move you and no money to pay you."

He said, "Henry, the God who has called me will help me. We will take the money from our savings, and we will move." Later Len came into my office and said, "Henry, my wife and I prayed and talked all night. I have worked bivocationally for 14 years, and I have no problem working to provide for my family. But the need here is so great and God's direction is so clear I believe I need to work full-time. My wife and I realized last night that the seven thousand dollars we have in the bank is God's, and He wants us to use that for our living expenses. When we have exhausted that, He will show us what to do next. So Henry, don't worry about my support."

When Len left the room, I fell on my face and wept before the Father. I said, "Father, I don't understand why such a faithful couple must make this kind of sacrifice." I saw in Len and Ruth a great faith that was demonstrated by their actions.

Two days later I received a letter from a Presbyterian layman in Kamloops, British Columbia. It simply said, "I understand a man named Len Koster has come to work with you. God has laid it on my heart to help support his ministry. Enclosed find a check for seven thousand dollars to be used for his support." When I opened that letter, I got back on my knees and wept before the Father again. This time I asked Him to forgive me for not trusting Him when He told me I could.

I called Len and said, "Len, you have placed your life savings on the altar of sacrifice, but God has something else in the bushes. The God who says, 'I am your Provider' has just provided!" Then I told him the news. Do you know what that did in Len's life? Can you imagine what it did in our church's life? We all grew in our faith to believe God. After that we stepped out in faith time and time again, and we saw God do amazing things. We never could have experienced God that way if we had not stepped out in faith to call Len. That experience helped us learn how to trust God.

When you encounter God, it will bring a crisis of belief. That crisis will require faith. Without that faith you will not be able to please God.

3 Describe a time in your life that required faith, but you did not respond because you lacked faith. _____
_____
_____

4 Describe a time in your life that required faith in God, and you responded in faith—a time when you could see no way to accomplish the task unless God did it through you or in you. _____
_____
_____
_____

5 What, if anything, do you know God wants you to do that you are not doing? _____
_____
_____

6 Why do you think you are hesitating? _____
_____

7 Have you ever wanted to pray like the disciples when they asked the Lord, "Increase our faith" (Luke 17:5)? ❑ Yes ❑ No When and why?
_____
_____
_____

8 Take time now to pray about your faith and what God wants to do through your life. Write a prayer to Him.
_____
_____
_____
_____
_____

SUMMARY STATEMENTS

When God speaks, my response requires faith.

Faith is confidence that what God has promised or said will come to pass.

Sight is the opposite of faith.

Faith must be in a Person.

Before I call myself, my family, or my church to exercise faith, I must be sure I have heard a word from God.

When God lets me know what He wants to do through me, it will be something only He can do.

What I believe about God will determine what I do.

Review today's lesson. Pray and ask God to identify one or more statements or Scriptures He wants you to understand, learn, or practice. Underline them. Then respond to the following.

What was the most meaningful statement or Scripture you read today?

Reword the statement or Scripture into a prayer of response to God.

What does God want you to do in response to today's study?

DAY 3

Encounters with God Are God-Sized

GOD IS INTERESTED IN THE WORLD'S COMING TO KNOW HIM.

God is interested in the world's coming to know Him. The only way people will know what God is like is to see Him at work in their world. They will know His nature when they see it expressed in His activity. Whenever God involves you in His activity, the assignment will have Godlike dimensions to it.

Some people say, "God will never ask me to do something that's impossible." On the contrary, if the assignment I sense God is giving me is something I know I can handle on my own, I assume it probably is *not* from God. The assignments God gave in the Bible were always God-sized. They were always beyond what people could do in their strength because He wanted to demonstrate His nature, His strength, His provision, and His love to His people and to a watching world. That is the only way the world will come to know Him.

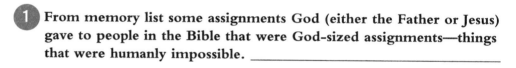 **From memory list some assignments God (either the Father or Jesus) gave to people in the Bible that were God-sized assignments—things that were humanly impossible.** _____

_____

You could name many God-sized assignments in Scripture. God told Abraham to father a nation when Abraham had no son and Sarah was past childbearing age. He told Moses to deliver the children of Israel, to cross the Red Sea, and to provide water from a rock. He told Gideon to defeat the giant Midianite army with only three hundred men. Jesus told the disciples to feed the multitudes and to make disciples of all nations. None of these things were humanly possible. When people see something happen that only God can do, they come to know God.

2 **Read the following biblical accounts of God's activity through His servants. Underline statements that indicate how people responded to God's activity when they observed it. I have underlined one for you.**

God told Moses to lead the Israelites to camp beside the Red Sea. God knew He was going to deliver them by dividing the sea and letting them cross on dry ground. He said, "I will gain glory for myself through Pharaoh and all his army, and the Egyptians will know that I am the Lord" (Ex. 14:4). What was the result? "When the Israelites saw the great power the Lord displayed against the Egyptians, <u>the people feared the Lord and put their trust in him</u>" (Ex. 14:31).

God commanded Joshua to lead the Israelites across the Jordan River at flood stage. Why? "He did this so that all the peoples of the earth might know that the hand of the Lord is powerful and so that you [Israel] might always fear the Lord your God" (Josh. 4:24).

A vast army came to attack Israel. King Jehoshaphat proclaimed a fast and led the people to seek God's counsel. He prayed, "O our God … we have no power to face this vast army that is attacking us. We do not know what to do, but our eyes are upon you" (2 Chron. 20:12).

God responded, "Do not be afraid or discouraged because of this vast army. For the battle is not yours, but God's. ... You will not have to fight this battle. Take up your positions; stand firm and see the deliverance the Lord will give you" (2 Chron. 20:15,17). Jehoshaphat sent a choir in front of the army singing praise to God for His enduring love. God destroyed the invading army before Jehoshaphat and Israel got to the battlefield. Then "the fear of God came upon all the kingdoms of the countries when they heard how the Lord had fought against the enemies of Israel" (2 Chron. 20:29).

Shadrach, Meshach, and Abednego chose to obey God rather than King Nebuchadnezzar. Before being thrown into a blazing furnace, they said, "The God we serve is able to save us from it, and he will rescue us from your hand" (Dan. 3:17). The soldiers holding them captive died, but God delivered these three faithful men.

King Nebuchadnezzar said, "Praise be to the God of Shadrach, Meshach and Abednego, who has sent his angel and rescued his servants. ... Therefore I decree that the people of any nation or language who say anything against the God of Shadrach, Meshach and Abednego be cut into pieces and their houses be turned into piles of rubble, for no other god can save in this way" (Dan. 3:28-29). This pagan king wrote to the whole nation, "It is my pleasure to tell you about the miraculous signs and wonders that the Most High God has performed for me. How great are his signs, how mighty his wonders!" (Dan. 4:2-3).

When Christians in the early church followed the directions of the Holy Spirit, God impacted their world. The disciples were filled with the Holy Spirit and spoke in foreign languages they had not learned. Then Peter preached. "Those who accepted his message were baptized, and about three thousand were added to their number that day" (Acts 2:41).

God used Peter and John to heal a crippled beggar in the name of Jesus. They preached, and "many who heard the message believed, and the number of men grew to about five thousand" (Acts 4:4).

God used Peter to raise Dorcas from the dead. "This became known all over Joppa, and many people believed in the Lord" (Acts 9:42).

3 Answer the following questions.

    a. When people saw God at work through His servants, who received the credit—God or the servants? _____

    b. What difference or impact do you see in the lives of people who saw or heard about God's activity? _____
_____

    c. How would you describe the response of the people in your community to what they see of God's activity in your church? _____
_____

What our world often witnesses today is a devoted, committed Christian or church serving God. But they are not seeing God. They don't see anything happening that can be explained only in terms of God's activity. Why? Because we are not attempting anything that only God can do.

Our world is not being attracted to the Christ we serve because they are not seeing Him at work in our lives. They see us doing good things for God and comment, "That's nice, but it's not my thing." The world is passing us by because they do not want to get involved in what they see in our lives. We are not giving them opportunities

Our world is not seeing God because we are not attempting anything that only God can do.

Let the world watch God at work, and He will attract people to Himself.

to encounter God. They are seeing only us. Let the world watch God at work, and He will attract people to Himself. Let Christ be lifted up, not in words but in life. Let people see the difference the living Christ makes in a life, a family, or a church; that will affect how they respond to the gospel. When the world sees things happening through God's people that cannot be explained except that God Himself has done them, the world will be drawn to such a God.

4 **Answer the following questions.**
a. How will the world come to know God? _____
_____
_____

b. Why are people in our world not being attracted to Christ and His church?
_____
_____

c. What kind of assignments does God give His people? _____

d. Why does God give God-sized assignments that an individual or a church cannot accomplish? _____
_____

e. What are you attempting to do that will happen only if God brings it to pass?
_____
_____

f. What is your church attempting to do that will happen only if God brings it to pass? _____
_____

g. Which of the following *best* describes the things you listed in the previous two questions? Check your response.
❑ They are things God led me/us to attempt.
❑ They are things I/we decided to ask God to do.

h. How are non-Christians responding to what they see God doing in your life and church?
❑ We are not attempting many God-sized tasks, and few people are responding to the gospel.
❑ We are not attempting many God-sized tasks, but many are responding to the gospel.
❑ We are seeing God do great things in and through our church, but few people are responding to the gospel.
❑ We are seeing God do great things in and through our church, and many people are responding to the gospel.

People come to know God when they see His nature expressed through His activity. When God does a work, He accomplishes something only He can do. When He does that, God's people and the world come to know Him in ways they have never experienced Him. That is why He gives God-sized assignments. The reason much of the world is not being attracted to Christ and to His church is that God's people lack the faith to attempt things only God can do. If you or your church is not responding to God and attempting God-sized tasks, you are not exercising faith. "Without faith it is impossible to please God" (Heb. 11:6). If people in your community are not responding to the gospel the way people responded in the New Testament, one possible reason is that they are not recognizing God in what you are doing as a church.

God is far more concerned with your walking with Him than He is interested in getting a job done for Him. You can complete an assignment but never experience God. He can accomplish His work anytime He wants. What is He concerned about? You and the world knowing Him and experiencing Him. So God will come to you and give you a God-sized assignment. When you start to do what He tells you to do, He brings to pass what He purposed. Then you and the people with you will rejoice that you have experienced Him. You and the people around you will know more of Him than you have ever known before.

Our church in Saskatoon was growing and needed more space. We sensed God leading us to enlarge our facility even though we had only $749 in the building fund. The building was going to cost $220,000. We didn't have the foggiest notion how to do it.

We did much of the work to save labor costs. Still, halfway through the building program we were $100,000 short. Those dear people looked to their pastor to see if I believed God would accomplish what He called us to do. God put confidence in my heart that the God who was leading us would show us how to do it.

God began providing the necessary funds, but we were about $60,000 short toward the end. We had expected some money from a Texas foundation. Delay after delay occurred that we could not understand. Then one day for two hours the **currency-exchange rate** for the Canadian dollar hit the lowest point in history. That was exactly the time the Texas foundation wired the money to Canada. That gave us $60,000 more than we would have received otherwise. After that the Canadian dollar went back up in value.

Does the Heavenly Father look after the economy in order to help His children? Nobody in the world would believe God did that for one church, but I can show you a church that believes God did it! When that happened, I magnified what the Lord had done in the eyes of the people. I made sure we gave Him the credit. God revealed Himself to us, and we came to know Him in a new way through that experience.

5 **Talk to the Lord about the level of your faith and that of your church. Ask for forgiveness for unbelief and for increased faith.**

God is far more concerned with your walking with Him than He is interested in getting a job done for Him.

SUMMARY STATEMENTS

When God's people and the world see something only God can do, they come to know God.

Let people see the difference a living Christ makes in a life, a family, or a church; that will make a difference in how they respond to the gospel.

Review today's lesson. Pray and ask God to identify one or more statements or Scriptures He wants you to understand, learn, or practice. Underline them. Then respond to the following.

What was the most meaningful statement or Scripture you read today?	Reword the statement or Scripture into a prayer of response to God.	What does God want you to do in response to today's study?

What You Do Reveals What You Believe

When God speaks to a person, revealing His plans and purpose, it will always cause a crisis of belief.

1 **As a review, complete the first two statements about this crisis of belief.**

The Crisis of Belief
1. An encounter with God requires _____.
2. Encounters with God are _____.
3. What you do in response to God's revelation (invitation) reveals what you believe about God.
4. True faith requires action.

2 **In each of the last two statements, circle one or two key words that might help you remember the points.**

What you do reveals what you believe about God, regardless of what you say. When God reveals what He is purposing to do, you face a crisis—a decision time. God and the world can tell from your response what you really believe about God. Your trust in God will determine what you do and how you live.

3 **In the following paragraphs, underline what David seems to have believed about God, based on what he said. I have underlined one for you.**

In 1 Samuel 16:12-13 God chose David and had Samuel anoint him to become the next king over Israel. In 1 Samuel 17 God brought David into the middle of His activity. While Saul was still the king, the Israelites were at war with the Philistines. Still a young boy, David was sent by his father to visit his brothers in the army. When David arrived, Goliath, a giant soldier nine feet tall, challenged Israel to send one man to fight him. The losing nation would become the slaves of the winner. Israel's army was terrified. David asked in amazement, "Who is this uncircumcised Philistine that he should defy the armies of the <u>living God</u>?" (v. 26). David faced a crisis of belief. He may have realized that God had brought him to the battlefield and had prepared him for this assignment.

David said he would fight this giant. He stated his belief: "The Lord who delivered me from the paw of the lion and the paw of the bear will deliver me from the hand of this Philistine" (v. 37). David refused to take the normal weapons of war. Instead, he chose a sling and five smooth stones. He said to Goliath, "You come against me with sword and spear and javelin, but I come against you in the name of the Lord Almighty, the God of the armies of Israel, whom you have defied. This day the Lord will hand you over to me … and the whole world will know that there is a God in Israel. All those gathered here will know that it is not by sword or spear that the Lord saves; for the battle is the Lord's, and he will give all of you into our hands" (vv. 45-47). David killed Goliath, and Israel went on to victory.

4 What did David say he believed about God? _____

_____

5 Based on David's response to Goliath, what do you think David believed about God? _____

_____

David's statements indicate he believed God was the living God and a Deliverer. He said God was almighty and would defend Israel's armies. David's actions verified that he really believed these things about God. Many thought David was a foolish young boy, and even Goliath laughed at him. However, God delivered the Israelites. He gave a mighty victory through David so the world would know there was a God in Israel!

God called Abram and promised to make his offspring as numerous as the stars. Abram questioned God about this promise since he remained childless in his old age. God reaffirmed, "A son coming from your own body will be your heir. Abram believed the Lord, and he credited it to him as righteousness" (Gen. 15:4,6).

Abram's wife, Sarai, was in her mid-70s at this time. Knowing she was past child-bearing years, she decided she would have to build a family in a different way. She gave her maid to Abram as a wife and asked for a child through her. Ishmael was born to Haggar a year later. Sarai's actions indicated what she believed about God.

6 Which of the following more closely indicates what Sarai seemed to believe about God? Check your response.
- ❑ a. Sarai believed God was almighty and could do anything, including giving her a child of her own even though she was advanced in years.
- ❑ b. Sarai believed God could not possibly give her a child at her age and needed her help in finding a way for Abram to become a father.

Sarai's actions revealed what she really believed about God. She did not have the faith to believe God could do the impossible and give her a child in her own age. Her belief about God was limited by her human reason. This act of unbelief was extremely costly. Ishmael caused Abram and Sarai much grief in their old age. Ishmael and his descendants have lived in hostility toward Isaac and his descendants from that time until today. What you do in response to God's invitation clearly indicates what you believe about God.

7 Read the following case studies. Evaluate the responses of the individuals and churches to determine what they believe about God. Check your response or write your own response to each situation.
1. Bill and Kathy, having just heard a missionary speaker, believe God wants them to go as missionaries to Africa. Kathy reminds Bill that her parents would never agree to let them move so far away with her parents' only grandchildren. They decide not to pursue that sense of calling to be missionaries but to seek to support missions where they live. What do you think Bill and Kathy believe about God?
   - ❑ a. God is Sovereign Lord and has the right to do anything in their lives that He pleases.
   - ❑ b. God is able to convince Kathy's parents that this is His purpose so they will accept her decision.

Unbelief was extremely costly.

❑ c. God may have been able to convince Pharaoh to let Israel go, but He would never be able to convince Kathy's parents to let Kathy, Bill, and the children go to Africa.
❑ d. Other _____

2. **Levona** has privately been praying that God would lead her to a place of service in the church. The Sunday School director, who has been praying for an adult Bible teacher, believes God is leading him to ask Levona to serve in that position. Levona responds, "I cannot accept that job. I don't have the abilities required. Besides, I have never done that before." What do you think Levona believes about God?
❑ a. The Holy Spirit will equip and enable me to do anything He calls me to do.
❑ b. God can't do anything through me that lies outside my giftedness.
❑ c. Other _____

3. A group of adults has been meeting together for six months and praying God would provide a church for their community, where there are currently no churches. As they pray, they sense God wants them to approach **Calvary Church** with an urgent plea to come and start the new church. Calvary's members say, "We are still paying off a debt on our building. We can't afford to sponsor a new church right now. Why don't you try First Church downtown." What do you think Calvary Church believes about God?
❑ a. God's resources for work through our church are limited to what our people already give.
❑ b. God owns everything in the world. He can provide resources to do whatever He purposes to do.
❑ c. Other _____

4. **First Church**'s budget committee prays together for a month prior to talking with leaders about next year's budget, and it asks the leaders to pray as well. They develop a challenging budget, based on what they believe God wants their church to do next year. The church prayerfully considers the budget and unanimously votes to adopt it. The deacons lead a pledge campaign that comes up with 10 percent less than the adopted budget. The church then requires the budget committee to trim the budget by 10 percent so the church will not overspend its income. What do you think First Church believes about God?
❑ a. God is faithful. He will provide for all He leads our church to do.
❑ b. God is uncaring. He leads us to agree to do many things, but then He won't give us what we need to get the job done.
❑ c. God won't do anything we as a church can't afford.
❑ d. Other _____

Bill, Kathy, Levona, Calvary Church, and First Church may have been dealing with many other variables, but one thing is sure: actions indicate what we believe and do not believe about God. When Bill and Kathy made a decision at their crisis of belief, they said far more about their belief in God than about Kathy's parents. Levona said far more about her belief in God's power than she did about her abilities. Calvary Church and First Church said far more about what they believed about God than they did about their own resources.

Actions Speak

When God invites you to join Him and you face a crisis of belief, what you do next reveals what you believe about God. Your actions speak louder than your words.

8 Read the following Scriptures and answer the questions.
a. Read Matthew 8:5-13. What did the centurion do to demonstrate his faith?

_____

b. What do you think the centurion believed about Jesus' authority and healing power? _____

c. Read Matthew 8:23-27. What did the disciples do to demonstrate their lack of faith in the middle of this storm? _____

_____

d. Read Matthew 9:20-22. What did the woman do to demonstrate her faith?

_____

e. What do you think the woman believed about Jesus' power to heal?

_____

f. Read Matthew 9:27-31. What trait of God (Jesus) did these two blind men appeal to (v. 27)? _____

g. On what basis did Jesus heal these two men (v. 29)? _____

9 Complete in your own words the third statement about the crisis of belief.

The Crisis of Belief
1. An encounter with God requires faith.
2. Encounters with God are God-sized.
3. What I do in response to God's revelation (invitation) … _____
_____
4. True faith requires action.

When the two blind men demonstrated that they believed Jesus was merciful and was the Messiah (Son of David), Jesus healed them according to their faith. The woman believed that touching Jesus' garment would allow His healing power to flow to her. She was willing to risk public ridicule to experience a miracle! When the storms of life overtake us as this tempest overtook the disciples, we often respond as if God does not exist or does not care about us. Jesus rebuked them, not for their human tendency to fear but for their failure to recognize His presence, protection, and power. "Just say the word, and my servant will be healed," the centurion claimed. Jesus commended the centurion's faith in His authority and power. What each of these people did indicated to Jesus what kind of faith they had.

10 Practice quoting your Scripture-memory verses aloud or write them on separate paper.

Review today's lesson. Pray and ask God to identify one or more statements or Scriptures He wants you to understand, learn, or practice. Underline them. Then respond to the following.

What was the most meaningful statement or Scripture you read today?

_____
_____
_____
_____
_____

Reword the statement or Scripture into a prayer of response to God.

_____
_____
_____
_____
_____

What does God want you to do in response to today's study?

_____
_____
_____
_____
_____

DAY 5

True Faith Requires Action

FAITH WITHOUT ACTION IS DEAD!

James 2:26 says, "As the body without the spirit is dead, so faith without deeds is dead." When you face a crisis of belief, what you do demonstrates what you believe. Faith without action is dead! Hebrews 11 is sometimes called the roll call of faith. Let's take a look at the actions of these individuals who demonstrated their faith.

1 **Turn to Hebrews 11. The following list on the left includes people commended for their faith in Hebrews 11. The verses of the chapter are in parentheses beside the name. Match the person on the left with the action on the right that demonstrated faith. Write the correct letters in the blanks. Some of the names will have more than one letter.**

____ 1. Abel (v. 4)
____ 2. Enoch (vv. 5-6)
____ 3. Noah (v. 7)
____ 4. Abraham (vv. 8-19)
____ 5. Joseph (v. 22)
____ 6. Moses (vv. 24-28)
____ 7. Israelites (vv. 29-30)
____ 8. Rahab (v. 31)

a. Chose to be mistreated along with God's people
b. Offered a righteous sacrifice to God
c. Left Egypt
d. Made his home in a foreign country
e. Marched around the walls of Jericho
f. Pleased God by earnestly seeking Him
g. Gave instructions to bury his bones in the promised land
h. Followed God without knowing where he was going
i. Kept the Passover
j. Passed through the Red Sea on dry ground
k. Welcomed and hid the Israelite spies
l. Considered God faithful to keep His promise
m. Built an ark to save his family
n. Offered Isaac as a sacrifice

Answers to activity 1 are: 1–b; 2–f; 3–m; 4–d, h, l, n; 5–g; 6–a, c, i; 7–e, j; 8–k.

2 In the previous list of actions, circle the word (the verb) in each lettered item that indicates an action taken as a demonstration of faith.

3 Based on Hebrews 11, is the following statement true or false? Circle one. Genuine faith is demonstrated by action.   True   False

Genuine faith is demonstrated by action. While you are studying Hebrews 11, you may notice that a faithful life does not always bring the same results in human terms.

4 Read Hebrews 11:32–38. Based on your own criteria, list the "good" outcomes of a faithful life on the left and the "bad" outcomes on the right. I have listed two to get you started.

"Good" Outcomes	"Bad" Outcomes
Routed enemies	*Stoned to death*

Verses 33–35a describe the victory and deliverance some people of faith experienced. Verses 35b–38 describe the torture, mockery, and death other people of faith endured. Were some more faithful than others? No. "These were all commended for their faith" (Heb. 11:39). They decided a "Well done!" from their Master was more important than life itself. Verse 40 explains God has planned something far better for people of faith than the world has to offer. Therefore, "Since we are surrounded by such a great cloud of witnesses, let us throw off everything that hinders and the sin that so easily entangles, and let us run with perseverance the race marked out for us. Let us fix our eyes on Jesus, the author and perfecter of our faith, who for the joy set before him endured the cross, scorning its shame, and sat down at the right hand of the throne of God. Consider him who endured such opposition from sinful men, so that you will not grow weary and lose heart" (Heb. 12:1-3).

Outward appearances of success do not always indicate faith, and outward appearances of failure do not always reflect a lack of faith. A faithful servant is one who does what his Master tells him, whatever the outcome may be. Consider Jesus: He endured the cross, but now He is seated next to the throne of God! What a reward for faithfulness! Don't grow weary in being faithful. A reward awaits faithful servants.

God has planned something far better for people of faith than the world has to offer.

151

5 Take a moment to review by filling in the blanks in the following four statements.

The Crisis of Belief
1. An encounter with God requires _____.
2. Encounters with God are God-_____.
3. What I do in response to God's _____ (invitation) reveals what I _____ about God.
4. True faith requires _____.

6 Write your Scripture-memory verse for this unit. _____

_____
_____
_____

I pray that you are trying to please God by earnestly seeking Him (see Heb. 11:6). In the next unit we will look more carefully at the cost of following God's will. Part of the action required to demonstrate your faith will be the adjustment you must make to God. Following God's will always requires adjustments that are costly to you and even to those around you.

7 Take time to review some of your responses at the end of each day in units 1–7. Has God asked you to do something you have not done because you lacked faith? ❑ Yes ❑ No If so, describe what you may need to do to demonstrate your faith in Him, His purposes, and His ways. _____

_____
_____
_____
_____
_____

8 Pray about your faithfulness. Ask God to increase your faith.

9 Review your Scripture-memory verses and be prepared to recite them to a partner in your small-group session this week.

Review today's lesson. Pray and ask God to identify one or more statements or Scriptures He wants you to understand, learn, or practice. Underline them. Then respond to the following.

What was the most meaningful statement or Scripture you read today?	Reword the statement or Scripture into a prayer of response to God.	What does God want you to do in response to today's study?

THE CRISIS OF BELIEF

DVD Message Notes

1. Your life becomes radically oriented to God.
2. Whenever God speaks to you, whatever you do next reveals what you believe about God, regardless of what you say.
3. What should be your response? An immediate "Yes, Lord."
4. When God speaks, it will create a crisis of belief.
5. When God speaks, it always has eternal dimensions about it. Your life response to God is going to affect eternity.
6. One word from God has the potential of an open-ended experience with God.
7. The smallest encounter with God has incredible dimensions about it.
8. No storm where the Master is present will ever overcome you.
9. Jesus never has sympathy with our unbelief.
10. Unbelief shuts down the activity of God.
11. "Nothing is impossible with God."
12. Do you have a mustard-seed faith?
13. God can do anything that's on His heart through the one who believes. The key is belief.
14. What has God been asking of you?
15. The key is obedience.
16. Your church will be as excited as you're willing to step out and believe God.
17. Most Christians are just one prayer away from God doing a mighty work.

Your Notes

_____

_____

_____

_____

Unit Review

In your own words write a statement of the fifth reality of experiencing God using the hint below (inside back cover).

Crisis: _____

_____

Fill in the blanks in the following four statements (activity 5, p. 152).

1. An encounter with God requires _____ .
2. Encounters with God are God-_____ .
3. What I do in response to God's _____ (invitation) reveals what I _____ about God.
4. True faith requires _____ .

Check your answers, using the pages cited in parentheses.

John 3:5
Matthew 13:11,16,31
Luke 8:22-25
Mark 9:17-24,28
Matthew 10:1
Matthew 17:19-21

Testimony

Bob Dixon

Sharing Time

- Activities 4–7, page 136. Compare your answers in activities 4–5 and discuss your responses to activities 6–7.
- Times in your life when faith was required and how you responded (activities 3–4, p. 141).
- Activity 4, page 144. Compare your answers to items a–d. Share, compare, and discuss your responses to items e–h.
- One of the most meaningful statements or Scriptures from this unit's lessons and your prayer responses to God. Choose one from pages 137, 141, 145, 150, and 152.

For Makeup or Review

Audio and video downloads are available at *www.lifeway.com*.

UNIT

8

VERSE TO MEMORIZE

"ANY OF YOU WHO DOES NOT GIVE UP EVERYTHING HE HAS CANNOT BE MY DISCIPLE."

LUKE 14:33

Adjusting Your Life to God

A Young Couple's Sacrifice

When a need arose in one of our mission churches 40 miles away, I asked the church to pray that God would call someone to move to that community to serve as the lay pastor of the mission. A young couple responded. Because the husband was attending the university, they had very little money.

If they took up residence in the mission community, he would have to commute 80 miles a day to the university. I knew they couldn't afford to do it. I said, "No, I can't let you do that" and named several reasons why that would not be fair.

This young couple was deeply grateful that God had saved them. The young man looked at me and said, "Pastor, don't deny me the opportunity to sacrifice for my Lord." That statement crushed me. How could I refuse? Yet I knew this couple would have to pay a high price because our church had been obedient to start new missions.

We had prayed for God to call a lay pastor, so I needed to be open to God's answering our prayers in an unexpected way. When this couple responded with a deep sense of commitment and personal sacrifice, our church affirmed their sense of call, and God provided for their needs!

Adjustments Are Necessary

YOU CANNOT STAY WHERE YOU ARE AND GO WITH GOD.

Critical Turning Points:

1. Crisis of Belief
2. Major Adjustments

God's revelation is your invitation to adjust your life to Him.

Many of us want God to speak to us and give us an assignment. However, we are not interested in making major adjustments in our lives. Biblically, that position is impossible. Every time God spoke to people in the Scripture about something He wanted to do through them, major adjustments were required. They had to adjust their lives to God. Once the adjustments were made, God accomplished His purposes through those He called.

Adjusting your life to God is the second critical turning point in your knowing and doing the will of God. The first turning point was the crisis of belief: you must believe God is who He says He is and that He will do what He says He will do. Without faith in God, you will make the wrong decision at this first turning point. Adjusting your life to God is another turning point. If you choose to make the adjustment, you can move on to obedience. If you refuse to make the adjustment, you will miss what God has in store for your life.

1 **If you have faith at the crisis of belief, what else is required as a demonstration of that faith? Fill in the blank below.**

Reality 5: God's invitation for you to work with Him always leads you to a crisis of belief that requires faith and _____.

Once you have come to believe God, you demonstrate your faith by what you *do* (your actions). Some response is required. This action is one of the major adjustments we will focus on in this unit. Your obedience will also be part of the action required. Your adjustments and obedience will be costly to you and to those around you.

> FAITH ▶ ACTIONS
> ACTION = ADJUSTMENTS + OBEDIENCE

2 **In your own words summarize what is stated in the preceding box.**

_____

_____

_____

Adjustments to God

When God speaks to you to reveal what He is about to do, that revelation is your invitation to adjust your life to Him. Your faith will be most clearly demonstrated by your actions. Actions you will take include the adjustments you must make to be in a position to obey the Lord. Once you've adjusted your life to the Lord, you act in obedience. Then God accomplishes through you what He has purposed to do. Adjustments prepare you for obedience. You cannot continue life as usual or stay where you are and go with God at the same time. This truth is demonstrated throughout Scripture. For instance:

- Noah could not continue life as usual and build an ark (see Gen. 6).
- Abram could not stay in Ur or Haran and father a nation in Canaan (see Gen. 12:1-8).
- Moses could not stay on the back side of the desert herding sheep and stand before Pharaoh (see Ex. 3).
- David had to leave his sheep to become king (see 1 Sam. 16:1-13).
- Amos had to leave the sycamore trees to preach in Israel (see Amos 7:14-15).
- Jonah had to leave his home and overcome a major prejudice in order to preach in Nineveh (see Jonah 1:1-2; 3:1-2; 4:1-11).
- Peter, Andrew, James, and John had to leave their fishing businesses to follow Jesus (see Matt. 4:18-22).
- Matthew had to leave his tax collector's booth to follow Jesus (see Matt. 9:9).
- Saul (later Paul) had to completely change directions in his life to preach the gospel to the Gentiles (see Acts 9:1-19).

These men had to make enormous adjustments! Some had to leave family and country. Others had to renounce prejudices and change their values. Others had to leave behind life goals, ideals, and desires. They had to yield everything to God and align their entire lives to Him. The moment they made the necessary changes, God began to accomplish His purposes through them. Each one, however, learned that adjusting one's life to God is well worth the cost.

3 **Your Scripture-memory verse for this unit speaks of a major adjustment that must be made to be a disciple of Jesus. Write Luke 14:33.**

_____

_____

_____

4 **Have you come to a place in your life where you are willing to yield everything to God in order to follow Him?** ❑ Yes ❑ No

5 **In the previous unit you studied the fifth reality in the sequence of God's working through His people. In this unit we will look together at the sixth reality. To review and preview, fill in the blanks in the realities below.**
Reality 5: God's invitation for you to work with Him always leads you to a
_____ of _____ that requires
_____ and _____.
Reality 6: You must make major _____
in your life to join God in what He is doing.

Adjusting one's
life to God is
well worth
the cost.

REALITY 6

ADJUST

You may be thinking, _But God will not ask me to make major adjustments._ Scripture shows that God most certainly requires adjustments of His people. He even required them of His own Son: "You know the grace of our Lord Jesus Christ, that though he was rich, yet for your sakes he became poor, so that you through his poverty might become rich" (2 Cor. 8:9). Jesus emptied Himself of position and wealth in heaven in order to join the Father in providing redemption through His death on the cross. That was a major adjustment!

If you want to be a disciple—a follower—of Jesus, you have no choice. You must leave where you are to follow Him. You must make major alterations in your life to

Isaiah 55:9

"As the heavens are higher
   than the earth,
   so are my ways higher
   than your ways
   and my thoughts than
   your thoughts."

follow God. Until you are ready to make any change necessary to follow and obey what God has said, you will be of little use to God. Your greatest single difficulty in following God may come at this point of full surrender.

We tend to want to skip making adjustments and go directly from believing God to obedience. If you want to follow Him, you don't have that choice. His ways are so different from yours (see Isa. 55:9) the only way you can follow Him requires an alignment of your life to His ways.

6 **Elisha and the rich young ruler were invited to join God and His activity. Read about them in 1 Kings 19:15-21 and Luke 18:18-27, respectively; then answer the following questions.**

The LORD said to [Elijah], "Go back the way you came, and go to the Desert of Damascus. When you get there, anoint Hazael king over Aram. Also, anoint Jehu son of Nimshi king over Israel, and anoint Elisha son of Shaphat from Abel Meholah to succeed you as prophet." …

So Elijah went from there and found Elisha son of Shaphat. He was plowing with twelve yoke of oxen, and he himself was driving the twelfth pair. Elijah went up to him and threw his cloak around him. Elisha then left his oxen and ran after Elijah. "Let me kiss my father and mother good-by," he said, "and then I will come with you."

"Go back," Elijah replied. "What have I done to you?"

So Elisha left him and went back. He took his yoke of oxen and slaughtered them. He burned the plowing equipment to cook the meat and gave it to the people, and they ate. Then he set out to follow Elijah and became his attendant (1 Kings 19:15-21).

A certain ruler asked him, "Good teacher, what must I do to inherit eternal life?"

"Why do you call me good?" Jesus answered. "No one is good—except God alone. You know the commandments: 'Do not commit adultery, do not murder, do not steal, do not give false testimony, honor your father and mother.'"

"All these I have kept since I was a boy," he said.

When Jesus heard this, he said to him, "You still lack one thing. Sell everything you have and give to the poor, and you will have treasure in heaven. Then come, follow me."

When he heard this, he became very sad, because he was a man of great wealth. Jesus looked at him and said, "How hard it is for the rich to enter the kingdom of God! Indeed, it is easier for a camel to go through the eye of a needle than for a rich man to enter the kingdom of God." (Luke 18:18-23).

a. What adjustment was required of each?
   Elisha: _____
   Rich young ruler: _____

b. What was the response of each?
   Elisha: _____
   Rich young ruler: _____

The **rich ruler** desired eternal life, but he didn't want to make the necessary adjustment to Jesus. He considered his money and wealth to be more important. Jesus knew that people cannot love God completely and love money at the same time (see Matt. 6:24). Jesus asked him to put away what had become his god—his wealth. The young ruler refused to change his priorities, and he missed experiencing eternal life. The rich young ruler's love of money and his greed made him an idolater (see **Eph. 5:5**). He missed coming to know the true God and Jesus Christ, whom God had sent. He wanted to gain eternal life, but he refused to do what was necessary to obtain it.

Elisha responded much differently. He had to leave family and career (farming) to follow God's call. You may have heard the phrase *burning your bridges behind you*. Elisha burned his farm equipment and killed his 24 oxen, cooking the meat and feeding the people of the community. He was not about to turn back! When he made the necessary adjustments, he was in a position to obey God. As a result, God worked through Elisha to perform some of the greatest signs and miracles recorded in the Old Testament (see 2 Kings 2–13). Elisha had to make major changes on the front end of his call. Not until he took those actions did God work through him to accomplish the miracles.

7 **As you come to know and do God's will, in what order do the following responses come? Number them in the correct order. Refer to the seven realities on the inside back cover if you need help.**

_____ obedience   _____ adjustments   _____ faith

When God invites you to join Him, the task will have such God-sized dimensions that it will cause you to experience a crisis of belief. Your response will require faith. Faith will be demonstrated by action. The first thing you will do is adjust your life to God. The second step will be to obey what God asks you to do. You cannot go on to obedience without first making the necessary adjustments. The order is (1) faith, (2) adjustments, (3) obedience. No one can sum up all God is able to accomplish through one solitary life that is wholly yielded, adjusted, and obedient to Him!

8 **Do you want to be someone who is wholly yielded, adjusted, and obedient to God? Answer carefully!** ❑ Yes ❑ No

9 **Begin memorizing your Scripture-memory verse for this unit and review your other verses.**

Review today's lesson. Pray and ask God to identify one or more statements or Scriptures He wants you to understand, learn, or practice. Underline them. Then respond to the following.

What was the most meaningful statement or Scripture you read today?	Reword the statement or Scripture into a prayer of response to God.	What does God want you to do in response to today's study?
_____	_____	_____
_____	_____	_____
_____	_____	_____
_____	_____	_____
_____	_____	_____

Ephesians 5:5

"Of this you can be sure: No immoral, impure or greedy person—such a man is an idolater—has any inheritance in the kingdom of Christ and of God."

SUMMARY STATEMENTS

When God speaks to me to reveal what He is about to do, that revelation is my invitation to adjust my life to Him.

Adjustments prepare me for obedience.

I cannot stay where I am and go with God.

No one can sum up all God is able to accomplish through one solitary life that is wholly yielded, adjusted, and obedient to Him!

DAY 2

GOD IS INTERESTED IN ABSOLUTE SURRENDER.

Kinds of Adjustments

What kinds of adjustments are required to position your life to be used by God? Trying to answer that question is like trying to list all the things God might ask you to do. The list could be endless. However, I can point you to some examples and give you some general categories of adjustments God might ask of you.

Adjustments may be required in one or more of the following areas.
- In your circumstances—job, home, finances, and others
- In your relationships—family, friends, business associates, and others
- In your thinking—prejudices, methods, your potential, about your past, and others
- In your commitments—to family, church, job, plans, tradition, and others
- In your actions—how you pray, give, serve, and others
- In your beliefs—about God, His purposes, His ways, your relationship with Him, and others

The list could go on and on. The major adjustment will come at the point of acting on your faith. When you face a crisis of belief, you must decide what you believe about God. That mental decision may be easy. The hard part is adjusting your life to God and taking an action that *demonstrates* your faith. You may be called to attempt things only *God* can do, whereas before you may have attempted only what you knew *you* could accomplish.

1 **List at least four areas in which God may ask you to make an adjustment of your life to Him. I have given you one.**
a. *beliefs* _____
b. _____
c. _____
d. _____

2 **Now go back and write one example for each area listed. For example in the area of beliefs you may have to make an adjustment to believe that nothing is impossible with God.**

3 **Read each of the following Scriptures. What kind of adjustment was (or is) required in each? Match the Scripture on the left with the correct adjustment required on the right. Some may call for more than one type of adjustment. Write a letter or letters in each blank.**

Scriptures	Adjustments
____ 1. Matthew 4:18-22	a. In circumstances
____ 2. Matthew 5:43-48	b. In relationships
____ 3. Matthew 6:5-8	c. In thinking
____ 4. Matthew 20:20-28	d. In commitments
____ 5. Acts 10:1-20	e. In actions
	f. In beliefs

Sometimes an adjustment may involve several of these areas at once. For instance, Peter's experience with Cornelius probably required adjustments in Peter's relationships with Gentiles, his thinking and beliefs about what is religiously pure, his commitments to the traditions of the Jews, and his actions regarding fellowship with Gentiles. Being able to place a title on an adjustment is not as important as identifying what change God wants you to make to Him, His purposes, or His ways. The primary adjustments I see in the Scriptures above are 1–a; 2–b or c; 3–e; 4–b, c, or e; 5–c or f. You may have seen others.

Some people have asked whether a *major* adjustment is always involved in joining God's work. Anytime you go from where you are to where God is working, from your way of thinking to God's way of thinking, from your ways to God's ways, or from your purposes to His purposes, a *major* adjustment will be required. Now, you may make adjustments at one point in your life that will prepare you for joining God at a future time. When the time comes for obedience, you will have already adjusted to God and you will not sense a major adjustment is required.

4 **Write *major* or *minor* beside each adjustment listed below.**

_____ a. Moving from my way of thinking to God's way of thinking

_____ b. Moving from my purposes to working on God's purposes

_____ c. Moving from my way of doing things to God's ways

_____ d. Moving from my human values to God's values

Did you write *major* beside each one? The distance from where we are to where God is in any one of these areas requires a major shift. The adjustments may be gradual over time so they don't seem so major at once, but these are all huge adjustments.

Absolute Surrender

God frequently requires adjustments in areas of your life that you have never considered or been open to in the past. You may have heard someone say something like this: "Don't ever tell God something you don't want to do. That is what He will ask you to do." God is not looking for ways to make your life difficult. However, He intends to be the Lord of your life. When you identify a place where you refuse to allow His lordship, that is a place He will go to work. He is seeking absolute surrender. God may or may not require you to do the thing you identified, but He will keep working until you are willing for Him to be Lord of all. Remember, because God loves you, His will is always best! Any adjustment God expects you to make is for your good. As you follow Him, the time may come when your life and future may depend on your adjusting quickly to God's directives.

You don't adjust your life to a concept. You align your life to God. You alter your viewpoints to resemble His. You change your ways to be like His ways. After you make the necessary adjustments, He will tell you what to do next to obey Him. When you follow Him, you will experience Him doing through you something only He can do.

5 **Describe at least one adjustment you have made in your thinking as you have studied this course. For example, someone might respond, "I had to accept the fact that I cannot do anything of Kingdom value apart from God. Instead of doing things for God, I am now watching and praying to see what God wants to do through me."**

_____

_____

Any adjustment God expects you to make is for your good.

6 Read the following statements that were made by godly men. Under each statement describe the kind of adjustment the person made or was willing to make. For example, one adjustment David Livingstone was prepared to make was to live in poverty as a missionary in Africa rather than to have wealth as a physician in his homeland.

David Livingstone (medical missionary to Africa): "Forbid that we should ever consider the holding of a commission from the King of Kings a sacrifice, so long as other men esteem the service of an earthly government as an honor. I am a missionary, heart and soul. God Himself had an only Son, and He was a missionary and a physician. A poor, poor imitation I am, or wish to be, but in this service I hope to live. In it I wish to die. I still prefer poverty and missions service to riches and ease. This is my choice."[1]
Adjustment: _____

Jim Elliot (missionary to Quichua Indians in South America): "He is no fool who gives what he cannot keep to gain what he cannot lose."[2]
Adjustment: _____

Bob Pierce (established World Vision and Samaritan's Purse): "Let my heart be broken by the things that break the heart of God."[3]
Adjustment: _____

Oswald J. Smith (missionary statesman of Canada): "I want Thy plan, O God, for my life. May I be happy and contented whether in the homeland or on the foreign field; whether married or alone, in happiness or sorrow, health or sickness, prosperity or adversity—I want Thy plan, O God, for my life. I want it; oh, I want it!"[4]
Adjustment: _____

C. T. Studd (missionary to China, India, and Africa): "If Jesus Christ be God and died for me, then no sacrifice is too great for me to give for Him."[5]
Adjustment: _____

Some adjustments these men made or were willing to make include the following.
- Livingstone considered a missionary work in Africa a high honor, not a sacrifice.
- Jim Elliot was willing to give up his life for heavenly reward. He was killed by South American Indians as he sought to spread the gospel to those who had never heard about Jesus.
- Bob Pierce was ready to be brokenhearted so he could be like the Father.
- Oswald Smith wanted God's plan for his life so much that he was willing to be content with any pleasure or adversity.
- C. T. Studd was open to make any sacrifice for Jesus' sake.

7 Draw a star in the margin beside the quotation that is most meaningful to you.

"If Jesus Christ be God and died for me, then no sacrifice is too great for me to give for Him."
—C. T. Studd

8 Think about the level of commitment that is reflected in that quotation. If you are willing to make a similar commitment to the lordship of Christ, spend a few moments in prayer expressing your willingness to adjust your life to Him.

You cannot stay where you are and go with God in obedience to His will. Adjustments must come first. Then you can follow in obedience. Keep in mind that the God who calls you is also the One who will enable you to do His will. In the remainder of this unit we will study the second and third points below.

Obedience Requires Adjustments

1. You cannot stay where you are and go with God at the same time.
2. Obedience is costly to you and to those around you.
3. Obedience requires total dependence on God to work through you.

When you are willing to surrender everything in your life to the lordship of Christ, you, like Elisha, will find the adjustments are well worth the reward of experiencing God. If you have not come to the place in your life where you have surrendered *all* to His lordship, decide today to deny yourself, take up your cross, and follow Him (see Luke 9:23).

From Cannibalism to Following Christ

A pastor approached me with a wonderful testimony while I was in Hawaii speaking at a pastors and staff retreat. He and others regularly took a mission trip to the mountain region of Fiji. He showed me a picture that astounded me, so I asked him to tell me the story behind it.

In the picture a man, smiling broadly, was pointing to some rough boards nailed together and a diagram of the seven realities of *Experiencing God* with words in his language over each of the realities. Behind him was a modest, thatched-roof building with open walls. The pastor told me that this man was the chief of his people. At one time in their past this tribe had been cannibalistic and had even eaten a missionary. Now, years later, they had repented and come to faith in Christ. This man in the picture was not only their chief but also their pastor. He was teaching *Experiencing God*. What an adjustment these people had made to God!

You cannot stay where you are and go with God!

Luke 9:23
"If anyone would come after me, he must deny himself and take up his cross daily and follow me."

SUMMARY STATEMENTS

God is interested in my absolute surrender to Him as Lord.

I adjust to a Person.

Adjustments are well worth the reward of experiencing God.

The God who calls me is also the One who will enable me to do His will.

Review today's lesson. Pray and ask God to identify one or more statements or Scriptures He wants you to understand, learn, or practice. Underline them. Then respond to the following.

What was the most meaningful statement or Scripture you read today?

Reword the statement or Scripture into a prayer of response to God.

What does God want you to do in response to today's study?

Obedience Is Costly, Part I

DAY 3

OBEDIENCE IS COSTLY TO YOU.

You cannot know and do God's will without paying the price of adjustment and obedience.

You cannot stay where you are and go with God. You cannot continue doing things your way and accomplish God's purposes. Your thinking cannot come close to thinking like God. For you to do the will of God, you must adjust your life to Him, His purposes, and His ways.

1 **In this unit we are looking at three statements about adjustments and obedience. Personalize each one from your perspective by writing in the blanks *I* and *me* instead of *you*.**

1. _____ cannot stay where _____ [am] and go with God at the same time.
2. Obedience is costly to _____ and to those around _____.
3. Obedience requires total dependence on God to work through _____.

Look at the second statement: obedience is costly to you and to those around you. You cannot know and do God's will without paying the price of adjustment and obedience. Willingness to pay the price of following His will is one of the major adjustments. At this point "many of his disciples turned back and no longer followed him" (John 6:66). Many churches will not know and experience the fulfilling of God's purposes through them because they are not willing to pay the price of obedience.

While I was pastoring a wonderful church in California, I received a call from a tiny congregation in Saskatoon, Canada, that said they would have to disband their church if I could not come as their pastor. As Marilynn and I prayed, we sensed God was moving our family from our comfortable church setting to an extremely challenging assignment. After driving for several days to move to the new church field, we finally arrived. We had barely eaten lunch when a car pulled up with six men in it. They were from a community 90 miles away. They said they had been pleading with God to send them a pastor who would start a church in their community, and they asked if I would be their pastor too. For the next two years every Sunday I would teach Sunday School and preach at my home church. Then I would drive 90 miles and teach Sunday School and preach at the mission church. Then I would drive 90 miles back and preach at our evening service and then teach adults in discipleship training. Every Tuesday afternoon I would also drive to our mission and lead them in a prayer meeting. There was a cost in accepting God's invitation, but the times of fellowship with those dear believers and with my Lord as I drove those highways for countless hours were a tremendous reward.

We say Christ is Lord, and He can interrupt our plans anytime He wants. We just don't expect Him to do it. We assume He will affirm everything we are doing and never ask us to change anything we have planned. If we want God to go down the channels we have already established and protect our personal plans and programming, we are in trouble. When God invites us to join Him, we will have to make major adjustments. Such a response can be costly.

2 **Read Acts 9:1-25 and describe the adjustment Saul had to make. Describe the cost He had to pay to follow Christ.** _____

_____

_____

3 **Why do you think a cost is often required to follow Christ?** _____

_____

Saul (later named Paul) had to make a total about-face in his life direction. He went from persecuting Christians to proclaiming that Jesus was the Christ. God will ask you to follow Him in ways that will require adjustments in your plans and directions. For Paul the adjustment was costly. It even put his life at risk. You will also have to pay a price for following Christ.

The Cost: Enduring Opposition

4 **As you read the following paragraphs, underline some of the costs of obedience. I have underlined one for you.**

In Saskatoon our church clearly sensed God was calling us to start new churches all across our province. Not everyone understood or agreed with what we were doing. Some actively opposed us at almost every mission church we started. Though we were totally convinced of the awesome spiritual darkness in Canada, some people did not see it. In Regina, the capital of our province, a full-page article appeared in the paper condemning us for daring to start a new church in this city of 150,000. In our efforts to have a Bible study in Humboldt, a delegation of leaders from another church group came to my office and urged me to stop. They said our efforts were of the devil and they would oppose the Bible study. In Deschambault our pastor was met on the street and cursed by a witch doctor. From Prince Albert I received letters condemning our efforts. In Blaine Lake we were told our prayer meetings would fail.

Some in our own denomination felt we were foolish to attempt new mission churches when we were so small ourselves. We were told not to ask the denominational office for help if we got into trouble with salary support for mission pastors or other staff workers. Those who had not been with us when God spoke to us saw our efforts as presuming on God. I soon discovered that every step of faith could be interpreted as presumption by others. Only obedience and God's affirmation of our obedience would reveal that we were doing God's will.

Later, as mission churches grew, flourished, and became self-supporting, some of our critics realized this work was indeed of God. Some were even encouraged to take these same steps of faith in starting new work themselves. God helped us remain faithful to Him, with a heart full of love toward others, but that was costly.

5 **List some of the costs that we had to pay in starting new churches.**

_____

_____

_____

6 **Read 2 Corinthians 11:23-33 on the following page and underline some of the costs Paul had to pay for following and obeying Christ. I've underlined one for you.**

Are they servants of Christ? (I am out of my mind to talk like this.) I am more. I have worked much harder, been in prison more frequently, been flogged more severely, and been exposed to death again and again. Five times I received from the Jews the forty lashes minus one. Three times I was beaten with rods, once I was stoned, three times I was shipwrecked, I spent a night and a day in the open sea, I have been constantly on the move. I have been in danger from rivers, in danger from bandits, in danger from my own countrymen, in danger from Gentiles; in danger in the city, in danger in the country, in danger at sea; and in danger from false brothers. I have labored and toiled and have often gone without sleep; I have known hunger and thirst and have often gone without food; I have been cold and naked. Besides everything else, I face daily the pressure of my concern for all the churches. Who is weak, and I do not feel weak? Who is led into sin, and I do not inwardly burn?

If I must boast, I will boast of the things that show my weakness. The God and Father of the Lord Jesus, who is to be praised forever, knows that I am not lying. In Damascus the governor under King Aretas had the city of the Damascenes guarded in order to arrest me. But I was lowered in a basket from a window in the wall and slipped through his hands (2 Cor. 11:23-33).

Sometimes obedience to God's will leads to opposition and misunderstanding. Because of his obedience Paul suffered much for the cause of Christ. The beatings, imprisonments, and danger listed in 2 Corinthians 11:23-27 sound like more than one person could bear. He concluded one letter by saying, "I bear on my body the marks of Jesus" (Gal. 6:17). Paul had not had these experiences before he began to do the will of his Lord. Obedience was costly to him. Even so, Paul could still say, "I want to know Christ and the power of his resurrection and the fellowship of sharing in his sufferings, becoming like him in his death, and so, somehow, to attain to the resurrection from the dead. Not that I have already obtained all this, or have already been made perfect, but I press on to take hold of that for which Christ Jesus took hold of me" (Phil. 3:10-12).

The Apostle Paul revealed the adjustments he made to do God's will when he said, "I have become all things to all men so that by all possible means I might save some" (1 Cor. 9:22). Your adjustments and obedience to Christ may be difficult as well.

7 **Have you ever had an experience in which your adjustment or obedience to God was costly?** ❑ **Yes** ❑ **No** **If so, briefly describe that experience and the cost you had to pay.** _____

_____

David Livingstone was a 19th–century missionary from Scotland who gave his life making Christ known in Africa. Perhaps his prayer may inspire your own commitment to pay the cost of following Christ:

> Lord, send me anywhere, only go with me.
> Lay any burden on me, only sustain me.
> Sever any tie but the tie that binds me to Thyself.

8 **Practice quoting or writing your Scripture-memory verses.**

SUMMARY STATEMENTS

Obedience is costly to me and to those around me.

I cannot know and do the will of God without paying the price of adjustment and obedience.

I must adjust my plans and program to what God is doing.

Review today's lesson. Pray and ask God to identify one or more statements or Scriptures He wants you to understand, learn, or practice. Underline them. Then respond to the following.

What was the most meaningful statement or Scripture you read today?

_____
_____
_____
_____
_____

Reword the statement or Scripture
into a prayer of response to God.

_____
_____
_____
_____
_____

What does God want you to do
in response to today's study?

_____
_____
_____
_____
_____

Obedience Is Costly, Part 2

DAY 4

OBEDIENCE IS
COSTLY TO THOSE
AROUND YOU.

One of the most demanding adjustments to doing God's will is deciding to obey even when obedience is costly to those around you. You as well as those around you may have to pay a price for *your* obedience.

1 **Answer the following questions. Read the Scripture passage if you do not already know the answer.**

    a. When **Moses** was obedient and told Pharaoh to let Israel go, what did it cost **the Israelites** (see Ex. 5:1-21)? _____

    _____

    b. When **Jesus** obeyed and went to the cross, how did it affect His mother, **Mary**, as she watched Him die (see John 19:17-37)? _____

    _____

    c. When **Paul** was obedient in preaching the gospel to the Gentiles at Thessa-lonica, what happened to **Jason** (see Acts 17:1-9)? _____

    _____

When Moses obeyed God, the workload of the children of Israel was increased, and the foremen were beaten. The Israelites paid a price for Moses to do God's will. When Jesus did the Father's will and died on the cross, His mother had to suffer the agony of watching her Son be cruelly killed. Jesus' obedience put Mary through a heartbreaking experience. His obedience brought fear and pain to the disciples. For Jesus to do God's will, others had to suffer. When Paul followed God's will in preaching the gospel, others were led to respond to God's work in their own lives. Jason and some others were arrested by a rioting mob and were accused of treason because of their association with Paul. Frequently, Paul's obedience to God's will endangered the lives of those who were with Him.

You must not overlook this element in knowing and doing the will of God: God will reveal His plans and purposes to you, but your obedience will impact you and others around you. When, for instance, a couple surrender their lives to missions, it may cost those around them, such as their church and elderly parents, as well as the church where they have served, more than it affects them. Yet not obeying God would be much worse.

2 **Fill in the blanks in the following statements.**
1. You cannot _____ where you are and go with _____ at the same time.
2. Obedience is _____ to you and to those _____ you.
3. Obedience requires total dependence on God to work through you.

Check your answers on page 163.

When Marilynn and I committed ourselves to do mission work, one of the great prices we had to pay was what it would cost our children for me to be gone so much. Our oldest child was eight when we moved to Saskatoon. Our youngest child was born a few months after we arrived. I was gone from home much of the time the children were growing up. Marilynn also had to pay a high price by rearing all five children during my frequent absence.

I have heard many Christians say, "I really think God is calling me to serve Him, but after all, my children need me. I can't put my family through that." Your children certainly need your care, but do you suppose that if you obediently responded to God's activity, He would provide for your children? We did!

We believed God would honor our obedience to Him. We trusted that He would show us how to rear our children. We believed the Heavenly Father, who loves His servants, could take better care of our children than we could. We were convinced that God would show us how to relate to our children in a way that would make up for the lost time with them. I could not let God's call become an excuse for neglecting my family, but when I was obeying the Father, I could trust Him to care for my family.

We baptized three persons the first year we were in Saskatoon. After 2½ years of hard and demanding labor, we were averaging 60 in attendance. Marilynn said to me, "Henry, Richard came to me today and said he really feels sorry for you. He said, 'Dad preaches such good sermons. He gives an invitation week after week, and nobody comes forward to make a decision.'"

I went to Richard and said, "Richard, don't ever feel sorry for your father. Even if God lets me labor for 10 years and see very little results, I will hardly be able to wait for the day when He brings the harvest." I had to help Richard understand what was taking place. I explained God's promise of a future harvest in **Psalm 126:6**. God worked through me at that moment to teach my son a deeply meaningful spiritual truth.

I remember a time when **Marilynn** hit a low point. She had grown discouraged. The next Sunday after I preached, Richard came down the aisle to make a decision, saying, "I feel called to the ministry." Behind him came another young man. Marilynn had spent many hours ministering to this young man who had grown up in a troubled home. He said, "I also believe that God has called me to the ministry." Then he turned and said, "And a lot of the credit goes to Mom Blackaby."

Another young man stood in that same service and said, "I want you to know that God is also calling me to the ministry. And I want you to know that it is due largely to Mom Blackaby." At a crisis time in his life, our family had ministered to him and encouraged him to seek God's will for his life. Marilynn had done much to show him love. At this critical time for Marilynn, God encouraged her.

Psalm 126:6

He who goes out weeping, carrying seed to sow, will return with songs of joy, carrying sheaves with him.

Ultimately, all five of our children sensed God's call to vocational ministry or mission work, and all five are serving in full-time Christian ministry today. Only God could have done such a beautiful work with our children. You can trust God with your family! I would rather entrust my family to God's care than to anyone else in the world.

3 **Can you recall an experience when your family had to pay a high price for you to do God's will?** ❏ **Yes** ❏ **No** **If so, briefly describe the experience.** _____

_____

4 **Can you recall a time when you chose not to obey God because of the high cost to those around you?** ❏ **Yes** ❏ **No** **If so, briefly describe the situation.** _____

_____

5 **What are some things you know about God that could help you trust God to care for your family? List several.** _____

_____

Let Christ Communicate with His People

If you ever ask God's people to seek the mind of the Lord, be prepared to accept what they tell you. Honor what they say. I have seen some leaders ask a church, a committee, or group to pray and seek God's will in a matter. The people expressed what they sensed God was saying. Then the leader would say something like "Now let me tell you what God wants us to do." If the people of God are the body of Christ, Christ is the Head. The whole body must come to Christ for an understanding of God's will for that body. We must learn to trust Christ to communicate with His people.

6 **Suppose your church began praying for a special financial need, and a retired person sensed God wanted her to give half of her four-thousand-dollar life savings to meet that need. How do you think you would respond? Check your response.**
  ❏ a. I would refuse her gift and ask the more financially secure people to give instead.
  ❏ b. I would receive the gift, thank God for answering prayer, and weep about the high cost she had to pay for our church to do God's will.
  ❏ c. I would receive the gift, but I would try to find a way to replace the money as soon as possible.
  ❏ d. I would ask her to pray for two more weeks to make sure this is what God wanted her to do.

I had to face this situation. One of our new missions needed a building. The financial agency we were working with required that a certain percentage of the cost be paid as a downpayment in order for us to obtain the loan. The mission was extremely small, so I asked our church members if they would be willing to pray about the possibility of contributing toward the downpayment. They agreed to pray and watch to see how God would provide. **Ivah Bates**, one of our diligent pray-ers, was a widow. In addition to a small pension, she had a total of four thousand dollars in the bank to last for the rest of her life. She gave a check for two thousand dollars to the building fund.

You can trust
God with
your family!

We must learn
to trust Christ
to communi-
cate with His
people.

Because I was her pastor, many emotions went through my heart. Although I was leading our church to do what we believed God wanted us to do, my heart ached when I saw what it was costing our dear people to respond. I talked with Ivah's daughter. She said, "Don't deny my mother the right to give. She has always trusted her Lord. She wants to do that now too."

Some pastors or finance committees say, "We can't ask our people to give too often, or it will hurt our ongoing budget giving." I learned never to deny God's people the opportunity to contribute. I never tried to pressure or manipulate people to give. That was not my job. Instead, I created the opportunity and encouraged them to contribute only what God led them to donate. Most of God's people will cheerfully do God's will. Some of them will respond with generosity, counting it an honor that God has allowed them to sacrifice for Him. Some will have life-changing experiences as a result of such an opportunity.

7 Do you know of a situation in which a person or a family had to pay a high price because your church followed God's will?
❏ Yes ❏ No **If so, briefly describe the situation.** _____

_____

8 Complete the first two statements; then check your answers on page 163.
a. You cannot stay where you are and _____

_____ .

b. Obedience is costly to _____

_____ .

c. Obedience requires total dependence on God to work through you.

Hudson Taylor, a great man of prayer and faith, responded to God's call to go to China as a missionary. Because his father had already died, he had to leave his widowed mother to go to China. By the end of his life in 1905, he had been used by God to found the China Inland Mission. There were 205 preaching stations, 849 missionaries, and 125,000 Chinese Christians—a testimony of a life absolutely surrendered to God. Hudson Taylor described something of the cost he and his mother experienced as he obeyed God's will to go to China as a missionary.

9 Imagine that you are Hudson Taylor. Your father is dead, and you realize that you may never see your mother again on earth. Slowly read Taylor's account of their parting and try to imagine the emotions they must have felt.

My beloved, now sainted, mother had come to see me off from Liverpool. Never shall I forget that day, nor how she went with me into the little cabin that was to be my home for nearly six long months. With a mother's loving hand she smoothed the little bed. She sat by my side, and joined me in the last hymn that we should sing together before the long parting. We knelt down, and she prayed—the last mother's prayer I was to hear before starting for China. Then notice was given that we must separate, and we had to say good-bye, never expecting to meet on earth again.

For my sake she restrained her feelings as much as possible. We parted; and she went on shore, giving me her blessing! I stood alone on deck, and she followed the ship as we moved towards the dock gates. As we passed through the gates, and the separation really commenced, I shall never forget the cry of anguish wrung from that mother's heart. It went through me like a knife. I never knew so fully, until then, what "God so loved the world" meant. And I am quite sure that my precious mother learned more of the love of God to the perishing in that hour than in all her life before.

Praise God, the number is increasing who are finding out the exceeding joys, the wondrous revelations of His mercies, vouchsafed to those who "follow Him," and emptying themselves, leave all in obedience to His great commission.[6]

10 **Based on this brief account, answer the following questions.**
   a. What did it cost Hudson Taylor to adjust his life to God and obediently go to China? _____

   b. What did it cost Hudson's mother for him to obey God's will? _____
   _____

   c. What did they learn about God's love through this experience? _____
   _____

Leaving home and family on a dangerous mission was a costly step for Hudson Taylor to take. His mother loved the Lord so much she was willing to pay the price of releasing her son to missions. Both of the Taylors had to pay a high cost for obedience. Yet they both experienced God's love in a way they had never known before. History reveals that God rewarded the faithfulness of His servant Hudson Taylor. God used him in miraculous ways to reach interior China with the gospel of Christ.

11 **How will you respond to God when He calls you to a sacrificial commitment? Check one: ❏ Yes, Lord!   ❏ No, that costs too much.**

You may think the last question is a little premature. Not really. That is what the lordship of Christ is all about. You should be able to answer the last question without knowing anything about what God may call you to. Your whole life should be lived with the attitude of "Lord, whatever You may ask of me today or in the future, my answer is yes!" Come to the place in your life where you are willing to surrender all to Him.

SUMMARY STATEMENTS

My obedience is costly to those around me.

I can trust God to care for my family.

Don't deny others the opportunity to sacrifice for their Lord.

I need to trust Christ to communicate with His people.

Lord, whatever You may ask of me today or in the future, my answer is yes!

Review today's lesson. Pray and ask God to identify one or more statements or Scriptures He wants you to understand, learn, or practice. Underline them. Then respond to the following.

What was the most meaningful statement or Scripture you read today?	Reword the statement or Scripture into a prayer of response to God.	What does God want you to do in response to today's study?

Total Dependence on God

OBEDIENCE
REQUIRES TOTAL
DEPENDENCE ON
GOD TO WORK
THROUGH YOU.

Another adjustment that is a part of knowing and doing the will of God is your coming to a total dependence on God to complete what He wants to do through you. Jesus said our relationship with Him would be like a vine and branches. He said, "Apart from me you can do nothing" (John 15:5). When you are God's servant, you must remain in an intimate relationship with God in order for Him to complete His work through you. You must depend on God alone.

The adjustment requires moving from doing work for God according to your abilities, your gifts, your likes and dislikes, and your goals to being totally dependent on God, His working, and His resources. This is a major adjustment, and it is never easy to make.

1 **Fill in the blanks to complete the statements we have been studying in this unit.**
1. You cannot _____ where you are and go with _____ at the same time.
2. Obedience is _____ to you and to those _____ you.
3. Obedience requires _____ _____ on God to work through you.

Check your answers on page 163.

2 **Read the Scriptures in the margin and below. Notice why you must depend on God to carry out His purposes. Answer the question that follows.**

> "The Lord Almighty has sworn,
>   'Surely, as I have planned, so it will be,
>   and as I have purposed, so it will stand' " (Isa. 14:24).

> "Do not fear, for I am with you;
>   do not be dismayed, for I am your God.
> I will strengthen you and help you;
>   I will uphold you with my righteous right hand" (Isa. 41:10).

> "I am God, and there is none like me. . . .
> My purpose will stand,
>   and I will do all that I please. . . .
> What I have said, that will I bring about;
>   what I have planned, that will I do" (Isa. 46:9-11).

Why must you totally depend on God to work through you? _____
_____

John 15:5

"I am the vine; you are the branches. If a man remains in me and I in him, he will bear much fruit; apart from me you can do nothing."

1 Corinthians 15:10

"By the grace of God I am what I am, and his grace to me was not without effect. No, I worked harder than all of them—yet not I, but the grace of God that was with me."

Galatians 2:20

"I have been crucified with Christ and I no longer live, but Christ lives in me. The life I live in the body, I live by faith in the Son of God, who loved me and gave himself for me."

Without God at work in you, you can do nothing to produce Kingdom fruit. When God purposes to do something, He guarantees it will come to pass. He is the One who will accomplish what He intends to do. If you depend on anything other than God, you are asking for failure in Kingdom terms.

Once a church asked, "O God, how do You want to reach our community through us and build a great church?" God led them to start a **bus ministry** and provide transportation for children and adults to come to church. They did what God told them to do, and their church grew into a great church.

They were flattered when people from all over the country began to ask, "What are you doing to grow so rapidly?" They wrote a book on how to build great churches through a bus ministry. Thousands of churches began to buy buses to reach their communities, believing the method was the key to growth. Later many sold the buses, saying, "It didn't work for us."

It never works. *He* works! The method is never the key to accomplishing God's purposes. The key is your relationship with a Person. When you want to know how God wants you to reach your city, start a new church, or be involved in His work, ask Him. Then when He tells you, don't be surprised if you can't find any church that is doing it that same way. Why? God wants you to know Him. If you follow someone else's plan, use a method, or emphasize a program, you tend to forget about your dependence on God. You leave the relationship with God and go after a method or a program. That is spiritual adultery.

3 **Answer the following questions by checking your responses.**

    a. Where do you usually go to find out how to accomplish God's purposes for your life or for your church? Check all that apply.
- ❑ 1. I go to the bookstore or library to find a good book on the subject—one written by a person who has a reputation for success in the area.
- ❑ 2. I talk to people or churches that are successful.
- ❑ 3. I contact the denominational office and ask which program to use to get the job done.
- ❑ 4. I spend time in prayer and the Word asking God to guide me (us) to do things His way.

    b. Which of the following is most important for you to know in seeking to do God's will? Check one.
- ❑ 1. What God wants to do where I am
- ❑ 2. A successful method
- ❑ 3. What program will work best in my situation
- ❑ 4. How other people or churches are succeeding in the Lord's work

Good books, successful methods, creative programs, and others' success cannot take the place of your relationship with God. They never do the work. God does the work. Apart from Him you can do nothing (see John 15:5). By focusing on anything other than God as the answer, you rob yourself and your church from seeing God at work. You keep yourself and your church from knowing God. That is a great tragedy for many in our day. May God deliver us from that.

Does that mean God will never lead you to develop an organized program or follow a method? No. But only God has the right to tell you what to do. Don't take the initiative to decide for yourself what you will do. Wait before God until He tells you what His will is for you.

It never works! *He* works!

Only God has the right to tell you what to do.

Read the following Scriptures and circle the word *wait* in each one.

> "In the morning, O Lord, you hear my voice;
>   in the morning I lay my requests before you
>   and wait in expectation" (Ps. 5:3).

> "We wait in hope for the Lord;
>   he is our help and our shield" (Ps. 33:20).

> "Wait for the Lord
>   and keep his way.
> He will exalt you to inherit the land" (Ps. 37:34).

> "I wait for you, O Lord;
>   you will answer, O Lord my God" (Ps. 38:15).

> "They that wait upon the Lord shall renew their strength; they shall mount up with wings as eagles; they shall run, and not be weary; and they shall walk, and not faint" (Isa. 40:31, KJV).

 Why do you think you should wait until you have heard a word of direction from the Lord? _____
_____
_____

You may think of waiting as a passive, inactive time. Waiting on the Lord is anything but inactivity. While you wait on Him, pray with a passion to know Him, His purposes, and His ways. Watch circumstances and ask God to interpret them by revealing His perspective to you. Share with other believers to find out what God is saying to them. As you wait on the Lord, actively ask, seek, and knock (see Matt. 7:7-8). While you wait, continue doing the last thing God clearly told you to do. By waiting, you shift the responsibility of the outcome to God, where it belongs.

When God gives you specific guidance, He will do more through you in days and weeks than you could ever accomplish in years of labor on your own. Waiting on Him is always worth the effort. His timing and His ways are always right. Depend on Him to guide you in His way and in His timing to accomplish His purpose.

The Holy Spirit Helps You Accomplish the Father's Will

The Holy Spirit will never misunderstand the Father's will for your life. The Father has a purpose to work out through your life, and He places His Spirit in you so you don't miss it. The Spirit's job is to guide you according to the Father's will. Then He enables you to do God's will. You are completely dependent on God for the knowledge and ability to accomplish His purposes. That is why your relationship with Him is crucial. That is why you need to wait until you have heard a word from Him about His purposes and ways.

Jesus is your example of One who never failed to know and do His Father's will. Everything the Father purposed to do through His life, the Lord Jesus did immediately. What was the key to His success? He was always rightly related to the Father! If you

Matthew 7:7-8

"Ask and it will be given to you; seek and you will find; knock and the door will be opened to you. For everyone who asks receives; he who seeks finds; and to him who knocks, the door will be opened."

walk in a consistent relationship with God's provision for you—the provision of His Son, His Holy Spirit, and His own presence in your life—then you should never come to a time when you do not know God's will. Nor should there be a time when you are not enabled to carry out His will.

In Jesus we have a picture of a solitary life in a love relationship with God, consistently living out that relationship. He is the perfect example. You and I quickly realize we are a long way from that. True! But the Christ who lived His life in complete obedience is fully present in you to enable you to know and do His will. We need to adjust our lives to God and consistently live out that relationship with absolute dependence on Him. He will never fail to lead your life into the middle of His purpose and enable you to do it.

6 **On a scale of 1 to 10, how would you rate the intimacy and quality of your walk with God? Circle one: 1   2   3   4   5   6   7   8   9   10**

Why did you rate it as you did? _____

_____

7 **What, if any, adjustments do you think God wants you to make to renew a consistent, right relationship with Him?** _____

_____

Adjustments in Prayer

When our church received a directive from God, I often experienced a crisis in my prayer life. I learned more about prayer at those times than at almost any other time. Only prayer could bring about certain things, and God often waits to act until we ask. The crisis was this: was I willing to pray until God brought it about? **Mark 11:24** has challenged me about the relationship of faith and prayer.

8 **Read Mark 11:24 again and write the promise in your own words.**

_____

_____

This verse is sometimes used to teach a name-it-and-claim-it theology. *You* decide what *you* want. *You* name that in *your* request and claim it, and it's *yours*. That is a self-centered theology. Remember that only God takes the initiative. He gives you the desire to do His will (see **Phil. 2:13**). His Holy Spirit guides you to pray according to God's will (see **Rom. 8:26-28**). The God-centered approach is to allow God to lead you to pray according to His will—in the name and character of Jesus. Believe that what He has led you to pray, He Himself will bring to pass. Then continue praying in faith and watching for it to come to pass.

When God encounters you, you face a crisis of belief that may require major adjustments in your life. You need to learn how to pray. However, realize that prayer will be exceedingly costly to you. God may wake you up in the middle of the night to pray. Times may come when you pray into the night or even all night. Becoming a person of prayer will require a major adjustment of your life to God.

Another cost will come as you try to guide the people around you to pray. Many churches have never learned how to pray. The greatest untapped resource is the prayer of God's people. Helping your church become a praying church will be a rewarding experience., but prayer will be costly. Every church needs to be a praying church!

Mark 11:24

"Whatever you ask for in prayer, believe that you have received it, and it will be yours."

Philippians 2:13

"It is God who works in you to will and to act according to his good purpose."

Romans 8:26-28

"The Spirit helps us in our weakness. We do not know what we ought to pray for, but the Spirit himself intercedes for us with groans that words cannot express. And he who searches our hearts knows the mind of the Spirit, because the Spirit intercedes for the saints in accordance with God's will. And we know that in all things God works for the good of those who love him, who have been called according to his purpose."

9 **Is your church known in your community as a house of prayer? Is your church a praying church? Which do you think is true? Check one.**
- ❑ Our church is widely known as a praying church.
- ❑ Our church is becoming a praying church, but we have a long way to go.
- ❑ Our church prays some but not very effectively. We need to become a praying church.
- ❑ Honestly, our church doesn't know how to pray. Our church needs to become a praying church.

10 **What, if anything, do you think God wants to do through you with regard to prayer in your church?** _____
_____

11 **Review your Scripture-memory verses and be prepared to recite them to a partner in your small-group session this week.**

A Leper Pays the Cost for His People to Experience God

A local church that responds to God's leading is God's strategy to change a lost world. It often begins when God moves in the heart of one member. This happened in the life of an Indonesian pastor on the east coast of Java. The pastor, who knew English, studied *Experiencing God,* and his life was dramatically changed. He wanted all of his people to have the opportunity to study this material as well, but they did not know English. He began the long, arduous task of translating the entire course into the language of his people. Missionaries saw him sitting at a manual typewriter three or four hours every day translating. Because he was a leper, his hands were badly marred, and he couldn't sit still long. But his pastor's heart kept him at his typewriter day after day until his people could have the material for themselves.

When I heard this, I wept. I asked the missionary who told me the story if she could get a picture of the man at his typewriter, showing his hands. She said he was very humble and might not let her. Several years later at a large meeting in Salt Lake City, I saw the missionary running toward me holding a picture. "I've got the picture. It is for you!" I have it hanging in my prayer room, where I can pray for this dear pastor and his people and be reminded of how precious to God are His people in every local church.

Review today's lesson. Pray and ask God to identify one or more statements or Scriptures He wants you to understand, learn, or practice. Underline them. Then respond to the following.

What was the most meaningful statement or Scripture you read today?

Reword the statement or Scripture into a prayer of response to God.

What does God want you to do in response to today's study?

ADJUSTING YOUR LIFE TO GOD

DVD Message Notes

1. As long as God knows where I am, He can cause anybody in the world to know where I am.
2. The safest place in all the world for your children is the center of God's will.
3. *Repent* means you are going in the wrong direction. You need to turn around and go in a different direction. The whole kingdom of God is right next to you.
4. It is impossible for you to stay where you are and go with God at the same time.
5. A call of God requires major adjustments.

Your Notes

Unit Review

Fill in the blanks to complete the statements we studied in this unit (p. 163).

1. You cannot _____ where you are and _____ with God at the same time.
2. Obedience is _____ to _____ and to those around you.
3. Obedience requires _____ _____ on God to work through you.

Which of the following is the best way to find God's directions for your life or your church? Check only one (p. 173).

❑ a. A good book   ❑ c. God
❑ b. Other people   ❑ d. A denominational agency

Answer the following.

1. Why must you totally depend on God to work through you to accomplish Kingdom purposes (activity 2, p. 172)? _____
_____
_____

2. Why should you "wait on the Lord" (activity 5, p. 174)? _____
_____
_____

Check your answers, using the pages cited in parentheses.

1. David and Naomi Shibley, *The Smoke of a Thousand Villages* (Nashville: Thomas Nelson Publishers, 1989), 11.
2. Elisabeth Elliot, *Shadow of the Almighty: The Life and Testament of Jim Elliot* (New York: Harper & Brothers Publishers, 1958), 247.
3. Franklin Graham with Jeanette Lockerbie, *Bob Pierce: This One Thing I Do* (Waco, Texas: Word Books, 1983), 220.
4. Shibley, *Smoke*, 90.
5. Ibid., 98.
6. J. Hudson Taylor, *A Retrospect* (Philadelphia: The China Inland Mission, n.d.), 39–40.

Scriptures Referenced

Mark 8:34-38
Matthew 10:37-39
Matthew 4:13-25

Testimony

Debbie Stuart

Sharing Time

- One of the most meaningful statements or Scriptures from this unit's lessons and your prayer response to God. Choose one from pages 159, 163, 167, 171, and 176.
- Adjustments you have made in your thinking during this course (activity 5, p. 161)
- The quotation that was most meaningful and why (activity 7, p. 162)
- An experience in which costly adjustment or obedience was required (activity 7, p. 166)
- How your church would be seen in regard to prayer and what God may want you to do regarding prayer in your church (activities 9–10, p. 176)

For Makeup or Review

Audio and video downloads are available at *www.lifeway.com.*

UNIT 9

VERSE TO MEMORIZE

"JESUS REPLIED, 'IF ANYONE LOVES ME, HE WILL OBEY MY TEACHING. MY FATHER WILL LOVE HIM, AND WE WILL COME TO HIM AND MAKE OUR HOME WITH HIM.'"

JOHN 14:23

Experiencing God Through Obedience

OBEDIENCE PROVIDED FUTURE BLESSING

We were still an extremely small church, and we were trying to staff and support three mission churches. We were asked to sponsor another mission in Winnipeg, Manitoba—510 miles from our church. Someone would have to drive this 1,020-mile round trip in order to meet with the people in the mission. At first glance this sounded like an impossible task for our little group.

I shared with our congregation that a faithful group of people had been meeting for more than two years and wanted to start a church. They had approached us to sponsor them. We had to determine whether this was God's work and whether He was revealing His work to us. Was this our invitation to join Him in what He was doing? The church agreed this was God's invitation, and we knew we had to obey. We agreed to sponsor the new mission. Then we asked God to show us how and to give us strength and resources to do it.

A number of times I drove to Winnipeg to preach and minister to the people. Sooner than for any of our other mission churches, God provided a pastor and a salary. However, the story of our obedience did not end there. That original church became the mother church to many other mission churches and started an entire association of churches.

When our oldest son, Richard, finished seminary, this church in Winnipeg called him to be its pastor. A year later the church called our second son, Tom, to be the associate pastor. Little did I know that this one act of obedience, which at first appeared impossible, held such potential for future blessing for my family.

DAY 1

Obedience, Part 1

YOU COME TO KNOW GOD BY EXPERIENCE AS YOU OBEY HIM, AND HE ACCOMPLISHES HIS WORK THROUGH YOU.

REALITY 7

OBEY & EXPERIENCE

Reality 1: WORK
Reality 2: LOVE
RELATIONSHIP
Reality 3: INVITATION
Reality 4: SPEAKS
Reality 5: CRISIS
Reality 6: ADJUST
Reality 7: OBEY

John 14:15,24

"If you love me, you will obey what I command. He who does not love me will not obey my teaching."

God has always been at work in our world. He is now at work where you are. God always takes the initiative to come to you and reveal what He is doing or what He is about to do. When He does, this will be His invitation for you to join Him in His activity.

Joining Him will require you to make major adjustments in your life so He will accomplish His will through you. When you know what God has said and what He is about to do and when you have adjusted your life to Him, there is yet one remaining response to God that is necessary. To experience God at work in and through you, you must obey Him. When you obey Him, He will accomplish His work through you, and you will come to know Him by experience.

This unit focuses on the last of the seven realities: you come to know God by experience as you obey Him, and He accomplishes His work through you.

1 **See if you can state the seven realities in your own words, using the hints in the margin. Check your answers on the inside back cover.**

2 **Below are three actions in reality 7. Number them in the order they occur as you follow God's will.**
____ a. You come to know God by experience.
____ b. You obey Him.
____ c. He accomplishes His work through you.

After God has taken the initiative to involve you in His work, you believe Him and adjust your life to Him. Only then do you reach a place of obedience. You must obey Him first. Then He accomplishes His work through you. When God does a God-sized work through your life, you come to know Him intimately by experience. The answer to activity 2 is a–3, b–1, c–2. In this unit you will more fully study each of these aspects of God's work.

If You Love Him, You Obey Him

In unit 4, day 3 (pp. 61–64) you studied the relationship between love and obedience. You learned that obedience is the outward expression of your love for God (see John 14:15,24). By way of review, here are some statements from that lesson.
• Obedience is the outward expression of your love for God.
• The reward for obedience and love is that God will reveal Himself to you.
• If you have an obedience problem, you have a love problem.
• God is love. His will is always best.
• God is all-knowing. His directions are always right.
• God is all-powerful. He can enable you to do His will.
• If you love God, you will obey Him!

3 **If in the past few weeks one of the previous statements has influenced the way you love and obey God, briefly describe how in the margin.**

4 **Your memory verse for this unit speaks of love and obedience. Begin memorizing it. Write it here.** _____

_____

_____

_____

Jesus said someone who has an intimate relationship with Him ("brother," "sister," "mother") is the one who does the will of the Heavenly Father (see **Matt. 12:50**). Jesus clearly indicated a person's obedience reveals his or her love relationship with God (see John 14:15-21).

James, in his letter to believers, strongly emphasized that faith that does not result in actions is dead (see **Jas. 2:26**). When the disciples obeyed Jesus, they saw and experienced God's mighty power working in and around them. When they did not act in faith and do His will, they did not experience God's power.

In many ways obedience is your moment of truth. What you *do* will …
* reveal what you believe about God;
* determine whether you will experience His mighty work in you and through you;
* decide whether you will come to know Him more intimately.

5 **Read 1 John 2:3-6 in the margin. Circle the word *know* each time it occurs. Underline the words *obey* and *obeys*. Draw a box around the word *love*. Then answer these questions:**

a. How can you be sure you have come to know God in Jesus Christ?

_____

b. What is one clear indication that a person does not know God?

_____

c. What does God do in the life of anyone who obeys His Word?

_____

6 **As a review of unit 4, fill in each blank in the following statements with the correct word from the following list.**

force   enable   right   true   best

a. Because God is love, His will is always _____.
b. Because God is all-knowing, His directives are always _____.
c. Because God is all-powerful, He can _____ me to do His will.

When you come to a moment of truth when you must choose whether to obey God, you will not obey Him unless you believe Him. You cannot trust Him unless you love Him. You will not love Him unless you know Him. Answers: a–best, b–right, c–enable.

The previous level of your walk with God will not be adequate for the new work God wants to do through you. Each new command of Jesus will require a fresh knowledge and understanding of Him. The Holy Spirit will teach you about Jesus so you can trust Him and obey Him. Then you will experience Him in new ways. This is how you grow in Him. As 1 John 2:3-6 says that when you come to know Him, you will obey Him. If you do not obey Him, that indicates you do not know Him.

Jesus stated it differently when He said, "Not everyone who says to me, 'Lord, Lord,' will enter the kingdom of heaven, but only he who does the will of my Father

---

Matthew 12:50
"Whoever does the will of my Father in heaven is my brother and sister and mother."

James 2:26
"Faith without works is dead" (KJV).

1 John 2:3-6
"We know that we have come to know him if we obey his commands. The man who says, 'I know him,' but does not do what he commands is a liar, and the truth is not in him. But if anyone obeys his word, God's love is truly made complete in him. This is how we know we are in him: Whoever claims to live in him must walk as Jesus did."

who is in heaven. Many will say to me on that day, 'Lord, Lord, did we not prophesy in your name, and in your name drive out demons and perform many miracles?' Then I will tell them plainly, 'I never knew you. Away from me, you evildoers!'" (Matt. 7:21-23). Obedience is crucial.

The Importance of Obedience

If you know God loves you, you should never question a directive from Him. It will always be right and best. When He gives you a command, you are not just to observe it, discuss it, or debate it. You are to obey it.

7 **Read the following Scriptures and circle the word *obey* in each. Answer the question that follows.**

"If you fully obey the Lord your God and carefully follow all his commands I give you today, the Lord your God will set you high above all the nations on earth. The Lord will send a blessing on your barns and on everything you put your hand to" (Deut. 28:1,8).

"If you do not obey the Lord your God and do not carefully follow all his commands and decrees I am giving you today, ... the Lord will send on you curses, confusion and rebuke in everything you put your hand to, until you are destroyed and come to sudden ruin because of the evil you have done in forsaking him" (Deut. 28:15-20).

How important is obedience? _____

8 **List benefits of obedience found in the following Scriptures.**

"Obey me, and I will be your God and you will be my people. Walk in all the ways I command you, that it may go well with you" (Jer. 7:23).
Benefit of obedience: _____

"Why do you call me, 'Lord, Lord,' and do not do what I say? I will show you what he is like who comes to me and hears my words and puts them into practice. He is like a man building a house, who dug down deep and laid the foundation on rock. When a flood came, the torrent struck that house but could not shake it, because it was well built. But the one who hears my words and does not put them into practice is like a man who built a house on the ground without a foundation. The moment the torrent struck that house, it collapsed and its destruction was complete" (Luke 6:46-49).
Benefit of obedience: _____

"Jesus answered, 'My teaching is not my own. It comes from him who sent me. If anyone chooses to do God's will, he will find out whether my teaching comes from God'" (John 7:16-17).
Benefit of obedience: _____

God blesses those who obey Him (see Deut. 28:1-14). The benefits of obedience are beyond our imagination, but they include being God's people (see Jer. 7:23), having

---

When He gives you a command, you are to obey it.

Psalm 119:33-35

"Teach me, O Lord, to follow your decrees;
then I will keep them to the end.
Give me understanding, and I will keep your law and obey it with all my heart.
Direct me in the path of your commands,
for there I find delight."

SUMMARY STATEMENTS

I come to know God by experience as I obey Him, and He accomplishes His work through me.

a solid foundation when the storms of life come against you (see Luke 6:46-49), and knowing spiritual truth (see John 7:16-17).

Rebellion against God is the opposite of obedience. Disobedience is a serious rejection of God's will. Deuteronomy 28:15-68 names some costs of disobedience. (For further study on the results of obedience and disobedience, see Deut. 30; 32.)

9 **How do you think God would describe your level of obedience to Him?**

_____

10 **What (if anything) do you know God wants you to do that you are not presently doing?** _____

_____

11 **Consider praying Psalm 119:33-35 (in the left margin) for your life.**

Review today's lesson. Pray and ask God to identify one or more statements or Scriptures He wants you to understand, learn, or practice. Underline them. Then respond to the following.

What was the most meaningful statement or Scripture you read today?

Reword the statement or Scripture into a prayer of response to God.

What does God want you to do in response to today's study?

Obedience, Part 2

Servants of God do what He commands. They obey Him. Servants do not have the option to decide what or when or how they will obey. Choosing not to obey in His way and on His timetable is rebellion, and such disobedience brings serious consequences. Delayed obedience is still disobedience.

What Is Obedience?

OBEDIENCE MEANS JOY AND UNINTERRUPTED FELLOWSHIP WITH GOD.

Many people today are self-centered They want to do their own thing. They do not consider what obedience could mean in their lives. Jesus told a parable about obedience: "What do you think? There was a man who had two sons. He went to the first and said, 'Son, go and work today in the vineyard.' 'I will not,' he answered, but later he changed his mind and went. Then the father went to the other son and said the same thing. He answered, 'I will, sir,' but he did not go" (Matt. 21:28-30).

1 Which son did his father's will? Circle one: first son   second son

2 What is the meaning of obedience? Check one.
❑ Saying you will do what is commanded   ❑ Doing what is commanded

3 At the end of each day's lesson, you are asked this question: What does God want you to do in response to today's study? Look back at your response to that question for each lesson. Pray before you begin this review, asking God to help you see your overall pattern of obedience or disobedience. Then review your response to the last question at the end of each day. Keeping in mind some of the things you have listed may be long-term commitments, mentally answer these two questions about each day's response:
   • Do I believe God clearly guided me to respond to the study that way?
   • Have I done all God has asked me to do up to this time?
Do not proceed until you have completed your review.

4 Respond to the following. If you do not have a response, go to the next item.
   a. What is one command or instruction you have obeyed? _____
   _____

   b. What is one long-term instruction to which you have only begun your obedience? _____

   c. What is one response that was probably your idea and not God's directive?
   _____

   d. What is one command you have not obeyed? _____
   _____

   e. Below is a scale from 0, complete disobedience, to 10, perfect obedience (only Jesus would qualify for a 10!). Place an X on the line to indicate how you think God would rate your obedience since you began studying this course.

   Complete Disobedience   Perfect Obedience

   0   1   2   3   4   5   6   7   8   9   10

   f. Why do you think He would rate you that way? _____
   _____

   g. If there is a level of disobedience, what do you sense is the root cause?
   _____

If this activity has not been a positive experience, don't despair. Let God use this time of evaluation to draw you back to Himself—into a relationship of loving obedience. God is interested in moving you from where you are to where He wants you to be in this love relationship. From that point you can experience all of the joys He has to offer.

Obey What You Already Know to Be God's Will

Some people want God to give them an assignment to do for Him. They vow that they will do whatever He asks. But when God observes their lives, He notices that they have not obeyed what He has already told them to do.

5 **Do you think God would give new assignments to a servant who had not obeyed what He previously commanded?** ❑ **Yes** ❑ **No** ❑ **Don't know**

When God gives you Ten Commandments, are you obeying them? When Jesus tells you to love your enemies, are you doing that? When Jesus tells your church to make disciples of all nations, are you doing all you know to obey Him? When God tells you through Scripture to live in unity with your Christian brothers and sisters, are you doing it?

God doesn't give you His commands so you can choose the ones you want to obey and neglect the rest. He wants you to obey *all* His commands from your love relationship with Him. When He sees you are faithful and obedient in a little, He will trust you with more. The Holy Spirit will guide you daily to the specific commands God wants you to obey.

Second Chances

Frequently, people ask me, "When a person disobeys God's will, does God give him or her a second chance?"

6 **Read Jonah 1:1-17 and answer these questions:**
   a. What did God ask Jonah to do (v. 2)? _____

   b. How did Jonah respond (v. 3)? _____

   c. How did God respond to Jonah (vv. 4-17)? _____

7 **Read Jonah 2:9–3:10 and answer these questions:**
   a. When God gave Jonah a second chance, how did Jonah respond (3:3)?

   _____

   b. When Jonah obeyed God, what did God do through Jonah's ministry (3:4-10)?

   _____

I am comforted to know God often gives a second chance. When God had a plan to call Nineveh to repentance, He asked Jonah to join Him in His work. Jonah disobeyed because he was prejudiced against these "pagan enemies." Jonah would have rather seen God destroy the evil city. Disobeying God is extremely serious. Jonah went through the trauma of being thrown into a raging sea and spending three days in the belly of a big fish. After Jonah confessed and repented of His disobedience, God gave him a second chance to obey.

The second time Jonah obeyed (though reluctantly). On his first day Jonah preached a one-sentence message, and God used his sermon to call 120,000 people to repentance. Jonah said, "I knew that you are a gracious and compassionate God, slow to anger and abounding in love, a God who relents from sending calamity" (Jonah 4:2).

God often gives a second chance.
_____

God's response to Jonah and Nineveh taught Jonah how deeply God cares for all peoples and wants them to experience salvation.

Some of the great people of God were broken by sin and disobedience; yet God did not give up on them. If God allowed people only one mistake, Moses would never have become the deliverer of his people. He made several mistakes (for example, see Ex. 2:11-15). Abraham began with a great walk of faith, but He made a side trip into Egypt and blew it—more than once (for example, see Gen. 12:10-20). David grievously sinned (for example, see 2 Sam. 11), and so did Peter (for example, see Matt. 26:69-75). Saul (Paul) began his mistaken "service for God" by persecuting Christians (see Acts 9:1-2).

Disobedience Is Costly

God doesn't take disobedience lightly. You read that Jonah's disobedience almost cost him his life. Moses' murder of the Egyptian consigned him to 40 years in the wilderness. David's sin with Bathsheba cost the life of his son. Paul's early ministry was greatly hindered because of his earlier murderous lifestyle: many people distrusted him because of his reputation as a persecutor of Christians.

Because God is interested in developing your character, at times He lets you proceed in your wrong direction, but He will never let you go far without disciplining you to bring you back to Him. In your relationship with God, He may let you make a wrong decision. Then the Spirit of God leads you to recognize it is not God's will, and He guides you back to the right path. He clarifies what He wants. He even takes the circumstance of your disobedience and works them together for good (see Rom. 8:28) as He corrects you and teaches you His ways.

Sometimes God does not give a second chance. Aaron's two sons, **Nadab and Abihu**, were disobedient in offering unholy incense to the Lord; and God instantly struck them dead (see Lev. 10). **Moses** stole God's glory in front of all Israel and struck the rock, saying, "Listen, you rebels, must we bring you water out of this rock?" (Num. 20:10). Notice the word *we*. God was the One who would bring water from the rock. Moses took God's glory, and God refused to take away the consequences of that disobedience: He refused to allow Moses to go with Israel into the promised land.

8 **Mark the following statements *T* (true) or *F* (false).**
____ a. God never gives second chances.
____ b. When God forgives the sin of disobedience, He also removes the consequences of the sin.
____ c. God can take the circumstances of disobedience and work them together for good for those who love Him.
____ d. God wants to develop your character.
____ e. Disobedience can be very costly.
____ f. God does not always remove the consequences of sin.

God loves you, and He wants what is best for you. That is why He gives you His commands and instructions. His instructions are not to limit or restrict you but to free you to experience the most meaningful life possible. Answers: a and b are false; the others are true.

Obedience brings joy and uninterrupted fellowship with God. A hymn by John H. Sammis reminds us of the relationship between obedience and fellowship with God:

God is interested in developing your character.

Read or sing the hymn and reflect on the benefits of obedience.

TRUST AND OBEY

When we walk with the Lord
In the Light of His Word
What a glory He sheds on our way!
Let us do His good will;
He abides with us still,
And with all who will trust and obey.
But we never can prove
The delights of His love
Until all on the altar we lay;
For the favor He shows
And the joy He bestows
Are for them who will trust and obey.

Then in fellowship sweet
We will sit at His feet
Or we'll walk by His side in the way;
What He says we will do,
Where He sends we will go;
Never fear, only trust and obey.

Refrain
Trust and obey,
for there's no other way
To be happy in Jesus,
But to trust and obey.

Affirmation

When we hear God invite us to join Him, we often want Him to give us a sign: "Lord, prove to me this is You, and then I will obey." When Moses stood before the burning bush and received his invitation to join God, God told him he would receive a sign that God sent him. God told Moses, "This will be the sign to you that it is I who have sent you: When you have brought the people out of Egypt, you will worship God on this mountain" (Ex. 3:12). In other words, "Moses, obey Me. I will deliver Israel through you. You will come to know Me as your Deliverer, and you will stand on this mountain and worship Me." God's affirmation that He had sent Moses would come after Moses obeyed, not before. This is most frequently the case in Scripture. Affirmation comes after obedience.

God is love. Trust Him and believe Him. Because you love Him, obey Him. Then you will fellowship with Him so much that you will come to know Him intimately. That affirmation will be a joyous time for you!

SUMMARY STATEMENTS

Obedience is doing what is commanded.

I should obey what I already know to be God's will.

When God sees that I am faithful and obedient in a little, He will entrust me with more.

God often gives second chances.

Sometimes God does not give a second chance.

Disobedience is costly.

God wants to develop my character.

Affirmation comes after obedience.

Review today's lesson. Pray and ask God to identify one or more statements or Scriptures He wants you to understand, learn, or practice. Underline them. Then respond to the following.

What was the most meaningful statement or Scripture you read today?

_____
_____
_____
_____
_____

Reword the statement or Scripture into a prayer of response to God.

_____
_____
_____
_____
_____

What does God want you to do in response to today's study?

_____
_____
_____
_____
_____

DAY 3

God Works Through You

YOU TOO WILL BE BLESSED WHEN GOD DOES A SPECIAL, GOD-SIZED WORK THROUGH YOU.

Reviewing Unit 7

1. When God calls you to join Him in a God-sized task, faith is always required.
2. When you face a crisis of belief, what you do next reveals what you believe about God.
3. Faith is in a Person.
4. Faith is confidence that what God has promised or said will come to pass.
5. When God speaks, He reveals what He is going to do—not what He wants you to do for Him.
6. If you have faith in the God who called you, you will obey Him, and He will bring to pass what He has purposed to do.
7. Obedience indicates your faith in God.
8. With faith you can confidently proceed to obey Him because you know He will accomplish what He purposes.

When you obey God, He will accomplish through you what He has purposed to do. When God does something through your life that only He can do, you will come to know Him more intimately. If you do not obey, you will miss some of the most exciting experiences of your life.

When God purposes to do something through you, the assignment will have God-sized dimensions. This is because God wants to reveal Himself to you and to those around you. If you can do the work in your own strength, people will not come to know God. However, if God works through you to do what only He can do, you and those around you will come to know Him.

The God-sized dimensions of an assignment from God create a crisis of belief. You must believe God is who He says He is and that He can and will do what He says He will do. When you obey Him, you must allow Him to do what He has said. He is the One who accomplishes the assignment, but He does it through you.

1 **Read the review statements from unit 7 in the margin. Circle the numbers of the ones that have been especially meaningful to you.**

2 **Briefly describe one thing God has done to bring meaning to your life through a God-sized task, faith, and obedience.** _____

_____

_____

_____

Moses Obeyed and God Accomplished

Only in the act of obedience did Moses begin to experience the full nature of God. Moses could believe in God while living in the wilderness, but he began to dramatically experience God only when he went to Egypt as God had commanded. What he began to know about God grew from his obedience to God. In Moses' life we can see this pattern of God speaking, Moses obeying, and God accomplishing what He purposed to do.

3 **Read Exodus 7:1-6 and answer these questions.**
   a. What was Moses commanded to do (v. 2)? _____

   b. What did God say He was going to do (v. 4)? _____

   c. What would be the result when Moses obeyed and God did what He said (v. 5)? _____

4 **Read Exodus 8:16-19 and answer the questions.**
   a. What did God command Moses and Aaron to do (v. 16)? _____

   b. How did Moses and Aaron respond (v. 17)? _____

c. Who turned the dust into gnats (v. 19)?   ❏ Moses and Aaron   ❏ God

We see this pattern throughout Moses' life:
- God invited Moses to join Him in what He was doing to deliver Israel.
- God told Moses what he was to do.
- Moses obeyed.
- God accomplished what He purposed to do.
- Moses and those around him came to know God more clearly and intimately.

When the people stood between the Red Sea and the oncoming Egyptian army, God told Moses to hold his staff over the sea. When Moses obeyed, God parted the sea, and the people crossed on dry ground (see Ex. 14:1-25). Then Miriam led the people in a hymn of praise describing their new understanding of God.

When the people were thirsty and had no water to drink, they complained to Moses. God told Moses to strike a rock with the staff. Moses obeyed, and God caused water to flow from the rock (see Ex. 17:1-7). We see this pattern in Moses' life again and again.

5 **The stages in this pattern of God's working through Moses are in the wrong order below. Number them in the correct order from 1 to 5.**
___ a. Moses and those around him came to know God more clearly
   and intimately.
___ b. Moses obeyed.
___ c. God told Moses what he was to do.
___ d. God accomplished what He purposed to do.
___ e. God invited Moses to join Him in what He was doing to deliver Israel.

When Noah obeyed, God preserved his family and repopulated the earth. When Abraham obeyed, God gave him a son and built a nation. When David obeyed, God made him a king. When Elijah obeyed, God sent down fire and consumed a sacrifice. Moses came to know God through experience as he obeyed Him. These people of faith came to know God by experience when they obeyed Him, and He accomplished His work through them. The correct order of stages in the pattern of God's working with Moses is e, c, b, d, a.

The Disciples Obeyed and God Accomplished

Luke recorded a beautiful experience of Jesus' disciples that follows this same pattern. Jesus invited **70 disciples** (72, NIV) to join Him in the Father's work. They obeyed and experienced God doing through them something only God could do.

6 **Read Luke 10:1-24 and answer the following questions.**
a. What did Jesus command the 70 followers to do—
   in verse 2? _____
   in verses 5 and 7? _____
   in verse 8? _____
   in verse 9? _____

b. What does verse 16 indicate about the relationship between servants
   and the Master, between the 70 and Jesus? _____
   _____
   _____

c. How do you think the 70 felt about their experience (v. 17)? _____

_____

d. What do you think the 70 came to know about God through this experience? _____

_____

Jesus gave these followers specific directions. They obeyed Him and experienced God working through them to heal people and cast out demons. Jesus told them their salvation should bring more joy than the submission of the spirits (see v. 20). Jesus praised God the Father for revealing Himself to these followers (see vv. 21-22). Then Jesus turned to His disciples and said, "Blessed are the eyes that see what you see. For I tell you that many prophets and kings wanted to see what you see but did not see it, and to hear what you hear but did not hear it" (Luke 10:23-24).

These disciples had been especially chosen by God to be involved in His work. What they saw, heard, and came to know about God was something even prophets and kings wanted to experience but could not. These disciples were truly blessed!

You will be blessed when God does a special, God-sized work through you. You will come to know Him in a way that will bring joy to your life. When other people see you experiencing God that way, they will want to know how they can experience God that way too. Be prepared to point them to God.

7 **Has God recently done something through you that caused you to rejoice?** ❏ **Yes** ❏ **No** **If so, briefly describe it.** _____

_____

If you are obedient, God will accomplish wonderful things through you. You will need to be careful that any testimony about what God has done gives glory only to Him. Pride may cause you to want to recount your experience because it makes you feel special. You will want to declare the wonderful deeds of the Lord, but you must avoid any sense of pride. Therefore, "let him who boasts boast in the Lord" (1 Cor. 1:31).

8 **Practice quoting or writing your Scripture-memory verses.**

Review today's lesson. Pray and ask God to identify one or more statements or Scriptures He wants you to understand, learn, or practice. Underline them. Then respond to the following.

What was the most meaningful statement or Scripture you read today?	Reword the statement or Scripture into a prayer of response to God.	What does God want you to do in response to today's study?

SUMMARY STATEMENTS

When I obey God, He will accomplish through me what He has purposed to do.

God wants to reveal Himself to me and to those around me.

I will be blessed when God does a special, God-sized work through me.

I need to be careful that any testimony about what God has done gives glory only to Him.

"Let him who boasts boast in the Lord" (1 Cor. 1:31).

You Come to Know God

God reveals Himself to His people by what He does. When God works through you to accomplish His purposes, you come to know Him by experience. You also come to know God when He meets a need in your life. In unit 4 you learned that in Scripture God's names indicate ways He has revealed Himself to humanity.

GOD REVEALS HIM-
SELF TO HIS PEOPLE
BY WHAT HE DOES.

1 As a review turn to page 70 and read "Knowing God by Experience." How does God reveal Himself to us? How do we come to know God?
_____
_____

In Scripture when God did something through obedient people, they came to know Him in new and more intimate ways (for examples see Ex. 31:13; Judg. 6:24; Ps. 23:1; Jer. 23:6). God revealed His personal name to Moses, "I AM WHO I AM" (Ex. 3:14). When God "became flesh and made his dwelling among us" (John 1:14), Jesus expressed Himself to His disciples by saying "I am …"

2 Read the list of I Am's of Jesus in the margin. Circle your favorite.

Jesus identified Himself with the I AM (the name of God revealed to Moses at the burning bush) of the Old Testament. Knowing and experiencing Jesus in these ways requires that you believe in Him (have faith in Him). For instance, when He says to you, "I am the way" (John 14:6), what you do next in your relationship with Him will determine whether you come to experience Him as the Way in your life. When you believe Him, adjust your life to Him, and obey what He says next, you come to know and experience Him as the Way. This is true about everything God reveals to you day by day.

The I Am's of Jesus

- "I am the bread of life" (John 6:35).
- "I am the light of the world" (John 8:12).
- "I am the gate" (John 10:9).
- "I am the good shepherd" (John 10:11).
- "I am the resurrection and the life" (John 11:25).
- "I am the way and the truth and the life" (John 14:6).
- "I am the true vine" (John 15:1).

3 Using "Names, Titles, and Descriptions of God" (p. 268), list names by which you have come to know God by experience.
_____ _____
_____ _____
_____ _____

4 Which name of God is most precious or meaningful to you at this point in your life? _____

5 Spend an extended time in prayer and thanksgiving to God for what He has revealed to you about Himself. You may want to use the worship helps on page 74 to guide your time of adoration.

6 After your time of prayer and worship, write a note in the margin or in your journal describing how you have come to know God by experience during this study of _Experiencing God_.

DAY 5

Questions and Answers

GOD WILL NEVER GIVE ME AN AS-SIGNMENT HE WILL NOT ENABLE ME TO COMPLETE.

Why Does God Seem to Work So Slowly in My Life?

Jesus had been with His disciples about three years when He said, "I have much more to say to you, more than you can now bear. But when he, the Spirit of truth, comes, he will guide you into all truth. He will not speak on his own; he will speak only what he hears, and he will tell you what is yet to come" (John 16:12-13). Jesus had more He wanted to teach them, but they were not ready to receive it. Jesus understood, however, that the Holy Spirit would continue to guide them into truth according to God's timetable.

You may be saying, "God, hurry up and make me mature." And God is saying, "I'm moving just as fast in your life as you will allow Me. When you are ready for your next lesson, I will bring a new truth into your life."

1 **Ask yourself these questions:**
- Am I responding to all God is already leading me to do?
- Have I obeyed all I already know to be His will?
- Do I really believe He loves me and will always do what is best and right?
- Am I willing to patiently wait on His timing and to obey everything I know to do in the meantime?

2 **Why do you think God sometimes works slowly in a person's life as He matures him or her?** _____

_____

Grass that is here today and gone tomorrow does not require much time to mature. A big oak tree that lives for generations requires much more time to develop. God is concerned about your life through eternity. Allow Him to take all the time He wants to shape you for His purposes. Larger assignments require longer periods of preparation.

3 **Would you be willing for God to take all the time He requires to prepare you for the assignments He has purposed for your life? If so, write a prayer to Him in the margin.**

Why Doesn't God Give Me a Big Assignment?

God might say to you, "You are asking Me to involve you in My great work, but I am trying to get you simply to understand how to believe Me. I can't give you that assignment yet." God has to lay some basic foundations in your life before you are ready for the larger tasks.

Have you ever said something like "Lord, if You just give me a great assignment, I will serve You for all I am worth"? God might respond, "I really want to, but I can't. If I gave you that kind of assignment, you would never be able to handle it. You are not ready."

Then you may argue, "Lord, I am able. I can handle it; just try me." Do you remember any of the disciples who thought they were able to handle a bigger assignment?

On the night before Jesus' crucifixion Peter said, "Lord, I am ready to go with you to prison and to death." Jesus answered, "I tell you, Peter, before the rooster crows today, you will deny three times that you know me" (Luke 22:33-34). Is it possible He also knows exactly what you would do? Trust Him. Do not insist that God give you something you think you are ready for. That could lead to your ruin.

God is far more interested in accomplishing His kingdom purposes than you are. He will move you into every assignment He knows you are ready for.

4 **How do you think you should respond when God has not given you the kind of assignment you want?** _____
_____

Let God orient you to Himself. The servant does not tell the Master what kind of task he wants. The servant waits on his Master for the assignment. Be patient and wait. Waiting on the Lord should not be an idle time for you. Let God use times of waiting to mold and shape your character. Let God use those times to purify your life and to make you a clean vessel for His service.

As you obey Him, God will prepare you for the assignment that is suitable for you. Any task, however, that comes from the Maker of the universe is important. Don't use human standards to measure the importance or value of the task God gives.

What Is Happening When I Obey and the Doors Close?

Suppose you sense God's call to a task, a place, or an assignment. You set about to do it, but everything goes wrong. Often people say, "I guess that was not God's will."

God calls you into a relationship with Himself. Be careful how you interpret circumstances. Many times we jump to a conclusion too quickly. God is moving us in one direction to tell us what He is about to do. We immediately jump to our own conclusion about what He is doing because our reasoning sounds logical. We start following the logic of our own thinking, and then nothing seems to work out. We tend to ignore our relationship with God and take things into our own hands. Don't do that.

Most of the time when God calls you or gives you a direction, He is not calling you to do something for Him. He is telling you what He is about to do where you are. For instance, God told Paul He was going to reach the Gentiles through him. God, not Paul, was going to reach the Gentiles. Paul started to go in one direction, and the Spirit prevented him (see **Acts 16:6-10**). He started to go in another direction. Again, the Spirit stopped him. What was God's original plan? To reach the Gentiles. What was Paul's problem? He was trying to figure out what he ought to do, and the door of opportunity closed. Did the door close? No. God was saying, "Listen to Me, Paul. Go and sit in Troas until I tell you where you are supposed to go."

In Troas Paul received a vision to go to Macedonia. What was happening? God's plan was to turn the gospel to the west toward Greece and Rome. God was at work in Philippi and wanted Paul to join Him.

When you begin to obey God and circumstances seem to close doors of opportunity, go back to the Lord and clarify what God said. Better yet, always try to make sure exactly what God is saying on the front end of a sense of call. Most often He is not calling you to a task but to a relationship with Him. Through that relationship He

God is far more interested in accomplishing His kingdom purposes than you are.

Acts 16:6-10

"Paul and his companions traveled throughout the region of Phrygia and Galatia, having been kept by the Holy Spirit from preaching the word in the province of Asia. When they came to the border of Mysia, they tried to enter Bithynia, but the Spirit of Jesus would not allow them to. So they passed by Mysia and went down to Troas. During the night Paul had a vision of a man of Macedonia standing and begging him, 'Come over to Macedonia and help us.' After Paul had seen the vision, we got ready at once to leave for Macedonia, concluding that God had called us to preach the gospel to them."

will do something through your life for His kingdom. If you start in a direction and then everything seems to come to a halt, go back and clarify what God said. Do not abandon what God said. Clarify what He said.

 Read about a couple who sensed God's call to student work. Watch for instructions on what to do when you begin to move in the direction you sense God is leading, but circumstances close the door. Underline or circle the instructions. I have underlined one example for you.

I talked with a wonderful couple who said God was inviting them to go to Saskatoon to do student work. They started the process for assignment as missionaries, but the mission board said no. The couple then concluded they had made a mistake about God's call. I advised them not to jump to that conclusion and cancel God's whole plan because one detail did not work out as they thought it would. Instead, I asked them to go back and <u>clarify what God had called them to do</u>. Was He calling them to missions? Was He calling them to student work? Was He calling them to Canada?

The couple sensed God was calling them to Canada and student work, so I said, "Keep that sense of call in place. Because one door closed, don't assume the assignment is canceled. Watch to see how the God who called you is going to implement what He said. When God speaks a word of direction, He will bring it to pass but in a way you might not have anticipated. Be careful not to let circumstances nullify what God said." God may have had a different city in mind for them. He may have wanted them to have a different means of financial support. Or He may have needed more time to prepare them for the assignment.

When God calls you, let Him work out the details in His timing. In the meantime, do all you know to do; then wait for the next word of instruction.

 What are some things you would do when faced with a circumstance that seemed to close the door on what you sensed God was telling you to do? After you make your list, read my suggestions in the margin.

_____
_____
_____

When Things Seem to Go Wrong

- Clarify what God said and identify what may have been your additions to what He said.
- Keep obeying what God has told you.
- Let Him work out the details in His timing.
- Do all you know to do.
- Wait on the Lord until He tells you what to do next.

God's great task is to adjust His people to Himself. It takes time for Him to shape us to be exactly what He wants us to be. Suppose you sense God is going to do something great because of what He has said to you in His Word and in prayer. You sense He is going to do it because of the way circumstances are working out and other believers (the church) agree. Then six months pass, and you still haven't seen anything significant happening. Don't become negative, depressed, or discouraged. Watch to see what God is doing in you and in the people around you to prepare you for what He is going to do. The key is your relationship with God. The God who initiates His work in a relationship with you is the One who guarantees to complete it.

How Can I Know Whether the Word I Receive Is from God, My Selfish Desires, or Satan?

Some people go to much trouble studying Satan's ways so they can identify when something appears to be his deception. I don't do that. I have determined not to focus on Satan. He is defeated. The One who is guiding me and is presently implementing His will through me is the Victor. The only way Satan can affect God's work through me is when I believe Satan and disbelieve God. Satan will always try to deceive you, but he cannot ultimately thwart what God purposes to do.

When Canadian Mounties train officers in anticounterfeiting work, they don't let a trainee see a counterfeit bill. Instead, trainees thoroughly study the genuine bill so they can readily identify anything that doesn't measure up to that standard.

7 **When you sense that God is leading you in a particular direction, you may ask yourself,** *Is this God, me, or Satan?* **How can you prepare yourself to know clearly a word from God?** _____

_____

_____

How should you approach spiritual warfare with Satan? Know the ways of God so thoroughly that if something doesn't measure up to God's ways, you will recognize it is not from Him and will turn away from it. That's what Jesus did when He was tempted. In essence Jesus said, "I understand what you are saying, Satan; but that is not the last word I had from My Father. The Scriptures say …" (see Matt. 4:1–11.) Jesus never debated with Satan. He never analyzed it. He just kept doing the last thing His Father told Him to do until the Father told Him what to do next. Our greatest weapon in spiritual warfare is obedience to God's Word.

Does God Have One Plan for My Life for Eternity?

Does God plan your life for eternity and then turn you loose to work out His intentions? God's desire is for a relationship. We get in trouble when we try to get God to tell us if He wants us to be a Christian business person, a music director, a schoolteacher, a preacher, or a missionary. We want to know if He wants us to serve in our home country or go to Japan or Canada. God doesn't usually give you a one-time assignment and leave you there forever. Yes, you may be placed in one job in one place for an extended period, but God's assignments come to you on a daily basis.

God calls you to a relationship in which He is Lord—in which you are willing to do and be anything He chooses. If you respond to Him as Lord, He may lead you to do and be things you would never have dreamed of. If you don't follow Him as Lord, you may lock yourself into a job or an assignment and miss something God wants to do through you. I've heard people say things like "God called me to be a _____, so this other thing couldn't possibly be His will." Or "My spiritual gift is _____, so this ministry couldn't be God's will for me."

God will never give you an assignment He will not enable you to complete. That is what a spiritual gift is—a supernatural empowering to accomplish the assignment God gives you. Don't focus on your talents, abilities, and interests in determining God's will. I have heard many people say, "I would really like to do that; therefore, it must be God's will." That kind of response is self-centered. Instead, become God-centered. When God is Lord, your response should be something like this: "Lord, I will do anything Your kingdom requires of me. Wherever You want me to go, I'll go. Whatever the circumstances, I'm willing to follow. If You want to meet a need through my life, I am Your servant, and I will do whatever is required."

God's desire is for a relationship.

_____

SUMMARY STATEMENTS

I will allow God to take all the time He needs to shape me for His purposes.

Any assignment that comes from the Maker of the universe is an important responsibility.

I won't ignore the relationship and take things into my own hands.

God calls me to a relationship.

Let God work out the details in His timing.

I must know the ways of God so thoroughly that if something doesn't measure up to God's ways, I will know it is not from Him and will turn away from it.

God will never give me an assignment He will not enable me to complete.

8 Suppose a teenager in your church came to you for counsel, saying, "I think God may be calling me to the ministry. Can you tell me how to know whether I should be a pastor, a missionary, or a youth minister? I want to be careful. I don't want to miss God's plan for my life." Outline what you would say.

_____

_____

_____

_____

Did you point him to God's plan as a relationship, not just a job description? Did you help him see his need to submit to Christ's lordship on a daily basis? I trust you would have helped him adopt a God-centered approach to knowing and doing God's will.

9 Review your Scripture-memory verses and be prepared to recite them to a partner in your small-group session this week.

Review today's lesson. Pray and ask God to identify one or more statements or Scriptures He wants you to understand, learn, or practice. Underline them. Then respond to the following.

What was the most meaningful statement or Scripture you read today?	Reword the statement or Scripture into a prayer of response to God.	What does God want you to do in response to today's study?
_____	_____	_____
_____	_____	_____
_____	_____	_____
_____	_____	_____
_____	_____	_____

Experiencing God: A Legacy of Life Change

My schedule was absolutely full! I was asked if I could now take on a role with two other major agencies, working with the presidents to counsel toward revival and spiritual awakening. One responsibility would be to travel extensively overseas. So I began to pray for God's guidance to know how to clear my calendar to take on added responsibilities. I began to cancel many assignments. But I came to one, Howard Payne University. I was about to cancel it when the Spirit of God put a clear check in my spirit. I was not to forgo this one. It didn't make sense to me, but the command to obey God's leading persisted. It was difficult even to get there, and so much went wrong on the way, but obedience kept ringing in my heart. I was to speak at Coggin Avenue Baptist Church on Sunday and be on campus Monday through Wednesday. It was soon obvious why God had commanded me to go: revival was breaking out! People were praying everywhere, especially the students.

On Sunday and during the days on campus, hundreds of lives were touched and radically changed. Every service, including an open luncheon for business people, was crowded. Open confession of sin broke out, testimonies were given spontaneously, people were saved, and many Christians had their faith renewed. This deep moving of God spread to other churches across Texas, then on to as many as three hundred college campuses. Lives touched during those weeks are still being greatly used by God today. When God speaks, obedience is crucial to His mighty work.

EXPERIENCING GOD THROUGH OBEDIENCE

DVD Message Notes

1. There is a difference between having Jesus as your Friend and you being a friend of Jesus.
2. Jesus clearly says, "When I look to see who's a friend of mine, there is one thing I look for, and that's obedience.
3. There is no substitute for obedience. Worship is not a substitute for obedience. Doctrine and right belief are not a substitute for obedience. Prayer is not a substitute for obedience.
4. There comes a point where you don't need to pray anymore; you just need to obey.
5. How do you experience the joy of your Master? You obey Him.
6. When God speaks, you need to obey and leave the results, the consequences to Him.
7. Obedience is always the avenue through which you find greater fellowship and intimacy with God.
8. The greatest single way you can engage in spiritual warfare is to obey whatever God tells you to do.
9. Don't ever blame anyone else for your disobedience.
10. You have all the power of heaven available to you to obey anything God tells you to do.

Your Notes

_____

_____

Unit Review

Now you have studied all seven realities of experiencing God. Using the hints below, write the seven statements in your own words.
1. God's work: _____
2. Love relationship: _____
   _____
3. God invites: _____
   _____
4. God speaks: _____
   _____
   _____
5. Crisis of belief: _____
   _____
6. Major adjustments: _____
   _____
7. Obey Him: _____
   _____

Check your answers, using the inside back cover of your book.

Scriptures Referenced

John 15:14
Luke 6:46
Isaiah 1:10-17
Matthew 25:21
Exodus 3–5

Testimony

Angela Temples

Sharing Time

- Statements that have influenced the way you love and obey God (activity 3, p. 180)
- Activity 4, page 184
- Statements that have been meaningful to you (activity 1, p. 188)
- Names by which you have come to know God by experience (activity 3, p. 191)
- One of the most meaningful statements or Scriptures from this unit's lessons and your prayer response to God. Choose one from pages 183, 187, 190, and 196.

For Makeup or Review

Audio and video downloads are available at *www.lifeway.com*.

UNIT

10

VERSE TO MEMORIZE

"In Christ we who are many form one body, and each member belongs to all the others."

ROMANS 12:5

God's Will and the Church

IVAH BATES WAS A "KNEE"

I've mentioned Ivah Bates before. A retired widow, she was one of the greatest pray-ers I have ever known. Our church was the body of Christ, and we called Ivah a knee. God put her in the body as a powerful pray-er.

When we had new believers in our church, Ivah taught them how to pray. She equipped many in our church to grow in their prayer lives. When we began our ministry to the university campus, Ivah didn't know how to reach college students. Our campus minister shared with Ivah how she could intercede for the campus. She did not change her role in the body but learned how to be the knee—the pray-er—for the campus. The students were told, "Whenever you are going to witness to somebody or have a particular assignment in our college ministry, tell Ivah about it. She will pray."

A student named Wayne said to Ivah, "Next Tuesday I will witness to Doug. Would you pray for me?" Ivah prayed through the noon hour while Wayne was witnessing. She did that every time the students told her what they were doing. The hand (Wayne) was touching the campus, but the whole body was fitly joined together to participate in that particular ministry. Each member functioned where God put it so the hand could be effective.

About three months later, a young man came down the aisle of our church during the altar call to place his trust in the Lord for salvation. I said to the congregation, "This is Doug. He has just become a Christian." I looked at Ivah, who was deeply moved and weeping. She had never met Doug, but she had prayed for him for three months. Who won Doug to the Lord? The body did!

The Church

WHEN A CHURCH ALLOWS GOD'S PRESENCE AND ACTIVITY TO BE EXPRESSED, A WATCHING WORLD WILL BE DRAWN TO HIM.

Church members need to know how to walk with God and to know how to hear Him speaking. They need to be able to identify things only God can do. As a pastor I was responsible for teaching members these things. During the first year of my ministry as a pastor, I took time to find out what God had been doing in the church before I arrived. Then I sought to lead members into the kind of relationship with God in which they understood what a church was and how it was to function.

In the Bible God gave direction to people and enabled the spiritual leaders He called. These leaders then led the people. Their walk with God and their sensitivity to what God was doing among the people were crucial. A picture of this pattern is seen in Acts 6.

Perhaps one of the greatest challenges for Christianity in our day is for churches to walk with God so closely that the world comes to know Him through their witness. When a church allows God's presence and activity to be expressed through them, a watching world will be drawn to Him. How can your church be that kind of congregation? First you must understand who you are in relation to God and to one another:

1. A church is a creation of Christ. He builds His church (see Matt. 16:18), using Spirit-directed pastors and leaders (see Eph. 4:11-13); therefore, spiritual leaders and members should respect the pastor. God also arranges the members in the church according to His will (see 1 Cor. 12:18). Every member has been placed in the church according to God's plan to accomplish His purpose for that place and time.
2. A church is a living body of Christ with many members (see 1 Cor. 12:27). The church is not a building or an organization. It is a group of people built into a living body.
3. A church is uniquely related to Christ as Head of the body (see Eph. 1:22; 4:15-16). All matters in a church are to come under His lordship.
4. Members of a church are uniquely related to every other member of the church (see 1 Cor. 12; Eph. 4:11-16). All members are interdependent and need one another.
5. A church is on mission with Christ in our world to carry out the Father's redemptive purposes (see Matt. 28:18-20; 2 Cor. 5:17-20). "We are God's fellow workers" (1 Cor. 3:9).

1 **In each of the following pairs of statements, one is human-centered, and one is God-centered. Check the God-centered statements.**
   a. ❑ (1) An effective church is built by strong leadership, the active participation of the laity, and good organization.
   ❑ (2) Christ builds His church through the Holy-Spirit-empowered service of the pastor, other spiritual leaders, and members of His body.
   b. ❑ (1) Jesus Christ gives life to the church, which is His living body.
   ❑ (2) A church is a group of people who have been effectively organized into an institution in a local community.
   c. ❑ (1) Every church needs a CEO and a board of directors.
   ❑ (2) Christ is the Head of the church.

    d. ❏ (1) When the church gathers, members experience God at work
            in the body through the lives of other members.
      ❏ (2) Church attendance is important to show our support for the organization.
    e. ❏ (1) A church watches to see where God is at work and joins Him
            in His redemptive mission.
      ❏ (2) A church sets worthy and reachable goals, and members give
            their best to achieve them.

The God-centered statements are a–2, b–1, c–2, d–1, e–1. God works through the pastor, other spiritual leaders, and people in the church to accomplish His purposes. Many statements commonly used around churches indicate, however, that often we are extremely human-centered in our religious work. We give our human intelligence and abilities far more credit than they deserve. God is the One who gets the glory rightfully due Him for kingdom work.

Being Is More Important than Doing

Like individuals, churches are often more interested in what God wants them to do than in what He wants them to be. Being the kind of people who please God is far more important than doing something for Him. Yes, God wants a church to obey Him by doing what He asks. Yet He doesn't want a church to violate His commands to get a task done. Can you imagine how God must feel when a church splits because one group wanted to do something for God and the other group refused?

 Circle your opinions below.
    a. God wants a church to complete an assigned task no matter what
       the cost to the church's unity.   Yes   No
    b. God wants His people to demonstrate love above all else.   Yes   No
    c. As long as a church is working for God, it can do it in whatever way
       it chooses.   Yes   No

For some people these are tough questions. Individuals often think a work for God can be done with whatever means are necessary. They don't hesitate to violate God's written will to accomplish something they think is His plan for them. God wants His people to be holy, clean, and pure. He desires unity in the church: "There should be no division in the body" (1 Cor. 12:25). He calls members to love one another, because the world will know we are His disciples by our love (see John 13:35). God will accomplish His work through His people in ways that are consistent with His commands and His nature. The New Testament expresses God's desires for the church. Keep these in mind as we study this unit together:

> 1. God wants His people to be holy and pure.
> 2. God wants His people to display unity.
> 3. God wants His people to love one another.

1. God wants His people to be holy and pure.
2. God wants His people to display unity.
3. God wants His people to love one another.

- God is always at work in and around a local church.
- God pursues a continuing love relationship with His church that is real and personal.
- God invites a church to become involved in His work.
- When a church sees where God is at work, that is its invitation to join Him.
- God speaks by the Holy Spirit through the Bible, prayer, circumstances, and the church.
- A church will face a crisis of belief when God invites it to become involved in a work only He can accomplish. Faith and action will be required.
- A church will have to make major adjustments to join God in His work.
- A church is totally dependent on God for accomplishing tasks of Kingdom value.
- Apart from God a church can do nothing of Kingdom value.
- As a church obeys God, it will come to know Him by experience as He does wonderful things through it.

3 **Read the following Scriptures. Match each Scripture with one of the three statements in the margin. Write the number of the correct statement on the line beside each Scripture.**

____ a. "I pray … that all of them may be one, Father, just as you are in me and I am in you. May they also be in us so that the world may believe that you have sent me. May they be brought to complete unity to let the world know that you sent me" (John 17:20-21,23).

____ b. "This is the message you heard from the beginning: We should love one another. Let us not love with words or tongue but with actions and in truth. This is his command: to believe in the name of his Son, Jesus Christ, and to love one another as he commanded us" (1 John 3:11,18,23).

____ c. "Do not conform to the evil desires you had when you lived in ignorance. But just as he who called you is holy, so be holy in all you do; for it is written: 'Be holy, because I am holy' " (1 Pet. 1:14-16).

____ d. "Do everything without complaining or arguing, so that you may become blameless and pure, children of God without fault in a crooked and depraved generation, in which you shine like stars in the universe as you hold out the word of life" (Phil. 2:14-16).

____ e. "Make every effort to keep the unity of the Spirit through the bond of peace" (Eph. 4:3).

4 **How would you evaluate your church's faithfulness to these commands? Is your church holy, pure, united, and loving? Write your response**

_____

_____

Answers are a–2, b–3, c–1, d–1, e–2.

Knowing and Doing God's Will as a Church

5 **Much of what you have studied about experiencing God applies to churches as well as individuals. Review the statements in the left margin that have been restated from a church perspective.**

The list could go on. In spite of these similarities, the way a church comes to know God's will and the way an individual comes to know God's will are different. A church is the body of Christ. A body functions as one unit with spiritual leaders and members. All are interdependent; they need one another. Each leader and member of the body needs the others to fully know God's will. Each member has a role in the body (see Gal. 6:1-5), and each leader has a responsibility to equip the members of the body (see Eph. 4:11-13). The pastor is responsible *for* the body as well as *to* the body.

Suppose your eye said to your body, "Let's walk down these train tracks (see the diagram in the opposite margin). The way is all clear. Not a train is in sight." So you begin to walk down the tracks.

Then suppose your ear says to the body, "I hear a whistle in the distance behind us."

Your eye argues, "But nothing is on the track as far as *I* can see. Let's keep on walking." So your body listens only to your eye and keeps on walking.

Soon your ear says, "That whistle is getting louder and closer!"

Then your feet say, "I can feel the rumbling motion of a train coming. We better get our body off these tracks!"

6 **If this were your physical body, what would you do? Check your response.**
- ❑ a. I would get off the train tracks as soon as possible!
- ❑ b. I would take a vote of all my body parts and let the majority rule.
- ❑ c. I would try to ignore the conflict and hope it went away.
- ❑ d. I would trust my eye and keep on walking. My eye has never let me down yet.

That may have seemed like a silly question. God gave our bodies many different senses and parts. When each member does its job, the whole body works the way it should. In our physical bodies we do not take votes based on majority rule, ignore conflicting senses, or listen only to one sense and ignore the others. To live that way would be extremely dangerous.

Because a church is the body of Christ, it functions best when spiritual leaders and members share with one another what they sense God wants the church to be and do. A congregation needs to hear the whole counsel of God through its spiritual leaders and members. Then it can proceed in confidence and unity to do God's will.

7 **Briefly summarize the difference between the way a church comes to know God's will and the way an individual comes to know God's will.**

_____

_____

8 **What questions do you have about the way a church comes to know God's will?** _____

_____

9 **Your memory verse for this unit focuses on the church as a body. Write it in the margin and begin memorizing it. Then review your other memory verses.**

When God wants to reveal His will to a church, He begins by speaking to one or more individuals. Because of the nature of his call and assignment from God, this is often the pastor, although it may be another member of the body. The pastor's job is to bear witness to the church about what he senses God is saying. Other members may also express what they believe God is communicating. The whole body looks to Christ—the Head of the church—for guidance. He guides all members of the body to fully understand His will.

You may have questions about how to practice these principles in your church. A church of 50 members would do this differently than one with 5,000 members. The most important factor is not a method but a relationship with a Person. Christ, the Head of His church, knows how each one can work uniquely with Him to understand His will. The Jerusalem church had more than 3,000 members, and Christ accomplished His work through them, with the guidance of the apostles as spiritual leaders.

As God moved and expressed His will to our church members, I guided them as their pastor to share with the other members of the body what they saw God doing. Everyone was given opportunities to testify, and each was encouraged to respond as God guided him or her. This happened not only in worship (usually at the close of a service) but also in prayer meetings, committee meetings, business meetings, Sunday School classes, home Bible studies, and personal conversations. Many called the church office and shared what God had said to them in their quiet times. Still others related

SUMMARY STATEMENTS

When a church allows God's presence and activity to be expressed, a watching world will be drawn to Him.

A church is on mission with Christ in our world carrying out the Father's redemptive purposes.

God wants His people to be holy and pure.

God wants His people to display unity.

God wants His people to love one another.

No one individual has the total vision for God's will for a local church.

A church needs to hear the whole counsel of God through the Bible, prayer, circumstances, and the church.

Sharing what God is doing in my life may help someone else encounter God in a meaningful way.

what they had experienced at work or at school. The entire church became experientially and practically aware of Christ's presence in our midst.

10 **When are some times members of a church body could tell others what they sense God wants the church to be and do? Include ideas from the previous paragraph and any other suggestions you may have.**

_____

_____

11 **Does your church take time for members of the body to share with the church what they sense God wants the congregation to be and do? ❑ Yes ❑ No If so, when?_____**

Sharing what God is doing in your life may help someone else encounter God in a meaningful way. For example, when someone was led to make a significant commitment to the Lord in one of our services, I gave that person an opportunity to share with the body. Sometimes that testimony prompted others to respond in a similar way.

Review today's lesson. Pray and ask God to identify one or more statements or Scriptures He wants you to understand, learn, or practice. Underline them. Then respond to the following.

What was the most meaningful statement or Scripture you read today?

_____

_____

_____

_____

_____

_____

Reword the statement or Scripture into a prayer of response to God.

_____

_____

_____

_____

_____

_____

What does God want you to do in response to today's study?

_____

_____

_____

_____

_____

_____

DAY 2

Discerning God's Will as a Body

A CHURCH COMES TO KNOW THE WILL OF GOD WHEN THE WHOLE BODY UNDERSTANDS WHAT CHRIST—THE HEAD—IS TELLING IT.

1 **Review day 5 in unit 6, "God Speaks Through the Church" (pp. 128-30). Write the most meaningful statement or Scripture you identified in that lesson. _____**

_____

_____

The church does not come to know God's will in exactly the same way an individual does. Individuals come to know God's will through an intimate love relationship with God. The Holy Spirit speaks through the Bible, prayer, circumstances, and the church to reveal Himself, His purposes, and His ways. A church comes to understand God's will when the whole body hears what Christ—the Head—is telling it.

2 **How does an individual come to know God's will?** _____

_____

3 **How does your church currently make decisions about what to be and do?** _____

_____

Before Pentecost (in the New Testament), the Holy Spirit did not dwell in the lives of all God's people. He came only on chosen individuals to accomplish God's purposes. In the Old Testament God spoke to His people through a leader—a judge, a prophet, a priest, or a king. For instance, God told Moses His will for Israel, and Moses told the people what they were to do. Israel then did what Moses said (most of the time; for an example see Num. 9:1-5).

4 **In the Old Testament how did Israel come to know God's will?**

_____

_____

Numbers 9:1-5
"The Lord spoke to Moses. … 'Have the Israelites celebrate the Passover. …' So Moses told the Israelites to celebrate the Passover, and they did so. … The Israelites did everything just as the Lord commanded Moses."

With the coming of the Holy Spirit on the church at Pentecost, God came to dwell in every believer. He created the body—a local church—so every member needed every other member. In the body of Christ, each believer has direct access to God. God can speak to any and every member of the congregation. He works through the whole body to reveal His will.

In the New Testament the Holy Spirit also led the apostles as they guided the church. God led the members and leaders in mutual interdependence as they served and made decisions. These New Testament examples illustrate joint decision making under Christ's lordship:
- Choosing Judas's replacement (see Acts 1:12-26)
- Selecting the seven (see Acts 6:1-7)
- Peter's witness to the Gentile conversions (see Acts 11:1-18)
- Sending out Barnabas and Saul (see Acts 13:1-3)
- The Jerusalem Council (see Acts 15:1-35)

Notice in these examples that different methods were used to arrive at corporate decisions. For example, the Jerusalem Council settled an important doctrinal and practical issue. After Peter and James had spoken, the "whole assembly … listened to Barnabas and Paul" (Acts 15:12) also. "Then the apostles and elders, with the whole church, decided" (Acts 15:22). "It seemed good to the Holy Spirit and to us" (Acts 15:28).

When God speaks to people about the church, they should relate to the body what they sense God is saying. As members tell what God is saying, the whole body goes to God in prayer to discern His will. In His timing God confirms to the body what He is saying. Individual opinions are not that important. God's will is crucial. No single method can be given for discerning God's will as a body. Pastors, other church leaders, and members are to have such deep relationships with God and the church body that spiritual guidance is the outcome. When Christ guides each spiritual leader and member of the body to function properly, the whole body knows and is enabled to do God's will.

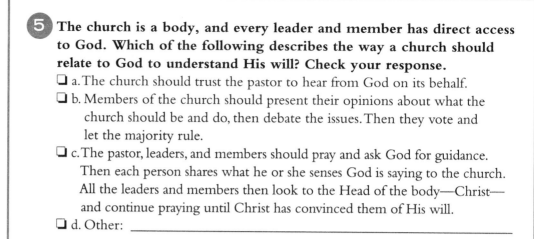

5 The church is a body, and every leader and member has direct access to God. Which of the following describes the way a church should relate to God to understand His will? Check your response.

❏ a. The church should trust the pastor to hear from God on its behalf.

❏ b. Members of the church should present their opinions about what the church should be and do, then debate the issues. Then they vote and let the majority rule.

❏ c. The pastor, leaders, and members should pray and ask God for guidance. Then each person shares what he or she senses God is saying to the church. All the leaders and members then look to the Head of the body—Christ— and continue praying until Christ has convinced them of His will.

❏ d. Other: _____

A church learns God's will when the whole body comes to understand what Christ wants it to do. For a church, knowing God's will may involve many members, not just one, although God often speaks to leaders about what He wants to do. The leaders then share with the body what they sense God is saying. The leader does not have to try to convince the church that this is God's will, nor does he have to ask the congregation to follow him without question. The leader encourages the body to go to Christ and get confirmation from the Head—Christ. The Head does the convincing on His timetable. Then the whole body follows Christ. This is why a church must learn to function as a body with Christ as its Head.

A new mission church agreed to buy land for its first building. The pastor led the church to purchase the land based on promises made by the realtor. Problems arose for the church because the realtor did not keep his commitments after closing the deal. The group ran into financial problems and grew discouraged. Finally, the pastor brought the church together and told them about the negotiations and problems. Two members said, "Pastor, we knew the realtor was dishonest because he has deceived us in business dealings before. We were afraid to disagree with your plans because it would have appeared that we were opposing God." Fortunately, God was gracious, and the problems were eventually resolved. This incident points out, however, that the church needs to function as a body, with every member free to share what he or she knows or senses as God's will.

6 How does a church come to know God's will? Write a brief summary.

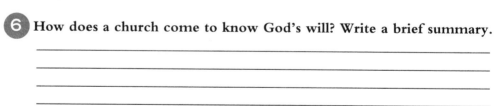

Church Decision Making

When God gave directions to our church in Saskatoon, He often provided them through members other than me, who sensed a clear direction of God and shared it with the body. We created opportunities for people to testify to what they sensed God was leading us to be or do. Our desire was not to find out who was for it and who was against it. In our business meetings we never took a vote, asking, "How many of you are for this, and how many of you are against it?" That is the wrong question. Every time you ask that question, you have a divided church, and you have acted as if our own opinions are more important than God's.

The Head
does the
convincing on
His timetable.

The right question is "With all the information we have heard and all our prayers, how many of you sense God is clearly directing us to proceed in this direction as a body?" This is a different question. It does not ask members for their opinions. It asks them to vote based on what they sense God is saying to His church. On critical issues we never voted at the time we discussed the issue. After discussion we would take time to pray and seek the mind of Christ.

Suppose 55 percent of the members voted, saying, "Yes, we sense God is clearly leading us to proceed in this direction." Forty-five percent voted saying, "We do not sense God is clearly leading us in this direction." What did we do? We never proceeded. That vote told me two things: (1) God seemed to be leading us in that direction. (2) However, the timing wasn't right, because the Head had not yet brought the rest of the body to the same sense of leading. We prayed, worked, and watched. We let the Head bring the body to understand what He wanted to do through us. God was in charge and was present to bring us to one mind and heart (see Rom. 15:5-6; **1 Cor. 1:10**). We trusted Him to do that.

People often ask, "Did you always wait until you got a 100 percent vote?" No, I knew one or more members could be out of fellowship with the Lord and couldn't hear His voice. Others might be purposely disobedient. However, we usually waited until the votes were almost unanimous.

I did not get angry or disappointed with those who did not agree with the rest of the body. Their disagreement indicated they might have a fellowship problem with the Lord. As the pastor I would place my life alongside them to see how God might want to work through me to help them return to proper fellowship with the Lord. I always prayed through this situation carefully and responded only as the Lord led me.

7 **Reflect on the following questions and check your response.**

a. Do you believe it is practical for God to bring the body to one heart and one mind about His will? ❑ Yes ❑ No

b. Do you believe God is able to bring His people to understand His will?
❑ Yes ❑ No

c. Do you believe God is able to bring your church to this kind of unity?
❑ Yes ❑ No

d. Would you be willing to wait on God until He has had time to adjust the members of the body to His will? ❑ Yes ❑ No

One evening I received a long-distance call from a man who told me he was at his church, where revival had broken out. He related that the church had scheduled a special business meeting that evening to address some extremely contentious issues. Tempers had flared, and people had leveled angry accusations at one another. Someone finally rose and tried to restore unity to the troubled and divided church. He shared that he and some others were meeting on Sunday evenings and studying *Experiencing God*. The hour before the business meeting that night, they had watched a video segment explaining how a church was to function. He suggested they all take a break from the meeting and watch a portion of the video. As they watched, the Holy Spirit brought conviction to many members who had not acted in a Christlike manner. At the close of the video segment, people rose and apologized for their behavior. Estranged church members were reconciled, and revival broke out. What had seemed

> The right question is "How many of you sense God is clearly directing us to proceed in this direction as a body?"

1 Corinthians 1:10
"I appeal to you, brothers, in the name of our Lord Jesus Christ, that all of you agree with one another so that there may be no divisions among you and that you may be perfectly united in mind and thought."

impossible only moments before was now occurring as God's people returned their focus to Him and His purposes for their church.

This may be another place where you have reached a crisis of belief. Ask God for help through this one. Can God bring a whole church to a sense of unity about His will? Yes: "May the God who gives endurance and encouragement give you a spirit of unity among yourselves as you follow Christ Jesus, so that with one heart and mouth you may glorify the God and Father of our Lord Jesus Christ" (Rom. 15:5-6).

 8 **What is God saying to you through the previous two verses?**

_____

_____

As a body we must wait on God's timing.

Good directions from God may be lost by missing God's timing. Not only does a church need to know *what* God wants it to do, but it also needs to know *when* He wants it to act. As a body we must wait on God's timing. God will seek to adjust us to Himself. Waiting on God develops confident patience in the Lord and loving trust in one another.

Real Motivation

I never tried to get members merely to support an organization, a program, or a person. Rather, I challenged them to ask God what He wanted. When they knew what God intended, the only realistic option was faithful obedience. That obedience could be and was often expressed through an organization, a program, or a ministry of the church.

9 **Which one of the following actions will best motivate God's people to faithful obedience to God's will? Check your response.**
- ❏ Ask them to find out what God wants as they walk in an intimate love relationship with Him. When He clearly speaks, they should obey Him.
- ❏ Ask them to support a program promoted by the denomination.
- ❏ Ask them to unquestioningly yield to their pastor's leadership.
- ❏ Ask them to go along with a committee's recommendation.
- ❏ Tell them, "I have a word from God" and expect them to accept it.

The churches I served had many traditions. I kept teaching until the Spirit of God, who is our common Teacher, brought us to one heart and one mind. We began to release ourselves to Him and to let God take all the time He needed. I believed my responsibility as a pastor was to lead God's people into such close relationships with Jesus Christ they would clearly know when He was speaking. Then I asked them to obey God, not follow a program, an influential lay leader, a committee, or me. God the Holy Spirit is a Christian's real Motivator.

Our business meetings became some of the most exciting times in the life of our church. People knew that at the business meeting we would clearly see God's directions and activity. They wanted to come to these meetings because they were such thrilling moments for our church to see God reveal His purposes and His ways to us.

The church is a body with Christ as its Head. The Spirit of God guides every believer. His indwelling presence can teach us and guide us. I always allowed my understanding of God's will to be tested in the life of the congregation, not because of what I thought the people were but because of what I knew the church was.

When I sensed God wanted our church to do something, as pastor I always asked the church family to work through it with me. If the people walked with God, I could

SUMMARY STATEMENTS

A church comes to know God's will when the whole body understands what Christ—the Head—is telling it.

Every believer has direct access to God.

trust God to guide them. This is true for pastors and other church members as well. If the people did not walk in right fellowship with God, I depended on God to guide me in helping them become what He wanted them to be. God doesn't give up on His people, so neither did I.

10 **What is God saying to you about your church and the way it currently makes decisions?** _____
_____
_____
_____

> Individual opinions are not that important. God's will is crucial.
>
> A church must learn to function as a body with Christ as the Head of His church.
>
> A church must wait on God's timing.

Review today's lesson. Pray and ask God to identify one or more statements or Scriptures He wants you to understand, learn, or practice. Underline them. Then respond to the following.

What was the most meaningful statement or Scripture you read today?
_____
_____
_____
_____
_____

Reword the statement or Scripture into a prayer of response to God.
_____
_____
_____
_____
_____

What does God want you to do in response to today's study?
_____
_____
_____
_____
_____

The Body of Christ, Part 1

DAY 3

Paul wrote to the church in Rome and gave the members instructions about how the body of Christ should function in relation to one another. A church needs to learn to act as the body of Christ. Paul's instructions will help you relate to your church as a member of Christ's body.

A CHURCH NEEDS TO LEARN TO FUNCTION AS THE BODY OF CHRIST.

1 **Turn in your Bible to Romans 12. Read the verses listed below and answer the questions.**
 a. Verses 1–2: What two things did Paul recommend to members of the body so the whole body would be able to discern God's will?
 • Offer your bodies as _____
 • Do not conform, but be transformed by _____

 b. Verses 3, 10, 16: What are specific things you can do to prevent problems caused by pride? _____
_____

c. Verses 4-6: "Members do not all have the same function, so in Christ we who are many form one body, and each member belongs to all the others. We have different gifts." Why are other members of the body important to you?

_____

_____

d. Verse 5 is your Scripture-memory verse this week. Write it below and begin memorizing it. _____

_____

Romans 12:9-21

❏ Love others sincerely.
❏ Bless those who persecute you.
❏ Hate evil.
❏ Rejoice with those who rejoice.
❏ Cling to what is good.
❏ Mourn with those who mourn.
❏ Be devoted to one another.
❏ Live in harmony with one another.
❏ Honor one another.
❏ Don't be proud or conceited.
❏ Serve the Lord with zeal.
❏ Associate with people of low position.
❏ Be joyful in hope.
❏ Don't repay evil for evil.
❏ Be patient in affliction.
❏ Do what is right.
❏ Be faithful in prayer.
❏ Don't take revenge.
❏ Share with God's people in need.
❏ Overcome evil with good.
❏ Practice hospitality.

e. Verses 9-21: Which of the many instructions given in these verses do you think members of your church need to practice more than they do? Read the list in the margin and check all that apply.

Living sacrifices and renewed minds are necessary to "test and approve what God's will is" (v. 2). Pride causes problems in the body. You should think of yourself with sober judgment, honor others above yourself, live in harmony, and associate with people of low position. Church members need to practice all of the instructions given in verses 9-21. Warning: following these instructions can be costly!

2 **Pause to pray for specific ways God may want your church to act more like the body of Christ.**

The Holy Spirit Equips Each Member to Function in the Body

The first part of 1 Corinthians 12 says the Holy Spirit enables each member. Verse 7 says, "To each one the manifestation of the Spirit is given for the common good" (1 Cor. 12:7). The Holy Spirit is the Gift (see Acts 2:38). The Holy Spirit manifests (makes visible, clear, known; reveals) Himself to each member of the body for the common good of the body.

3 **Check the correct answer to each of the following questions.**
a. To whom does the Spirit manifest Himself?
❏ Only to a few spiritual individuals
❏ Only to church leaders
❏ To every believer

b. Why does the Holy Spirit manifest Himself to believers?
❏ So the individual can be blessed
❏ So the individual can fulfill his or her ministry
❏ So the whole body can benefit from His work

The Holy Spirit is the Gift.

Did you check the last item in both questions? Good! All members of the church—Christ's body—are gifted with the Holy Spirit's presence. Each person's experience of the Holy Spirit is for the good of the entire body, not for himself or herself. That is why we need one another. Without a healthy, functioning body, a church will miss much of what God provides for a church.

The Old Testament is the kindergarten for understanding the Holy Spirit's work. In the Old Testament the Spirit came on individuals to help them achieve particular assignments God had given them. Moses had a task as an administrator, so God equipped him by His Holy Spirit to administer.

God gave each of the judges an assignment. Then the Spirit of God came on each one and equipped him or her to complete the assignment that was given. David was called to be the king when he was a shepherd. How could such a young, inexperienced man rule during that dangerous time? The Spirit of God came on him and equipped him for the task. Ezekiel was called to be a prophet. How could he be a prophet? Scripture says the Spirit of God came on him and caused him to do everything God asked of him (see Ezek. 2–3).

Here is the pattern we see in the Old Testament:
1. God gave an assignment to a person.
2. God gave the Holy Spirit to that person to equip him or her to accomplish the task.
3. The proof of the Spirit's presence was that the person was able to complete the assignment effectively through His supernatural enabling.

The workmen who built the tabernacle clearly illustrate this pattern. God gave Moses specific details for building the tabernacle (see Ex. 25–31). Then God said, "I have chosen **Bezalel** son of Uri, the son of Hur, of the tribe of Judah, and I have filled him with the Spirit of God, with skill, ability and knowledge in all kinds of crafts. Moreover, I have appointed **Oholiab** … to help him. Also I have given skill to all the craftsmen to make everything I have commanded you" (Ex. 31:2-3,6). How would Moses know whether the Spirit of God was on those men? He watched them at work. If God enabled them to carry out the assignment He had given, Moses would know God's Spirit was on them.

Throughout the Old Testament the Spirit of God was always present to equip individuals to carry out divine assignments. God didn't give things. He gave Himself. The Spirit manifested His presence by equipping people to function where God assigned them.

4 **What is the pattern for the Holy Spirit's work in the Old Testament? Use the hints below and describe the pattern.**
Assignment: _____
The Gift: _____
The proof: _____

When members of a church begin considering spiritual gifts, they sometimes run into difficulty by thinking God gives them a *thing,* like an ingredient called administration. He doesn't give a thing; He gives Himself. The Gift is a Person. The Holy Spirit equips you with *His* administrative ability so His administration becomes your administration. When you see a spiritual gift exercised, you are observing a manifestation of the Holy Spirit—the Holy Spirit equipping and enabling an individual with His abilities to accomplish God's work.

5 **Read John 14:10 and 1 Corinthians 12:7 in the margin. Which of the following is the better definition of spiritual gift? Check your response.**
❏ A spiritual gift is a manifestation of the Holy Spirit at work in and through a person's life for the common good of the body of Christ.
❏ A spiritual gift is a special ability God gives a person so he or she can accomplish the work God has assigned to the church.

John 14:10
"It is the Father, living in me, who is doing his work."

1 Corinthians 12:7
"To each one the manifestation of the Spirit is given for the common good."

SUMMARY
STATEMENTS

The Holy Spirit is the Gift.

A spiritual gift is a manifestation of the Holy Spirit
at work in and through a
person's life for the common
good of the body of Christ.

The Spirit decides whom
to give assignments and
enables spiritual leaders
and members to accomplish
His work.

God puts spiritual leaders
and members in the body
where He wants them to be.

The body is not complete
without all the spiritual
leaders and members God
has given the body.

Members of the body should
have equal concern for one
another.

Spiritual leaders and
members of the body have
different assignments from
God for the good of the
whole body.

Jesus said, "It is the Father, living in me, who is doing his work" (John 14:10). Even in Jesus' miracles the Father was manifesting Himself. The Father was in Jesus, and He worked through Jesus to accomplish His purposes. The first definition above focuses on God and what He does through us. The second definition focuses more on what I receive so I can do something for God or His church. Jesus said, "Apart from me you can do nothing" (John 15:5). A spiritual gift is a manifestation of God at work through you.

The Body of Christ in 1 Corinthians 12

The first part of 1 Corinthians 12 says the Holy Spirit manifests Himself in different ways. He reveals Himself in every believer. The second part of that chapter talks about the body.

6 **Read the following list of summary statements. Then read 1 Corinthians 12:11-31 and try to find at least one verse that supports each statement. Write the numbers of the verses beside the statements.**

Verse(s) _____ a. The Holy Spirit decides whom to give assignments and enables each spiritual leader and member to accomplish God's work.

Verse(s) _____ b. The body is a single unit made up of many parts.

Verse(s) _____ c. Members of the body do not determine their roles in the body.

Verse(s) _____ d. God puts spiritual leaders and members in the body where He wants them to function.

Verse(s) _____ e. The body is not complete without all the spiritual leaders and members God has given the body.

Verse(s) _____ f. Members of the body need every other member of the body.

Verse(s) _____ g. The body should be united as one, not divided.

Verse(s) _____ h. Members of the body should have equal concern for one another.

Verse(s) _____ i. Spiritual leaders and members of the body have different assignments from God for the good of the whole body.

You may have identified fewer verses or different verses, but here are some possible answers: a, verse 11; b, verses 12-14; c, verses 15-17; d, verse 18; e, verses 17-20; f, verses 21-24; g, verse 25; h, verses 25-26; i, verses 28-30.

Review today's lesson. Pray and ask God to identify one or more statements or Scriptures He wants you to understand, learn, or practice. Underline them. Then respond to the following.

What was the most meaningful statement or Scripture you read today?	Reword the statement or Scripture into a prayer of response to God.	What does God want you to do in response to today's study?

The Body of Christ, Part 2

Paul wrote to the Corinthian church, a local body of believers, "You are the body of Christ, and each one of you is a part of it" (1 Cor. 12:27). Just as your physical body needs every part in order to experience a normal and healthy life, the church depends on every member in order to live a normal, healthy church life. No member can say of any other member, "I don't need you." Apart from the other members of the church (the body) you will not be able to experience the fullness of life God intends for you. When one member is missing or is not functioning as God designed, the rest of the body will miss the fullness of life God provides for the church.

God places members in the body as it pleases Him. If He makes a person an "eye," the Holy Spirit will equip him to see. If God makes a person an "ear," the Holy Spirit will equip her to hear. If He makes a person a "hand," the Holy Spirit will equip him to function as a hand. In New Testament Scriptures describing the body of Christ, the Holy Spirit's work enables a person to function in the assignment where God puts him in the body. Not every member is an apostle, a prophet, a teacher, and so forth, but each one has a God-given function. Each one serves where God puts him or her in the body so the whole body works together as it should.

When I was a pastor, a woman in my church approached me and said she wanted to lead the church's hospital-visitation ministry. I soon discovered that despite her enthusiasm, God had not equipped her for that ministry! When I stopped by the hospital, I discovered church members weeping because this misguided woman had visited them! She invariably told the sick church member that she knew someone else who previously had the same illness—and the person had died!

I had to gently take this sincere woman aside and tell her that the Holy Spirit had clearly not equipped her for a hospital ministry. However, I said, I had noticed that God always seemed to answer when she prayed. I asked her if she would be willing to serve as an intercessor. She agreed. I gave her a long list of names of people who were not Christians to whom our church was ministering and asked her to pray for them. Soon we regularly began to see those people coming to faith in Christ. The church and I grew to depend on her for prayer about every major need in the church. Even after I left that church, I continued to call and ask her to lift me up in prayer. God had uniquely equipped this woman for a special ministry in her church body, but she needed her pastor to help her find where that place was.

1 **On the following page are some statements church members might make. They may reflect an incorrect view of the church as the body of Christ. If you heard a member of your church make the statement on the left, which biblical principle on the right could you use to help the person understand how God intends for the church to function? You may list more than one principle that may apply. Write the number of the principle beside each statement on the left. If you agree with a statement, write agree beside it. If you have serious questions about any of the statements, write your questions in the margin for discussion in your small-group session.**

I UNDERSTAND THE WILL OF GOD FOR MY CHURCH WHEN I LISTEN TO THE WHOLE BODY EXPRESS WHAT THEY ARE EXPERIENCING IN THE LIFE OF THAT BODY.

Statements	Principles
_____ a. "I think we should clean up our church's rolls and get rid of the names of people who don't attend anymore."	1. The Spirit decides whom to give assignments and enables members to accomplish His work.
_____ b. "Bill got himself into trouble by breaking the law. It serves him right to spend time in jail."	2. The body is a single unit made up of many parts.
_____ c. "I think I should be elected as the chairman of the deacons. After all, I have been a faithful member of this church for 25 years."	3. Members of the body do not determine their roles in the body.
_____ d. "If I can't be a Sunday School teacher, I'll just quit coming to this church."	4. God puts members in the body where He wants them to be.
_____ e. "I don't care that the rest of the church thinks God is leading them to ask me to serve in that role. I have never been a _____, and I know I couldn't do it. I don't have the necessary talents."	5. The body is not complete without all the members God has given the body.
_____ f. "If those 10 families can't agree with the majority, that's tough. In this church the majority rules. If they don't like what we are doing, they can go somewhere else."	6. Members of the body need every other member of the body.
_____ g. "Because God has told me what His will is for this church, you should listen to me. Anybody who doesn't agree with me is unspiritual and outside God's will."	7. The body should be united as one, not divided.
	8. Members of the body should have equal concern for one another.
	9. Members of the body have different assignments from God for the good of the whole body.

I believe each of these statements may reflect an incorrect understanding of the church as the body of Christ. Some of the principles I would use are a–5, 6; b–8; c–3, 4; d–1, 3; e–1; f–7; g–2, 5, 6. Anytime you evaluate the way a church body functions, you should keep at least three concerns in mind:

God's Concerns for the Body of Christ

1. Jesus is the Head of the body. The body ought to be Christ-centered.
2. God wants the body to maintain unity and oneness of heart.
3. Love like that described in 1 Corinthians 13 should prevail. Members of the body ought to love one another as they love themselves.

2 **In the list of three concerns above, circle one or two key words in each that might help you remember them. As you read the following responses, underline statements that will help you function correctly**

in the body of Christ. If you have questions or concerns, write them in the margin for discussion in your small-group session.

Statement a. "I think we should clean up our church's rolls and get rid of the names of people who don't attend anymore." The first question this church needs to ask is, Are these people members of the body of Christ—are they Christians? If God added them to your body because that is where He wanted them (see 1 Cor. 12:18), do you have a right to delete them? A church needs all the members God has given the body (principles 5 and 6). This church should pray and ask God to show them how to reclaim these wayward members for active fellowship.

Statement b. "Bill got himself into trouble by breaking the law. It serves him right that he has to spend time in jail." When one member suffers, everyone feels the pain (see 1 Cor. 12:26), even if the suffering is the consequence of sin. Members of Christ's body are commanded to love one another. Read 1 Corinthians 13 to see how love would respond in the body. Show concern for all members of the body (principle 8).

3 Are you remembering to underline statements that will help you function rightly in the body of Christ? Be sure to do so.

Statement c. "I think I should be elected as the chairman of the deacons. After all, I have been a faithful member of this church for 25 years." This could be a self-centered desire. We serve in the church by God's assignment (principles 3 and 4). We do not choose our own function. If God intends for you to serve in a particular capacity, the Head, Jesus Christ, can bring the rest of the body to recognize that. Will you trust Him to do that through your church?

Statement d. "If I can't be a Sunday School teacher, I'll quit coming to this church." The church needs to be sensitive to what others sense God may be leading them to do. Principles 1 and 3 focus attention on the fact that God is the One to decide where someone functions in the body. Trust Him to let the body know. A nominating committee for church-leadership positions must prayerfully discern God's will. Both the individual and the church must carefully seek God's will and trust Him to make His will clear.

Statement e. "I don't care that the rest of the body thinks God is leading them to ask me to serve in that role. I have never been a _____, and I know I couldn't do it. I don't have the necessary talents." One problem we face in the body is that we seldom see God at work. We just see people. I try to see God at work in His people. Principle 1 points out that the Holy Spirit enables a person to carry out any assignment God gives him or her. Just because you have never done something before or because you don't think you have the skills does not necessarily mean God is not giving you that assignment. Moses gave some objections like this one when God was calling him at the burning bush. Take very seriously what the body believes to be God's will. Talk to the Lord about what the body senses about you and trust God to guide you correctly.

Be willing to respond as to the Lord. Serve with all your heart as to the Lord. That assignment in your church could become an exciting place of God's activity. Don't do it just to fill a job. Do it because your Lord has led you to.

Can teaching unruly teenage boys become a special assignment from God? Shortly after I began teaching teenage boys at a church in California, 23 leather-jacketed teenagers walked into the church at the end of an evening service. None of them were Christians. God had put me in the midst of a group of hurting young people. Within three months 22 of the 23 teenagers had come to saving faith in Christ.

A church needs all the members God has given the body.

———

God decides where someone should function in the body.

———

Their changed lives broke up a gang called **the Untouchables**, and the crime rate dramatically dropped in the low-rent housing area where they lived. God can take your service in any part of the church body to impact your congregation and your world for Him.

God can display Himself anywhere in your church you are willing to let Him place you. Ask God to fill that ministry in the life of the church with His presence. You could become the catalyst to turn your church completely upside down.

4 **In statements a–e review the things you underlined that might help you function more effectively in the body of Christ. Which one strikes you as the most important for your life right now?**

_____

_____

Statement f. "If those 10 families can't agree with the majority, that's tough. In this church the majority rules. If they don't like what we are doing, they can go somewhere else." The church functions by the rule of the Head—Jesus Christ. We often settle for majority rule because we don't want to wait until the Head has time to convince the body of His will. If we are willing to sacrifice the unity of the body so the majority can have its way, we are not taking 1 Corinthians 12:25 (principle 7) seriously. Didn't Jesus pray for the unity of the church in **John 17** so the world would believe in Him? We ought to have a similar burden for unity. Give Jesus—the Head—time to do the convincing. When He has brought the body to an understanding of His will, His timing will be perfect for you to proceed! Each member is precious to God. In God's kingdom, _how_ you do something is as important as _what_ you do.

Statement g. "Because God has told me what His will is for this church, you should listen to me. Anybody who doesn't agree with me is unspiritual and outside God's will." Principles 2, 5, and 6 apply here. When the eye begins to see, the eye has a tendency to say, "Hand, why don't you see what I see? You're not spiritual." Then the hand says, "I can't see because I'm a hand." The eye has forgotten that the body is not one part but many (see 1 Cor. 12:14). The Spirit of God manifests Himself to every person. Why? For the common good. When the eye sees, it is not for the eye alone. His sight is for the body. Sight is not for the eye's sake so he can say, "I thank God I have the gift of seeing. I wish all the rest of you did too." Sight is for the body's sake. All of the other members depend on the eye to tell them what it sees. As I illustrated with the parable of the train tracks in day 1, the eye will seldom get the whole picture of what God has for a church. The body needs everyone to express what he or she senses. When the church puts together what each member senses, the body comes to know God's will. No one individual can fully know all of God's will for a church. Leaders understand God's will for the church when they listen to the whole body express what it is experiencing in the life of that body.

I may come with a sincere heart and share what I sense God is saying through me as the pastor, but I never assume I know all God has for the church. I share and then listen to what the rest of the body says. Often I find that the blending of what God is saying through me and what He is communicating through someone else is God's will. Neither one of us knew the whole will of God. At other times I share and realize the Lord wants us to begin making some adjustments, but the timing is not right to start the work now. When God brings the body to unity, we know the timing is right. What I sense God wants us to do may not be wrong; it is just not complete. I need to hear what the other members are saying in order to understand fully what God is saying to me.

John 17:20-21

"My prayer is ... that all of them may be one, Father, just as you are in me and I am in you. May they also be in us so that the world may believe that you have sent me."

SUMMARY STATEMENTS

Jesus is the Head of the body.

God is concerned about the body maintaining unity.

5 **Review your underlining in the preceding material. As the questions apply to you, respond to the following.**

a. What questions do you have that you would like to discuss in your small-group session? Write the letters: _____

b. What is one thing you think God would like to change in the way your church functions as a body? _____
_____

c. What is one thing you think God wants you to do differently as you relate to other members of the body of Christ—your church? _____
_____

6 **Practice quoting or writing your Scripture-memory verses.**

Review today's lesson. Pray and ask God to identify one or more statements or Scriptures He wants you to understand, learn, or practice. Underline them. Then respond to the following.

What was the most meaningful statement or Scripture you read today?	Reword the statement or Scripture into a prayer of response to God.	What does God want you to do in response to today's study?

Godlike love ought to prevail in the body.

God decides where I ought to function in the body.

I understand God's will for my church when I listen to the whole body express what it is experiencing in the life of that body.

Each member is precious to God.

Life in the Body

DAY 5

RIGHT RELATIONSHIPS WITH GOD ARE FAR MORE IMPORTANT THAN BUILDINGS, BUDGETS, PROGRAMS, METHODS, CHURCH PERSONNEL, SIZE, OR ANYTHING ELSE.

I was speaking at a church's morning and evening services. That morning during the altar call, a young girl came to the altar and prayed. No one from the congregation joined her, so I came to stand beside her and discovered she was praying for her nine-year-old friend to become a Christian. At the close of the evening service, I saw this same girl walking down the aisle with another girl. Sure enough, her friend was declaring her decision to become a Christian. At the close of the service, the pastor began to do what the church always did by asking the congregation to formally vote to receive the new convert into membership. I interrupted him and said, "Pastor, you are hiding the activity of God from the people!" I recounted to the congregation how God had spoken to that young girl during the morning service and how she had cried out to God for the salvation of her friend. Now, only a few hours later, we were witnessing the miracle of someone's eternal salvation, and the church was responding by merely calling for a vote of membership. That dear pastor wept before his people as he realized the church had been practicing religion but had not been watching for

217

God's activity among its members. God was actively and powerfully at work in this young girl's life. As that church learned to recognize God's activity in the life of each member, an entirely new, exciting dynamic was created in the church.

As you and your church allow God to teach you how to effectively live as a body, you will see love and unity spring forth that you may not have experienced before. Effective body life begins when each individual is rightly related to God in an intimate love relationship. It continues as all members become rightly related to Jesus Christ as the Head of the church. Right relationships with God are far more important than buildings, budgets, programs, methods, church personnel, or size.

The Scriptures teach a church body how to be rightly related to one another.

1 **Read each of the following Scriptures. Under each one write a brief statement or summary of God's will for relationships in the church body. You may want to look these up in your Bible to see the context for the verses.**

a. "Accept him whose faith is weak, without passing judgment on disputable matters. Each of us will give an account of himself to God. Therefore let us stop passing judgment on one another. Instead, make up your mind not to put any stumbling block or obstacle in your brother's way" (Rom. 14:1,12-13).
God's will: _____

b. "Nobody should seek his own good, but the good of others" (1 Cor. 10:24).
God's will: _____

c. "Each of you must put off falsehood and speak truthfully to his neighbor, for we are all members of one body" (Eph. 4:25).
God's will: _____

d. "Do not let any unwholesome talk come out of your mouths, but only what is helpful for building others up according to their needs, that it may benefit those who listen" (Eph. 4:29).
God's will: _____

e. "Get rid of all bitterness, rage and anger, brawling and slander, along with every form of malice. Be kind and compassionate to one another, forgiving each other, just as in Christ God forgave you" (Eph. 4:31–32).
God's will: _____

f. "Speak to one another with psalms, hymns and spiritual songs. Sing and make music in your heart to the Lord, always giving thanks to God the Father for everything" (Eph. 5:19–20).
God's will: _____

g. "Submit to one another out of reverence for Christ" (Eph. 5:21).
God's will: _____

h. "Bear with each other and forgive whatever grievances you may have against one another. Forgive as the Lord forgave you. And over all these virtues put on love, which binds them all together in perfect unity" (Col. 3:13–14).
God's will: _____

As you read the New Testament, you will find many instructions that speak specifically to the way God's people ought to live in relation to others. These guidelines are not in the Bible just for you to study, memorize, discuss, or debate. They are written so you can know how to experience abundant life in Christ. When you have doubts about how to apply a Scripture, take your concern to the Lord. His Spirit can help you understand spiritual truth. Here are some of my summary statements for activity 1.

1. Be patient and accepting of those whose faith is weak or those who are immature.
2. Don't be quick to judge others in matters that are disputable.
3. Don't be selfish. Seek the good of others even at your own expense.
4. Be absolutely truthful in all you say.
5. Don't be critical and tear people down with your speech. Don't focus your conversation on unwholesome subjects.
6. Be an encourager. Build people up. Keep their needs in mind as you speak.
7. Forgive one another as Christ forgave you. Don't let a root of bitterness remain between you and another.
8. Get rid of anger, inside fighting, and slander. Don't intentionally try to hurt another person (physically, emotionally, or spiritually).
9. Encourage one another in your joint worship of God. Make music together.
10. Die to self daily and submit to one another. Do this in reverence for Christ, who submitted Himself to death on the cross for you.
11. Be patient with one another, even when you have been mistreated or offended. Forgive even the worst offenses as God does.
12. Love one another.

This unit is not long enough for me to share all I want to express. You may finish today's lesson and say, "I wish Henry had told me what to do in this circumstance." I have some good news for you! You don't need for me to do that. The God who led my church to function as the body of Christ is also present in your church. Christ alone is the Head of your church. You don't need a method from me; you need instructions that are especially customized for your church from its Head. He will take the Scriptures and guide you to live in a way that will honor and please Him.

Let me take the remaining space to share about a few subjects the Lord may want to use in your life or your church.

A Covenant Relationship

First Corinthians 12:7,18 tells us God adds members to the body as it pleases Him for the common good of the whole body. When God added a member to our body, we rejoiced and immediately began talking about what being the body of Christ meant. As the pastor I led the congregation to establish a covenant relationship with the person. (A covenant is a sacred pledge or agreement.) Though I varied the process depending on the individual's experience, the covenant making usually went something like this.

I asked the persons desiring membership to briefly share their personal testimonies. Then I asked the persons to respond to the following.

• Do you affirm before this congregation that Jesus Christ is your Savior and Lord?
• Have you obediently followed the Lord in believer's baptism? (Or do you desire to follow the Lord in believer's baptism?)
• Do you clearly believe God is adding you to this body of Christ? (Or tell us how you have come to sense God is adding you to this body.)

Then I said, "God is adding you to our church for a reason. He wants to do something through your life to help us become all He wants us to become."

- Will you allow God to work through you to make this body more complete?
- Will you open your life to allow this body to minister to you and help you grow into all God wants you to become?

After the person answered these questions, I turned to the congregation and asked:

- From the testimony you have heard, do you believe God is adding this person to our body?
- Would you allow God to work in your life through him or her?
- Would you allow God to work through each of you to help this person become all God has purposed for him or her?

Then I reminded the church, "None of us know what this person may go through in the days to come. God may have added him to our body because He knew he was going to need our ministry. Will you covenant with this person to let God use you to help him become all God wants him to be? If you will so pledge yourself, please stand and let's thank God for adding this person to our body. Because God added this person to our church, we will be better equipped to respond to what God asks us to do next."

We took this covenant relationship seriously. Once a young woman asked me to remove her name from our membership roll because she had joined a cult. I told her, "We cannot do that. We entered a sacred covenant agreement with you. We believe you are making a mistake in this decision. Though you have broken your part of the covenant, we are committed to keep our covenant with you. Our church family will continue to love and pray for you. Whenever you need us, we will be here for you."

A few months later she came back, having realized that she had been deceived. She said, "Thank you for continuing to love me. Thank you for not giving up on me." That's what the body of Christ is all about. The body cares for each member of the body so that together all members become more complete in love and in Christ.

2 **Read 1 Corinthians 12 once more. Ask God to speak to you about your church and how it can better function as the body of Christ. Ask Him to speak to you about your relationship to the body of Christ. Record anything you sense God is saying to you through His Word.**

For my church: _____

For me: _____

3 **If you want to continue letting God speak through His Word, read Romans 12 again and ask God to speak to you about how you and your church can function as the body of Christ should. On a separate sheet of paper record what you sense God is saying to you.**

God Builds the Body to Match the Assignment

If you wanted to be a weightlifter, you would train your body so it could lift weights effectively. If you wanted to be a sprinter, you would train your body differently. When you want to do a job well, you train your body to match the assignment.

When God builds a local church as the body of Christ, He adds members to the body and trains them to match the assignment He has for that body. He builds a local church body in a way that enables it to respond to Him. Then God accomplishes His purposes through it.

Let me illustrate. In the early days in Saskatoon, our church had about 15 or 20 members. We sensed God wanted to use us to start churches in towns and villages all across Canada. As we prayed about this, we sensed God wanted to work through us to reach students on the university campus. We came to believe that if we would be faithful to witness on that campus, God would save many students. If we would then involve them in the life of the church, we believed God would call many of them to be pastors, church leaders, and missionaries who would dramatically impact our nation for Christ.

We had two major problems: we didn't have a single college student, and we didn't know how to reach students on a university campus. But we had an assignment. We began to pray and watch to see what God would do to help us become the kind of church that could fulfill that assignment to the campus. The first persons I baptized were a professor at the university and his daughter. Then God began to bring other students into the church, and the body began to grow.

God led us to **Robert Cannon**, an experienced college minister at a university in Texas. He sensed God was calling him to join us in Canada to work with students, but we had no money to move him or pay him. Yet Robert came, and God provided. When Robert arrived, I said, "Robert, you are here to equip the body so the body can fulfill its ministry of reaching students for Christ on the campus. The assignment for campus ministry has been given to our church."

4 Read Ephesians 4:11-13 in the margin. Do you follow what we were doing? Who had the assignment to reach the campus for Christ? Circle one: Robert Cannon   our church

5 Where did the assignment come from? _____

6 What was Robert's primary job? Check one.
❑ Start a Christian-student organization on campus.
❑ Witness door to door in the dorm.
❑ Equip the body to carry out its ministry to the campus.

The assignment came from God to the church. God added Robert to our body to equip it to carry out its ministry to the campus. Robert helped our intercessors know how to pray for the campus. He encouraged those with the gift of hospitality to link with students who needed a home away from home. He equipped others to witness. He helped the church know how to minister to the needs of the campus.

At least 50 students went on to seminaries to train for ministry. Many are now serving in churches. God built the body, gave it an assignment, and equipped it so He could accomplish His will through the members. The church was faithful, and God did what He told us He would do.

Because I know God builds the body to match the assignment, I pay close attention to the people He adds to it. Sometimes that indicates an assignment God is preparing us for. Over a short period of time, several persons in the medical profession joined our church, so we began praying to learn why God had added them to our congregation. When God assigned us to reach native Indians on reservations, this group felt led to be part of that work. They went to the reservations and provided a

Ephesians 4:11-13
"It was he who gave some to be apostles, some to be prophets, some to be evangelists, and some to be pastors and teachers, to prepare God's people for works of service, so that the body of Christ may be built up until we all reach unity in the faith and in the knowledge of the Son of God and become mature, attaining to the whole measure of the fullness of Christ"

SUMMARY STATEMENTS

Right relationships with God are far more important than buildings, budgets, programs, methods, church personnel, size, or anything else.

God doesn't add members to the body accidentally.

God builds the body to match the assignment.

God builds the body, gives it an assignment, and equips it to carry out its assignment.

I will pay close attention to the people God adds to my church.

wide variety of free medical help. While people waited in line to receive help, other members of the church talked to them and witnessed. The medical clinic opened doors for us to start Bible studies, lead people to the Lord, and start churches with the native Indians. Pay attention to the people God adds to your church.

7 **Think about the people in your congregation. Pray now and ask God to guide you and others in your church to identify the assignments He has already prepared you for.**

8 **Have any ideas come to your mind as you have prayed? Write them below.** _____

_____
_____

Continue praying for God's guidance. If the ideas grow into a burden, share with other members of the body what you are thinking and feeling. Their responses may help you understand what God wants to do in your midst.

9 **Review your Scripture-memory verses.**

Review today's lesson. Pray and ask God to identify one or more statements or Scriptures He wants you to understand, learn, or practice. Underline them. Then respond to the following.

What was the most meaningful statement or Scripture you read today?

Reword the statement or Scripture into a prayer of response to God.

What does God want you to do in response to today's study?

Enriched Fellowship and Fullness of Joy

When I wrote *Experiencing God,* I did not intend it to be a theological treatise or an exhaustive book on the Christian life. I was simply trying to share what God had taught me through Scripture and as I walked with Him and His people for many years. The result of sharing these truths with others has been incredible. It has led to opportunities for me to speak in almost two hundred countries. It has allowed me to share God's truths in churches of every size and denomination. It has brought invitations to speak a word for God at the White House and the United Nations. It has resulted in a ministry to Christian CEOs of many of America's largest companies. Most significantly for me, it has resulted in the testimonies of countless people who have shared that through this course they learned to experience God for themselves for the first time. What a joy for me to know that as God walked with an ordinary person like me, He would do so much to encourage God's people around the world. Don't settle for less than all God intends to do through your life and your church as He walks with you.

GOD'S WILL AND THE CHURCH

DVD Message Notes

1. The church is a living organism.
2. God is the Author of the church, and He has placed His Son, Jesus Christ, to be the Head of the church.
3. God is the One who builds the church.
4. God has a specific assignment for each and every church.
5. God makes the body interconnected.

Your Notes

Unit Review

In your own words write three concerns God has for the body of Christ (p. 214).

1. _____
   _____
2. _____
   _____
3. _____
   _____

Write your response to the following.

1. Why do you think God has added you to your present church body?
   _____
   _____
   _____

2. What do you do in your church that most effectively helps build up the body of Christ? _____
   _____
   _____

Check your answers, using the pages cited in parentheses. The last two questions ask for your own viewpoint.

Scriptures Referenced

1 Corinthians 12:18
1 Corinthians 12:26

Testimony

John Thomas

Sharing Time

• What you sense God is saying about the way our church makes decisions (activity 10, p. 209)
• Last two questions in the review at left
• Things that might help you function more effectively in the body (activity 4, p. 216)
• Activity 5, page 217
• Instructions from Romans 12 and 1 Corinthians 12 for your church and for you (activity 1e, p. 210, and activity 2, p. 220)
• One of the most meaningful statements or Scriptures from this unit and your prayer response to God (pp. 204, 209, 212, 217, and 222).

For Makeup or Review

Audio and video downloads are available at *www.lifeway.com*.

UNIT | II

VERSE TO MEMORIZE

"IF WE WALK IN THE LIGHT, AS
HE IS IN THE LIGHT, WE HAVE
FELLOWSHIP WITH ONE ANOTHER,
AND THE BLOOD OF JESUS, HIS
SON, PURIFIES US FROM ALL SIN."

1 JOHN 1:7

Kingdom People

A WORLD-MISSIONS STRATEGY CENTER

Gary Hillyard was the pastor of Beverly Park Church in Seattle, Washington. Church attendance ran about 110 on Sundays. Forty church members took training to learn to pray, and 8 committed themselves to pray daily for God to show them how He wanted to grow their church. Nineteen members began a study of *Experiencing God*.

When immigrants from the Ukraine began attending Beverly Park, members joined God in what He was doing. One day a new family arrived, and the man asked Gary if the church would like to have his father's house in Lugansk, a city of 650,000. Gary called me to ask to whom they should give the house. I responded that this sounded like God's invitation for the church to get involved in world missions.

Though behind in its budget, Beverly Park voted to accept the house, and members began praying. Within weeks Don English called Gary. "Do you remember our prayer time seven years ago [before the fall of Communism] when I sensed God would one day call me as a missionary to the Soviet Union? Well, God has told me that now is the time to go."

Gary replied, "I have good news for you. We have your house, and it's in Lugansk, Ukraine." Beverly Park voted to call Don and his family to be its missionaries. But Gary called me again and said the church had only $21 in the bank. "Now what do we do?" he asked.

I suggested they clarify that this was indeed the Lord's leading. Then they needed to trust the Lord to provide for what He had called them to do. And I said, "Don't hesitate to allow God's people to give." They spent their Sunday-evening service in prayer for God's provision. Following the prayer time, they had $2,400 on the front pew, including two pledges for $1,000 and $500. By the end of the week, they had $4,000 to send Don and his family to Lugansk.

Once there, Don received invitations to lead Bible studies in homes, at the elementary and high schools, for university faculty, and even for five hundred people at the medical center. When the government heard about Don, they asked to have a ceremony to thank America for their city library, which had been partially funded by the Marshal Plan following World War II. Don agreed. The national television station that broadcast the ceremony asked Don to say a few words. Less than two months into his work, Don was on national television telling the Ukraine about Jesus. Later he was invited to speak to the parliament.

Don also worked with the local churches to hold evangelistic meetings, and between four hundred and five hundred people were saved in a week. They wanted to distribute Bibles in the Lugansk region, so Don called his home church to request prayer. One hour after Beverly Park's prayer meeting, a church in Texas called and said it wanted to buy Bibles for the Ukraine. The government asked for food and medical supplies for the elderly, handicapped, and children in the city. Again Don called his home church. The next day Bob Dixon called from Texas Baptist Men. They had been asked by the State Department to oversee the distribution of food in the former Soviet republics. He had three 40-foot shipping containers of food that could be sent immediately.

Workers also started a Bible college, provided medical equipment, planted churches, and worked with orphans. In one conversation Gary wept as he explained how their church at one time had struggled to pay the electric bill. But now significant financial and personnel resources were being funneled through the little church to touch the world.

On Mission to the World

DAY 1

YOU CANNOT BE IN RELATIONSHIP WITH JESUS AND NOT BE ON MISSION.

John 20:21

"As the Father has sent me, I am sending you."

When you respond to God's invitation to an intimate love relationship with Him, He brings you into a special partnership with Himself. God has added you to a local body of believers. Together you are the body of Christ in your community. As the Head of your church, Christ Himself is guiding and working through your congregation to accomplish the will of the Father.

The Spirit who bonds you to other believers in a local church also connects you to *all* believers around the world. God's people from every local body of Christ are part of God's kingdom. Christians are kingdom people, and Christ Himself is the eternal King over His kingdom. He "has made us to be a kingdom and priests to serve his God and Father" (Rev. 1:6). In this relationship with Christ as King, you become involved in His mission to reconcile a lost world to God. To be related to Christ is to be on mission with Him. You cannot be in relationship with Jesus and not be on mission. Jesus said, "As the Father has sent me, I am sending you" (John 20:21).

God Has the World on His Heart!

"God so loved the world that he gave his one and only Son, that whoever believes in him shall not perish but have eternal life" (John 3:16). God fashioned Christ's first body by the Holy Spirit and placed Him in Mary. Christ became flesh and dwelled among us (see John 1:14). Jesus provided for our salvation through His death and resurrection. When Jesus returned to heaven, God fashioned a new body of Christ through the Holy Spirit. This body is the believers God has added to the church.

Jesus now functions as the Head of His body, the local church, to guide it in carrying out the will of the Father. God established each church as a body of Christ so He could continue His redemptive work in the world. When Christ functions as the Head of His church, God will use that body to carry out His will in every part of the earth.

1 **Reflect on the following questions. Check yes or no for each.**
   a. Did Christ know the Father's will while He was on earth?   ❏ Yes   ❏ No
   b. Did Christ ever misunderstand the Father's purposes?   ❏ Yes   ❏ No
   c. Did Christ ever fail to do the Father's will?   ❏ Yes   ❏ No
   d. If Christ is allowed to be the Head of a local congregation, will He ever misunderstand what the Father wants to achieve through that body of believers?   ❏ Yes   ❏ No
   e. Can Christ reveal to the members of His body how they are to be involved in the Father's purposes?   ❏ Yes   ❏ No

Every congregation is a world-missions strategy center.

A church is a living organism, a body with Christ as its Head. Each part of that body is related to Christ and to one another. Anytime God guides His people, He can impact a world through that congregation. Jesus gave us a commission to "go and make disciples of all nations" (Matt. 28:19). As they obey that command, every congregation is a world-missions strategy center. God can impact the world through one church if it adjusts itself to God's activity.

Impacting the World

 Read the account of Philip and the Ethiopian in Acts 8:26-39. Then answer the following questions.

a. Who guided Philip to become involved in what God was going to do for the Ethiopian (vv. 26,29)?

_____

b. At the beginning how much information did Philip have about what to do (v. 26)? _____

c. When Philip saw the Ethiopian, he was watching to see what the Father was doing. What do you think he saw of God's activity (vv. 27-28)?

_____

d. What did the Spirit tell Philip to do next (v. 29)? _____

e. How did Philip find out what God was doing in this man's life (v. 30)?

_____

f. What did God do in this Ethiopian's life through Philip (vv. 35-39)?

_____

_____

g. Based on what we know of the Ethiopian (v. 27), what impact do you think this encounter could have had on the spread of the gospel?

_____

_____

Answers: a. An angel of the Lord—the Spirit—guided Philip. b. He knew only that he was to travel south on the road from Jerusalem to Gaza. c. He saw a God-fearing man who had been to Jerusalem to worship. Because the Ethiopian was reading from Isaiah, Philip saw a man who was seeking God, a man interested in spiritual matters. Philip knew that only God could draw a person to Himself like that. d. The Spirit told Philip to approach the chariot. From that place Philip could then find out what he needed to do to join God in His activity. e. Philip asked a probing question. f. God used Philip to tell the good news about Jesus Christ. The Ethiopian believed the gospel message, was saved, and was baptized. g. God evidently had a plan for getting the gospel message to Ethiopia. He chose a key leader in the government and used Philip to lead him to Christ. God used Philip's obedience on a single day to carry the gospel to a strategic kingdom in Africa.

One Sunday while preaching in a church in Florida, I spoke about the woman at the well in John 4:1-41. I stated that when the woman faithfully shared with her countrymen what Christ had done in her life, she saw her entire region come to faith in Christ. Then I asked, "Who will be the woman at the well for those places who still do not know Jesus?" The altar call elicited a tremendous response as many people wept in prayer. One man approached me and said, "God told me I am to be the woman at the well for my people in Pakistan. A woman approached and said, "God told me I am to be the woman at the well for my country, Ghana." People from all over the world lined up to tell me God had convicted them that they were to return to their native countries to share with their people what Christ had done in their lives.

Acts 8:26-39

[26] "Now an angel of the Lord said to Philip, 'Go south to the road—the desert road—that goes down from Jerusalem to Gaza.' [27] So he started out, and on his way he met an Ethiopian eunuch, an important official in charge of all the treasury of Candace, queen of the Ethiopians. This man had gone to Jerusalem to worship, [28] and on his way home was sitting in his chariot reading the book of Isaiah the prophet. [29] The Spirit told Philip, 'Go to that chariot and stay near it.'

[30] "Then Philip ran up to the chariot and heard the man reading Isaiah the prophet. 'Do you understand what you are reading?' Philip asked.

[31] "'How can I,' he said, 'unless someone explains it to me?' So he invited Philip to come up and sit with him.

[32] "The eunuch was reading this passage of Scripture: 'He was led like a sheep to the slaughter, and as a lamb before the shearer is silent, so he did not open his mouth. [33] In his humiliation he was deprived of justice. Who can speak of his descendants? For his life was taken from the earth.'

[34] "The eunuch asked Philip, 'Tell me, please, who is the prophet talking about, himself or someone else?' [35] Then Philip began with that very passage of Scripture and told him the good news about Jesus.

[36] "As they traveled along the road, they came to some water and the eunuch said, 'Look, here is water. Why shouldn't I be baptized?' [38] And he gave orders to stop the chariot. Then both Philip and the eunuch went down into the water and Philip baptized him. [39] When they came up out of the water, the Spirit of the Lord suddenly took Philip away, and the eunuch did not see him again, but went on his way rejoicing."

The pastor of the church was weeping. God had brought the world into his church, but his church had not necessarily had the world on its heart. Too often a church receives new members who are natives of other countries and merely adds them to its membership roll without asking God why He brought people from around the world to join their church body. God intends for every local church to be a world-missions strategy center. God will equip each church to carry out the Great Commission if it will be a careful steward of every person God sends to it.

 Think about your community. How could God use a person in your community to impact world missions? Check persons below or list others you think of.
❏ International students at the local college or university
❏ International business personnel at local companies
❏ Tourists from foreign countries
❏ International seamen on ships in port
❏ Ethnic persons who have contact with their native countries
❏ Local individuals who do business in foreign countries
❏ Christian youth and college students whom God might call to be missionaries
❏ Laypersons who would be willing to serve as volunteers in short-term international mission projects (evangelism, medical and health care, disaster relief, agriculture, teaching English)
Others: _____

4 Pray and ask God if He wants you to become involved in some way with one of these groups.

When you adjust your life to God and become a Kingdom-oriented person, He will involve you in His work anywhere in the world He chooses. He is at work all over the world building His kingdom.

I was speaking at a conference in **Minneapolis-Saint Paul** about participating with God to touch a world. A pastor from an inner-city church said, "That's how God told me to function as a pastor! We began to look for what God was doing. Someone from Jamaica joined our church and asked, 'Would you come and preach in our country. We need the Lord so much.' I took some people with me, and we started three churches. The next month God added to our church someone from another Caribbean nation. We went there and started churches. Now we sponsor mission churches in three Caribbean nations." Then he smiled and said, "Last Sunday we had a man join our church from Ghana in west Africa. I don't know what God is up to, but we're ready to see!"

This congregation discovered they were Kingdom citizens. To experience God and to know and do God's will is to put your life alongside His activity and to let His Spirit show you why that happened in your church. Adjust your life to Him and let Him work through you to draw a world to Himself.

Isn't it tragic when we become so self-centered we enter God's presence and say, "O God, bless me. Bless my family. Bless my church"?

Then God says, "I've been trying to do that all along but in a completely different way than you anticipated. I want you to deny self. Pick up your cross and follow Me. I will lead you to places where I am working, and I'll include you in My activity. You will be an instrument in My hand so I use your life to touch a world. When I do that through you, you will truly experience My blessings."

Review today's lesson. Pray and ask God to identify one or more statements or Scriptures He wants you to understand, learn, or practice. Underline them. Then respond to the following.

What was the most meaningful statement or Scripture you read today?

_____
_____
_____
_____
_____

Reword the statement or Scripture into a prayer of response to God.

_____
_____
_____
_____
_____

What does God want you to do in response to today's study?

_____
_____
_____
_____
_____

Koinonia

DAY 2

YOU CANNOT BE IN TRUE FELLOWSHIP WITH GOD AND OUT OF FELLOWSHIP WITH OTHER BELIEVERS.

In the mind and teaching of Jesus, a church was a vital, living, dynamic fellowship of believers. The Greek word *koinonia*, most frequently translated *fellowship*, is the best way to describe what a church ought to be. In this unit I will use the word *koinonia* to mean the fullest possible partnership and fellowship with God and with other believers.

1 **Underline in the following paragraph words and phrases that help you understand the meaning of *koinonia*.**

Koinonia, or intimate fellowship, in the church is based on personal *koinonia* with God and individual believers. *Koinonia* with God comes only from a real, personal encounter with the living Christ and surrender to Him as the absolute Lord of your life. This is the intimate love relationship we have talked about. God pursues that kind of a relationship with you.

2 **How would you define *koinonia*?** _____
_____

3 **Which of the following words can you use to describe your relationship with God? Check all that apply.**
❑ alive   ❑ close   ❑ cold   ❑ distant   ❑ growing   ❑ intimate
❑ personal   ❑ removed   ❑ stagnant   ❑ real   ❑ uneasy   ❑ vibrant

4 **Read 1 John 1:1-7 below and circle the word *fellowship (koinonia)* each time it occurs. Then answer the questions that follow.**
[1]"That which was from the beginning, which we have heard, which we have seen with our eyes, which we have looked at and our hands have touched—this we proclaim concerning the Word of life. [2]The life appeared; we have seen it and testify to it, and we proclaim to you the

eternal life, which was with the Father and has appeared to us. ³We proclaim to you what we have seen and heard, so that you also may have fellowship with us. And our fellowship is with the Father and with his Son, Jesus Christ. ⁴We write this to make our joy complete.

⁵"This is the message we have heard from him and declare to you: God is light; in him there is no darkness at all. ⁶If we claim to have fellowship with him yet walk in the darkness, we lie and do not live by the truth. ⁷But if we walk in the light, as he is in the light, we have fellowship with one another, and the blood of Jesus, his Son, purifies us from all sin" (1 John 1:1-7).

a. What are some words in verses 1-3 indicating that John had a personal, dynamic relationship with the living Lord Jesus Christ? _____

_____

b. Why did John write about what he had seen and heard of Jesus (v. 3)?

_____

c. What are two benefits to believers because of their fellowship with God and one another (vv. 4,7)? _____

_____

d. What is indicated when a person says he has fellowship *(koinonia)* with God, but he walks in sin and darkness (v. 6)? _____

_____

e. What is true of a person who walks in the light as God is in the light (v. 7)?

_____

Answers: a. John said he had seen, heard, and touched Jesus. John had an experiential knowledge of Jesus. He had come to know Him as the "eternal life" (v. 2). John also recorded Jesus' words "This is eternal life: that they may know you, the only true God, and Jesus Christ, whom you have sent" (John 17:3). Eternal life means knowing God by experience in a real, personal way. This is *koinonia*—fellowship with God. b. John proclaimed Jesus so others would believe in Him and have fellowship with John and other believers. c. When we fellowship with God and when others come into fellowship with Him and with us, our joy is made complete, and we experience the cleansing work of Jesus' blood. d. Such a person is a liar. His or her life is a lie. e. If a person walks in the light as God is in the light, he or she has fellowship with other believers and experiences forgiveness and the cleansing of sin.

Fellowship Among Believers

Our *koinonia* as believers is with God and His Son, Jesus Christ. This fellowship is an intimate partnership. It is the sharing of all God is with us and all we are with God. To me, *koinonia* is the most complete expression of a love relationship with God. When you live in this kind of love relationship with God, you will have the same quality of loving fellowship with other believers.

First John clearly states that your relationships with your Christian brothers and sisters are an expression of your relationship with God. You cannot be in true fellowship with God and out of fellowship with other believers.

5 **Read each of the following Scriptures. Circle the words** *brother* **and** *brothers*. **Underline the words** *love* **and** *loves*.

"Anyone who claims to be in the light but hates his brother is still in the darkness. Whoever loves his brother lives in the light, and there is nothing in him to make him stumble. But whoever hates his brother is in the darkness and walks around in the darkness" (1 John 2:9-11).

"This is how we know who the children of God are and who the children of the devil are: Anyone who does not do what is right is not a child of God; nor is anyone who does not love his brother" (1 John 3:10).

"We know that we have passed from death to life, because we love our brothers. Anyone who does not love remains in death. Anyone who hates his brother is a murderer, and you know that no murderer has eternal life in him" (1 John 3:14-15).

"This is how we know what love is: Jesus Christ laid down his life for us. And we ought to lay down our lives for our brothers. If anyone has material possessions and sees his brother in need but has no pity on him, how can the love of God be in him?" (1 John 3:16-17).

"Let us love one another, for love comes from God. Everyone who loves has been born of God and knows God. Whoever does not love does not know God, because God is love" (1 John 4:7-8).

"Since God so loved us, we also ought to love one another. No one has ever seen God; but if we love one another, God lives in us and his love is made complete in us" (1 John 4:11-12).

"If anyone says, 'I love God,' yet hates his brother, he is a liar. For anyone who does not love his brother, whom he has seen, cannot love God, whom he has not seen. And he has given us this command: Whoever loves God must also love his brother" (1 John 4:20-21).

"Everyone who loves the father loves his child as well. This is how we know that we love the children of God: by loving God and carrying out his commands" (1 John 5:1-2).

6 **How is your relationship with God reflected in your relationship with your "brother"?** _____

_____

7 **If you are in a right relationship with God, how will you treat your Christian brothers and sisters?** _____

_____

8 Suppose a person claimed to be a Christian and to love Jesus; yet he treated his Christian brothers and sisters harshly. He was unkind and unforgiving toward them and regularly argumentative. He publicly ridiculed them or slandered their name or reputation. He was unwilling to help them when they were in need. In light of 1 John, what would you say about this person's relationship with God? Check one or more responses that you agree with or write your own response.

❏ I would take this person's word that he is a Christian who really loves Jesus.
❏ I would question whether this person really knows and loves God.
❏ I would think this person has a serious problem in his relationship with God.
❏ Other: _____

9 Read 1 Corinthians 13:4-8 (in the margin) and write in the columns below words and phrases that describe what Christian love is and is not. I have written one for you.

Love Is ...	Love is not ...
patient	

> ### 1 Corinthians 13:4-8
>
> "Love is patient, love is kind. It does not envy, it does not boast, it is not proud. It is not rude, it is not self-seeking, it is not easily angered, it keeps no record of wrongs. Love does not delight in evil but rejoices with the truth. It always protects, always trusts, always hopes, always perseveres.
>
> "Love never fails. But where there are prophecies, they will cease; where there are tongues, they will be stilled; where there is knowledge, it will pass away."

If you love God, your love for your fellow Christians will be obvious. You will be patient and kind. You will not be envious, boastful, proud, rude, self-seeking, or easily angered. You will not hold grudges. You will rejoice in truth and righteousness, not in evil. You will protect and trust your Christian brothers and sisters. You will hope for the best in others, and you will persevere in your love. This Godlike love grows from an intimate love relationship with God. In John 13:35 Jesus said, "By this all men will know that you are my disciples, if you love one another."

10 Take time to pray, asking God to reveal the truth to you about your fellowship (love relationship) with Him and with your Christian brothers and sisters. Remember that anyone who is in Christ is a brother or sister in the Lord.

a. What do you sense God is saying about your fellowship with other Christians?
_____
_____

b. What do you sense God is saying about your fellowship with Him?
_____
_____

SUMMARY STATEMENTS

A church is a vital, living, dynamic fellowship of believers.

Koinonia is the fullest possible partnership and fellowship with God and with others.

I cannot be in true fellowship with God and out of fellowship with other believers.

These two evaluations of your fellowship ought to be similar. If you say your fellowship with the Lord is good, but your fellowship with other Christians is poor, something is wrong. If you walk in intimate fellowship with God, you will enjoy warm fellowship with your brothers and sisters in Christ.

Review today's lesson. Pray and ask God to identify one or more statements or Scriptures He wants you to understand, learn, or practice. Underline them. Then respond to the following.

What was the most meaningful statement or Scripture you read today?	Reword the statement or Scripture into a prayer of response to God.	What does God want you to do in response to today's study?
_____	_____	_____
_____	_____	_____
_____	_____	_____
_____	_____	_____
_____	_____	_____
_____	_____	_____

A Laotian Refugee

In Vancouver I served as the interim pastor of a small church. A Laotian refugee family had joined the church the week before I came. I knew God never adds to the body by accident. My responsibility as the pastor was to learn what God was doing when He added this family to our church.

Thomas, the father, had been saved in a refugee camp in Thailand. His life was so gloriously transformed he wanted all the Laotian people to know Jesus. He went all over our community trying to find his Laotian brothers and lead them to Christ. The first week Thomas led 15 adults to the Lord. The next week he led 11 to the Lord, and he wept because he felt he was unfaithful to the Lord.

In our next church business meeting I said, "We need to start a Laotian mission church." I shared all I knew of what God was doing. "I believe God is leading those people to the Lord so we can start a Laotian mission," I explained. Then I asked the church to decide how they sensed God wanted us to respond. They voted to start a Laotian mission church.

Then I said, "We ought to call Thomas as the pastor." I told them what God was doing in Thomas's life. God had given him a pastor's heart. He had a burden for evangelism. He had just enrolled in a local Baptist theological college to train for anything God wanted to do through him. The church voted to call Thomas as the pastor of the new mission.

Two months later, Thomas was invited to a meeting for ethnic pastors in Saint Louis. Thomas asked, "Can I take some friends with me?" I didn't know what that meant until he said he wanted to take 18 friends with him. Then he said, "Henry, would you mind if I came back through all the major cities of Canada? My relatives are in all of these cities. God wants me to go and lead some of them to the Lord. If God will help me, I'll find a pastor for them. Then they can have a church in every major city of Canada."

Then I knew God was doing something special. I said, "Oh, Thomas, please go!" He did. Later that year at Christmas, Laotian people from all across Canada came to celebrate the new life in Christ they had found.

Later the Laotian government granted permission to start churches. Thomas returned to Laos and preached the gospel, and 133 relatives and friends came to know the Lord. He started four mission churches. He linked the church in Vancouver with the Laotian churches with the desire to see all Laotian people come to know the Lord.

When Thomas joined our church, all we saw was one Laotian refugee. What did God see? He saw a people and a whole nation being drawn to Himself. When God honors your church by placing a new member in the body, ask God to show you what He is up to. He wants to touch your community and maybe even the world through your church.

DAY 3

Koinonia in the Kingdom

KOINONIA TAKES ON NEW DIMENSIONS, NEW POSSIBILITIES, AND NEW RICHNESS AS CHURCHES RELATE IN THE WIDER CIRCLES OF THE KINGDOM.

Daniel 3:17

"The God we serve is able ... and he will."

Ephesians 3:20-21

"To him who is able to do immeasurably more than all we ask or imagine, according to his power that is at work within us, to him be glory in the church and in Christ Jesus throughout all generations, for ever and ever!"

We considered everything each of us possessed as belonging by love to one another.

Kingdom people are interrelated with other members and believers in the Kingdom worldwide. After serving 22 years as a pastor, I became the director of missions for an association of 11 churches and mission churches in the greater Vancouver area of British Columbia, Canada. Guiding a church to walk with Christ as the Head of His body is one matter. Guiding an association of 11 congregations to walk together with God with one heart and one mind is quite different. I had to face some serious questions:

- Would God speak to the churches individually and then bring them to one mind as they functioned together as an association?
- Would the churches respond to God when He spoke?
- Would the churches have the same kind of *koinonia* (fellowship) with one another as believers have with other Christians in a local church?
- Would churches be willing to give freely of themselves in order to experience the fullest life God has to offer (see Luke 9:23-24)?
- Would godly fellowship be expressed by the free sharing of resources with churches that had needs?

I came to this new assignment with the conviction that "the God we serve is able ... and he will" (**Dan. 3:17**). Biblical principles of God's working with His people do not change. Helping a group of churches learn to walk with God in intimate *koinonia* with Him and with one another took time, but God is the One who does that kind of miraculous work. I was only a vessel through whom He chose to work.

Though we were a small band of congregations, God manifested His presence in the lives of the churches and the association. God led our churches to walk by faith as we witnessed to the people attending the World's Fair. God worked through our association to begin ministry to East Indians. In four years the number of churches and missions in our association doubled. Student work grew from one part-time student director to five full-time directors. Almost one hundred people expressed a sense of call into ministry or mission work. Once strained relationships with other church groups were healed and flourished into dynamic, cooperative efforts of fellowship and outreach. God did so much more than we could ever ask or think, according to the Holy Spirit's enabling power at work in His churches (see **Eph. 3:20-21**).

1 **As you read the following paragraphs about the relationships among churches in our association, underline some things that indicate we had functioning *koinonia* among the churches.**

While I served as a pastor in Saskatchewan, the Holy Spirit developed unique *koinonia* among the sister churches. Together our churches developed a network to reach the entire province for Christ. Much like the New Testament churches, we considered everything each of us possessed as belonging by love to one another (see Acts 4:34-35). A church's resources don't belong to the people themselves. The church is merely a steward of them. Everything a church has belongs to the Kingdom. Anything our church had was available to all the others. When one church called a student minister, he became a resource for every other church for helping to develop their student ministry. When our church had a summer youth program, we invited small churches to participate with us. We also shared copy machines and other material resources. If one church needed financial help, we didn't hesitate to let God's people know. Then we took an offering. Once we even mortgaged our building to help a mission church purchase its own.

This kind of sharing developed a deep sense of *koinonia* among our churches. We belonged to one another. We needed one another. We went out of our way to help one another and meet each church's needs. We learned to love one another. We planned times to get together for fellowship and mutual encouragement. That is what Christ's kingdom ought to be like. The watching world should be able to say, "Look how they love one another." That unique quality of love can come only from God. When people see Godlike love, they will be drawn to Christ and to His church.

2 **What kinds of things indicate the churches had functioning *koinonia*? List them in the margin.**

When *koinonia* exists among churches, it is evident in their relationships. We cooperated in our commission to reach our world for Christ. We were able to do things together that no one church alone could have done effectively. We shared anything we had if it would meet the need of a sister church. We spent time together and loved one another.

Can that kind of *koinonia* exist among churches not only on an associational level but also on a state, provincial, national, or international level? Yes! Can Godlike *koinonia* exist among churches of different denominations as they cooperate to achieve greater Kingdom purposes? Yes! However, humans left to their own ways cannot achieve those kinds of relationships. Only God through His Holy Spirit can create and sustain *koinonia* among His people. He wants to be the King, Ruler, and Sovereign over all His kingdom. When He is allowed to rule, barriers erected by humans inevitably fall.

When we have *koinonia* with God, the same quality and nature of that *koinonia* will be reflected when we relate to—

- brothers and sisters in our local church;
- other churches in a local area;
- other churches in a state or province;
- other churches in a nation;
- other churches in the world;
- other Christian denominations.

3 **Based on the relationships your church has with other churches and denominations in your local area and worldwide, what kind of *koinonia* would a watching world see?** _____

_____

4 **What does your church do or fail to do that indicates a lack of *koinonia* with other churches or Christian groups? For instance, some church-league sports teams develop a poor reputation in the community because of their displays of anger, jealousy, rudeness, violence, and hatred. That reflects a deep fellowship problem.**

_____

If your church has a *koinonia* problem with other Christian churches or groups, that indicates a deeper *koinonia* problem with the Lord. I am not suggesting that doctrinal differences ought to be compromised, but we can act like brothers and sisters who love one another. *Koinonia* takes on new dimensions, new possibilities, and new richness as churches relate in the wider circles of the Kingdom. This is the same way love works.

Sharing developed a deep sense of *koinonia* among our churches.

Loving on a New Level

Suppose, on a scale of 1 to 10, you are loving at level 2—you love your parents and family who love you, and you love your friends who care about you. Suppose God enables you to love your archenemy, as Jesus commanded in Matthew 5:43-48. If you can love your enemy at level 10, your capacity to love other persons will increase. All others you have been loving will receive a greater dimension of concern than you have previously been able to give them.

5 **Evaluate your Christian love life. Check statements that are true of your Christian love.**
❑ I don't genuinely love anybody.
❑ I love my family.
❑ I love those who love me.
❑ I love those I trust.
❑ God has helped me love those around me who are irritable and unfriendly.
❑ God has taught me to love those in my community who are unlovely— people who are different from me.
❑ God has taught me to show love for people who are openly living in sin.
❑ God has given me grace to love my enemies.

You and I usually do not try to improve our capacity to love by loving those who are difficult to love. Often when we try to love our enemy, frustration and anger result instead of a new kind of love. Then we respond, "Lord, I didn't want You to bring anger into my life. I wanted You to bring love into my life." But God can deepen our capacity to love as He enables us to care for the unlovely. When we learn to love on a deeper level, our capacity to love others grows.

While I was leading an association of churches, we made a commitment to love everyone and to help every person in our city know the Lord. Isn't that what Jesus commanded us in the Great Commission (see Matt. 28:18-20)? God placed me in a relationship with a person who had a deep love for anarchists—young adults who were angry at everybody and wanted to destroy established order and authority. This man said, "Henry, go with me to the anarchists' restaurant. I want you to listen to this group of people express their anger and bitterness. I want you to see how God can bring the gospel to them."

That was a life-changing experience for me. I sat in that restaurant for three hours listening to an outpouring of hatred and bitterness. By the aid of the Spirit of God, with my heart, mind, and life I came to love those people. Consequently, I was able to pour out greater love on the next Christian I met. By teaching me to love anarchists, God brought me to a deeper capacity to love.

6 **Is God impressing you to demonstrate your love to a specific individual, a particular group of people or perhaps people who are different from you? Ask Him. If God is impressing you to demonstrate your love at a deeper level, write the name of the one or ones He wants you to love.** _____
_____
_____
_____
_____

Cooperative Relationships Among Churches

The churches of the New Testament were interdependent. Each was independent before the Lord; yet they needed one another. They helped and encouraged one another. They had cooperative relationships that enhanced their experience of God.

 As you read about each of the following relationships, underline or write in the margin examples that clearly indicate the New Testament churches had *koinonia* with one another. I've given you one example.

The young church in Jerusalem. On the day of Pentecost three thousand people came to trust in Christ. We do not know how many of these remained in Jerusalem after the Jewish feast was over. We know, however, the Jerusalem church had many members. Early on, they met in the temple courts and in many smaller groups in individual homes. They met daily for teaching, fellowship, meals, and prayer. <u>They shared their material resources with any believer who had a need</u> (see Acts 2:42-47). These many small congregations were interdependent. Because of *koinonia* they were "one in heart and mind" (Acts 4:32).

Jerusalem shares with Antioch. When the gospel began to bear fruit among the Greeks in Antioch, the Jerusalem church sent Barnabas to investigate and help the young church. When Barnabas saw God's activity there, he enlisted Saul (Paul) to come and help. Together they remained in Antioch teaching the new converts (see Acts 11:19-26).

Antioch provides for needs in Jerusalem. Word came to the church in Antioch that their Christian brothers and sisters in Judea were suffering from a famine. Because of *koinonia* "the disciples, each according to his ability, decided to provide help for the brothers living in Judea. This they did, sending their gift to the elders by Barnabas and Saul" (Acts 11:29-30). These churches were not totally independent. They were bound together by their common *koinonia* with Christ. They cared for one another's needs from their love for one another.

Antioch sends out Barnabas and Saul. The church at Antioch was missions-minded, sharing Christ's heart for a lost world. One day "while they were worshiping the Lord and fasting, the Holy Spirit said, 'Set apart for me Barnabas and Saul for the work to which I have called them.' So after they had fasted and prayed, they placed their hands on them and sent them off" (Acts 13:2-3). The church at Antioch had freely received leaders, and they freely gave them for the advancement of the Kingdom.

Notice Barnabas and Saul (Paul) had already been called to take the gospel to the Gentiles. Saul's conversion and call had occurred several years before (see Acts 9:1-19; Gal. 1:16-24). Only in the midst of the body of Christ did they come to know the right timing for their missionary work. God spoke to them by the Holy Spirit and through the church. Don't be afraid to trust God and your church to help you know God's will and His timing for your Kingdom assignments.

Jerusalem helps maintain sound doctrine. When a dispute arose about the nature of salvation, Paul and Barnabas went to Jerusalem for consultation. The apostles, elders, and church in Jerusalem helped settle the dispute. Then they sent two of their own members to the church in Antioch to instruct, encourage, and strengthen the Gentile Christians.

Other churches cooperate for Kingdom purposes. Throughout Paul's letters we read about ways the churches cooperated with other Christians for the Kingdom's sake.

• The faith of the Roman Christians encouraged others all over the Christian
   world (see Rom. 1:8-12). Paul planned to receive assistance from this church
   for a journey to Spain that he was planning (see Rom. 15:24).

- Churches in Macedonia and Achaia sent contributions to the poor Christians in Jerusalem (see Rom. 15:26-27).
- The church in Philippi frequently provided financial support for Paul so he could preach the gospel and start churches in other cities (see Phil. 4:14-16).
- The churches at Colosse and Laodicea shared workers (Epaphras) and letters from Paul (see Col. 4:12-16).
- The believers in the church at Thessalonica inspired and became models to all of the believers in Macedonia and Achaia (see 1 Thess. 1:6-10).

8 **Which of the following best describes the relationship among churches in the New Testament? Check your response.**
- ❑ a. The churches were isolated and independent. They each focused their ministries solely on their own communities.
- ❑ b. The churches were interdependent. They cared about one another, and they encouraged and helped one another.

9 **Describe one way your church has experienced *koinonia* because of a cooperative relationship with another church or Christian group.**

_____

_____

_____

A small group of Christians felt burdened for the inner city of a major city and did not know of any other evangelical church that was reaching that massive district. God led some of them to quit their jobs, raise their own financial support, and by faith start a new church in that area. After they had begun, it was announced that a megachurch was going to sponsor a new church in the same area and intended to invest massive financial and human resources in order to build the church quickly. When the small church heard the news, rather than fearing the "competition," they rejoiced. News that God had motivated a second church to reach the same area confirmed God truly wanted to reach that vast population for Christ. The little church raised funds to fully equip the second church's nursery. They even asked to place the second church in its budget, even though it was not in their denomination and had far more resources at its disposal than the original church did. The small church's burden to reach the people of that community led them to invest in the ministry of the second church. Every time someone came to Christ in the second church, the people of the first church could celebrate that another person had been added to the kingdom of God.

Experiencing More of God

A believer cannot experience God in all the dimensions God intends for him or her apart from the body of Christ—a local church. As the body goes on mission together to the ends of the earth, Christians begin to experience the fuller dimensions of life in God's kingdom. As you experience *koinonia* with other groups of God's people, you experience greater dimensions of God's presence at work in your world. God has created channels through which you and your church can touch the world for Him. Allow Him to break down any barriers that may prevent you from experiencing God through *koinonia* with others. Go to Him and watch for His initiative. He can show you how, with whom, and when He wants to use you.

SUMMARY STATEMENTS

Everything each church possessed belonged by love to one another.

Everything a church has belongs to the Kingdom.

When *koinonia* exists among churches, it is evident in their relationships.

10 **Fill in the blank in the following statement.**
The churches of the New Testament were not independent. They were
_____. They needed fellowship with one another
to experience the greater dimensions of God and the *koinonia* He creates.

11 **Write your Scripture-memory verse, 1 John 1:7.** _____
_____
_____
_____

12 **Review your Scripture-memory verses and be prepared to recite
them to a partner in your small-group session this week.**

When Christ is allowed to rule, barriers erected by humans inevitably fall.

The churches of the New Testament were interdependent.

As my church experiences *koinonia* with other groups of God's people, we experience greater dimensions of God's presence at work in our world.

**Review today's lesson. Pray and ask God to identify one or more statements or Scriptures He
wants you to understand, learn, or practice. Underline them. Then respond to the following.**

What was the most meaningful statement or Scripture you read today?
_____
_____
_____
_____
_____

Reword the statement or Scripture into a prayer of response to God.
_____
_____
_____
_____
_____

What does God want you to do in response to today's study?
_____
_____
_____
_____
_____

Essentials of *Koinonia*, Part I

DAY 4

KOINONIA WITH GOD IS AN EXPERIENCE OF HIS PRESENCE.

Koinonia with God is the basic element of salvation and eternal life (see John 17:3).
God takes the initiative to invite you into a love relationship. He places His Holy Spirit
in you to enable you to live in right relationship with Him. No human method or list
of steps to follow can maintain fellowship with God. *Koinonia* with God is an experience of His presence. Although God takes the initiative, you must respond to Him in
order to fully experience His presence.

1 **The seven realities of experiencing God identify the way you come to
know God by experience. I have personalized the statements for you
below. Check your memory and fill in the blanks. Then check your
work on the inside back cover.**
Reality 1: _____ is always at work around you.

Reality 2: God pursues a continuing love _____ with you that is real and _____.

Reality 3: God invites you to become _____ with Him in His _____.

Reality 4: God speaks by the Holy _____ through the Bible, _____, circumstances, and the _____ to reveal Himself, His _____, and His ways.

Reality 5: God's invitation for you to work with Him always leads you to a crisis of _____ that requires _____ and action.

Reality 6: You must make major _____ in your life to join God in what He is doing.

Reality 7: You come to know God by _____ as you _____ Him and He accomplishes His work through you.

Notice that the last three realities identify your response to God's initiative: You must act on *faith* in Him. You must make major *adjustments* to Him. You must *obey* Him. When you respond to God's initiative, you come to know Him intimately by experience. Living in faithful obedience to Him allows you to experience His presence. This is *koinonia* with God. Continuing in fellowship with God does not happen by accident. This fellowship can be broken. Sometimes what seems to be a good intention can threaten fellowship with God and with Christian brothers and sisters. To guard against broken fellowship, we need to identify and understand some essentials of genuine *koinonia* with God.

Essentials of *Koinonia*

1. We must love God with our total being.
2. We must submit to God's sovereign rule.
3. We must experience God in a real and personal way.
4. We must completely trust in God.

1. We must love God with our total being.

"This is the first and greatest commandment" (Matt. 22:37-38). If you love God, you will obey Him (see John 14:21-24). If you love Him, you will also love your brother (see 1 John 4:21; 5:3). If your fellowship with God is right—if you love Him with your total being—you will even be able to love your enemies.

The threat to fellowship is anything that causes you to lose your first love for God. This was the problem with the church at Ephesus (see Rev. 2:1-7).

2️⃣ **Read 1 John 2:15-16 in the margin and list things that can threaten or compete with your love for God.** _____

_____

_____

Matthew 22:37-38

"Jesus replied: ' "Love the Lord your God with all your heart and with all your soul and with all your mind." This is the first and greatest commandment.' "

1 John 2:15-16

"Do not love the world or anything in the world. If anyone loves the world, the love of the Father is not in him. For everything in the world—the cravings of sinful man, the lust of his eyes and the boasting of what he has and does—comes not from the Father but from the world."

Loving money or things more than God will break your fellowship with Him. Your sinful cravings and lust can capture your first love. You can even fall in love with what you have or what you are able to do. When your love is not pure toward God, fellowship with God is broken. Your fellowship with others will then reflect your broken fellowship with God.

Suppose a person begins to love things more than God. When fellowship with God is broken, love for others will suffer. A person who loves things more than God will become stingy and greedy. When he sees a brother in need, he will keep his possessions to use for himself. He will not give to help others. He may start using God's tithe (tenth) for himself. Greed is a dangerous threat to fellowship with God (see Eph. 5:5; 1 John 3:17).

Materialism is a terrible trap that robs many people of their love for God. Churches can also be selfish and greedy, primarily using God's resources to satisfy themselves rather than to help a lost and needy world.

3 **What is one essential of *koinonia*?** _____

_____

4 **Name at least two things that can threaten *koinonia* by interfering with your love for God.** _____

2. We must submit to God's sovereign rule.

God is your Master. Because of His perfect love for you, He demands absolute obedience. As the Head of the church, Christ demands submission to Him and obedience to His will. Absolute surrender to His lordship is necessary for right fellowship with God.

When people become "a law to themselves" (Hab. 1:7) and do what is right in their own eyes (see Judg. 17:6), the experience of *koinonia* becomes impossible in their lives and in the life of a church. Yielding your loyalty or allegiance to anyone other than Christ is spiritual adultery. If a pastor, the deacons, influential business persons, or a committee tries to run or rule the church, *koinonia* is threatened.

The problem always starts with an individual's or a church's relationship with God. When a person refuses to deny self and follow Christ, fellowship with God is broken. When self is in control, all other authority relationships will be out of control. Asserting self in the body of Christ robs Christ of His rightful authority as the Head of the body.

Fellowship is broken not only when an individual tries to be the head of the church but also when the church expects its pastor or another individual or group to rule the church. No individual or group can function as the head of the body if that church is to be a healthy body. It may look healthy on the outside, but God sees the rebellion against His Son's rule and deplores it. Every member of the church must submit to Christ's lordship over his life and to Christ's headship over the church.

5 **In your opinion, to whom does your church look as the head of your church?** _____

In 1 Corinthians 1–3 divisions (broken fellowship) existed in the church because some were following Paul, some were following Apollos, and some were following Peter (Cephas). Paul condemned this kind of rebellion and rebuked any attempt to follow anyone other than Christ. To follow him or Apollos would be childish, worldly, and ungodly (see 1 Cor. 3:1-4). The church must have the mind of Christ (see 1 Cor. 2:16) and must follow Christ alone.

Every member of the church must submit to Christ's lordship over his life and to Christ's headship over the church.

Koinonia is impossible if a church is made up of individuals who are unwilling to submit to the lordship of Christ in the body of Christ. The same impossibility exists in a larger body of fellowship, such as an association or a denomination, in which pastors and other participants refuse to submit to Christ's lordship and will not function in that body under Christ's rule. Anything or anyone who hinders or usurps God's lordship in your life, in the church, or in the larger bodies of the Kingdom causes broken fellowship with God. When fellowship with God breaks down, it is reflected in broken relationships with others.

6 **In your opinion, who is looked to as the head of your denomination?**

_____

7 **What is the second essential of *koinonia*?**
1. We must love God with our total being.
2. _____

8 **Describe the way interference with Christ's rule threatens *koinonia* in a church.** _____
_____

9 **In all honesty before God, who is the Lord and Master of your life? Check one or write your own.**
❏ Jesus Christ is.   ❏ I am.   ❏ Money and possessions are.
❏ My job is.   ❏ My spouse is.
❏ Other: _____

10 **Pray through this lesson and specifically bring the following matters to the Lord.**
- Ask God whether anything in your life is causing you to lose your first love for Him. Do you love anything more than Him? If He reveals anything, confess it and return to your first love.
- Ask God whether you are absolutely surrendered to His lordship in your life.
- Ask God whether you are allowing Jesus to function as the Head of your church.
- Pray for your spouse, your family, your church, and your denomination that God will be allowed to rule in every heart.

SUMMARY STATEMENTS

Koinonia with God is an experience of His presence.

Koinonia with God is the basic element of salvation and eternal life.

I must love God with my total being.

I must submit to God's sovereign rule.

Koinonia is possible only if a church is made up of individuals who are willing to submit to the lordship of Christ in the body of Christ.

Review today's lesson. Pray and ask God to identify one or more statements or Scriptures He wants you to understand, learn, or practice. Underline them. Then respond to the following.

What was the most meaningful statement or Scripture you read today?	Reword the statement or Scripture into a prayer of response to God.	What does God want you to do in response to today's study?

Essentials of *Koinonia*, Part 2

Yesterday you learned that *koinonia* with God requires that you love God with your total being and that you submit to His sovereign rule in your life. Many people, things, and influences in your life and in your church can threaten your fellowship with God if you allow them to distract you from loving Him and following Him. Today we will look at two more essentials of *koinonia* and possible threats to fellowship with God.

> ONLY A PERSONAL ENCOUNTER WITH THE LIVING CHRIST WILL RESULT IN EFFECTIVE KOINONIA.

3. We must experience God in a real and personal way.

Your *koinonia* with God is based on your personal experience with Him. No substitutes will do. You cannot rely on the personal experience of your spouse, your parents, your pastor, your Sunday School teacher, or your fellow church members. Your *koinonia* with God must be real and personal.

Koinonia is threatened when you allow anyone or anything to make you a spectator rather than an active participant in relationship to God. You must encounter God firsthand, or you will become passive and apathetic. If you do not continually encounter God firsthand, your fellowship with God will grow cold. You will quit caring about God's concern for His church, His kingdom, and the lost world.

1 **What are some things that happen in churches that can tempt a person to become more of a spectator than an active participant?**

_____

_____

2 **What is one way you have substituted a spectator religion for a real and personal experience of God?** _____

_____

Although church organizations and programs are designed to promote outreach, growth, and ministry, they can lead to shallow relationships and indifference. If a church is not careful, it may help people experience a program but miss a personal encounter with the living Christ. Well-organized programs, plans, methods, and Bible studies are valuable, but they must not take the place of the Holy Spirit's personal guidance. Churches must make sure their organization encourages personal experiences with God.

Spiritual truths and realities that others have already experienced must not be taught just for the sake of knowledge. Instead, people must be led to experiences in which God reveals to them the same spiritual truth or reality in a personal way. Secondhand experiences will not suffice.

Agencies of a denomination, for instance, have a place in doing God's will in ways individual churches cannot accomplish alone. Yet individuals and churches must not allow the work of the denomination to become a substitute for their personal involvement in God's work. When that happens, the result is social and spiritual indifference rather than responsible involvement and participation. Only a personal encounter with the living Christ will result in true *koinonia*.

3 What are some things your denomination can do that most churches cannot do alone? _____

_____

4 In what way could reliance on these good things, if misused, become a hindrance to a real and personal encounter with God? _____

_____

This is not an either-or situation. It is both-and. Denominations, programs, methods, prepared study materials, and so forth are helpful tools for churches. But they must not become substitutes for personal encounters with God. Each individual needs to experience the Lord's presence at work in his or her life. Individuals experience *koinonia* when they follow God's leadership and are empowered by the Holy Spirit to accomplish God's purposes.

When programs and ministries become ends instead of means, activity for activity's sake, or superficial signs of success, *koinonia* is in grave danger of being obscured and lost. Churches must not concern themselves only with numerical results. They must carefully look at the motive and inner spirit of their work. Are lives being transformed? Are broken people finding spiritual and emotional healing? Are people personally encountering the living Christ at work in the church? If not, something is wrong with members' personal relationships with God.

5 What is the third essential of *koinonia*?
1. We must love God with our total beings.
2. We must submit to God's sovereign rule.
3. _____

6 What are some things in a church that can take the place of a real and personal encounter with God? _____

_____

7 What is one thing in your past that you allowed to take the place of a personal experience with God? For example, someone might say, "I gave money to the church, but I avoided getting personally involved in God's work. I never experienced a sense of personal involvement in what God was doing through my church." _____

_____

_____

4. We must completely trust in God.

To experience genuine *koinonia* with God, you must depend on God to do the things only He can do. You must trust in God alone.

Once when Israel was faced with trouble, it turned to Egypt for help rather than to the Lord. God said to the nation, "Woe to those who go down to Egypt for help, who rely on horses, who trust in the multitude of their chariots and in the great strength of their horsemen, but do not look to the Holy One of Israel, or seek help from the Lord" (Isa. 31:1).

 8 What are some things or people in which a church may be tempted to place its trust? For instance, a church may trust in wealthy givers who provide financial stability rather than in the God who provides through His people. _____

_____

Placing your trust in anything other than God breaks your fellowship with Him. Here are some examples of things in which you can be tempted to place your trust to accomplish God's work instead of trusting in God.

- Yourself, your abilities, your resources
- Other people, their abilities, their resources
- Programs or methods
- Manipulation or coercion
- Pressure tactics or guilt
- Deceit

God provides people, relationships, resources, methods, and programs to be used by a church. However, a congregation that yields to the temptation to trust in these rather than the Lord displeases Him. Your church may be tempted to trust in yourselves; your pastor; a well-organized Bible-study program; a denominational agency; a bank; an outreach method; the government; or other organizations, people, or things. When you depend on any of these rather than God to accomplish His work in a church, fellowship with God and with other believers is broken. Sometimes leaders try to use pressure tactics to get members to do God's will. This tactic denies God's power to guide His people. When conflict arises, leaders may depend on a manual on handling church conflict instead of leading people back to trust in God and to love Him alone.

The Holy Spirit manifests Himself through believers and empowers them to accomplish God-sized tasks. God grows His church. The Holy Spirit produces unity. Christ brings forth spiritual fruit. You and your church must depend on God to accomplish His purposes in His ways through you. Completely depend on God.

Yes, God will call you to join Him. Yes, He will ask you to do things through which He will work. Often He will lead you to a program or method to help you organize and function to accomplish what He purposes. He will call you to use your money, resources, skills, and abilities. But in everything you must depend on God's guidance, provision, gifts, and power if you hope to bear lasting fruit. Without Him you can do nothing (see John 15:5). His presence creates and maintains fellowship, and He bears lasting spiritual fruit through an obedient and trusting people.

9 What is the fourth essential of *koinonia?*
1. We must love God with our total beings.
2. We must submit to God's sovereign rule.
3. We must experience God in a real and personal way.
4. _____

10 Name one thing in which you have been tempted to place your trust rather than God. _____

John 15:5
"I am the vine; you are the branches. If a man remains in me and I in him, he will bear much fruit; apart from me you can do nothing."

11 Take time to pray. Pray through today's lesson. Ask God to identify ways you have missed experiencing Him by substituting religious practices for personal encounters with Him. Ask Him to reveal any ways you trust in other people or other things rather than in the Lord your Provider. Also pray about ways your church may unknowingly encourage people to substitute religion for personal experiences with God. Pray that your church will always trust in the Lord alone.

12 Practice quoting or writing your Scripture-memory verses.

Review today's lesson. Pray and ask God to identify one or more statements or Scriptures He wants you to understand, learn, or practice. Underline them. Then respond to the following.

What was the most meaningful statement or Scripture you read today?

Reword the statement or Scripture into a prayer of response to God.

What does God want you to do in response to today's study?

A GOD-GIVEN BURDEN FOR THE WORLD

When my wife, Marilynn, and I were teenagers, God placed a burden for the world on our hearts. Early in our marriage we heard a missionary issue a call to those who were willing to go wherever God called them. We both went forward and surrendered our lives to go anywhere God sent us. Our denominational mission agency preliminarily approved us to serve in Africa, but then our oldest son, Richard, came down with a mysterious illness. The mission agency encouraged us to delay going to Africa until doctors could determine the nature of Richard's condition. Over the next few months God made it clear He was calling us not to Africa but to Canada. When we arrived in Canada, doctors discovered that Richard no longer had the illness. We served for the next 18 years in mission work in Canada. During that time God taught me much about walking with Him by faith, and I was eventually asked to write about what I had learned in the course *Experiencing God*.

Over the years I have learned that although God does not call everyone to be an author or a preacher, He expects all of His children to have the world on their hearts. Can God impact the world through one life or one church? Certainly. He is looking for those people and churches today.

KINGDOM PEOPLE

DVD Message Notes

1. God's strategy for taking God's good news to the ends of the earth was through these disciples.
2. If God has somebody with faith the size of a mustard seed, there is no limit to what God can do.
3. There is no small involvement of God.
4. As go God's people, so goes the redemption of the rest of the world.
5. We have such a focus on evangelism that we have missed discipleship.
6. "As go My people, so goes My glory in the world."
7. Is my life bringing honor to Christ?

Your Notes

_____

_____

_____

_____

_____

_____

_____

_____

_____

Unit Review

Using the hints below, write four essentials of *koinonia*. Then check your answers on page 240.

1. Love: _____
2. Submit: _____
3. Experience: _____
4. Trust: _____

Respond to the following.

1. How is your relationship with God reflected in your relationship with your "brother" (activity 6, p. 231)? _____
_____

2. What do you need to do to experience *koinonia* more completely in your church?
_____

3. What do you sense God wants your church to do to experience *koinonia* more completely in the Kingdom? _____
_____

Check your answers, using the pages cited in parentheses.

Scriptures Referenced

Matthew 4:17
John 17:4
John 17:8
John 17:18
John 17:4
John 17:9-10
John 17:10
John 17:15-18
John 20:21
Mark 16:15
Acts 1:8

Testimony

Kyle Hebert

Sharing Time

• Last three questions in the review at left
• One of the most meaningful statements or Scriptures from this unit's lessons and your prayer response to God. Choose one from pages 229, 233, 239, 242, and 246.

For Makeup or Review

Audio and video downloads are available at *www.lifeway.com*.

12

VERSE TO MEMORIZE

"LET US CONSIDER HOW WE MAY SPUR ONE ANOTHER ON TOWARD LOVE AND GOOD DEEDS. LET US NOT GIVE UP MEETING TOGETHER, AS SOME ARE IN THE HABIT OF DOING, BUT LET US ENCOURAGE ONE ANOTHER—AND ALL THE MORE AS YOU SEE THE DAY APPROACHING."

HEBREWS 10:24-25

Experiencing God in Your Daily Life

A Church Member Without a Relationship

I was preaching in a church one Sunday about the way Christ's presence dramatically affects daily living. At the close of the service, a man came forward weeping. The pastor had him share with the congregation the commitment he had just made. The man confessed that a decade earlier his wife had urged him to come with her to church. When he attended, he liked the people, enjoyed worship, and decided to join the church. Later, he heard that the church needed teachers in the Children's Sunday School Department, so he volunteered. Over the years he served in numerous capacities in the church, including being a deacon and a Sunday School teacher. Yet as I preached that morning, the Holy Spirit awakened him to the fact that he did not have a personal relationship with Jesus. This good man had been practicing religion without a genuine, life-changing relationship with Christ.

As I spoke of how the Holy Spirit walks with us to guide us each day, the man realized he was not hearing the Holy Spirit speak to him. As I talked of God's love for us, he saw that he served God but did not have a love relationship with Him. To his and the church's surprise, this man suddenly recognized that for all his service and attendance at church, he did not have an experiential relationship with God.

This man is not alone. One comment I hear from people who study *Experiencing God* is "I thought I knew what it meant to be a Christian and to walk with God. But after taking this course, I realize I was a religious person, but I did not really know what it meant to enjoy a personal relationship with Him."

This is the heart of this course: to move you from merely being religious to having a vibrant, real, growing relationship with God. In this unit we will address what it means to walk daily with God in a personal relationship with Him.

Returning to God

RETURN TO GOD,
AND HE WILL
FORGIVE YOU
AND REESTABLISH
YOUR FELLOWSHIP
WITH HIM.

Christians can encounter times when they lose their intimacy with God. Even the most zealous Christian can find that his love for God has cooled if he is not careful. The drift away from the Lord can be so subtle that you fail to recognize the loss until it is fairly severe. The Scriptures describe some ways you can know whether you are in a right relationship with the Lord or if you have departed.

1 **Listed below are some evidences that you have departed from the intimacy of your fellowship with God. Read the Scriptures in the left margin and John 15:10-11 in the margin on the next page. Write the Scripture reference beside the corresponding evidence listed below. Some may have more than one reference.**

_____ a. You no longer hear from God.
_____ b. You lose your joy.
_____ c. You do not produce spiritual fruit.
_____ d. You no longer have victory in your life.

2 **Using these evidences of lost intimacy with the Lord, what can you conclude about your closeness to the Lord today?**
❑ a. I may have begun to drift away.
❑ b. Thank the Lord, our intimacy is growing deeper.
❑ c. I'm farther away than I thought.
❑ d. Other: _____

#1 answers: a–Deuteronomy 30:17 and Amos 8:11-12; b–John 15:10-11; c–John 15:4-5; d–Deuteronomy 28:25

Deuteronomy 28:25

"The LORD will cause you to be defeated before your enemies. You will come at them from one direction but flee from them in seven."

Deuteronomy 30:17

"If your heart turns away so that you do not hear ..." (NKJV).

Amos 8:11-12

"The days are coming ... when I will send a famine through the land— not a famine of food or a thirst for water, but a famine of hearing the words of the LORD."

John 15:4-5

"No branch can bear fruit by itself; it must remain in the vine. Neither can you bear fruit unless you remain in me. ... If a man remains in me and I in him, he will bear much fruit."

How does this loss of intimacy happen? Three parables of Jesus in Luke 15 illustrate how. In one parable a sheep is lost (vv. 3–7). Sheep typically get lost from the shepherd when they turn aside to distractions. In the second parable a valuable coin is lost (vv. 8–10). Generally, valuables are lost through carelessness. No one means to lose something precious. But by not taking precautions, we can misplace even the most valuable possessions. In the third parable a son is lost (vv. 11–32). In this story the prodigal son deliberately chose to leave to indulge in a wasteful lifestyle that dishonored his father.

3 **Match the way the loss occurred on the right with the parable on the left. Write a letter beside each number.**

____ 1. Lost sheep   a. Turning aside to distractions
____ 2. Lost coin   b. Intentional choice
____ 3. Lost son   c. Carelessness, not taking precautions

In similar ways, you can lose your intimate fellowship with God. Like a sheep (a), you can focus on the world and the things of the world, on pleasures and activities, or on other people and relationships. You lose your focus on the Lord, and before long you realize you have drifted far away. Like the carelessness that lost a valuable coin (c), you may fail to guard your heart and mind. When temptations come, your strength to resist is not strong. Then sin robs you of your intimacy by breaking fellowship with your Lord. Or like the prodigal son (b), you may intentionally resist the Father's will through disobedience and the pursuit of sinful behaviors and activities.

Whenever you depart from God to any degree, He disciplines you in increasing measure until you return to Him. God loves you as His child and, as your Heavenly Father, will correct you until you turn from your rebellion (see Heb. 12:5-11). He will continue to bring discipline until it reaches a moment of crisis at which you must make a serious choice. You cry out to God in your distress.

Scripture promises that "if we confess our sins, he is faithful and just and will forgive us our sins and purify us from all unrighteousness" (1 John 1:9). You confess your sin when you agree with God about the awful nature of your wrong. Confession and repentance go together. When you repent of sin, you turn away from the sin and return to God. When your fellowship with God is broken because of sin, agree with Him about your condition and turn from it. Return to God, and He will forgive you and reestablish your fellowship with Him. This responding to God's discipline that results in restoration of life and vitality with the Lord is called revival. Another important Scripture that describes revival is 2 Chronicles 7:13-14.

 Read 2 Chronicles 7:13-14 in the margin.
a. When God brings judgment on His people, what four things should they do?
1. _____ 2. _____
3. _____ 4. _____

b. What three things does God promise to do when His people return to Him? Underline them in the text.

God's remedy for restored fellowship with Him involves humility, prayer, seeking His face (seeking the experience of His presence), and repentance (turning from sin). He promises to hear, forgive sin, and heal the land. When we return to God (and not merely to religious activity), He returns to us in a fresh, close relationship and begins once again to fulfill His purposes for us (see **Zech. 1:3; 2 Chron. 15:2**). Revival means the life of God returns to our soul. This can happen to an individual, a church, a denomination, or a nation.[1]

5 **If you find that your heart is not as enthusiastic and devoted to God as it once was, take a moment now and pray. Confess your sin and return to Him now so you can begin to experience His presence returning to your life. If you have not departed from God, pray about your commitment to remain steadfast and true to Him.**

Confessing and returning to the Lord are good, but prevention is even better. Scripture gives much helpful counsel for keeping your heart from departing from the Lord.

6 **As you read the following counsel, underline a key word or phrase in each that will help you properly focus on your intimacy with God.**

1. Proverbs 4:23 cautions, "Keep your heart with all diligence, for out of it spring the issues of life" (NKJV). Guard your heart. Our hearts are desperately wicked and, if left unchecked and unguarded, will be quickly drawn away from God (see **Jer. 17:9**). Be careful what you allow into your mind and your heart!

John 15:10-11
"If you obey my commands, you will remain in my love. . . . I have told you this so that my joy may be in you and that your joy may be complete."

2 Chronicles 7:13-14
"When I shut up the heavens so that there is no rain, or command locusts to devour the land or send a plague among my people, if my people, who are called by my name, will humble themselves and pray and seek my face and turn from their wicked ways, then will I hear from heaven and will forgive their sin and will heal their land."

Zechariah 1:3
" 'Return to me,' declares the LORD Almighty, 'and I will return to you,' says the LORD Almighty."

2 Chronicles 15:2
"The LORD is with you when you are with him. If you seek him, he will be found by you, but if you forsake him, he will forsake you."

Jeremiah 17:9
"The heart is deceitful above all things and beyond cure."

2. Proverbs 11:14 advises, "Where there is no counsel, the people fall; but in the multitude of counselors there is safety" (NKJV). Surround yourself with godly counselors who will encourage you and warn you if they see your heart beginning to shift.

3. Jesus said, "Love the Lord your God with all your heart and with all your soul and with all your mind" (Matt. 22:37). Make every effort to love God with all your being. Loving God is a choice you make. Keep your heart, mind and soul in a constant posture of love for God.

4. Jesus also said, "Everyone who hears these words of mine and puts them into practice is like a wise man who built his house on the rock" (Matt. 7:24). Adopt a lifestyle of obedience. Make it your habit to immediately obey anything God says. Obedience brings you into fresh experiences of God working in and through you. Jesus said, "If anyone loves me, he will obey my teaching. My Father will love him, and we will come to him and make our home with him" (John 14:23).

You may have identified other words, but here are my summaries: *(1) guard your heart, (2) godly counselors, (3) love God,* and *(4) obey* or *obedience.*

Review today's lesson. Pray and ask God to identify one or more statements or Scriptures He wants you to understand, learn, or practice. Underline them. Then respond to the following.

What was the most meaningful statement or Scripture you read today?	Reword the statement or Scripture into a prayer of response to God.	What does God want you to do in response to today's study?
_____	_____	_____
_____	_____	_____
_____	_____	_____
_____	_____	_____
_____	_____	_____

DAY 2

Experiencing God as Couples

IF GOD HAS GIVEN YOU A LIFE PARTNER, YOU WILL WANT TO BE INVOLVED IN THE GREAT WORK GOD INTENDS TO DO IN HIS OR HER LIFE.

Today's lesson for couples and tomorrow's lesson for parents may not be applicable to your circumstances. You may want to study them anyway. But if you prefer, use these two days for review and prayer.

People often ask me, "Henry, how do you explain how God has used your life to accomplish so much for His kingdom?" My response is always twofold. First, I am an extremely ordinary person. I have not done anything. I think God wanted to demonstrate what His incredible power could do in the lives of ordinary people, and He chose to work in my life. I have sought with all my heart to surrender my life to God, and the consequences of that commitment have amazed me. But the second thing I quickly add is this: "When God intended to use an ordinary life like mine for

His purposes, He chose to match my life with a life partner perfectly suited to me and God's direction for my life."

By nature I am a shy, introverted Canadian. My wife, Marilynn, is an extrovert who was born and reared in Oklahoma. We could not be more opposite if we tried. Yet God had an eternal purpose for both of us from the beginning of time. Both of our parents raised us to be active in our local churches. Our fathers were deacons. Both of our parents helped start new churches. Having grown up in such homes, we both surrendered our lives to do whatever our Lord commanded us to do and to go wherever He told us to go. Early in our lives we grew to love the local church and missions.

God's plans for me included learning to walk by faith through some extremely challenging times as a mission pastor in Canada and eventually traveling millions of miles around the world teaching others what God had instructed me. For me to fulfill God's will for my life, I would require a life partner with a unique calling of her own. Now God just had to get the two of us together! God did that by having me meet Marilynn at my roommate's wedding, where I was the best man, and she was the maid of honor. We were married a year later. What a joy to experience God's will together for these past 47 years!

1 List below some ways you are like your spouse and some ways you are different. Consider your personality, your interests, your backgrounds, your values, and so forth.

Similar	Different

As you yield yourselves to the Lord, He can take your similarities and differences and maximize your usefulness as a couple for His kingdom. For several years Marilynn and I led "Experiencing God as Couples" conferences across the country. It was marvelous to invite couples to stand together before God to see what He intended for their marriages. Ultimately, a course with videos was made of this teaching.[2] An unusually high percentage of the couples at these events felt called into Christian ministry. Many marriages were restored. Once couples came to understand God's purpose for their marriages, they discovered a new and exciting dimension to their lives together. Today we will look at ways you can experience God together with your spouse.

God's Purpose for Marriage

Jesus said this of marriage: "Haven't you read … that at the beginning the Creator 'made them male and female,' and said, 'For this reason a man will leave his father and mother and be united to his wife, and the two will become one flesh'? So they are no longer two, but one. Therefore what God has joined together, let man not separate" (Matt. 19:4-6). Marriage is God's joining together a man and a woman to create a union through which He can accomplish His purposes and be glorified. Marriage is not merely a human contract or agreement. It is a divine creation. God has a special purpose for each couple He unites. He is so committed to the sanctity of marriage that He hates divorce (see Mal. 2:16).

Once couples came to understand God's purpose for their marriages, they discovered a new and exciting dimension to their lives together.

What does it mean to be one flesh? It implies that your life is not your own. You are not two separate individuals trying to work out a coexistence. You are one. When your spouse feels pain, you suffer too. When your spouse experiences spiritual victory, you are victorious as well. When God has a plan for the wife, it means God's activity will affect the husband.

 Describe one way you and your spouse have experienced an unusual God-given oneness.

_____

_____

At times someone says to me, "I want to go forward with God, but my wife is unwilling. Should I go on without her?" My response is "You are one flesh. You cannot leave your spouse behind." Others have said, "My wife clearly senses that God wants us to be more involved in missions, but I haven't heard God say anything to me." My response: "You are one flesh. If God spoke to your spouse, He has just spoken to you!" Because you are one flesh, you need to adjust your life to a word God speaks to your partner. Pray together and trust the Holy Spirit to bring clarity and assurance about the direction of His calling. Then you can walk together with confidence.

This is why I always strongly advise couples coming to me for premarital counseling to consider carefully where God is leading their potential partner. After they are married, God's directives to one will directly affect the other. I have known people who had a clear sense of God's leading in their lives in one direction, but after they married, they rejected everything God had previously said to them because their spouse was not interested in those things. When I asked Marilynn to marry me, I knew God had been working in her life long before she met me. Marilynn almost died when she was five, and after that she had a strong sense that her life belonged to God. So I asked her, "Marilynn, what has God told you He intends to do through your life? And what promises have you made to God? If I marry you, I vow to spend the rest of my life helping you keep every promise you ever made to God."

If you have not already done so, take time with your spouse and list on separate paper some things you know God has done and said to each of you. What commitments have you made to Him? What do you sense He desires from you that has not yet come to pass? How have you sensed God leading you both to join Him in His work? Check here when you have taken such a time with your spouse. ❏

Being one with your spouse is critical to your ability to hear from God. That is why the apostle Paul warned believers not to marry unbelievers (see **2 Cor. 6:14**). Paul said it is like trying to mix light and darkness. They cannot become one spiritually because they are opposite in their fundamental nature. The spiritual intimacy you have with your spouse will affect your walk with God. The apostle Peter said a husband who mistreats his wife will find that his prayers are hindered (see **1 Pet. 3:7**). That is also why it is wise never to allow your anger or a damaged relationship to remain unresolved (see **Eph. 4:26**).

You may be studying this course and realize you are unequally yoked with an unbeliever. If that is the case, share this fact with your group and your church. Invite them to pray with you and walk with you and your spouse until he or she comes to faith in Christ.

2 Corinthians 6:14

"Do not be yoked together with unbelievers. For what do righteousness and wickedness have in common? Or what fellowship can light have with darkness?"

1 Peter 3:7

"Husbands, in the same way be considerate as you live with your wives, and treat them with respect as the weaker partner and as heirs with you of the gracious gift of life, so that nothing will hinder your prayers."

Ephesians 4:26

" 'In your anger do not sin': Do not let the sun go down while you are still angry."

Joining God's Activity
in Your Spouse's Life

One of the most exciting things you can do is to look to see where God is working in your spouse's life and join Him! You can do this in several ways:

1. **Regularly pray for and with your spouse.** God knows what your spouse is going through better than you do. He knows her fears and insecurities. God knows what He intends to do through your spouse's life. Praying regularly for your spouse enables you to gain God's perspective on your spouse. Couples can easily frustrate each other. If you look at your spouse solely from a human perspective, you will see his or her limitations, failures, and weaknesses. When you look at your spouse from God's perspective, you will see his or her unlimited potential in the hands of God. As you pray, God can alert you that you need to take a specific action, such as offering a particular word of encouragement or giving a note or a gift. God may show you abilities in your spouse that she does not see in herself. As I prayed for Marilynn, God affirmed to me that she has some wonderful insights into walking with God that can encourage many others. Although I have been the "professional" speaker throughout our marriage, I encouraged my wife to accept invitations that came her way because I sensed she needed to be a steward of what God had done in her life and such opportunities would richly bless others.

4 **How would you characterize your prayer relationship with your spouse up to this point in your marriage? Check one choice or write your own.**
   ❏ a. We have learned to pray in agreement and unity—what a blessing!
   ❏ b. We have had our own prayer times but have not prayed together regularly.
   ❏ c. My spouse hesitates or will not pray with me.
   ❏ d. I am hesitant to pray aloud with my spouse.
   ❏ e. Other: _____

5 **What, if anything, do you sense the Lord wants you to do differently regarding your prayer relationship with your spouse?**

   _____

   _____

2. **Regularly ask your spouse spiritual questions.** Some Christian couples never speak to each other about God's activity. They may assume God is working, but they never talk about it. Ask each other questions like "What has God been showing you in your quiet times lately? Has God placed a particular burden on your heart as your have prayed? You seemed very intent during the sermon today. What was God saying to you?" I have also found my spouse is the best person for me to share God's activity in my life. As I relate what I have been hearing God say, my wife recognizes things I missed. Together we hear far more from God than we do separately.

3. **Review your spiritual markers as a couple.** As God leads couples in their marriage, they will experience key moments when God clearly, unmistakably speaks. Identify these spiritual markers and periodically review them as a couple. This helps in two ways. First, it prepares you to understand where God is leading you. When I came to my official age of retirement, I, like everyone else my age, had to decide what to do. Should I join a country club and buy a set of golf clubs? As we reviewed what God had done in our lives as a couple, we realized that all of our married life had prepared us for what God wanted to do through us next. We ultimately formed

Spiritual Questions

1. What has God been showing you in your quiet times lately?
2. Has God placed a particular burden on your heart as you have prayed?
3. You seemed very intent during the sermon today. What was God saying to you?

Blackaby Ministries International so we could respond to God's invitations around the world to continue ministering. When our oldest son, Richard, sensed God leading him to join our ministry, we recognized again that this fit perfectly with the spiritual markers in our lives. We can respond to each new invitation God gives us because we have a clear sense as a couple of the way God has led us to this point in our lives. A second benefit of reviewing your spiritual markers as a couple is that it provides a wonderful opportunity to celebrate God's activity in your lives. Each morning Marilynn and I have coffee together and reflect on God's goodness to us for almost five decades. What joy that brings!

6 **What are two benefits of reviewing your spiritual markers as a couple?**
1. _____
2. _____
Take time this week to review your spiritual markers as a couple.

4. ***Minister together as a couple.*** God led you to your spouse for a reason. He had a purpose in mind. One purpose is to produce godly offspring (see Mal. 2:15). If couples look for God's activity together, they will discover there are ways God wants to work uniquely through them together to accomplish His kingdom purposes. I know couples who regularly go on mission trips together, teach a Sunday School class, teach English to immigrants, intercede for others, host a home Bible study, take international students into their home, and adopt foreign children. They find tremendous rewards in ministering for Christ together as a couple.

One couple had separate ministries for years. The husband served in the church as a deacon; the wife went on mission trips. After several years the wife finally convinced her husband to go with her on a mission trip. The man was overwhelmed by the experience. In tears he confessed to his wife, "Now I understand what you have been talking about all this time!" They had been missing the privilege of serving their Lord together.

7 **What are some ways you and your spouse are presently joining God's activity together?** _____
_____

8 **What are some ways you would like to?** _____
_____

5. ***Give together.*** Many Christian couples faithfully put their offerings in the offering plate each Sunday but have never discovered the joy of giving together. God is at work in the world around you. He wants you to become involved both personally and financially. Marilynn and I have found great joy in determining together where God wants us to invest the money He has given us. We support not only our local church but also various ministries around the world. This involves far more than writing a check. It includes seeking together how God wants us to invest our finances in His kingdom. Together we are laying up treasures in heaven.

God has called all of us to be on mission with Him. One of the first places we must seek His activity is in the life of the person we are most intimately related to. If God has given you a life partner, you will want to be involved in the great work God intends to do in his or her life.

SUMMARY STATEMENTS

Regularly pray for and with your spouse.

Regularly ask your spouse spiritual questions.

Review your spiritual markers as a couple.

Minister together as a couple.

Give together.

Review today's lesson. Pray and ask God to identify one or more statements or Scriptures He wants you to understand, learn, or practice. Underline them. Then respond to the following.

What was the most meaningful statement or Scripture you read today?	Reword the statement or Scripture into a prayer of response to God.	What does God want you to do in response to today's study?
_____	_____	_____
_____	_____	_____
_____	_____	_____
_____	_____	_____
_____	_____	_____

Joining God's Activity in Your Children's Lives

DAY 3

OUR GREATEST SINGLE CONTRIBUTION TO GOD'S KINGDOM IS TEACHING OUR CHILDREN TO WATCH TO SEE WHERE GOD IS AT WORK AROUND THEM AND THEN JOIN HIM.

Marilynn and I were married in 1960 in California. Those were turbulent times! We were in Los Angeles during the Watts riot. I was doing graduate work near Berkeley University during the student protests. The local elementary schools regularly had air-raid drills to teach the schoolchildren what to do in the event of a nuclear attack. Many people discouraged us from bringing children into such a dangerous and unsettled world. But I noticed that throughout Scripture when times were difficult, God's answer was often to send a baby into the world. Isaac, Moses, Samuel, Samson, John the Baptist, and of course Jesus were God's response to difficult times. Ultimately, Marilynn and I had five children, four boys and a girl. All five are serving in full-time Christian ministry, and now our grandchildren are beginning to sense God's call to ministry as well.

When our first child, Richard, was born, I spent all night praying over him after we brought him home from the hospital. I believed that God had given him to us for a particular purpose. I sensed God wanted to use him in Christian ministry when he grew up. I also knew that being raised in a pastor's home, he would feel pressure from some people to simply follow in his father's footsteps. I never told him what I thought God wanted him to do. Instead, I prayed and asked God to show me how to raise Richard so he would have a heart to know and do God's will. There were some difficult times along the way. Richard experienced serious health problems as a child. During his teen years he had to decide if he would go God's way or the world's. When he entered the university, he began to prepare to be a high-school social-studies teacher. Believing that he was running from God's will, I prayed and sought to help Richard enter a walk with God in which he would obey what God told him.

Halfway through his freshman year at the university, I noticed Richard walking down the aisle of the church auditorium during the altar call. In tears he explained to me that he knew God was calling him into Christian ministry and that he had been running from God. He didn't want to be a pastor just because his dad was or because everyone expected him to be, but he would resist no longer. For the first time I told my oldest son I had known all his life that God was calling him into ministry. With a startled look, he asked, "Well if you have known for so long, why didn't you tell me?"

"I wanted you to hear it from God" I replied. Today Richard is the president of my ministry! Likewise, God gave us opportunities in each of our children's lives to help walk with God so they would not miss anything God intended to do in their lives. Scripture indicates:

> Sons are a heritage from the LORD,
>   children a reward from him.
> Like arrows in the hands of a warrior
>   are sons born in one's youth.
> Blessed is the man
>   whose quiver is full of them.
> They will not be put to shame
>   when they contend with their enemies in the gate (Ps. 127:3-5).

Not everyone will be married or have children. For those to whom God entrusts them, children are a special assignment as well as a reward from the Lord. Wise parents understand that God has a special purpose for each child He gives to them, and they should carefully watch to see where God is at work in their lives.

1 **Notice some of the unique purposes God had for children in the Bible. Choose two or more of the people listed in the margin and read the Scriptures under their names. Write their names below and God's purpose for their lives.**
    1. _____
    2. _____

Although it is true that these biblical characters had unique assignments, God has a purpose for each person He creates. The psalmist described this truth about himself.

2 **Read Psalm 139:13-17 below and underline words that describe when God determined a purpose for the "days ordained" for the psalmist.**

> You created my inmost being;
>   you knit me together in my mother's womb.
> I praise you because I am fearfully and wonderfully made;
>   your works are wonderful,
>   I know that full well.
> My frame was not hidden from you
>   when I was made in the secret place.
> When I was woven together in the depths of the earth,
>   your eyes saw my unformed body.
> All the days ordained for me
>   were written in your book
>   before one of them came to be.
> How precious to me are your thoughts, O God!
>   How vast is the sum of them! (Ps. 139:13-17).

Margin:

❑ Isaac
    Genesis 17:19
❑ Joseph
    Genesis 37:5-11
❑ Moses
    Exodus 2:1-10;
    3:9-10
❑ Samson
    Judges 13:1-5
❑ Samuel
    1 Samuel 1:11;
    3:19-21
❑ David
    1 Samuel 16:1,
    11-13
❑ Jeremiah
    Jeremiah 1:4-10
❑ John the Baptist
    Luke 1:13-17

God has a unique purpose for each life. As He did for the psalmist, God determines that purpose before we are born. Just as God intended for Jeremiah to be His prophet before he was born, God has purposes for each of us. The apostle Paul identified one of God's eternal purposes for every person: "Those God foreknew he also predestined to be conformed to the likeness of his Son, that he might be the firstborn among many brothers. And those he predestined, he also called; those he called, he also justified; those he justified, he also glorified" (Rom. 8:29-30).

3 **What is one thing God wants for every person?** _____
_____

God's eternal purpose for each of your children is that they be conformed to the image of Christ. If they are willing and responsive, God will draw each of your children into a unique love relationship with Him. He will speak to your children and will use the circumstances in their lives to fashion them into Christlikeness. There are several ways you can join in God's activity in your children's lives:

1. Pray with and for your children. Prayer is not primarily for us to tell God what we want Him to do for our children. It is for God to adjust our lives so we can be God's instrument in their lives. We don't always know what is best for our kids. We aren't aware of all they experience at school. We don't see all the temptations, criticisms, threats, or pressures they undergo. God does not make our children immune to difficulty, but He alerts parents so they can be God's spokesperson when their children need to respond to the circumstances in their lives. God also knows what the potential of each child is when placed in His hand. As much as we love our children, we can't begin to imagine all God has in His heart for them (see **1 Cor. 2:9**). That is why we rob our children if we merely seek to have them meet our expectations. We need to be on God's agenda for our kids' lives so they can experience the abundant life God intends for them (see **John 10:10**).

4 **List your children's names on the following lines and take a few minutes to pray for each one. Beside each one write the primary prayer you are praying for him or her. Use the margin if you need more space.**

_____
_____
_____

2. Talk with your children about God's activity. Parents talk to their children about numerous things, but no topic is as important as discussing God's activity in their lives. Deuteronomy 6:6-9,20-25 instructs parents to regularly talk with their children about God's activity. Parents should rehearse with their children God's acts throughout their family history. Parents ought to recount to their children how they met Christ personally, how God led them to be married, how God guided them in their careers, how God led them to their church, and how God has walked with them through the years. Parents should point out to their children God's ongoing activity in their lives so they learn to recognize God's activity for themselves.

5 **Write on the following lines two or more spiritual markers or ways God has worked in your life (or in your lives as parents) that you could share with your children. Watch for a time this week when you could tell them about God's activity in your life.**

God's eternal purpose for each of your children is that they be conformed to the image of Christ.

1 Corinthians 2:9
"No eye has seen,
   no ear has heard,
no mind has conceived
   what God has prepared
   for those who love him."

John 10:10
"I have come that they may
   have life, and that they may
   have it more abundantly"
(NKJV).

_____

_____

_____

_____

As Marilynn and I raised our children, we constantly pointed out God's activity to them. When God provided for a financial need we faced, we were careful to give God the praise before our children. When God answered our prayers, we would help them see the connection between what we prayed and what happened next. As a result, walking with God daily became a natural part of our children's lives.

I also learned to ask my children God-centered questions. Instead of "What would you like to be when you grow up?" I would ask, "What do you sense that God wants you to do?" When my children came to me with a question, they learned to expect me to point them to God: "What do you think God wants you to do?" was my usual reply. If I had merely given my children my opinion every time they came to me for help, they would have learned to come to me for answers instead of to God. I wanted my kids to learn to put their trust in God, not in their parents. As my children grew older, I regularly asked them, "What has God taught you lately?" Those times always provided many opportunities to discuss important issues with them.

6 **Review the previous paragraph and underline questions you might ask your children to help them focus on God and His activity.**

3. Minister with your children. One of the greatest joys we had as parents was ministering alongside our children. We often invited people to our home, and through those times our children learned to care for others. When I was a pastor, I would often take one of our children with me when I spoke at one of our mission churches. At times I would take one of them to visit a widow or someone in the hospital. Our kids served in Vacation Bible School and youth camps.

I know families who go on mission trips together every year. Some families openly discuss their family budgets and decide as a family what causes beyond the support of their local church they will contribute to that year. Many of history's greatest missionaries and ministers were taught as children to be on mission with God.

7 **From the following list identify a ministry activity (or write your own) in which you can and will participate with one or more of your children. Better yet, let your children help you decide on a project.**
- ❑ Visit someone in a nursing home or a hospital or a shut-in at home
- ❑ Assist a widow or a senior adult with yard work or home repairs
- ❑ Serve a meal in a local rescue mission or homeless shelter
- ❑ Participate in a mission trip or local mission project
- ❑ Train for and participate in disaster relief
- ❑ Prayerwalk your neighborhood or city and pray for people you encounter
- ❑ Lead or participate in a worship service in a park, recreational area, campground, or assisted-living facility
- ❑ Prepare and deliver a meal to a grieving family or someone who has recently returned from the hospital
- ❑ Other: _____

_____

> I wanted my kids to learn to put their trust in God, not in their parents.

As my kids have grown older, I have had the privilege of speaking and writing with all five of them. Last year I had a new first. I spoke at a men's conference along with my oldest son, Richard, and his oldest son, Mike—three generations of Blackabys all ministering for their Lord together! It is important to model for our children how to join God's activity. When we heard of a new opportunity for ministry God had given, we shared it with our children and asked them what they thought God wanted us to do in response. As our children grew older, they recognized God at work around our family and suggested ways they thought our family should become involved. As Marilynn and I have watched our children mature, we have realized our greatest single contribution to God's kingdom is teaching our children to watch to see where God is at work around them and then join Him.

8 **Describe a time when your family ministered together. If necessary, complete one of the suggestions in activity 7 and record it below.**

_____

_____

_____

SUMMARY STATEMENTS

Pray with and
for your children.

Talk with your children
about God's activity.

Minister with your children.

Review today's lesson. Pray and ask God to identify one or more statements or Scriptures He wants you to understand, learn, or practice. Underline them. Then respond to the following.

What was the most meaningful statement or Scripture you read today?

_____
_____
_____
_____
_____

Reword the statement or Scripture into a prayer of response to God.

_____
_____
_____
_____
_____

What does God want you to do in response to today's study?

_____
_____
_____
_____
_____

Experiencing God in the Marketplace

DAY 4

WHY WAS SO MUCH OF GOD'S ACTIVITY ACCOMPLISHED IN THE MARKETPLACE? BECAUSE THAT IS WHERE PEOPLE LIVED THROUGHOUT THE WEEK.

For too long Christians have assumed God's activity generally occurs at a church building on Sunday. In reality, throughout Scripture God was continually at work in the marketplace. When God launched His great work to bring salvation to all humanity, He called Abraham, one of the most successful businessmen of his day (see Gen. 24:35). Abraham's son Isaac also prospered in the marketplace (see Gen. 26:12-14). Likewise, Isaac's son Jacob became wealthy through his business acumen (see Gen. 30:43). Joseph served God not as a preacher or a missionary but as a grain administrator (see Gen. 41:37-57). Moses had a profound encounter with God while working as a shepherd (see Ex. 3:1-6). Elisha was invited to join God's activity while plowing a field (see 1 Kings 19:19-21). Amos declared that he was not a prophet or the son of a prophet but a sheep breeder and a tender of sycamore trees (see Amos 7:14). Daniel served God as a government official.

Jesus was trained as a carpenter. When He began calling the 12 men who would walk with Him as His disciples, He called fishermen (see Mark 1:16-20), a tax collector (see Mark 2:14), and other career people. I believe one reason Jesus called businesspeople is that they are not intimidated by the world. They live and thrive in the marketplace. Once these businesspeople had experienced life-transforming encounters with Jesus, they were prepared to turn their world upside down! Joseph of Arimathea was a businessman who, though fearing the religious leaders, had the courage to approach the Roman leader Pilate for Jesus' body (see Mark 15:42-43; John 19:38). Lydia, a businessperson, was a key member of the church in Philippi (see Acts 16:14-15). Two of the apostle Paul's supporters in his church-planting ministry were Aquila and Priscilla, also businesspeople (see Acts 18:1-2).

1 **Mark the following statements as _T_ (true) or _F_ (false).**
____ a. In the Bible God only used priests and other religious leaders to do His work.
____ b. Many of the best-known Bible characters were ordinary businesspeople who were available to God for His work.
____ c. The only significant religious activity in our nation takes place inside church buildings on Sundays.

#1 answers: true–b; false–a and c

Why was so much of God's activity accomplished in the marketplace? Because that is where people lived throughout the week. The same is true for believers today. Church on Sunday provides an opportunity for the saints to be equipped for their mission work throughout the week at their job sites.

2 **Read Ephesians 4:11-12 in the margin and match the persons on the left with the task assigned to them in the body of Christ.**
____ 1. Apostles and prophets   a. Equip others for works of service
____ 2. God's people (members)   b. Perform works of service to build
____ 3. Evangelists, pastors, teachers   up the body of Christ

One of the greatest movements of God I am seeing today is His work in the marketplace. I work with a group of Christian CEOs of some of America's largest companies. These men and women have realized God has placed them in their positions for a purpose. These business leaders impact the lives of tens of thousands of employees. They control huge advertising budgets. They have access to world leaders that missionaries do not. One businessman's company produced power plants. He provided one free to a village in Africa on the condition that he could tell the villagers why he was helping them. By the time the power was turned on in that village, the chief and almost all the people had become believers. Another CEO gives Bibles to world leaders as gifts when he visits their country on business.

Many people are discovering that God has placed them in their companies so they can be witnesses to their colleagues as well as to customers. I could tell you numerous stories of people who led their colleagues to faith in Christ. I know business leaders who lead Bible studies for their staffs during the lunch hour. Some physicians pray with and share Christ with patients. Many of the people who meet Christ in a workplace would never have dreamed of visiting a church on Sunday, so Christ sends

---

Church on Sunday provides an opportunity for the saints to be equipped for their mission work throughout the week at their job sites.

Ephesians 4:11-12

"It was he who gave some to be apostles, some to be prophets, some to be evangelists, and some to be pastors and teachers, to prepare God's people for works of service, so that the body of Christ may be built up."

#2 answers: 1–a, 2–b, 3–a

His servants to job sites where they encounter people who need to hear about Him. I believe churches ought to have commissioning services for those who go into the marketplace every Monday morning in the same way we pray over missionaries who travel to other countries to share the gospel.

3 **If your church had commissioning services of marketplace missionaries (members who are on mission with God in their workplaces) what are some of the groups you might commission? Check groups that are most numerous in your church.**

❑ schoolteachers ❑ salespersons ❑ medical professionals
❑ factory workers ❑ pilots ❑ government workers
❑ accountants ❑ lawyers ❑ government leaders
❑ artists ❑ flight attendants ❑ business managers, CEOs
❑ media personnel ❑ firefighters ❑ law-enforcement personnel
❑ bankers ❑ cab drivers ❑ IT personnel
❑ scientists ❑ engineers ❑ mechanics
❑ farmers ❑ judges ❑ entertainers

Others: _____

God is at work among businesspeople around the world. Many of their hearts are restless as they realize that reaching the top of the corporate ladder or achieving their financial goals does not bring the peace and contentment they have sought.

One businessman was at work when the Holy Spirit drew his attention to a particular colleague. Although the Christian did not know the other man well, he felt impressed to ask to have lunch with him. Over lunch the man confessed that just that morning he had left his wife. Before that day was over, the Christian had led his troubled coworker to place his trust in Christ and to be restored to his wife.

As a salesman made the rounds in his community, the Lord drew his attention to a house for sale. A few weeks later he noticed a moving van in the driveway of that house. Two weeks later he spied a wheelchair ramp being installed to the front door. Every time this Christian drove by that home, he felt the Spirit nudging him to find out who lived there. Finally one day as he drove by, he strongly felt that he should stop and visit the new home, so he approached the house and rang the doorbell. The house was not far from his church, so he decided to invite the stranger to his church. He was met by a disabled man with a bitter, lonely story. He was deeply grateful someone had cared enough to come by. The man said he had noticed the church and wondered whether its people were friendly. Now he knew.

Other businesspeople have discovered that God has granted them prosperity so they can invest their wealth in the kingdom of God. Suddenly, rather than being absorbed in their work, these men and women have found that a new world of God's activity in His kingdom has opened to them. Some have begun using their resources to build church buildings around the world. Others have invested in Bible colleges and seminaries that are training people for Christian ministry. Others have supported orphanages and ministries to those suffering from hunger and disease. Jesus commanded those who would be His followers, "Seek first his kingdom and his righteousness, and all these things will be given to you as well" (Matt. 6:33). This command is not just for people in full-time Christian ministry. Jesus expects every disciple to make his or her first priority to be involved in the building of God's kingdom and then to see how God provides for all their other needs.

I believe churches ought to have commissioning services for those who go into the marketplace every Monday morning in the same way we pray over missionaries who travel to other countries to share the gospel.

———

4 **Pray, asking the Lord to open your eyes and touch your mind and heart with ways you can serve Him on mission in your workplace or through the platform and resources your work provides. Consider (but don't be limited to) some of the following.**

❏ Minister to needy people in the name of Christ
❏ Seek justice and alleviate human suffering
❏ Share the good news about Christ with coworkers, vendors, and/or customers
❏ Testify to Christ and His goodness in public
❏ Invest financial resources in Kingdom work and share with those in need
❏ Demonstrate holiness and love to those who need an example of Christlikeness
❏ Pray for God's work in the lives of others
❏ Provide a listening ear and wise counsel to people facing problems
❏ Influence leaders and governments for Kingdom causes
❏ Take a stand for truth, righteousness, justice, honesty, and purity
❏ Use your expertise to serve churches, ministries, or mission enterprises
❏ Lead a Bible study or a discipleship class at lunch or before or after work
Others: _____
_____

Review today's lesson. Pray and ask God to identify one or more statements or Scriptures He wants you to understand, learn, or practice. Underline them. Then respond to the following.

What was the most meaningful statement or Scripture you read today?	Reword the statement or Scripture into a prayer of response to God.	What does God want you to do in response to today's study?

DAY 5

Continuing to Experience God

Two persons were walking together on their way to Emmaus, a town roughly seven miles from Jerusalem (see Luke 24:13-35). They were discouraged. They had chosen to follow Jesus, and they had been excited about all He had done and taught. Then Jesus had been cruelly taken from them. Now they were bewildered, not knowing what to do next. Suddenly a stranger joined them and asked what they were talking about. They explained what had happened and that they could no longer follow Jesus as they had intended. Over the next few miles the stranger explained to them that the events surrounding Jesus' death were not the end but the beginning of an exciting new opportunity to walk daily with the Son of God. Rather than being taken from them, Jesus was now closer to them than they could have imagined!

Many people who study *Experiencing God* feel a letdown when they finish the course and stop meeting regularly with their small group. Many tell us they hated coming to the end of the course because they feared their Christian life might go back to the way it was before. Let me encourage you by saying that this does not need to be the case. Your encounter with Christ through this material has not been an end but a beginning. I pray God has shown you how you can experience a love relationship with Him that is real and fresh every day. I trust that you have been challenged to watch to see where God is at work and then to join Him. I hope you have made the adjustments in your life that God has asked for and are now obeying everything He has told you to do. But all of this is only the beginning! God wants you to know and experience more of Him. He wants you to understand new truths that will set you free (see John 8:32). There is far more of God's nature, His purposes, and His ways that He wants to reveal to you. This course should be only the starting point for a whole new adventure in following Christ daily. As you prepare to move to the next stage in your walk with God, consider adopting a few practices that will help you to continue going deeper with your Lord.

1. *Stay immersed in God's Word.* Remember God's instruction to Joshua: "Do not let this Book of the Law depart from your mouth; meditate on it day and night, so you may be careful to do everything written in it. Then you will be prosperous and successful" (Josh. 1:8). Make it your habit to read God's Word daily. God has many more truths to reveal to you if you will give Him the opportunity.

① **Take some time to review your Scripture-memory verses. Which one has been the most meaningful to you and why?** _____

_____

2. *Remain intimately involved with a church family that will love and nurture you.* Hebrews urges us: "Let us not give up meeting together, as some are in the habit of doing, but let us encourage one another—and all the more as you see the Day approaching" (Heb. 10:25). God made us interdependent on one another. You cannot experience all God has for you apart from the rest of the body of Christ.

② **What do you sense you should do next to stay connected in the body of Christ? Consider the following options or write your own.**
  ❑ a. Lead a new group study of *Experiencing God* for others
  ❑ b. Participate in a group study of one of the following discipleship courses:
    • *When God Speaks: How to Recognize God's Voice and Respond in Obedience*
    • *Fresh Encounter*
    • *The Family God Uses*
    • *Experiencing God as Couples*
    • *The Man God Uses: Moved from the Ordinary to the Extraordinary*
  ❑ c. Get involved on a ministry team: _____
  ❑ d. Accept a place of service as _____
  ❑ e. Other: _____

3. *Pray regularly.* Scripture indicates that Daniel made it a habit to pray three times daily (see Dan. 6:10). As a result, he had a powerful prayer life in which God spoke to him and answered him the moment he began praying (see Dan. 9:23). One of the best ways to prevent your heart from growing cold is to regularly talk with God. As

To order any of these resources, write to LifeWay Church Resources Customer Service; One LifeWay Plaza; Nashville, TN 37234-0113; e-mail *orderentry@lifeway.com*; fax (615) 251-5933; phone toll free (800) 458-2772; order online at *www.lifeway.com*; or visit the LifeWay Christian Store serving you.

Daniel 6:10

"Three times a day he got down on his knees and prayed, giving thanks to his God."

Daniel 9:23

"As soon as you began to pray, an answer was given, which I have come to tell you, for you are highly esteemed."

you commune with Him, you will keep your focus on Him and be reminded that you are to follow Him daily.

3 **Pause now to pray. Ask the Lord to cultivate in you an intimate, consistent communion with Him.**

4. *Strive to keep your vows to God.* Ecclesiastes warns, "When you make a vow to God, do not delay in fulfilling it. He has no pleasure in fools; fulfill your vow. It is better not to vow than to make a vow and not fulfill it" (Eccl. 5:4-5). Throughout this course God has spoken to you. You may have made several commitments to Him in response.

4 **Review your spiritual journal or the daily-review activities in this book. On separate paper make a list of commitments you have made to God. Keep that list in your Bible where you can review it regularly.**

Remember that God takes our promises to Him extremely seriously. God is not mocked. Be diligent to follow through with everything you promised God you would do. Remember, a good intention is not the same as obedience. There are no substitutes for obedience!

5. *Take time to process what God has said to you or done in your life through this course.* God may have spoken to you many times over the past weeks. If you do not let this material soak into your heart and life, however, it may be like the seed that fell on stony ground and was soon taken away (see Matt. 13:20-21). Processing God's Word means allowing God to explain and apply all He has said to you. It is not enough to agree with what God said in your mind. You must also apply God's Word in your heart and life.

If, for instance, God spoke to you about forgiveness, it is not enough to believe in forgiveness. You must ask God to examine your heart and relationships to see if you have not truly forgiven someone. If God reveals someone to you, ask Him to show you what action you must take to be reconciled. Don't treat God's truth as a doctrine to be believed but as a reality that must be lived and experienced. If there are special truths God revealed to you during this study, don't let them be lost when you put this book on your bookshelf and go on to your next study. Identify all the truths God revealed to you and meditate on them until you are assured that you understand and experience everything God intended when He revealed them to you.

5 **As time allows before your final small-group session, review the most meaningful statements or Scriptures you listed at the end of each day in this study. Of all those statements or Scriptures, which one has had the most profound impact on your thinking, your actions, or your life?**

_____

_____

6 **As you come to the end of this course, take a moment to write on separate paper a prayer of commitment to the Lord. Tell Him how you intend, with His help, to walk with Him in the coming days. Sign and date your prayer so you can return to it in years to come.**

I am so glad you chose to take this course and to study it right until the end. I trust that God will honor your faithfulness and will bring you into an ever-deepening walk with Him as you continue to experience God.

There are no substitutes for obedience!

SUMMARY STATEMENTS

1. Stay immersed in God's Word.

2. Remain intimately involved with a church family that will love and nurture you.

3. Pray regularly.

4. Strive to keep your vows to God.

5. Take time to process what God has said to you or done in your life through this course.

EXPERIENCING GOD IN YOUR DAILY LIFE

DVD Message Notes

1. This study is a way of living every day where you open your eyes to see what God is doing all around you.
2. Ask, "God, where are You at work around me today?"
3. Today perhaps the greatest movement and working of God we see is in the marketplace.
4. God is at work where you go to work every day.
5. Pray, "God, would You open my eyes to see what You're doing, and when I see, help me have the courage to join You?"

Your Notes

_____

Unit Review

Find a partner. Using the key words below, state in your own words the seven realities of experiencing God. Alternate statements: you state 1, 3, 5, and 7, and your partner states 2, 4, and 6. If time permits, swap assignments and state the other realities you did not state the first time.

• First person: (1) God's work, (3) invitation, (5) crisis of belief, (7) obey
• Second person: (2) relationship, (4) God speaks, (6) adjust

Check your answers, using the pages cited in parentheses.

---

1. For a more detailed study on revival for individuals and groups, see Henry Blackaby and Claude King, *Fresh Encounter: Seeking God Together for Revival in the Land* (Nashville: LifeWay Press, 2006).
2. For a more detailed study for couples, see Henry and Marilynn Blackaby, *Experiencing God as Couples* (Nashville: LifeWay Press, 2000).

Scripture Referenced

Mark 8:18

Testimony

Don and Lena Gibson

Sharing Time

• How you would evaluate your intimacy with God (activity 2, p. 250)
• What you sense you should do next (activity 2, p. 265)
• One of the most meaningful statements or Scriptures from this unit's lessons and your prayer response to God. Choose one from pages 252, 257, 261, and 264.

For Makeup or Review

Audio and video downloads are available at *www.lifeway.com*.

NAMES, TITLES, AND DESCRIPTIONS OF GOD

The following are representative names, titles, and descriptions of God found in the New International Version of the Bible. At least one Bible reference is provided for each name.

FATHER

A faithful God (Deut. 32:4)
A forgiving God (Neh. 9:17)
A fortress of salvation (Ps. 28:8)
A glorious crown (Isa. 28:5)
A jealous and avenging God (Nah. 1:2)
A Master in heaven (Col. 4:1)
A refuge for his people (Joel 3:16)
A refuge for the oppressed (Ps. 9:9)
A refuge for the poor (Isa. 25:4)
A sanctuary (Isa. 8:14)
A shade from the heat (Isa. 25:4)
A shelter from the storm (Isa. 25:4)
A source of strength (Isa. 28:6)
A stronghold in times of trouble (Ps. 9:9)
An ever–present help in trouble (Ps. 46:1)
Architect and builder (Heb. 11:10)
Builder of everything (Heb. 3:4)
Commander of the army of the LORD (Josh. 5:14)
Creator of heaven and earth (Gen. 14:19)
Defender of widows (Ps. 68:5)
Eternal King (Jer. 10:10)
Father (Isa. 9:6; 63:16; Matt. 5:16)
Father of compassion (2 Cor. 1:3)
Father of our spirits (Heb. 12:9)
Father of the heavenly lights (Jas. 1:17)
Father to the fatherless (Ps. 68:5)
God (Gen. 1:2)
God Almighty *(El Shaddai;* Gen. 17:1)
God and Father of Jesus Christ (1 Pet. 1:3)
God Most High (Gen. 14:18–22)
God my Maker (Job 35:10)
God my Rock (Ps. 42:9)
God my Savior (Ps. 18:46; 27:9)
God my stronghold (Ps. 144:2; 2 Sam. 22:3)
God of Abraham, Isaac, Jacob (Ex. 3:16)
God of all comfort (2 Cor. 1:3)
God of all mankind (Jer. 32:27)
God of glory (Ps. 29:3)
God of gods (Deut. 10:17; Ps. 136:2)
God of grace (1 Pet. 5:10)
God of peace (1 Thess. 5:23)
God of retribution (Jer. 51:56)
God of the living (Matt. 22:32)
God of the spirits (Num. 16:22)
God of truth (Ps. 31:5)
God our Father (Col. 1:2)
God our strength (Ps. 18:2)
God over all the kingdoms (Dan. 4:17)
God the Father (Col. 3:17)
God who avenges me (Ps. 18:47; 94:1)
God who relents from sending calamity (Joel 2:13)
Great and awesome God (Deut. 7:21)

Great and powerful God (Jer. 32:18)
Great, mighty, awesome God (Deut. 10:17)
He who blots out your transgressions (Isa. 43:25)
He who comforts you (Isa. 66:13)
He who forms the hearts of all (Ps. 33:15)
He who raised Christ from the dead (Rom. 8:11)
He who reveals His thoughts to man (Amos 4:13)
Helper of the fatherless (Ps. 10:14)
Him who is able to do more than all we ask or imagine (Eph. 3:20)
Him who is able to keep you from falling (Jude 24)
Him who is ready to judge the living and the dead (2 Tim. 4:1)
Holy Father (John 17:11)
Holy One (Rev. 16:5)
Holy One among you (Hos. 11:9)
I AM WHO I AM (Ex. 3:14)
Jealous (Ex. 20:5)
Judge of all the earth (Gen. 18:25)
King of glory (Ps. 24:7–10)
King of heaven (Dan. 4:37)
Living and true God (1 Thess. 1:9)
Lord Almighty (2 Cor. 6:18)
Lord God Almighty (Rev. 4:8; 16:7; 21:22)
LORD is Peace (Judg. 6:24)
LORD Most High (Ps. 7:17)
LORD is my Banner (Ex. 17:15)
LORD my Rock (Ps. 28:1)
LORD of all the earth (Mic. 4:13; Zech. 4:14)
Lord of kings (Dan. 2:47)
LORD our God (Deut. 1:6,10)
LORD our Maker (Ps. 95:6)
LORD who heals you (Ex. 15:26)
LORD who is there (of Jerusalem; Ezek. 48:35)
Lord who makes you holy (Heb. 2:11)
LORD who strikes the blow (Ezek. 7:9)
LORD will provide (Gen. 22:14)
Love (1 John 4:8)
Maker of all things (Eccl. 11:5; Jer. 10:16)
Most High (Gen. 14:18–22)
My advocate (Job 16:19)
My Comforter in sorrow (Jer. 8:18)
My confidence (Ps. 71:5)
My helper (Ps. 118:7; Heb. 13:6)
My hiding place (Ps. 32:7)
My hope (Ps. 25:5,21)
My light (Ps. 27:1)
My mighty rock (Ps. 62:7)
My refuge in times of trouble (Ps. 59:16)
My song (Ex. 15:2)
My strong deliverer (Ps. 140:7)
My support (2 Sam. 22:19)
One to be feared (1 Chron. 16:25)
Only wise God (Rom. 16:27)
Our dwelling place (Ps. 90:1)
Our help and our shield (Ps. 33:20)
Our judge (1 Sam. 24:15)
Our lawgiver (Isa. 33:22)

Our leader (2 Chron. 13:12)
Our Mighty One (Isa. 33:21)
Our Redeemer (Isa. 47:4: 63:16)
Our refuge and strength (Ps. 46:1)
Righteous Father (John 17:25)
Rock of our salvation (Ps. 95:1)
Shepherd (Ps. 23:1)
Sovereign Lord (Acts 4:24)
The Almighty (Gen. 49:25; Ruth 1:20)
The compassionate and gracious God (Ex. 34:6)
The Eternal God (Gen. 21:33)
The consuming fire (Isa. 33:14)
The everlasting God (Isa. 40:28)
The exalted God (Mic. 6:6)
The faithful God (Deut. 7:9)
The gardener (husbandman; John 15:1)
The glorious Father (Eph. 1:17)
The glory of Israel (Mic. 1:15)
The God who saves me (Ps. 88:1)
The God who sees me (Gen. 16:13)
The great King above all gods (Ps. 95:3)
The just and mighty One (Job 34:17)
The living Father (John 6:57)
The Majestic Glory (2 Pet. 1:17)
The Majesty in heaven (Heb. 1:3)
The one who sustains me (Ps. 54:4)
The only God (Jude 1:25)
The potter (Jer. 18:6)
The rock in whom I take refuge (Ps. 18:2)
The spring of living water (Jer. 2:13)
The strength of my heart (Ps. 73:26)
The true God (1 Thess. 1:9)
You who judge righteously and test the heart and mind (Jer. 11:20)
You who love the people (Deut. 33:3)
Your glory (Ps. 57:11)
Your praise (Isa. 38:18; Ps. 71:8; 138:1)
Your very great reward (Gen. 15:1)

SON (JESUS)

A Nazarene (Matt. 2:23; Mark 14:67)
All (Col. 3:11)
Alpha and Omega (Rev. 1:8)
Anointed One (Acts 4:26; Ps. 2:2)
Apostle and high priest (Heb. 3:1)
Author and perfecter of our faith (Heb. 12:2)
Author of life (Acts 3:15)
Author of their salvation (Heb. 2:10)
Branch of the LORD (Isa. 4:2)
Bread of God (John 6:33)
Bread of life (John 6:48)
Bridegroom (Luke 5:34–35)
Chief cornerstone (Eph. 2:20)
Chief Shepherd (1 Pet. 5:4)
Chosen and precious cornerstone (1 Pet. 2:6)
Christ Jesus my Lord (Phil. 3:8)
Christ Jesus our hope (1 Tim. 1:1)
Christ of God (Luke 9:20)

Consolation of Israel (Luke 2:25)
Crown of splendor (Isa. 62:3)
Eternal life (1 John 5:20)
Faithful and True (Rev. 19:11)
Faithful and true witness (Rev. 3:14)
First to rise from the dead (Acts 26:23)
Firstborn from among the dead (Col. 1:18)
Firstborn over all creation (Col. 1:15)
Firstfruits of those who have fallen asleep (1 Cor. 15:20)
Fragrant offering and sacrifice to God (Eph. 5:2)
Friend of tax collectors and "sinners" (Matt. 11:19)
God over all (Rom. 9:5)
God's Son (John 11:4)
Great high priest (Heb. 4:14)
Great light (Matt. 4:16)
Great Shepherd of the sheep (Heb. 13:20)
Guarantee of a better covenant (Heb. 7:22)
He who comes down from heaven and gives life to the world (John 6:33)
He who searches hearts and minds (Rev. 2:23)
Head of every man (1 Cor. 11:3)
Head of the body, the church (Col. 1:18)
Head of the church (Eph. 5:23)
Head over every power and authority (Col. 2:10)
Heir of all things (Heb. 1:2)
Him ... who died and came to life again (Rev. 2:8)
Him who loves us and has freed us from our sins (Rev. 1:5)
His one and only Son (1 John 4:9)
Holy and Righteous One (Acts 3:14)
Holy One of God (John 6:69)
Holy servant Jesus (Acts 4:27,30)
Hope of Israel (Jer. 17:13)
Horn of salvation (Luke 1:69)
Image of the invisible God (Col. 1:15)
Immanuel (God with us; Matt. 1:23)
Indescribable gift (2 Cor. 9:15)
Jesus (Matt. 1:21)
Jesus Christ (John 1:17)
Jesus Christ our Lord (Rom. 1:4; 5:21)
Jesus Christ our Savior (Titus 3:6)
Jesus of Nazareth (Mark 1:24; Matt. 26:71)
Judge of the living and the dead (Acts 10:42)
KING OF KINGS (Rev. 19:16)
King of the ages (Rev. 15:3)
Lamb of God (John 1:29; 1:36)
Light for revelation to the Gentiles (Luke 2:32)
Light of men (John 1:4)
Light of the world (John 8:12)
Living bread that came down from heaven (John 6:51)
Lord and Savior Jesus Christ (2 Pet 3:18)
Lord (Kurios; Josh. 3:11,13)
Lord of glory (1 Cor. 2:8)
LORD OF LORDS (Rev. 19:16)
Lord of peace (2 Thess. 3:16)

Lord of the harvest (Matt. 9:38)
Lord of the Sabbath (Matt. 12:8)
Lord (Rabboni; John 20:16)
Man accredited by God (Acts 2:22)
Man of sorrows (Isa. 53:3)
Master (Luke 8:24; 9:33; Col. 4:1)
Mediator of a new covenant (Heb. 9:15; 12:24)
Merciful and faithful high priest (Heb. 2:17)
Messenger of the covenant (Mal. 3:1)
Messiah (John 1:41)
Morning star (Rev. 2:28)
My friend (Jer. 3:4)
My intercessor (Job 16:20)
One who makes men holy (Heb. 2:11)
One who speaks to the Father in our defense (1 John 2:1)
One who will arise to rule over the nations (Rom. 15:12)
Our glorious Lord Jesus Christ (Jas. 2:1)
Our God and Savior Jesus Christ (2 Pet. 1:1)
Our only Sovereign and Lord (Jude 1:4)
Our Passover lamb (1 Cor. 5:7)
Our peace (Eph. 2:14)
Our righteousness, holiness and redemption (1 Cor. 1:30)
Physician (Luke 4:23)
Prince and Savior (Acts 5:31)
Prince of Peace (Isa. 9:6)
Prince of princes (Dan. 8:25)
Prince of the hosts (Dan. 8:11)
Ransom for all men (1 Tim. 2:6)
Refiner and purifier (Mal. 3:3)
Resurrection and the life (John 11:25)
Righteous Judge (2 Tim. 4:8)
Righteous One (Acts 3:14; 7:52)
Rock eternal (rock of ages; Isa. 26:4)
Ruler of God's creation (Rev. 3:14)
Ruler of the kings of the earth (Rev. 1:5)
Savior of the world (John 4:42)
Second man (1 Cor. 15:47)
Shepherd and Overseer of your souls (1 Pet. 2:25)
Son of Man (John 3:13-14; 5:27; 6:27)
Son of the Blessed One (Mark 14:61)
Son of the living God (Matt. 16:16)
Son of the Most High God (Luke 8:28)
Source of eternal salvation (Heb. 5:9)
Sure foundation (Isa. 33:6)
Teacher (Matt. 23:10)
The Amen (2 Cor. 1:20)
The Beginning and the End (Rev. 21:6)
The bright Morning Star (Rev. 22:16)
The exact representation of His (God's) being (Heb. 1:3)
The First and the Last (Rev. 1:17)
The gate (door; John 10:7,9)
The good shepherd (John 10:11)
The Head (Eph. 4:15; Col. 2:19)
The last Adam (1 Cor. 15:45)
The life (John 14:6)
The Living One (Rev. 1:18)
The living Stone (1 Pet. 2:4)

The LORD Our Righteousness (Jer. 23:6)
The man from heaven (1 Cor. 15:49)
The man Christ Jesus (1 Tim. 2:5)
The most holy (Dan. 9:24)
The One and Only (John 1:14,18)
The only God our Savior (Jude 1:25)
The radiance of God's glory (Heb. 1:3)
The rising of the sun (Isa. 59:19)
The stone the builders rejected (1 Pet. 2:7)
The testimony given in its proper time (1 Tim. 2:6)
The true light (John 1:9)
The true vine (John 15:1)
The truth (John 14:6)
The way (John 14:6)
The Word (logos; John 1:1)
True bread from heaven (John 6:32)
Wisdom from God (1 Cor. 1:30)
Wonderful Counselor (Isa. 9:6)
Word of God (Rev. 19:13)
Word of life (1 John 1:1)
Your life (Col. 3:3)
Your salvation (Isa. 30:15; Eph. 1:13)

HOLY SPIRIT

A deposit (earnest; 2 Cor. 5:5))
Another Counselor (John 14:16,26)
Breath of the Almighty (Job 32:8)
Holy One (1 John 2:20)
Holy Spirit (John 1:33)
Holy Spirit of God (Eph. 4:30)
Seal (2 Cor. 1:22)
Spirit of Christ (1 Pet. 1:11)
Spirit of counsel and of power (Isa 11:2)
Spirit of faith (2 Cor. 4:13)
Spirit of fire (Isa. 4:4)
Spirit of glory (1 Pet. 4:14)
Spirit of grace and supplication (Zech. 12:10)
Spirit of his Son (Gal. 4:6)
Spirit of holiness (Rom. 1:4)
Spirit of Jesus Christ (Phil. 1:19)
Spirit of judgment (Isa. 4:4)
Spirit of justice (Isa. 28:6)
Spirit of knowledge and of the fear of the LORD (Isa. 11:2)
Spirit of life (Rom. 8:2)
Spirit of our God (1 Cor. 6:11)
Spirit of sonship (adoption (Rom. 8:15)
Spirit of the living God (2 Cor. 3:3)
Spirit of the LORD (Isa. 63:14; Luke 4:18)
Spirit of the Sovereign LORD (Isa. 61:1)
Spirit of truth (John 14:17; 1 John 4:6)
Spirit of wisdom and of understanding (Isa. 11:2)
Spirit of wisdom and revelation (Eph. 1:17)
The gift (Acts 2:38; 10:45)
The promised Holy Spirit (Acts 2:33)
The same gift (Acts 11:17)
Voice of the Almighty (Ezek. 1:24)
Voice of the LORD (Hag. 1:12; Isa. 30:31)

EXPERIENCING
GOD
Group Covenant

I, _____

covenant with my Experiencing God *group to do the following.*

1. *Complete the study of the* Experiencing God *workbook each week before the group session.*

2. *Pray regularly for my fellow group members.*

3. *Participate in all group sessions unless urgent circumstances beyond my control prevent my attendance. When unable to attend, I will make up the session at the earliest possible time with the group leader or with the assigned group member.*

4. *Participate openly and honestly in the group sessions.*

5. *Keep confidential any personal matters shared by others in the group.*

6. *Be patient with my Christian brothers and sisters and my church as God works in us all to make us what He wants us to be. I will trust God to convince others of His will. I will not try to manipulate or pressure others to do what I think is best. I will simply bear witness of what I sense that God may be saying to us and watch to see how the Spirit uses that witness.*

7. *Pray at least weekly for my pastor and my church.*

Others: _____

_____

_____

_____

Signature _____ *Date* _____

Experiencing God *Group Members*

_____   _____

_____   _____

_____   _____

_____   _____

_____   _____

KEEPING A SPIRITUAL JOURNAL

Throughout this course you will have experiences in your spiritual life that you will want to record for later reference. When God speaks to you, write down what He says. You will also have opportunities to pray specifically for members of your group and for your church.

You will need a notebook for creating your spiritual journal. Assignments in the notebook will fall into four general categories. You may choose to create other categories if you want to, but sections in your journal should include at least the following.

1. TESTIMONIES. This section is for diary accounts of what God is doing in, around, and through your life and what you have learned about Him, His purposes, and His ways.

2. DAILY REVIEW. At the end of each day's work, you will be asked to review the lesson, identify the most meaningful statement or Scripture, and then respond to God. The daily-review section of your journal provides extra space for you to record summaries of what God is saying to you through His Word, prayer, circumstances, and the church. It can also include summaries of adjustments that you sense God wants you to make, directions that you sense God is calling you to follow, steps of obedience God is calling for, and other responses God may be calling you to make to Him.

3. WEEKLY REVIEW. Keeping a spiritual journal will help you remember the important things God says to you and the things He does in your life. Use the following questions to review God's activity in your life each week during this course of study. You need to respond only to the questions that apply to what God has done or revealed.
   • What has God revealed to you about Himself? (His name, His character, His nature)
   • What has God revealed to you about His purposes? (His will, His plans, His desires, His activity around you, His assignment to you, His goals, His objectives)
   • What has God revealed to you about His ways? (How He acts, what He does, how He responds in given circumstances, the kind of persons He uses, the ways He involves persons in His work, the ways He accomplishes His purposes)
   • What has God done in your life or through your life that has caused you to experience His presence?
   • What Scriptures has God used to speak to you about Himself, His purposes, or His ways?
   • What particular person or concern has God given you a burden to pray for? What has He guided you to pray for this person or concern?
   • What has God done through circumstances that has given you a sense of His timing or direction about any aspect of His will?
   • What word of guidance or truth do you sense that God has spoken to you through another believer?
   • What adjustment is God leading you to make in your life?
   • What acts of obedience have you taken this week?
   • What acts of obedience do you know God wants you to take?

4. SPIRITUAL MARKERS. The times God clearly spoke to you that are recorded in your spiritual journal can become spiritual markers in your life. Go back and review your journal six months, one year, and two years later. Observe ways God has been faithful to do what He promised. Examine whether you have been faithful to obey what you knew God was telling you to do. It can be rewarding to see how much you have grown spiritually since you wrote in your journal in times past. When you face times of transition in your life, what God said to you in your journal can also provide clear direction for you as you make decisions today.

5. PRAYER REQUESTS. You will use this section in each group session to record prayer requests and answers to prayer for individuals and your church. Put a date on the prayer requests as you record them. Then be sure to go back and put the date beside the concern when God answers. This practice will enable you to praise God for answered prayer. It can be divided to include requests such as the following.
   • Personal requests
   • Requests for group members
   • Requests for your church
   • Other special requests

EXPERIENCE
EVEN MORE.

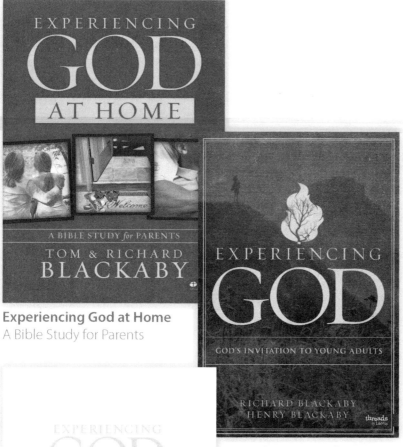

Experiencing God at Home
A Bible Study for Parents

Experiencing God
God's Invitation to
Young Adults

Experiencing God
A Documentary

**Experiencing God Audio
Devotional CD Set**

When we first read Henry Blackaby's words more than thirty years ago, we never imagined the *Experiencing God* family of Bible studies would become one of the most powerful and life-changing tools we've been privileged to offer churches. We, too, have experienced God.

Now, there are new studies and additional resources in the *Experiencing God* family for you and your family. To learn more about these and others, go online, call 800.458.2772, or visit the LifeWay Christian Store serving you.

lifeway.com/eg